Memories of an Ant

Memories of an Ant

GRIGORY SCHMERLING

THE SHERWOOD PRESS

First published 1987

© Grigory Schmerling 1987

The Sherwood Press Ltd, 88 Tylney Road, London E7 0LY

ISBN 0 907671 18 7

Typeset in Times by BookEns, Saffron Walden
Printed and bound by Redwood Burn Ltd., Trowbridge, Wiltshire

Contents

PART ONE: ROOTS

1 Origins   3
2 Ancestral landscape   13
3 The grandparents   27
4 Father   49
5 Mother's people   56
6 Childhood in Moscow   67
7 War   76
8 The Revolution   88
9 Flight from the Bolsheviks   111

PART TWO: IN EXILE

10 In Czargrad   129
11 With the victors   139
12 In defeated Germany   146
13 Madness   159
14 In war-time England   186
15 The aftermath   221
16 $E = m.c^2$ 243
17 The shadows lengthen   248
Epilogue   250
Select Bibliography   252
Index   253

Foreword

All events mentioned in this narrative are real. They are described as accurately as possible. All persons mentioned are real. Sometimes their name is altered; it is then marked with *.

This is not a complete life story—large parts of that are of no interest to anyone, as I am not a public figure. On the other hand, I have tried to sketch the background of wars and revolutions against which the episodes of my life took place.

The book contains the truth and nothing but the truth.

I am grateful to Dr. K. W. Watkins for his helpful advice and to James Shepherd, who edited this book.

PART ONE:

Roots

1

Origins

Our family was saved from dire peril three times by armed forces: once by the Imperial German Army, once by the Royal Navy and once by the Royal Air Force. How it happened will be described in this narrative.

In AD 1213 the Tartar hordes burst forth from Mongolia. Headed by the Genghis Khan, they conquered China and the whole of Asia to the Urals and the Caspian. After the death of the Genghis Khan in 1227, his son Ogadai, the new supreme ruler, decided to add the European peninsula to the Tartar *Lebensraum*. Ogadai's horsemen were commanded by his nephew, Batu, who, in several lightning campaigns, subjugated Moscow, Kiev and all the other Russian principalities, devastated Poland and Hungary, but turned back in 1241 because of the sudden death of Ogadai, an event which probably saved Central and Western Europe from a Mongol conquest. Batu then settled on the lower reaches of the Volga, where he founded the dreaded Golden Horde that was to rule over Russia for the next two hundred and fifty years, greatly impeding the progress of that gifted nation.

The bubonic plague had been endemic in China for many years. The bacillus was carried by various rodents, particularly by the black-rat population of the towns. From time to time there was an outbreak of the plague among the rats; the fleas, which inhabited the dead rats, transferred to humans. The blood of an infected rat may contain some hundred million pest bacilli per millilitre (a fifth of a teaspoon); a flea might ingest five thousand bacilli during one feeding. The Chinese knew well that a sudden dying of the rats presaged a human plague epidemic.

In the Middle Ages the city-state of Genoa was the leading maritime

3

trading power in the Mediterranean. In 1261 it concluded the Treaty of Ninfeo with Byzantium, which gave Genoa the right to trade on the Black Sea. The Genoese established a fortified trading post at Kaffa (now Feodosia) in the Crimea. The empire of the sea and the empire of the steppes were now on a collision-course. The clash occurred in the next century.

Khan Janibeg of the Golden Horde decided to add the Crimea to his dominions. The fortress of Kaffa dominated the Crimean coastline, and in 1347 Janibeg laid siege to it. The Tartar horsemen made little headway against the city fortifications and lacked siege machinery. At that time there occurred in Asia one of the periodic outbreaks of bubonic plague, and the disease reached Janibeg's horsemen, greatly weakening his forces. A brilliant stratagem occurred to the wily Tartar. As his horsemen died of the dreaded disease the disfigured corpses were catapulted into Kaffa. It was the first recorded case of bacteriological warfare. In the confines of the beleaguered city the plague spread like wildfire; the panic-stricken Genoese embarked in their ships and fled, leaving only a small garrison behind. Janibeg founded the Crimean Horde, with Bakhchisarai as his capital, where his descendants ruled (from 1475 under Turkish suzerainty), threatening the Russian principalities (even burning down Moscow in 1571), until in 1783 the last Khan was deposed by Catherine the Great and the Crimea was incorporated into Russia.

When the stricken ships returned home, having lost many diseased men at sea, the plague disembarked with them. Soon the whole of Genoa was dying of the strange and terrifying affliction. During 1348 the plague spread through southern Europe and in 1349 through Germany and the Low Countries. A ship sailing from Calais brought the infection to England, and it reached Bristol in 1348 and London in 1349. Only by 1351 had the epidemic burnt itself out in Europe. In four years some twenty-five million people, a quarter of Europe's population, had died of the Black Death, as the terrible disease became known. The ravages of Batu pale into insignificance compared with the calamity inflicted upon Europe by his wretched descendant. Nor was this the end of the matter. With the Crusaders' ships, returning from the Middle East, arrived the Asiatic black rat, the natural habitat of the plague bacillus. During the Black Death epidemic the bacillus established itself in Europe's thriving black-rat population, and periodic outbreaks of the ratborne disease were to plague Europe for the next five centuries (as in London in 1665). Even to this day, the bacillus may well be lying dormant in more than one European sewer.

Jews and Judaism were widespread throughout the Greek Hellenic Empire, and, after the Roman Conquest, throughout the entire Roman Empire from Alexandria to York. Judaism attracted many converts from

the pagans of the Hellenic, and later, the Roman periods. Even after
Constantine the Great made Christianity the state religion around AD 325,
Judaism was still a proselytising religion, with a steady intake of converts,
until perhaps, the tenth century, when the Christian Church became
dominant in Europe. There are very few families (except, perhaps, some of
the Roman nobility), and certainly no Jewish families who could trace their
ancestors back for two thousand years. The bearers of family names like
Levi and Cohen (Russion Kagan, sometimes abbreviated to Katz) are, of
course, descended in direct male line from the Levites and the *Cohanim*
(Temple Priests), thus representing the oldest lineage in Europe. There are
no records of ancestors on the distaff side. For the average European Jew
like myself, I would assume that, at the time of the Roman conquest of
Judea, perhaps half of my ancestors were Jews of Hebrew stock, spread
throughout the Hellenic Empire, and the other half were pagan Europeans,
mainly of Mediterranean stock, whose descendants later became converted
to Judaism, and were absorbed in the Jewish community.[1]

The historic German territory between the Rhine and the Elbe (east of
the Elbe was Slav territory before the German *Drang nach Osten*) was part
of the Roman Empire and contained many Jewish communities; the Jewish
community in Cologne is, in fact, mentioned in two edicts of Constantine
the Great in 321 and 331. After the break-up of the Roman Empire the
Jewish communities continued in their native countries, and there were
such communities in most towns of what is today Western Germany, representing an important element of the population. Through conversion and
intermarriage over centuries, a fair sprinkling of German blood had been
absorbed. The religious fanaticism of the Crusades, about 1000–1300
(when Europe was passing through a Khomeini period), resulted in many
persecutions (in fact, all Jews were expelled from England by Edward I in
1290 and were re-admitted only by Cromwell), and there were indeed persecutions in Germany (for example, the notorious *Findfleisch pogróm* in
which the Jewish community of Nurnberg was annihilated in about 1300),
but the Jewish communities in Germany remained in being until the Black
Death struck in 1349. As the strange and terrifying disease wiped out whole
towns and villages it soon became evident to the populace that *the Jews had
poisoned the wells*. No other explanation was possible (in Moscow, when
there was a terrible plague epidemic in 1771, the populace, there being no
Jews, blamed the clergy and murdered the Archbishop). Gangs of men,
crazed with fear, many delirious, roamed the countryside, spreading the
disease even further, and murdering Jewish men, women and children.
Before the double onslaught of bacillus and mass hysteria the surviving
Jews fled the country in which they had lived for a thousand years and part
of which they were. They fled to the New World that was then opening up in

the East. Their family names often show, to this day, the native German city from which they fled: the Kellner from Koeln (Cologne), the Mintz from Mainz, the Trèves, Triefus or Dreifus from Trier (Trèves), the Spiro (Russian, Shapiro) from Speyer, the Halpern (Russian, Galperin) from Heilbronn, the Ginsburg from Gunzburg, the Landau (from the town of that name) and many others.

The kingdom of Poland (which then included Silesia) extended eastwards from the Odra (in German, Oder) and was ruled by the ancient dynasty of the Piast, with Cracow as its capital. It was a completely feudal country, with a population of peasants ruled by an aristocracy. The country had been badly ravaged and depopulated by the Mongol invasion of 1239–40. King Casimir the Great (1333–70) was endeavouring to rebuild and repopulate the country and to develop trade and industry. To this end, the king desired to attract skilled immigrants from all over Europe and Asia Minor, artisans and craftsmen, traders and merchants, apothecaries and physicians. Thus the king welcomed all fleeing German Jews, to whom he extended the full protection of the Crown. Beyond Poland lay Lithuania, a vast and quite undeveloped territory extending from the Baltic to the Black Sea, and including, in addition to ethnic Lithuania, Byelorussia and Malorussia (Ukraine) up to the Dnieper and beyond. In 1386 Casimir's successor died without male issue, leaving his 13-year-old daughter Jadwiga heir to the throne, and the nobles negotiated her marriage to Jagiello, the Prince of Lithuania, thus founding the Jagiellon dynasty, under which both countries were united. The new kingdom comprised ethnic Poland, with Silesia and Pomorze (Pomerania), and ethnic Lithuania with Byelorussia and Malorussia (Ukraine), and, extending from the Odra (Oder) to beyond the Dnieper, it became the leading power in Eastern Europe, by far overshadowing Muscovy. Casimir the Great's open-door policy of encouraging immigration from Europe was continued by the Jagiellons, and the protection and privileges granted by Casimir extended to all the domains of the new realm. Landless German peasants, Jews fleeing from persecution, Armenians escaping from Mongol rule (the Mongols conquered Armenia in 1236–42) all flocked to the new realm and contributed to its development.

The Jewish immigrants brought their German language with them. Augmented by some Slavonic words (and, confusingly, spelt with Hebrew characters which they all knew from the Scriptures) but still unmistakenly German, it became, over the centuries, the Yiddish dialect spoken by millions of East European Jews, when, six hundred years later, the second Black Death struck, and Hitler's black-attired SS murder squads descended, Mongol-like, upon Eastern Europe and annihilated half the Jewish population (together with millions of other human beings), an improvement on the plague bacillus that generally only killed a quarter of the afflicted population.

Partitions of Poland

The great Polish Realm, the haven of all Europeans driven by persecution or poverty to seek a new future, flourished for some centuries. As part and parcel of it, the Jewish communities prospered too. It was said that, at the time, about four-fifths of the Jewish population of Europe lived there. They must have included most of my forebears. Later, after the great Jagiellon dynasty had become extinct, the kingdom became a Republic with an elected 'King' and an Assembly requiring a *unanimous* vote for all decisions of importance; there was much internal strife and dissension, and the Government was powerless. As always, the warring factions sought support from the neighbouring states, now grown very powerful. The country was in a state of anarchy and civil war, and, in 1773, Catherine the Great of Russia (Muscovy had, in the meantime, become the Russian Empire), Frederick the Great of Prussia and Maria Theresia of Austria intervened with their troops, restored order and availed themselves of the opportunity to annex large territories ('First Partition'). Russia recovered part of Byelorussia (ethnically and historically Russian), Frederick the Great took Pomorze (Pomerania), and other ethnically Polish territories, thus joining Brandenburg and Prussia (and cutting Poland off from the sea), and Maria Theresia, a fellow-Catholic, whilst deploring the fate of the once-great kingdom, annexed Galicia, without any particular justification at all. As Frederick the Great is said to have remarked acidly: 'She wept, but she took.' The part of Byelorussia ceded to Russia included the cities of Mogilév and Vitébsk, the home towns of Father's and Mother's families. In England, the sandwich was invented.

There were further troubles and, in 1793, it came to the Second Partition, when Russia received the remainder of Byelorussia including Minsk and Pinsk, and Prussia took Gdansk (Danzig) and the *ethnically Polish* province of Poznan (Posen). Finally, in 1795, the once-great Realm was finally destroyed ('Third Partition'). Russia acquired the whole of ethnic Lithuania, with Kovno, Wilna and Grodno. Ethnic Poland was divided between Prussia, who received the Duchy of Warsaw, and Austria, who received Cracow, the historic capital. Finally, at the Congress of Vienna (1815) Prussia ceded the Duchy of Warsaw to Russia. The wheel of history had now swung full-circle. In past centuries Poland had threatened Muscovy often enough, and through the union with Lithuania, had acquired Byelorussia, parts of Malorussia (Ukraine) and other ethnically Russian territories. After the death of Czar Boris (Godunov) in 1605 the Poles, in fact, occupied Moscow and forced the election of the Polish heir to the throne as Czar, aiming at the incorporation of Muscovy as the fifth state into the Polish Realm. So, in 1815, Czar Alexander I must have felt some satisfaction at turning the tables and becoming Czar of Poland, not foreseeing the century of trouble he was laying in store for his country.

The three partitions, and the Congress of Vienna, transferred some ten million people to the suzerainty of the Czar, and some three million to Prussia and Austria (mostly ethnic Poles or Polish Jews). The large population transferred to Russia included several million Jews. The break-up of the great Polish Realm and the transfer of millions of people to new statehoods, and new majority nations, caused considerable problems for the vanquished as for the victors. In effect, the Partitions created in Europe some ten to twelve million *displaced persons*, except that it was not that people had been moved away from their home territories but that national homes themselves vanished in the course of a generation.

The problem was particularly grave for the Polish and Lithuanian Jews transferred to Russia. In the Polish Realm the Jews had been involved in its development from the beginning (as they later were in the United States); they were not intruders, but an old-established, respected and, in many ways, privileged, community. Poland was then, as now, a devoutly Catholic country, and Catholicism the state religion, but the country was not intolerant and not infected by western fanaticism and bigotry. Now several million Polish and Lithuanian Jews found themselves living in what had become, quite suddenly, a remote, conquered province of an empire whose language they did not understand and whose religion and culture were quite alien to them. It was like emigration to a new country. Moreover, the Jews were not settled on the land—they were never allowed to in medieval Europe—but lived in towns, all engaged in urban occupations. In fact, the position of the Jews after the Partitions has been compared with that of the Asians in British East Africa after the end of the Empire. With the Partitions the Polish and Lithuanian provinces rapidly became economic backwaters, trade stagnated and declined and a large number of town-dwelling Jews (in towns such as Minsk or Vilna half the population was Jewish) found themselves without any means of earning their living (*Luftmenschen*, people living on air).

The new rulers

The Norsemen, or Vikings, conquered Russia about two centuries before they invaded England. In 862, Norsemen under Rurik crossed the Baltic and founded a colony based on Novgorod on Lake Ilmen. (Fifty years later, in 912, other Norsemen, headed by Rollo, crossed the North Sea and settled in what became Normandy and served as a base for the conquest of England in 1066, and from there, another century later, the conquest of Ireland.)

The precise date of 862 for the conquest of Novgorod is disputed; however, in 1862, Czar Alexander II erected a monument at Novgorod to celebrate the millennium of the foundation of the Russian State. From Novgorod, Rurik's successor, Oleg (Helgi), followed the river-route down to Kiev, and founded the first Russian state, Rus, with Kiev as its capital, which flourished until destroyed by the Mongols in 1241. The Rurik dynasty continued in the various principalities and finally in Moscow, where it ended in 1598, after seven hundred years, with the death of Ivan the Terrible's only surviving son.[2]

The Russian state was thus founded by seafaring people, and the seafaring and colonising tradition has always been alive in Russia, even if at times, particularly during the Tartar rule, submerged. Through the depredations of the Teutonic Orders on the Baltic coast, and later of the Tartars followed by the Turks, on the Black Sea, Russia became dislodged from the sea, leaving only the White Sea coast with Archangel, ice-bound for most of the year. When Tudor England opened relations with Russia in 1553 it was through the White Sea (the English ships were actually looking for the North-east passage to China and reached the Russian coast by accident), and the Muscovy Company, founded in 1554, received from the Czar important trading privileges in Archangel. It was only Peter the Great who retrieved the Baltic coast from Sweden in 1700, and Catherine the Great (1762–96) who secured the Black Sea coast.

In 1582 the merchant–adventurers Stroganoff gained western Siberia for the Russian Crown with 840 men. The Russians continued to advance through Siberia, most sparsely populated by primitive wandering tribes, and reached the Pacific in 1648. From the Pacific coast, Bering sailed in 1728 to discover whether Asia and America were joined, and navigated the strait now perpetuating his name, later discovering Alaska, and claiming it for Russia (it was purchased by America in 1867 for the risible sum of $7 million). In fact, the Russians established trading posts along the American Pacific coast as far south as California until repulsed by Spanish troops (the only military engagement ever between Russia and Spain). The Prelestnaya (beautiful) river north of San Francisco still bears its Russian name.

In 988, Saint Vladimir, the Prince of Kiev, great-grandson of Rurik, embraced Greek Orthodox Christianity for himself and the Russian people, and married the sister of the Byzantine Emperor.[3] After the fall of Constantinople and the Byzantine Empire in 1453 Muscovy considered itself as the repository and guardian of Orthodox Christianity, and Moscow as the

'Third Rome' (Constantinople being the Second). In 1547 the Princes of Muscovy assumed the title of Caesar (Czar); Europe now had two Caesars, the Catholic Caesar (Kaiser) in Vienna and the Orthodox Caesar in Moscow. Each adopted the double-headed eagle as a symbol of the joined Eastern and Western Roman Empire, and each claimed the Christian Imperial succession. The ensuing Russian state, with the Orthodox Church as state religion, was intolerant of other religions, whether Catholic, Uniate (Orthodox Rite affiliated to Rome), Old Believers (Orthodox Dissent) or Jewish, though Russia never went as far as Spain, or France, in totally suppressing all non-conforming religions. So the millions of Polish and Lithuanian Jews who became subjects of the Orthodox Russian Czar were eyed with alarm and hostility in St Petersburg, and so were, of course, the Polish Catholics. Even after the First Partition (1772) Catherine had decreed that the Jewish inhabitants of the newly won territories were not allowed to move from what now became the Pale of Settlement, and live in pre-Partition Russia. With various easements (exemption of Merchants of the First Guild, university graduates and other categories) promulgated by Alexander II (1855–81), the great and enlightened Czar-Liberator, the ignominious Pale of Settlement was in existence with varying degrees of severity until the end of autocracy in 1917.

In Russia a system of selective conscription with an active service period of *twenty-five years* had been in force since Peter the Great (replaced in 1874 only by Alexander II with universal conscription and six years' active service). In England, it is true, the military service period was twenty-one years, but by voluntary enlistment. The press gangs operated only for the Navy, and in any case did not abduct mere boys from their parents' homes. Nicholas I (1825–55), a narrow-minded though fair disciplinarian interested chiefly in military matters and a great admirer of Prussia (in fact he married Princess Charlotte, the daughter of King Frederick William III), applied the twenty-five year conscription with all severity in the new provinces. This time-honoured system of conscription was excessively harsh for everyone, and universally hated, but it bore down most heavily on minority groups. Under the conditions of the period the system meant that a lad, often a boy of thirteen, was conscripted into an army whose language he did not understand and was completely cut off from his family, his background and his religion for twenty-five years. There was, of course, no home leave and no mail, and the regiment would probably be stationed several months' march away, in Central or Eastern Russia, or in Asia, where there were no Jewish, or other minority, communities, and, of course, the army had no religious facilities other than Orthodox. Jewish families in the Pale certainly considered the twenty-five-year conscription a calamity, when a boy would probably never see his parents again, much like the Janissaries of the

Sultan (who were children of Christian parents forcibly conscripted).

Soon an underground escape-route came into being, along which con-scripted Jewish boys disappeared into Prussian or Austrian (formerly Polish) territory, where they were looked after by the Jewish community. Naturally, these escapes did not endear his new Jewish subjects to the Czar, who considered them desertions, and probably did not understand at all why parents did not want their boys to serve in his army. As far as I know, the twenty-five-year conscription did not befall any members of my family on either side but, before Hitler, I knew several German Jews whose great-grandfathers had fled from Poland or Lithuania under Nicholas I. Golda Meir's grandfather was conscripted, and a brief account of his twenty-five years' service can be read in her autobiography. However, Nicholas I was not generally anti-Jewish, and, for instance, visited a Jewish school in 1837 in Odessa.

The attitude to the new masters was somewhat different with Lithuanian and with Polish Jews, in line with the different attitudes of the main com-munity. The Poles, Catholic, proud of their great history as the leading power in Eastern Europe, at one time very close to incorporating Muscovy into their Realm, never accepted the loss of their independence, their possessions and their considerable—almost excessive—civil liberties and their subjection to an Orthodox empire. The Poles spent the whole nineteenth century in insurrection, with major armed rebellions, savagely crushed, in 1830 and 1863. The Polish Jews, having enjoyed, during Europe's darkest centuries, freedom and protection under the Polish Crown supported the Polish aspirations and fought with their Polish compatriots. The Lithuanians (not to mention the Byelorussians and Malorussians of the First Partition) were very close to the Russians, largely Orthodox, and soon felt at home in the new empire. The transfer of Vilna to Russia in the Third Partition was particularly welcomed by the Byelorussian and Lithuanian Jews transferred to Russia in the previous Partitions, as Vilna had always been their spiritual capital; all theological seminaries and Hebrew printing presses were in that city. Now, the whole community was, at least, under one rule and the Lithuanian Jews, or *Litvaks*, were mainly concerned with coming to terms with their new masters, an attitude not made easier by the forbidding figure of Nicholas I and his stern methods.

Notes

1   There were also the Khazars, a turkic people who embraced Judaism around AD 740. When their state declined and was finally destroyed in the tenth to twelfth centuries many Jewish Khazars fled to Eastern Europe, particularly ethnically related Hungary, and were also absorbed by the Jewish com-munities.

2   The Reign of Ivan IV ('the Terrible'), who became deranged in the latter part of his life, had most unfortunate consequences for the constitutional progress of Russia, because in 1570 the Czar destroyed the ancient self-governing city of Novgorod, from where the highly developed civic spirit might have permeated the whole of the political life of the country.

3   About the same time, Poland became converted to Catholic Christianity. The religious, and consequently cultural, division of the Slavonic populations between Latin and Greek Christianity has caused unfortunate tensions that are with us to this day.

2

Ancestral Landscape

The Dnieper, the Borysthenes of the Ancients, descends from the Valdai Hills west of Moscow and flows majestically, in a slow broad stream, through the heartlands of Russia, past Smolénsk, past Kiev, until at the end of its 1400—mile course the Black Sea is gained. The great river was the main part of the famous Great Waterway from Byzantium to Scandanavia, used since antiquity as a highway for trade and travel and military movement through a roadless, forest-covered Eastern Europe. It was the main artery of Rurik's Russian empire. Between Smolénsk and Kiev the Dnieper flows past Mogilév, an important trading-town and river port. Mogilév (German and Yiddish, Mohilev), being in Byelorussia, had belonged to Lithuania, then to the Polish Realm, and was returned to Russia in the First Partition (1773). A century later Mogilév, with a population of some 100,000, had a fine Russian (Orthodox) cathedral and a few Russian churches, a Polish 'Castel' (Catholic church), a German (Lutheran) church, and some forty synagogues. Only two or three were purpose-built stone edifices: the rest were wooden prayer-sheds serving a neighbourhood.

As in most towns in the Pale, a third to a half of the population was Jewish, and spoke Yiddish, the basically German language preserved for five hundred years. The clergy, civil service and garrison-officers were Russian Orthodox, the landowners in the country were Poles since the days of the Polish supremacy. The Russian government did not like it but respected private property, that great safeguard of minorities, and could do nothing about it. Socialist methods of dispossession were not practised in Czarist Russia (nor was there any arbitrary arrest). The peasants were Orthodox Byelorussians and thought to be speaking a kind of Russian dialect; no-one knew, because no-one talked to the peasants, except the farm bailiffs, and

13

they were Germans, the hard-working NCOs of Russian society, hated by the peasants, derided by their Polish masters, an object of fun to the Russians.

A visitor from London

Sir Moses Montefiore (1784–1885) was an Italian-born Jew who came to London as a young man and made a fortune in the City. He was one of the first Jews to receive a knighthood and used his great wealth and his station as nobleman (which counted heavily in post-Napoleonic, aristocratic Europe to intercede for Jews wherever they were persecuted. Montefiore[1] travelled in state, in a coach and four,[2] and with a large retinue, as befitted a nobleman, and was received by all princes and potentates.

On several occasions Montefiore journeyed to Russia, and was even received in 1846 by Czar Nicholas I in person (the audience was conducted in French), and obtained cancellation of an anti-Jewish edict proposed by the government. When travelling through the Pale Montefiore visited all the important centres, stopping at each to meet the local Jewish community. It is difficult to exaggerate the effect on morale of Sir Moses' tour; even at the turn of the century, three generations later, the Jewish population in the Pale was still talking about the visit, and the name of Montefiore vied with that of Rothschild as one of the great Jewish benefactors who used their wealth and influence to intercede for their oppressed brethren. For this reason Montefiore is much revered in Israel today, and the Israeli government in fact asked for his remains to be disinterred at Ramsgate, in Kent, to which he had retired and where he died a centenarian, to be transferred to a Heroes' Cemetery in Israel. Fortunately this request was refused; Moses Montefiore, whilst interceding for his persecuted co-religionists everywhere, was greatly attached to the country of his adoption, his success and his ennoblement, and would not have wished to be laid at rest anywhere but in his beloved Ramsgate, where he had a mausoleum built, a copy of Rachel's Tomb in the Holy Land which he had restored.

When Sir Moses reached Mogilév a great reception was arranged for him by the Jewish community. All the leading Jewish citizens were present, and one of them was my great-grandfather, Solomon. Solomon was still a young man; his father, the first Schmerling to be born under Russian rule, had died early, of the cholera, I believe, and young Solomon had to take charge of the family business of local building contractors.

Nothing is known about the pre-Partition Schmerlings; according to family tradition, they lived in Lithuania throughout the eighteenth century. The Schmerlings were not *cohens*, or levites; they could not boast of any rabbis, or great scholars, and they earned their living in the various occupations open to Jews in the Polish lands. A few were innkeepers; I always like to think that the landlord of the inn on the Lithuanian border in *Boris Godunov* could have been one of my ancestors. And, of course, smuggling was a favourite pastime in border-countries and, no doubt, not eschewed by some of the Schmerlings.

Napoleon had been and gone: from the *Grande Armée* of 600,000 men (and 300,000 horses) launched against Russia, barely 100,000 limped home; half a million perished at the hands, mainly, of *Generals Janvier et Fevrier*. The Russian language was permanently enriched with the words *cheval* (meaning *carrion*!) and *shury mury* (cher amour)—the Corsican's only enduring monument.

Shortly after the Napoleonic invasion was over, Solomon's father, my great-great-grandfather, built a stone house (most houses in Russia were wooden) off Mogilév's main square. It was an unpretentious, squat building with heavy walls and small windows to keep the cold out, as well as marauding soldiers and robbers. There was, however, a large walled garden with fruit trees. Three generations of Schmerlings were born in the family home.

John McAdam (1756–1836) was a Scotsman with an eminently practical bent, like so many of his compatriots, who invented the surfacing of roads with a self-sealing layer of pebbles. This was a most useful invention and, in the beginning of the nineteenth century, streets and roads in Britain were being 'macadamised' (the tar macadam, or tarmac, came later).

At the reception in Mogilév Sir Moses Montefiore was describing this great improvement of England's streets and roads, and he found a receptive listener in young Schmerling. Soon Solomon was experimenting with local stone in the builder's yard, and, in a year or two, obtained contracts for the surfacing of streets and roads. Finally, Schmerling was appointed official road-building contractor in the counties of Mogilév and Smolénsk, and laid out, or resurfaced, several major highways in the region. The technical obstacles, though daunting, were overcome; more difficult were the formidable commercial problems. Negotiating with the authorities was not easy, particularly if one was a 'non-believer' and only a second-generation Russian. Also in Russia (as in most countries of the world, even today) the underpaid officials expected bribes, in fact depended on them, as a waiter depends on gratuities, and this was something Solomon Schmerling much disliked. In a play in Moscow's state-owned Maly Theatre, *The Price of Life*, a contractor was shown waiting in a quartermaster's outer office. Each time he asked the clerk when His Excellency would be free the clerk replied '*Nadozhdat*', a pun meaning either *nado zhdat* (one has to wait) or *nadozh dat* (but one has to give). This was at the beginning of this century, but in Solomon's time things were not much better. There were also the road-building gangs—hardly any machinery was available. The men were generally hard-working and conscientious but, on pay-day, liable to get senselessly drunk and run amok, with the contractor expected to pay for the damage to save trouble. In spite of all these difficulties the business flourished, and in the middle of the century Solomon Schmerling was elected to the First Merchant Guild of Smolénsk. This would have been a great honour for everyone, as the First Guild of Smolénsk was one of the premier merchant guilds of all Russia. For a Jew it was a special honour, and Schmerling was the only Jewish member of the Guild.

The military particularly liked the new metalled roads: the troops could march much faster and the roads were also easier for the officer's horses. Czar Nicholas I greatly encouraged road-building in the new territories because it would strengthen the military position. Unfortunately, by concentrating on the defence of the Western Region, as the newly won territories were called, the Czar neglected communications to the South, and when the Crimean War came in 1854 it took the troops three months to march from St Petersburg to the Crimea, over a thousand miles of dirt roads that were dustbowls when dry and quagmires in the wet season, with the horse-drawn cannon bogged down. In fact, the seaborne communications of the British from the Channel ports (let alone the French from Toulon) to Varna, the Allied base on the Black Sea, were better and faster than the Czar's (the British Admiralty even disposed of some steamships). Czar Nicholas died in 1855, a broken man after the disaster of the Crimea, and was followed by his son, Alexander II (1855–81).

This enlightened monarch was the very antithesis of his father, and set about improving political and social conditions and bringing Russia firmly into the second half of the nineteenth century.

The liberation of the peasants

Czar Alexander's crowning achievement was the liberation of the peasant serfs in 1861. The attachment of the peasants to the land had actually been enacted in the Roman Empire by Constantine the Great in 332 in order to safeguard food supply. The peasants were therefore serfs in most successor-states of the Roman Empire. In England, the serfdom of the villeins gradually declined after the Black Death and was formally abolished in Tudor times. England was the first country to abolish serfdom. France followed suit after the Revolution of 1789, and the peasant became the *fermier*, or farmer, paying a firm rent to the landowner, rather than being his serf. In Austria–Hungary serfdom was abolished by that great reformer, Joseph II (1780–90) (though it still prevailed in Bosnia as late as 1914). One of the last German states to abolish serfdom was Pomerania (1806).

So when Alexander II came to the throne in 1855 Russia was the only country left in Europe in which serfdom, or villeinage, flourished. Government and public opinion in Russia had been fully aware of the need to abolish serfdom since the beginning of the century. Alexander I (1801–25) gave the land-owners the right to *voluntary* liberation of their serfs—to the Czar's astonishment very few landowners availed themselves of this privilege. Nicholas I (1825–55), Alexander's younger brother (Alexander I died childless), carried out various reforms restricting abuses and the Imperial Committee on serfdom deliberated almost continuously. But still the peasants remained tied to the land. It was left to Alexander II the Liberator (1855–81) to take the momentous decision, and one which required immense courage. In the famous Imperial Manifesto of 1861 serfdom was abolished throughout Russia, and some twenty million peasants were free men, at a stroke of the Imperial pen. In the same year, in America a Civil War had to be fought in order to abolish slavery, at a cost of 600,000 lives. Moreover, in Russia each liberated peasant received a small holding of three to thirty acres, depending on the area and other circumstances. This was not much; the peasants wanted more, and they had to pay the landlords in instalments, in money or in kind. At any rate, the liberated peasants were not left free but destitute and forced to hire out their labour. The landlords were greatly impoverished, but not destroyed. The freed American slaves, as far as I know, received nothing. In the British Empire slavery had been ended in 1833, a generation before Russia and America.

Alexander II was a great reformer in many other fields. He introduced an independent judiciary and trial by judge and jury (abolished by the Soviets) and improved and expanded the educational system. Censorship was greatly eased and completely abolished for books (of over 160 pages). Many time-honoured restrictions on Jews were eased, and, no doubt, the Czar was moving towards their complete abolition. In an unprecedented gesture, Alexander II, Supreme Head of the Orthodox Church, attended the Sabbath service in the synagogue at Taganrog. The canker of serfdom removed, one more great reform was needed; this was representative, parliamentary government.

The Czar was an absolute autocrat and Alexander II knew that, now that the Russians were all free men they, or their children, would expect com-mensurate civil liberties and a say in the government of the country. So he instructed his ministers to prepare the introduction of constitutional govern-ment and parliamentary institutions. The required legislation was sub-mitted to the Czar, who approved it and *signed* it on 1 March (old style; 13 March new style) 1881. A few hours later, Alexander II, the Liberator, was dead, assassinated by terrorists. There had been secret revolutionary and terrorist societies in Russia throughout the century, inflamed by the ideas of the French Revolution of 1789. Alexander II's enlightened and humane government, introducing reform after reform, culminating in the Liberation of 1861, had no moderating influence on the revolutionaries. They were wholly doctrinaire. They were dedicated republicans *on principle*, and believed that once the monarch was assassinated everything would come right. *Three* attempts on Alexander II's life had failed, but the fourth, organised by a fanatical young woman (Sophie Pérovskaya, daughter of a Governor-General of St Petersburg) succeeded. Czars had been murdered before: Catherine the Great's consort, Czar Peter III, in 1762 and Czar Paul I, Alexander II's grandfather, in 1801. But these Czars, both psychopaths, had been killed by courtiers and guards officers in palace coups, in the interest of the dynasty. Alexander II was assassinated by radical terrorists attacking the monarchy as an institution.

Alexander's life was snuffed out at the age of 63. Had he been allowed to live out his full span it seems possible that constitutional and parliamentary government would have taken root in Russia, and the subsequent history of Russia and indeed of Europe and the world would have been entirely different. We are still reliving today the consequences of those fatal shots of 1881. Alexander II's eldest son, the Cesaréwitch Nicholas, on whom his father had pinned great hopes, died of meningitis (before the discovery of penicillin, almost incurable) in 1865. By all accounts this gifted young man would have been a worthy heir of his father.

Alexander III

The succession now fell upon the second son, Alexander III (1881–94). He was very different by nature, his education had been neglected, and he was entirely under the influence of his tutor, Pobedonóstsev, who abhorred the ideas of the French Revolution, considered the people as quite unworthy of any say in the government of the country and was a fanatical believer in autocracy, or absolute monarchy. It was a bad day for Russia and the world when this fanatic became the power behind the throne, at the precise moment when large sections of the population, the new professional and middle classes, the emancipated serfs, or their sons, and even the tiny minority of factory workers, had become politically conscious, demanding a say in government.

Alexander III intensely disliked his father, who had lavished all his care and affection on the first-born son; also Alexander II had married his mistress (thirty years younger than himself) a few months after the death of the Empress, Alexander III's mother, and the new Czar considered this an affront to his mother's memory. Alexander III was therefore quite determined, with the active encouragement of Pobedonóstsev, to undo all the reforms his great father had carried out. The peasants could not, of course, be re-tied to the land after twenty years of liberty, but Alexander's first act was to suppress the liberal constitution signed by his father, now his Last Will, and for it to be disregarded. Russia took the wrong turning and it proved the road to disaster.

Because of the then-prevailing custom within European royalty of inter-marrying with reigning houses only, Alexander III was almost wholly of German descent (his father, Alexander II, had married a Hesse, his grandfather, Nicholas I, a Hohenzollern, his great-grandfather, mad Paul I, a Württemberg, and, of course, Paul I's mother was Catherine the Great, née Anhalt-Zerbst. All these kingdoms and principalities were sovereign states until the German unification of 1870. In spite of his German descent (or was it because of it?), Alexander III was the first Czar to think not only on state-national but also on Russian-ethnic lines, and his government pursued a policy of 'Russification', particularly in the Western Region, discriminating against all minorities and suppressing the use and teaching of Polish, German, Yiddish and all other non-Russian languages spoken by large sections of the local population (similar policies were, of course, pursued, somewhat more covertly, by Prussia in her Eastern Region—the notorious *Ostmarkenverein*—and by Austria in Galicia and Bohemia).

In particular, Alexander III's government oppressed the Jewish popu-lation. Volumes have been written analysing the reasons behind this anti-Jewish policy. There was, undoubtedly, religious fanaticism, certainly on Pobedonoʌstsev's part (and, consequently, on Alexander III's part). There were anti-Jewish movements in Prussia and Austria, the other Partition powers, caused by the inability of these countries to come to terms with the large and alien populations acquired with the new territories. And Russia always tried to keep abreast with the latest developments abroad. Above all, there was Disraeli.

The Russian claim to Constantinople

It is probably difficult for an Englishman to imagine the amount of hatred the Earl of Beaconsfield engendered in Russia. To the Orthodox, if Jerusalem was the birthplace of Christianity, Constantinople was the cradle of the Christian Church, the city where the great Caesar Constantine called in 325 the Council in nearby Nicaea to write the Creed; the city where he declared Christianity an official religion of the Roman Empire, the city where he built Hagia Sophia, the mother-church of Christendom, forcibly converted into a mosque by the Turkish infidels. And, of course, with Christianity Russia's entire culture had come from Constantinople.

The Czars were the protectors of the Orthodox faith, and for centuries it had been the aim of Orthodox Russian policy to recover Constantinople (called Czargrad, or Caesar's city, in Russian), for Christendom, and to protect the four Orthodox patriarchs (Constantinople, Antioch, Jerusalem and Alexandria), all under Turkish domination, and their oppressed flocks. In 1472 Prince Ivan III of Muscovy married Sophie, niece and heiress of the last Byzantine Emperor Constantine Paleologus, who died on the city-ramparts defending Constantinople from the Turks. In dynastic terms the Russian ruling house were considered legitimate heirs to the Byzantine dynasty and its possessions. This was quite a valid consideration: many European territories had come to their rulers through marriage; from Lithuania (to the Polish crown) to the Shetland Islands (from Norway to the Scottish crown).

When the Tenth Russo-Turkish War came in 1877 it had for Russia the character of a crusade. After some delay at Plevna the Russian armies were soon within sight of Constantinople, the supreme goal of four centuries. The Christian peoples of the Balkans were being persecuted by the Turks. In Bulgaria alone (under Turkish domination since the battle of Nicopol, 1396) 12,000 men, women and children had been massacred (by European pre-1917 standards, an enormity). The Bulgarian atrocities caused a storm of protest throughout Europe. In Russia, public opinion (which considered the Bulgars as brothers) clamoured for action, as always, ahead of the Czar.[3] In Britain, Gladstone published his celebrated pamphlet *Bulgarian Horrors* and, a few years later, conducted his Midlothian election campaign against British pro-Turkish policy.

Now was a chance for Russia to fulfil its historic mission and roll back Islam from Europe, stopped by Martel at Tours and Poitiers in 732 and finally pushed out by the Spaniards at the other end of the Mediterranean. But it was not to be.

Apart from its religious and historic significance (often underestimated in Britain), Constantinople and the Straits also had immense strategic importance (precisely the reason why Constantine founded his capital there). It is the counterpart to Gibraltar, the key to the eastern entrance of the Mediterranean. Particularly after the opening of the Suez Canal by the French in 1869 and the purchase of the Egyptian ruler's shareholding for Britain by Disraeli in 1875 (and ultimately the British occupation of Egypt in 1882) it was a cardinal aim of British policy to safeguard the sea-route to India, East Africa, Malaya and Australia, the main artery of the Empire, by dominating the Mediterranean, and the possible emergence of a Sebastopol-based Russian fleet astride the main British line of communications simply could not be tolerated (except, of course, in alliance with Russia, and that, in the face of the Kaiser's threat, was thirty years away, and unthinkable in

1877). Seven thousand Indian troops were transported to Malta, a gesture whose meaning was not lost in St Petersburg. As the Russian armies crossed the Danube, the British Mediterranean fleet, now wholly steam, sailed eastwards, negotiated the 50-mile-long Dardanelles, hugging the Gallipoli coast, in the narrows only a mile or so wide, and anchored in the Sea of Marmara. As the Russians approached Constantinople the Fleet moved north and anchored off the Princes Islands (Turkish, Kizil Adalar), its big guns trained on the Russian headquarters at San Stefano, a few miles south of Constantinople on the Marmara shore. Europe was watching the duel with bated breath. Through diplomatic channels, Disraeli made it clear that a Russian entry into Constantinople would be considered a *casus belli*.

Alexander II knew that, in the event of war, Britain would be supported by France and Austria (then a Mediterranean power through its long Adriatic seaboard), and that the newly forged Germany would support Austria. He could not take on the whole of Europe. It would be the Crimea all over again, with even more extended lines of communication for his troops, and correspondingly shorter ones for the enemy. He certainly would not want to conclude his reign with a catastrophe, like his father in 1855. With a heavy heart Alexander II gave way. He had seen himself, perhaps, entering Czargrad in solemn procession on a white charger, acclaimed by the Greek population of the city, witnessing the re-consecration of the great cathedral by the Holy Patriarch, ending the four centuries of shameful oppression by the kinsmen of the Tartars.

Alexander's dream was shattered. His name would be inscribed in the pages of history as Liberator of the peasants but not also as Liberator of Czargrad and the oppressed Christian peoples.

The Russian troops preparing for the final assault were halted, and peace concluded with the Turks at the Russian headquarters at San Stefano in 1878. The provisions of the Peace Treaty were very generous to the Turks: Turkey retained Constantinople and a slice of the Balkan peninsula, and recognised the total independence of Serbia, Romania and Montenegro. A principality of Bulgaria was to be formed, with a large territory including Macedonia. Even so, the British government considered the San Stefano Treaty unacceptable, which in those days meant that it could not come into force. The main British objection was that, Bulgaria being expected to become in practice a Russian dependancy, Constantinople would have been outflanked, placing it militarily at the mercy of Russia, who could therefore have enforced the passage of the Black Sea Fleet through the Straits at any time. The French and Austrians also did not want a Russian fleet in the Mediterranean, remembering the havoc wrought by Russian warships in the Eastern Mediterranean in 1770 (Cesme) and 1798.

Alexander had to agree to a second humiliation, to set aside the Treaty of San Stefano, and to take part in a peace conference, hosted by Bismarck's officially neutral Germany, flushed with the victory of 1870 and flexing its muscle, in Berlin. Not in Vienna this time. The Austrians were left in no doubt as to who was the senior partner now.

The Congress of Berlin (1878) was dominated by the personality of Disraeli, who proved a skilful, if decidedly ungentlemanly, negotiator, not averse to brinkmanship (ordering his special train to be got ready in mid-conference), and taking every advantage of the inadequacy of the chief Russian delegate, the elderly and high-living *grand seigneur* Prince Gorchákoff. In the event, Disraeli obtained much greater concessions than London had ever envisaged. There was going to be only a small Principality of Bulgaria north of the Balkan mountains, under the nominal suzerainty of the Sultan and in no way threatening the Straits. South of the Balkan range the autonomous province of Eastern Rumelia was formed. Austria received Bosnia and Hercegovina, thus balancing Russian influence in the Balkans. Russia gained the Black Sea coast south of the Caucasus, with Batum (now the major port for Baku oil). Turkey retained Albania on the Adriatic and a broad swathe across the Balkan peninsula, with Macedonia (including Salonika) and Thrace (including Adrianople), thus separating Greece from Serbia and Bulgaria. A grateful Sultan gave Cyprus to Britain, a convenient base to guard the Eastern Mediterranean and the approaches to the Suez Canal (the Greek population of the island had not been asked, but was, of course, jubilant to be freed of Turkish misrule). Queen Victoria gave the Garter to Disraeli, and he returned to London in triumph to become a national hero.

Indignation in Russia

Solomon Schmerling's grandson, Boris, my father, was born a few years after the Congress of Berlin. When he was a schoolboy of fourteen at the Gymnasium (grammar school) of Mogilév, the history teacher, otherwise a decent and considerate man, described the war of 1877 with the victorious Russian armies at the gates of Czargrad, and added: 'But the Yid Disraeli robbed Russia of the fruits of her victory.' Generally, there was no anti-Jewish feeling whatsoever at the Gymnasium, either among the teaching staff or among the schoolboys; the worst Father ever experienced was some friendly teasing by his classmates' getting him to pronounce the word *kukurúsa* (maize), it being generally thought that Jewish boys could not pronounce the rolling Russian 'R' (similar to the Scotch 'R')—I certainly cannot.

When Alexander III, urged on by Pobedonóstsev, embarked on the anti-

Jewish policy, in the eyes of many Russians he was avenging the humiliation of Berlin. Public opinion in Russia was indeed incensed. Educated
classes felt much stronger about Constantinople and the persecuted
Bulgarians (of all Slavonic peoples, closest to the Russians) than Alexander
II himself, who was accused of being half-hearted about the war because of
his German protestant antecedents. Turgénev, a liberal and anglophile,
wrote his celebrated poem *Croquet at Windsor*, depicting the Royal
Family playing croquet with the severed heads of the Bulgarian children
(the Turks had no gas-chambers and simply butchered). Disraeli, the first
statesman of Jewish descent on the European scene, had made a tremendous impression in all the chanceries; in Russia he was now cast in the role
of the Devil incarnate. Some people in Russia, even in government circles,
believed in a Jewish world conspiracy, whose agent was Disraeli (just as, a
generation later, Hitler and his followers believed that Karl Marx was the
agent of a Jewish world conspiracy). Hardly anyone in Petersburg
appreciated that Disraeli simply acted in the British interest, as perceived
by the British government and by British public opinion at the time. (Now, a
century later, it is possible with hindsight to arrive at a different conclusion:
with Russian control of the Straits the war might have been won in 1917
before the Bolshevik Revolution, which could never have taken place in
peacetime.)

Of course, Russia was a civilised and Christian country with a civilised
government. There were no arbitrary arrests, no concentration camps, no
mass murders. No deportations and no confiscation of property. Torture
had been abolished by Catherine the Great and the prohibition was complied with (until torture was re-introduced under Lenin). In schools, boys
were never beaten (the Army schools were said to be an exception).
Teachers were trained to maintain perfect discipline without any corporal
punishment, and addressed all secondary school pupils with the formal
'you' instead of the 'thou' that their parents would use. In the secondary
school Mother went to in Moscow, all girls were addressed as Mademoiselle
from the day of entry. Criminals and active revolutionaries were indeed sentenced to be transported to Siberia (in Britain, transportation to Australia
and Tasmania was ended in 1864, in France—to Cayenne—only in 1945).
Conditions were harsh by European pre-1917 standards, particularly on
Sakhalin; by Soviet and National Socialist standards it was paradise.[4]
Before the railway was built, the chain-gangs on the Vladimirka—the trunk-
road to Siberia via Vladimir—were a pitiful sight (so, no doubt, were the
British chain gangs in Australia and Tasmania[5]). The villagers used to give
the convicts food and tobacco; characteristically, they were allowed to do
this. And a whole folklore grew up about the life of the exiles in Siberia, with
songs about the Holy Baikal (the 450-mile-long lake) and the tarred barrels

in which prisoners escaped. There was, of course, no systematic ill-treatment of convicts. A prisoner could indeed be flogged for assault on a warder, and similar offences, but corporal punishment required the minister's signature in each case.[6] I well remember talks at home about public protests and interpolations in the Duma because the flogging of some unfortunate prisoner had been ordered; sometimes the protests were effective and the flogging order was rescinded. All this was, of course, outrageous by the highly civilised standards of pre-1917 Europe. I also remember indignant dinner-table talks at home about the allocation of handkerchiefs—yes, handkerchiefs—to revolutionaries exiled to Siberia. They were only allowed two handkerchiefs annually, and—under the primitive conditions prevailing, probably washing in a stream—the handkerchiefs never lasted a full year, so that part of the time the exiles had no handkerchiefs. Somehow I do not recall ever hearing complaints about the allocation of handkerchiefs in Hitler's concentration camps, or the Gulag labour camps. Presumably the prisoners were all well supplied with clean linen.

The anti-Jewish policy of Alexander III

As part of his reactionary and chauvinist policy, Alexander III oppressed the Jewish population of his realm. The instrument of the policy were the notorious discriminatory Temporary Regulations of 1882. According to this infamous ordinance, the Pale of Settlement residence restrictions, eased under the Czar Liberator, were again tightened, even excluding rural areas within the Pale. Travel to other parts of the country was severely restricted. Jews were totally excluded from the Civil Service (from university professors and judges to postmen and nightwatchmen) and all Jewish civil servants dismissed. A very onerous *numerus clausus* was introduced for secondary schools and universities (generally, for secondary schools 10 per cent in the Pale of Settlement, 5 per cent elsewhere and 3 per cent in Petersburg and Moscow; for universities, even less). Jewish children all received a primary education in the Jewish parochial schools, and were all literate (whereas 80 per cent of the general population were, at the time, illiterate peasants, just liberated from serfdom), and the *numerus clausus* meant that the majority were denied secondary education, and not admitted to universities (or had to study abroad, which was expensive and beyond the means of most). There were numerous other irksome restrictions, even a requirement to use on official documents the Yiddish form of first names (such as Shloima instead of Solomon which, though closer to the Hebrew original Shlomo, sounds ridiculous in Russian).

The Regulations had been called Temporary because Alexander III had appointed a Commission, presided over by Count Pahlen, to advise on the

position of the Jews in Russia and on any changes desirable in the legislation affecting them. They were issued pending any advice proffered by the
Pahlen Commission (in the event, the advice of the Commission, given after
five years of hearings and deliberations and recommending gradual complete abolition of all restrictions and disabilities, was ignored by the
Government), and remained in force until the February Revolution of
1917, though in many ways eased during World War I.

Furthermore, at the behest of the Ministry of the Interior an assembly of
the representatives of all Jewish communities was called in Petersburg to
discuss the position of the Jews in Russia. Solomon Schmerling, my great-
grandfather, proud member of the First Merchant Guild of Smolénsk, was a
delegate, and addressed the Assembly with an impassioned plea for the
abolition of all disabilities and restrictions with the aim of complete inte-
gration of the Jewish community. 'Trust us,' he said to the Government representatives, 'and you will find that we respond.' Great-grandfather
completed his speech with an expression of loyalty to the throne, and . . .
dropped dead in a final mute appeal.

Schmerling's sudden death obviously created a deep and lasting impression, and Father used to tell me that, even thirty years later, he would often
be introduced as Solomon Schmerling's grandson.

The *pogróms*

In addition to the formidable legal apparatus now harassing the Jewish
population there was an additional weapon in Pobedonóstsev's armoury;
the *pogróm*. Under Polish rule, there had been occasional attacks on Jewish
communities, to be sure. But they had all been spontaneous. It sometimes
happened that the Host was exposed for a long period in a Catholic church
and, if the temperature and humidity were right, a *red-coloured mould*
would develop.[7] The ignorant population believed that the Host was bleeding, and was demanding vengeance on the 'Christ-killers'. A mob, such as
can be found in any part of the world, would seize the occasion and rush into
the Jewish quarter, pillaging and murdering. Such riots were invariably put
down by the Polish authorities, and the Jews were allowed to keep weapons
and defend themselves. The only systematic and sustained persecution was
in 1648, when a revolt of the Cossacks in the then Polish part of Malorussia
occurred under Chmielnicki, who murdered in the most barbaric way all
Jews, Poles and Catholic priests in sight. A similar revolt and persecution
broke out in 1768. On the whole, however, the Jewish population was
always effectively protected by the Polish Crown.

Under Russian rule, after the partitions there were no attacks against the
Jewish population for a century. There was administrative hostility and

many restrictions, but no violence. The supposedly spontaneous *pogróms*, or anti-Jewish riots, commenced quite suddenly in the Alexander III–Pobedonóstsev era, rendered possible, it must be admitted, by the considerable anti-Jewish feeling within a section of Russian public opinion after the Congress of Berlin.

In Britain the last sectarian (anti-Catholic) *pogróm*, organised by Lord Gordon, took place in London in 1780. Now, a century later, this contemptible and, in the end, boomeranging method of persecuting minorities by mob violence, supposedly spontaneous, appeared in Russia.

Notes

1   Bishop Montefiore is, I believe, his great-great-great-grandson.
2   The coach is now preserved in the Montefiore Museum in Jerusalem.
3   Tyutchev sang:
      The dome of ancient Sophia
      In restored Byzantia
      Once again hallowed by the altar of Christ,
      Prostrate before it, Czar of Russia
      And arise as all-Slav Czar.
4   In 1913 the total number of convicts in penal servitude in Siberia was 32,826; today the Gulag population is 4–5 million, over a hundred-fold increase.
5   The thousand-mile journey, in leg-fetters, to Irkutsk took three months.
6   Flogging was carried out with the *knout* (pronounced knoot), said to be less barbaric than the 'cat', but, of course, the 'cat' was last used in England in 1797.
7   The bread of the Orthodox Eucharist is leavened and, apparently, not attacked by this red-coloured mould which has caused so much bloodshed in Germany and Poland.

3

The grandparents

After Solomon Schmerling's sudden death the conduct of the family business was taken over by his son Moses, my grandfather. Grandfather Moses had married a Sandomírsky, of a distinguished, if somewhat impoverished, family obviously originating in Sandomír, the Polish fortress-city on the Vistula (Act III of *Boris Godunov* is set in Sandomír). However, at the time of the marriage the family lived in Chernígov, one of the oldest cities in Malorussia (Ukraine), on a tributary of the Dnieper. It was somewhat unusual for 'Litvaks' and 'Pollaks' to intermarry, the 'Litvaks' considering themselves, for no particular reason, as decidedly superior. On the other hand, the Sandomírskys had some renowned rabbis in the family, something the Schmerlings had always been lacking. The marriage was a most happy one.

Even in Solomon's time, the importance of the road-building business had declined. The Railway Age had come to Russia somewhat belatedly. Only one line, the main line from St Petersburg to Moscow, had been built by the end of Nicholas I's reign in 1855. The Imperial Commission that had been sent to England to inspect the new railways arrived at Vauxhall Station, then the terminus for the Channel ports, as the railway bridges across the Thames had not yet been built. The Commission therefore gained the impression that Vauxhall was simply the English word for a railway terminus, and to this day all railway termini in Russia are called *voksál* (e.g. the celebrated Finlandski Voksál in Petersburg, where Lenin arrived in 1917, loaded with German money, to organise the revolt against the Republican Government). There was not much railway-building for the next decade or two, but after that the Railway Age came with a vengeance, and no more trunk-roads were being built. Moreover, Alexander III had concluded an alliance with France (no longer, it seems, considered in Petersburg a revolutionary power and soundly anti-British) in 1891. The French generals ascribed their military disasters in the Franco-Prussian War of 1870, and particularly the débacle of Sedan (where almost 100,000 French troops, with Napoleon III at their head, were taken prisoner) with some justification to the fact that Prussia by that time had a system of strategic railways which enabled it to move troops rapidly along the front, whereas the French armies were still marching. France, with the black-draped statues of Alsace and Lorraine at the Place de la Concorde daily before the eyes of the generals at the War Ministry, gave large loans to the Russian government for the building of railways, particularly in the Western region, in order to speed up the Russian mobilisation period to fourteen days, and generally provide better mobility for the Russian Army.

There was now no trunk-road building whatsoever, and, before the century was out, Grandfather liquidated the family business and took an early retirement. The inherited family fortune was 600,000 roubles, most of it invested in Russian government bonds. The coupon was, as far as I recall hearing from Father, between 3 and 4 per cent which, in the absence of inflation and of income tax, gave a most acceptable income of some 20,000 roubles. Very few Jewish families were in this enviable position.

Travel to the Crimea and the Caucasus was forbidden to Jewish residents of the Pale; in fact, these areas facing Turkey were forbidden to all Jews, even those exempt from the general residential restrictions, as someone in Petersburg apparently though that most Jews were Turkish spies. Generally, the small minority of Russians, non-Jews and Jews, who could afford foreign travel went to Germany and Austria; the aristocracy travelled to France. Robespierre, after all, had now been dead for a century.

The Schmerlings, I believe the only Jewish family in Mogilév able to afford foreign travel, journeyed each summer to Austria, where Grandfather took the cure at Bad Ischl, a delightful spa offering many pleasant walks and excursions. And in the *Kurpark* one could walk literally within a few yards of the Emperor Francis-Joseph, a dignified old gentleman accompanied by a very small suite. To a visitor from Russia, where the Czar could not generally be approached to within a mile, particularly after the calamitous assassination of Alexander II, this was a unique and elevating experience. On the way home the family would stop at Vienna, then one of the great European capitals, and spend a few days shopping, with a visit or two to the Opera perhaps (there was none in Mogilév, and Moscow was out of bounds).

Grandfather is bitten by a rabid dog

On one occasion, though, my grandparents did travel to France. In 1887, or 1888, Grandfather was bitten by a rabid dog (fifty years later, six million Jewish people were). This was quite a usual occurrence at the time in Russia, as it is today even in many European countries, not to mention India. However, the only treatment then known—cauterising the wound with a red-hot iron—did not help, and Grandfather developed the dreaded symptoms of hydrophobia, one of nature's many cruel forms of attack upon man. The virus lodges in the nervous system, through which it progresses very slowly, but steadily. Swallowing becomes progressively more difficult, and lethal convulsions may occur in a matter of days. There was just one possibility, said the doctor. He had read that in Paris a young French doctor had cured a child bitten by a rabid dog by injecting some fluid taken from an infected animal. Although it did not seem to make sense to inject more of the infection, Dr Pasteur, the Frenchman, was apparently treating patients with reasonable success—whether the success was permanent it was too early to say. There was not a day to lose, said Grandmother. As the railway reached Mogilév only in 1904, Grandmother drew a thousand gold roubles from the bank, packed some wicker trunks and ordered a *troika* sleigh to take Grandfather, now seriously ill, and herself through the winter snows to Orsha Junction, the nearest point on the railway, some fifty miles away. They were pursued by a pack of ravenous wolves but managed to shake them off, and reached Orsha without losing their way—a common hazard in the snow-covered landscape. Back to civilisation, at Orsha, Grandparents took the train to Minsk, where they boarded the Moscow–Paris express, which brought them, via Warsaw and Berlin, to Paris in about 48 hours. There was, of course, a change of carriages, at Warsaw, I believe, as the Russian railways were built on the wide 5-foot gauge, and the Central- and West-European network on 4 foot 8½ inches. The adjustable bogies which can surmount the 3½-inch difference had not yet been invented.

Within four days of leaving the family home, Grandfather was being examined by Dr Louis Pasteur. Fortunately, the great man had some vaccine in store, laboriously prepared from the spinal cord of infected rabbits. This source of the remedy was concealed from Grandfather as rabbits, like pigs and hares, are on the list of prescribed animals that are not *kosher*. Grandfather underwent a course of injections which brought almost immediate alleviation of the hydrophobia symptoms, and after some three weeks he was a cured man, living for another thirty years or more, rather than dying a horrible death. So ended Grandparents' one and only visit to Paris. I doubt if they saw any of the sights of that great city, probably not even the Arc de Triomphe with the familiar names of Smolénsk, Vítebsk and Mogilév chiselled in the marble (though not the names of the million men who died on both sides in that most senseless campaign to satisfy one man's vanity).

Daily life at Mogilév

Apart from the annual expedition to Bad Ischl, life was uneventful for the Schmerling family. Grandparents had three sons and two daughters. The youngest son, Boris, was my father. Grandfather took a great interest in the education of the boys and their scholastic progress; each of the three brothers had his own study, with desk and oil lamp, of the latest type, and was expected to be top of the form.

In the morning the whole family, which included a few maiden or widowed aunts, would breakfast together, on the usual home-baked rye bread, quite delicious, home-made jam and China tea, which in Russia was drunk from glasses, with lemon or apple slices. Tea was not sugared but, as widely practised in Russia, a lump of sugar was held in the mouth when drinking; this was not considered good manners in polite society, but was more economical, there being a heavy excise duty on sugar. Butter, always a luxury in Russia, was only served with the cold breakfast on the Sabbath. Grandfather, although quite wealthy by the standards of the Pale, disapproved of commoners' adopting 'von Baron' habits and would never permit butter on weekdays.

After breakfast, with the boys off, on foot, to the Gymnasium Grandfather would repair to his study with its print of the Temple Wall, cover his head with the *yermolka* skullcap and don the philacteries (two tiny leather satchels of cubic shape containing the Ten Commandments and other biblical texts and fixed with leather straps to the forehead, left arm facing the heart). He would then drape the black and white striped *tallit* prayer shawl over his shoulders and say the full morning prayers, in Hebrew, followed by reading of the Scriptures and of the commentaries on the passage, all in Hebrew (or Aramaic). The standard Hebrew Bible, as published by the rabbinical authorities in Vilna, consisted of a few lines from the Pentateuch, printed in, perhaps, quarter-inch letters in the centre of the page, and surrounded in small print, by the appropriate passages from the six leading bible commentators (Rashi, Maimonides and others). If it was the anniversary of the death of one of Grandfather's parents he would have the memorial candle burning since the previous night, and say, as behoves the eldest son, three times a day, the *Kaddish*:

Magnify and hallow the Name of the Lord . . .

The Sabbath began, as all Jewish feasts and anniversaries, on the preceding evening. The house was tidied up and spotless. After Grandfather's return from evening service the family, in their Sabbath best, would sit down for a meal, generally the traditional fish (carp, perhaps) with stuffing, known as *gefilte fisch*, in the many very poor families often the only proper meal of the week. Grandfather would pronounce the blessing over the bread and wine. It was the last hot meal for twenty-four hours; no work was permitted on the Lord's Day, and this meant just that: no cooking, no lighting of fires. All the roads leading out of Mogilév had a signpost indicating, for the benefit of the Jewish population, how far one was permitted to *walk* on the Sabbath. Driving was strictly prohibited. To make non-Jewish servants work was considered particularly reprehensible, taking advantage, as it were, of their ignorance of God's Commandments. Most Jewish families had no servants in any case. The Schmerlings had. Alexei, the old porter-cum-gardener, himself a devout Orthodox Christian, knew well what Grandmother, to whom he was devoted, expected of him. On the Sabbath, when Grandfather came home for a brief rest between the three services of the day (not counting the Sabbath Eve service), the faithful Alexei repaired to his quarters, took off his left boot and, using it in the time-honoured manner as a bellows to get the charcoal aflame in the samovár, launched into his favourite *Anglichánin Mudréts*:

> The clever Englishman
> To help the work
> Invented the machine
> But the Russian peasant
> To speed the work
> Sings a song . . .

When the samovár was steaming, Alexei brewed the tea in the teapot, placed it on top of the samovár and came up deferentially to Grandfather. I have just got the samovár going *for myself*, he would say, and would the *bárin* (squire) like a glass of hot lemon tea. This was, of course, quite lawful, and Grandfather readily agreed. Fortified, Grandfather would then walk back to the main Synagogue where he was generally called to read a Lesson. The curtain of the Ark was drawn, the handwritten bible scroll, standing upright, carried out with reverence, the silver crown, often with little bells, lifted and the heavy, gold-embroidered velvet cloak removed. The scroll was opened at the right place and Grandfather called to read the final (eighth) Lesson for the day (a mark of distinction).

Shortly after Pentecost (a Jewish holiday too) Grandparents moved to their *dácha*, or summer house, at Páshkovo in the woods nearby. Actually, the *dácha*, as opposed to the town house, was not owned by the Schmerlings, as even in the Pale Jews could not own rural property. Obviously, the appearance of a Jewish estate-owner could not be tolerated; it was already bad enough that so many estates were owned by Catholic Poles, schismatic azymites, crossing themselves the wrong way round. The bankrupt cherry orchards were generally acquired by liberated serfs, or their descendants, as in the Chekhov play. Most Jews, in any case, were too poor to move out for the summer. However, Solomon Schmerling had acquired a very long lease of a pleasant *dácha*, next to the Archdeacon's summer residence with its extensive grounds (confiscated by the Bolsheviks and, in the last war, a Gestapo headquarters, complete with mobile gas chamber—these horrors were mercifully beyond the horizon). Father remembers one summer when there was a drought; this was a calamity for the whole region, as it could have meant a famine. No grain was imported—there was then nowhere to import it from in such quantities. Tables covered with white cloth were moved into the fields, serving as altars, and the Archdeacon and his priests held special Services of Supplication. The rain came at the last moment, and the harvest was saved.

The Schmerling family spent the summer at the *dácha*, except for the month in Austria, and returned to the town house in time for the Ten Days of Awe of the Lord's Judgment, commencing with the New Year, and culminating on Yom Kippur, the day on which the Judgment is delivered. This is a Fast Day which, in the Jewish religion, means that everyone, men and women, starting from the age of 13, are not allowed to partake of any food or drink for twenty-four hours, not even a glass of water. There was no way in which the faithful Alexei could help here. Pious Jews would spend the previous evening, and the whole day, in the synagogue, in their stockinged feet, praying for forgiveness of their sins. I cannot think of many sins Grandfather may have committed, except possibly eating freshly pre-pared meals on the Sabbath at the hotel in Bad Ischl and similar offences, but naturally he spent the day at the synagogue like everyone else. It was a very exhausting day (the reason why it was chosen by Egypt for the attack on Israel in 1973). Pious people, like Grandfather, only returned home after sunset, to a traditional breakfast of a piece of herring with black bread, and a glass of hot lemon tea. Before that, however, in a traditional gesture of supererogation, one would drive in a few nails for the tabernacle that would be required within the next few days.

Naturally, some local customs grew up which verged on the superstitious. There was an ancient synagogue somewhere near Vilna where during the Palm branch Procession round the synagogue on the Day of the Great Hosanna everyone bowed deeply at a certain point. No-one knew why. Was it, perhaps, where a martyr had met his death? The reason became apparent when medieval drawings of the Procession were found showing a low stove pipe crossing at that point.

The *pogróm*

Winter came soon. One day, when Grandfather was in his study at morning prayers, a policeman called with a verbal message from the Chief of Police. Grandfather could not be disturbed, so Grandmother took the message, which caused great worry. Grandfather was invited to call at the Police Chief's house after the mid-day meal for a game of cards. Grandmother knew what this meant, and so did Grandfather. He walked across to the bank and drew out five hundred roubles. Wealthy Jews (and not only Jews) were expected to play cards with the Chief of Police (and lose heavily) from time to time. This was natural. Nor was Russia unique in this respect. It happened in all the numerous countries where there was no public account-ability and no elected parliament to watch over the rights of the citizen and prevent abuses of power. But the next game of cards was not due until after Easter. Why today? After a hurried meal, and fearing the worst, Grandfather walked across through the uncleared snow to the Chief's head-quarters. A uniformed policeman opened the door, greeted Grandfather deferentially, as he would any *bárin*, and conducted him to the Chief's study. The nickel-plated samovár was steaming, with the large white and blue china teapot warming at the top. The Chief offered Grandfather a glass of tea, with a slice of lemon and a lump of sugar, and did not keep him in sus-pense much longer. A telegram had arrived from Petersburg. A *pogróm* had been arranged for the next day. The Schmerling home would be protected—the Chief would find a way—and generally he would try to keep the disorder to the minimum required to satisfy them in Petersburg. Grandfather could give a few discreet warnings but no preparations must be seen, otherwise the scoundrels would notice, and report him to the Ministry, and the next time, it would be murder. Synagogues would not be attacked but must not be used as shelter. The police would not be allowed to interfere, except, of course, if the riot got out of hand and Christian persons or property were attacked, as happened recently in the neighbouring province.

The only house officially protected by the police, was that of the Fiscal Rabbi. Towns in the Pale had two rabbis: Spiritual and Fiscal. The Fiscal was, in effect, Registrar of Births, Marriages and Deaths for the Jewish population (as the Christian clergy were for their communities), and the Registers were used by the authorities for tax and conscription purposes. It would never have done for the Registers to go up in flames.

Like all policemen, the Chief hated *pogróms*, not for humanitarian reasons (although he was, at heart, quite a decent person) but because he prided himself on the maintenance of law and order in Mogilév, where nothing worse than a drunken Sunday evening brawl ever occurred. There were no murders and few burglaries. And now he had, on the orders of some incompetent court-favourite in Petersburg, to put up with the spectacle of a mob rioting and looting with impunity.

Grandfather returned home a sad man. So the *pogróms* had reached Mogilév. He sent discreet messages to the elders of the community, and various inobtrusive and largely futile precautions were taken. Expectant mothers, whose confinement was imminent, were taken into Grandfather's home, together with the midwife, ostensibly to help with the housework. As the railway had not yet reached Mogilév the nearest town that had a Jewish community and where some refugees could have been placed was inaccessible over the snow-bound roads.

An extreme, ultra-chauvinistic organisation had been founded, the Union of the Russian People, with a paramilitary wing, the *Black Hundreds*. This theatrically secretive organisation, a kind of Russian version of the Ku Klux Klan, was devoted to maintaining by violence ethnic Russian supremacy against all *inoródtsy*, or ethnically non-Russians, and particularly Jews, though not exclusively. The Black Hundred had spread word that the 'Christ-killers' were the enemies of the Czar, and tomorrow they would be taught a lesson and could be relieved of their ill-gotten possessions with impunity.

Whilst Grandmother was busy preparing the house as a shelter (and a possible maternity home), Grandfather repaired to his study, praying for the intercession of the Archangels Gabriel and Michael, the protectors of Israel: *El moléh rachamim*, God full of Mercy, he would chant, *Avinu Malkénu*, Our Father, our Lord, let this affliction pass Thine people. At the same time, the faithful Alexei went to his married quarters, and touched the ground three times with his forehead, in front of the *kivót* (the console with the icons, standing in the corner of the living-room, as customary in Orthodox households), exclaiming *Góspodi Pomílui*, Lord have Mercy, each time.

In the meantime a liquor store was broken into, and a drunken mob of layabouts, as can be found in any town around the world, went on the rampage in the narrow streets of Mogilév in an orgy of destruction. Houses known to be lived in by Jewish families were broken into, with the occupants mostly cowering in the cellar. Oil lamps, cutlery and anything useful was looted, and furniture and bedding thrown out of the broken windows and set alight. Some houses were set alight too, mostly unintentionally. Any Jews encountered would, of course, be beaten up.

As the police were forbidden to protect Jewish property, the Chief had seen to it that a fireman in full uniform was posted in front of the Schmerling house. To the drunkards on the rampage one blue uniform was as good as another, and the rioters left well alone. After some hours of passive observation the Chief reckoned enough damage had been done to enable him to send a satisfying report to Petersburg. A posse of policemen was despatched to tell the rioters that they had done their duty to the Czar and the party was over. Police instructions were, at that time, generally obeyed in Russia, and the mob dispersed, carrying featherbeds and tablecloths as booty to pacify their irate spouses.

It had been an exceedingly mild *pogróm*, as *pogróms* went. No-one got killed, and only one young woman raped (non-Jewish, mistaken for Jewish). Some young men who attempted to resist the attackers were injured, one severely. The Schmerling home had been protected, as the Chief had promised, with all inmates. There had been no premature births.

Dissatisfied with the lack of support from the population, evidenced during the *pogróm*, the Union of Russian People stepped up their vicious propaganda. A year or two later the doctor prescribed Grandmother a glass of fresh milk daily—I believe she was inclining to consumption. Milk of reasonable quality was difficult to obtain, and Grandfather purchased a milch-cow which the faithful Alexei took to the common to graze. When he called in the evening to collect the animal the cow was in agony, a piece of paper attached to its tail, with the clumsy handwriting: 'No Yid cows wanted here.' The animal had been fed ground glass and had to be destroyed. That was, as far as I know, the only success the pernicious Union managed to achieve in sober Mogilév. When a *pogróm* was organised in a neighbouring provincial capital the instruction telegram from the Ministry was intercepted and leaked to a liberal national newspaper which proclaimed that a *pogróm* had been ordered for the day in that city. When the senior officials reached their desks at the Ministry their frantic countermanding telegrams could no longer stop the *pogróm*, which was by now in full swing, nor could they stop the trains carrying the correspondents of the world press.

In the meantime, in Petersburg a forgery was produced, *The Protocols of the Elders of Zion*, in which Jewish politicians and bankers from all countries meet in secret to discuss plans for a Jewish world government. There are several versions, I believe. In the one I read some fifty years ago the conspirators meet in the Jewish cemetery in Prague (with the author hiding in a tomb, as recording equipment had not yet been invented), at midnight, and I remember my astonishment at this venue, knowing how much typical Jewish bankers disliked draughts. Dr Goebbels did not make much use of the *Protocols*, probably because they had been proved a forgery in a court case in Berlin in 1923, and in many courts round the world, but the *Protocols* are found even today in anti-Jewish armouries in South America and other more remote countries.

The new Czar

Czar Alexander III died suddenly of kidney disease in 1894, only fifty years of age, at Livadia, his sumptuous *dácha* in the Crimea (President Roosevelt's residence during the Yalta Conference of 1945). When Alexander had it built, all Jewish families established at Yalta since Turkish times were expelled, as the Czar, or his advisers, considered it unseemly, possibly dangerous, for Jews to live within a mile or two of the Imperial residence. Alexander's elder son became Czar Nicholas II. Generally, in autocratic Russia a change of monarch heralded a change of policy. This system worked, after a fashion, rather like the periodic changes of government under a parliamentary two-party system. There were many hopes that the new Czar would resume his grandfather's liberal policy, bring autocracy to an end and introduce constitutional government. The Jewish population in particular, hoped for an abolition of the hated Temporary Regulations, and the grant of full civil rights. Very soon, all these hopes were dashed. Nicholas II was 26 years of age, by nature and upbringing a landed gentleman, with a love of country pursuits and dislike of affairs of state, in which he was totally inexperienced. The new Czar proved conscientious and well meaning, but weak in the extreme, without any will of his own, acceptable, perhaps, in a constitutional monarchy, in the absence of any crisis, but disastrous for an autocrat, and in a crisis. Nicholas chose the line of least resistance by continuing the misguided policies of his father, Alexander III. The fanatical and incorruptible Pobedonóstsev remained. The incompetent and corrupt courtiers remained. The monarchy continued on the road to ruin.

The accession of the new Czar was marred by a major disaster. As all the Czars before him, Nicholas II was crowned in the great Cathedral of the Assumption in the Kremlin, built by the Italian architect Fioraventi, whom the Empress Sophie, the heiress to the throne of Byzantium and consort of Czar Ivan III, had brought to Moscow. The coronation was celebrated by a great popular festival organised in the Khody˙nka field on the outskirts of Moscow. Several hundred thousand Muscovites were entertained with military bands and free refreshment. The field was, in fact, normally used for military exercises and was criss-crossed by deep trenches. The authorities had ordered these trenches to be covered up but, whether from incompetence or graft or both, the covering planks were far too thin. When a rush occurred for some reason, the planks gave way, and people started falling into the deep trenches. This caused a panic, with more and more people piling up in the trenches and crushing and suffocating those beneath them. Finally mounted Cossacks appeared to restore order and trampled more people underfoot. Altogether over a thousand people died; the exact figure will never be known. As there was no public accountability of ministers, no Parliament where questions could be asked and no coroner (a unique English institution)—in fact, none of the traditional safeguards of good administration—there was no public enquiry and probably no private enquiry either. This disaster had a shattering impact in Russia and was considered a bad augury for the new reign.

Under the new Czar, with Pobedonóstsev continuing at his side, there was no let-up in the Government's action against the Jewish population. Particularly when Plehvé, of East Prussian extraction, and a Jew-hater, became Head of Police and then, in 1902, Minister of the Interior, *pogróms* increased in intensity and frequency. At the notorious Easter *pogróm* in Kishinev in 1903, Plehvé's masterpiece, some *fifty* people were killed and six hundred injured, and over a thousand homes looted and destroyed, with their inhabitants rendered homeless.[1] The riot lasted two or three days with the police under strict orders, as always, not to intervene. The culprits were not apprehended (they never were) although their identity was well known. As it happened, by that time, as an unavoidable result of political repression, revolutionary terrorism was quite ripe in Russia. There were many assassinations, and when Plehvé was murdered in 1904 by (non-Jewish) revolutionaries religious Jews considered his assassination as just retribution by the Lord.[2]

The Jewish population of the Pale numbered some six million. Hemmed in and restricted in many ways by the Temporary Regulations of 1882, a large part of the population simply had no opportunity of earning a decent living, and were condemned to an existence of poverty and squalor. And now they were exposed to deliberately organised mob violence.

Life in the Pale has been described in the many stories by Sholem Alechem (S. Rabbinówicz)—on whose 'Tawje the Milkman' the play *Fiddler on the Roof* is based—and by Mendele Mocher Sephorim (J. Abrámovicz) and life of the Russian immigrants on New York's East Side by Sholem Ash ('East River') and numerous other writers.

A small part of the population succeeded in breaking out, perhaps by acquiring a university degree, or by wealth (inherited or acquired, mostly legitimately, sometimes by hook or by crook). And, of course, there was the unheroic possibility of disingenuous conversion to the Orthodox Church which immediately removed all the disabilities and restrictions heaped upon Jews (the racialist theory had not yet been invented, or if it had, in a sense, by Gobineau, it had not yet reached the realm of politics). Quite a few academics, conservatoire teachers and others chose this way rather than being forced by a bigoted government to give up their life's work.

Altogether, from a Jewish population of some six million, about two hundred thousand, or just over three per cent, qualified for various reasons for residence outside the Pale. These privileged few generally lived in comfortable conditions, and a handful became millionaires. They never forgot the misery in the Pale.

Emigration

For the majority in the Pale of Settlement there was only one way out: emigration. Between 1881 and 1914 something like two and half million Jewish people emigrated, mostly to the USA, a small number to Britain,[3] until the passing of the anti-immigration Aliens Act of 1905 reduced immigration to Britain to a trickle. The immigrants to Britain included the Soskices and the Shinwells, the Sieffs, the Wolfsons and the Weinstocks, Lord Grade's parents, Moiseiwitsch and Solomon, and many other families now distinguished in public and commercial life and the arts.

Return to the land

Not everyone in the Pale wanted to emigrate to America. The squalor of the New York sweatshops (fully reported in letters home) did not frighten them—it frequently offered an improvement on conditions in the Pale—and, above all, there was no political persecution. But emigration to a foreign country (something fortunately outside the ken of the British emigrant) required a fairly robust character, and entailed a clear break with the past (however unpleasant this past may have been for many emigrants). True, by the turn of the century a fairly cohesive Russian–Jewish community (Yiddish-speaking) had been built up in New York City, and immigrants often had relatives to go to. However, America was, a hundred years ago, still a fairly raw and brash country, where none of the unwritten laws and taboos of the homeland operated, which softened the harsh conditions of life. In Minsk one did not evict a widow with small children if she was in arrears with the rent; on New York's East Side one could and did. In 'Anatevka' (the imaginary but typical locale of the *Fiddler on the Roof*) if one had been swindled one would complain to the *rebbe*, and he would cause the swindler to make amends. In New York there were dozens of rabbis, but none had temporal authority. Moreover, a large part of the Jewish population of the Pale was essentially rural in outlook—the market towns were small, the economy rural and life was dominated by the growing and harvesting of crops, by hay and timber, cattle and horses. Many Jews—though in Europe always barred from the soil—had the age-old yearning to nurture with their own hands the produce they were dealing with. Moreover, many young Jews were smarting from the gibe that all Jews were middlemen, parasites who could not with their own hands produce the basic necessities of life, and who were only exploiting the labour of others.

One answer were the agricultural settlements organised by the Jewish Colonization Association (ICA), founded in 1891 by the great philanthropist Baron von Hirsch, the Brussels banker and railway magnate. The colonies, in the Argentine and elsewhere including even Russia (where the Government allowed some Jewish settlement in the Crimea and the under-populated southern steppes acquired from Turkey) were for a while quite successful and offered thousands of young people the opportunity of earning their living by the sweat of their brow. All the same, there was always the Sword of Damocles of political hostility hanging above them—they were there on sufferance and they knew it. The real answer to the desire of many Jews, to lead a life of honest toil on the land in a community of like-minded people of the same ilk, the same background and tradition lay in *Zionism*.

There were many strands that came together to form the political movement of Zionism. The Jews had never given up their hope of regaining possession of the Land of Israel lost through Roman aggression. In the parochial schools every Jewish schoolboy in the Pale, while studying, almost dissecting, the Bible learnt that the Lord had given Eretz Israel (the Land of Israel) to the Jews in all perpetuity (the word 'Palestine' does not exist in Hebrew; it is of Greek origin and referred initially to the southern coastal strip inhabited by the Philistines). An old and pious Jew, widowed and feeling that his days were numbered, would, as Father told me, quite often sell his meagre possessions, scrape together the fare for the voyage and travel to Jerusalem in order to spend his last days there. There was, throughout the centuries, a permanent Jewish presence in the Old City, praying daily at the *Kotel*, the West wall of the Temple Mount (whose ascent is forbidden by the rabbinical authorities to Orthodox Jews lest they inadvertently step on to the site of the Holy of Holies). Only during the brief period of Arab rule from 1948 to 1967 were the Jews expelled and totally excluded from the Old City, and latrines built against the Western Wall, the only relic of the Temple.

The Paschal Meal always ends with the time-hallowed words: *Leshonó haboóh b'Jerusholáim*—next year in Jerusalem. 'Jerusalem, lest I forget thee, may my right hand wither,' sang the Psalmist.

In previous centuries there had been false Messiahs who claimed they would bring the Jews back to the Holy Land. In the seventeenth century, Sabbatai Zwi, a Turkish-born Jew, almost assembled the Jewish equivalent of a crusade to settle in the ancestral home. In 1700 a convoy of Polish Jews led by one Judah he Hasid arrived in Jerusalem and settled in the Jewish Quarter.

The idea of a Jewish resettlement in the Promised Land was always alive. The Jews have never recognised the Roman, Arab and Turkish conquests. As early as 1855 Sir Moses Montefiore purchased an estate near Jaffa to be used for Jewish settlement. George Eliot's Daniel Deronda (1876) departs for 'Palestine' to establish a home for the Jews there. After the Temporary Regulations of 1882 the Movement of Return to the ancestral land naturally received new impetus in Russia. An organisation sprung up, the *Chovevé Zion* (Friends of Zion), buying derelict and uninhabited land in Palestine and reclaiming it. A whole generation of committed Russian–Jewish youth went out and toiled in the malaria-infested swamps, draining the marshes and creating flourishing vegetable gardens and orange groves from neglected waste-land. One of Father's cousins from Mogilév, although with an economically assured future in Russia, joined these pioneers who died young so that future generations might live. Another young man who emigrated from Russia (1906) was the future Prime Minister of Israel, David Ben-Gurion; yet another, one of his successors, Levi Eshkol. In 1909, Tel Aviv, the first modern city built by Jews for Jews, was founded. Baron Edmond de Rothschild, then in Paris, acquired undying fame by supporting these early colonies.

After World War I the Jewish resettlement of Israel was mainly sustained by emigration from re-created Poland (and Romania). Professor Weizmann, the first President of Israel (*Trial and Error*, London, 1949, p. 119) makes the important point that every country has a *saturation point* for Jews (or any other minority), depending not on the Jews and their behaviour but on the 'solvent power' (he was a chemist!) of that country. Poland, as constituted at Versailles, had inherited a Jewish population of some 10 per cent, an utterly indigestible minority figure for any country; even more so if the country is a re-emerging one, trying to find its own character, and further aggravated if the minority is not spread through all levels but, for historic reasons, is concentrated in the towns of a largely rural country, in overcrowded and degrading conditions (the 'Judennot', the misery of the Jews).[4] The Jewish youth of Poland, led by Menachem Begin, realised that out of ten of them, nine had no future (except as unwanted and despised middlemen) and emigrated to Israel to the extent possible. Unfortunately in 1939 there were still millions left to be exterminated by Hitler.

It was left to Theodor Herzl (1860–1904), an Austrian-born writer and journalist, to provide the political framework for the Jewish repatriation movement.

This was the time of the inevitable European backlash resulting from the destruction (actually self-destruction) of the Polish Realm, and the emancipation of the Jews throughout Europe (except Russia). In Vienna, Karl Lueger, a precursor and teacher of Adolf Hitler, inveighed against the Jews, and managed to get himself elected Lord Mayor in 1897. Fortunately, under the Emperor, he could do only limited harm. In Germany, Adolf

Stoecker was Court Preacher (yes, he was actually a Protestant pastor) and organised political anti-semitism. Even in France, the cradle of *Egalité*, Captain Dreyfus (the family evidently originally came from Trèves) was in 1894 deliberately framed, convicted of espionage for Germany, publicly degraded and condemned to penal servitude on Devil's Island off the French Guiana coast. Herzl was reporting the trial for the *Neue Freie Presse* of Vienna, and was so shocked by the ensuing crude anti-Jewish agitation in France that he came to the conclusion that it was necessary to create a territory to which Jews who were not wanted in their countries of birth or who felt alienated there could emigrate, and sustain themselves by honest toil without becoming a burden to anyone. Herzl expressed his thoughts in his famous book, *Der Judenstaat* (1896), the title of which means The State of the Jews (often mistranslated as The Jewish State). It is some fifty years since I read the book, but I remember clearly that Herzl envisaged the new state with little specific Jewish religious or ethnic attributes. The flag, I believe, was going to be not the historic Blue and White adopted by the State of Israel but Eight Stars, symbolising the Eight-hour Day (at the turn of the century considered the highest goal of all social endeavour; even Britain, in the vanguard of progress, was still ruled by the seventh Earl of Shaftesbury's Ten-hour Bill). And the language of Herzl's Judenstaat? All settlers should speak their native tongues and, in the end, one of them would prevail. It was generally assumed that this would be Yiddish, or modern German. There is no doubt that the vast majority of the young people without any prospect of a decent and productive life in their homelands who went to reclaim Eretz Israel would have done so on the basis of *Der Judenstaat*.

A year later, in 1897, Herzl organised the First Zionist Congress in Basel in Switzerland, which adopted the aim 'To create for the Jewish people a home in Palestine secured by public law'. Grandfather attended the Congress as observer—Bad Ischl was not far away—and was most impressed with the political framework to be provided for the existing and future Jewish colonies in the Holy Land

In 1901 the KKL Fund was established, with the aim of buying neglected waste-land in Palestine and organising Jewish colonies in order to reclaim the land and grow food. The land the Fund bought was mostly derelict or otherwise non-arable, and certainly not settled; until 1947 not a single Arab had been displaced or evicted by the Jewish colonisation (what happened after the War of Independence is described later). The fact was that Palestine was grossly underpopulated. After the Arab Conquest, and even more under Turkish rule, the old irrigation systems had been allowed to go to ruin, the forests were destroyed without replanting and the entire country had become a wilderness. When Allenby captured Palestine from the Turks in

1917 in a brilliant feat of arms, the total Arab population of the *whole* of Palestine—cis- and transjordanian—numbered 600,000 and led a wretched, semi-nomadic existence. Under the British mandate and Jewish colonisation there was very considerable *Arab* immigration into Palestine, attracted by the greatly improved living conditions and opportunities.

Now Israel alone, without the 'West Bank' territories, supports a total population of 3.9 million (including 600,000 Arabs) and a million Arabs live in the 'West Bank' and a further over 1.5 million (not counting the still-unintegrated inmates of the Camps) in transjordanian Palestine (where Jews are barred from settling). The total Arab population of Palestine has therefore increased fivefold, and their standard of living is, in Israel, improved beyond recognition. In peace, with a reduced defence burden, the standard of living of Jews and Arabs could be further considerably improved.

The KKL Fund did *not* approach the many wealthy Jews of Western Europe or even the handful of Jewish millionaires in Russia. The idea was that the poor Jews of the Pale should themselves collect the money to redeem the land, thus redeeming themselves. There was about a million Jewish households in Russia, and *every* household had the celebrated pale-blue money box at the entrance door into which every visitor was expected to drop a coin on leaving. A quarter kopeck, perhaps, or maybe half a kopeck or, if one was better off, even a whole kopeck (visitors to our home in Moscow dropped in roubles, but that was a great exception). A household in the Pale would collect perhaps one or two roubles in a year, and this meant one or two million roubles for the Fund, for which quite a lot of derelict land could be bought in Israel.

In the meantime, in 1898 Herzl had travelled to Palestine and had also obtained an audience with the Sultan, Abdul Hamid, in Constantinople, endeavouring to obtain a *firman* (charter) for Jewish mass settlement with an autonomous administration. The Sultan was interested. Clearly, the taxes paid would be much increased. However, he had previously, in 1895, ordered or condoned terrible massacres of the Armenians in Turkey (a dress-rehearsal for the genocide attempt in 1915, when almost a million Armenians perished). The massacres, like the previous Bulgarian atrocities, caused an outcry in Europe, supported particularly by the liberal press in Austria and Germany. The Sultan's answer to Herzl was, therefore, in substance: 'You undertake to stop the "Jewish press" in Vienna and Berlin from interfering in our internal affairs, relating to my Armenian subjects, and you can have your charter.' Herzl indignantly refused. He and the Zionists had no influence on the editorial policy of the liberal press, and if they had had, they would never secure Jewish settlement with the blood of innocent Armenians. So Herzl's mission proved abortive.

In 1903 the British Government offered the Zionists to open Uganda, then a British colony, for Jewish mass settlement. This suggestion was particularly supported by Israel Zangwill, the Anglo-Jewish writer, as a means of obtaining immediate relief for the oppressed Jews of Russia and Romania. Plehvé was tightening the screw, and it was the year of the Kishinev *pogróm*. However, the Seventh Zionist Congress of 1905, still held in Basel, rejected, though with gratitude, the Uganda option, believing that the idealism of Jewish youth could only be mobilised in reclaiming with their own hands the ancestral land (in 1905 there were no general doubts as to the future of European settlement in Africa).

One of the few really wealthy Jews in Russia was the tea-merchant Basil Wissotzky. All Russia was drinking his tea, commonly believed to come from China by the caravan route, its subtle fragrance unimpaired by the salty sea air. In truth, Wissotzky's salesmen never claimed this, and it was very good tea, but, as Father always said, they did not contradict the persistent belief either. No doubt, originally the tea drunk in Russia did come by the caravan route, but since the opening of the Suez canal the China tea was shipped, securely packed in air- and watertight chests, to London where it was sold at the tea-auctions. Wissotzky himself was an early supporter of the Zionist cause; he gave, for instance, large sums of money for the foundation of the celebrated Technion in Haifa, a technical institute designed to develop the modern skills required in Israel for agriculture. Wissotzky's London agent was A. Ginzberg (1856–1927), who, even before he came to London, was supported by Wissotzky in his activities as author and journalist. Under the pen-name Achad Haam (One of the People) Ginzberg wrote a series of books and articles developing the idea, complementary to Herzl's, of Jewish settlement in Palestine as a cultural centre based on a renascence of the Hebrew language (which had not been used as a lay language for two thousand years) and on Jewish traditions. In a way, Achad Haam's ideas were comparable with the aspirations of the Gaelic League founded in Ireland in 1893. Ben Yehuda (Elieser Perelman, 1858–1922) spent his lifetime modernising the Hebrew language.

The ideas of Herzl and Ginzberg became amalgamated in the Zionist movement, and in Israel today Hebrew has been successfully revived as an everyday language.

Another great Jewish benefactor of the period was Baron Horace Günzburg (1833–1909), a Jewish banker in Petersburg, knighted by the Grand Duke of Hesse in 1872. Like Sir Moses Montefiore, he used his position and influence to moderate or stave off many proposed anti-Jewish measures.

Emigration to America, or Return to Israel, could reduce the pressure on the Jewish population of the Pale but it could not provide the complete answer. Many Jews felt that, in spite of all persecution, this was their country, had been for perhaps four or five centuries, and that they meant to stay and fight for their rights. A popular movement expressing this attachment to the native soil was the *Autonomism*, led by Professor Dubnov, the celebrated Jewish historian (born 1860, murdered by the National Socialists in 1941 together with the entire Jewish population of Riga). The autonomists demanded the formation, under the Imperial Crown, of a special autonomous province centred on the area of Jewish concentration in Byelorussia and Lithuania, with home rule and a provincial government elected by universal suffrage. This scheme has been sadly overtaken by events, but had at the time a lot to commend it. Had this plan been adopted, a competent and progressive provincial government would probably have ensued, developing the economic potential of the area and releasing the energy and enterprise of the population, and the Czar would have gained a well-run wealthy model province, with millions of contented and loyal subjects.

Rehabilitation at home

A more mundane approach to alleviate the *Judennot*, the Jewish misery in the Pale, was taken by a group of Jewish philanthropists in Petersburg and Moscow in 1881. Although the Jews in the Pale were barred from agriculture and many other occupations, there were still many possibilities of earning one's living as an artisan which were not taken up because Jewish young men lacked the necessary skills. An organisation was therefore founded, known as ORT (an acronym of the Russian words Society of Manual Trades), opening training schools in the Pale to teach young people (who were only familiar with shopkeeping and peddling) the skills of carpentry, brick-laying, metal-working and other trades. ORT was a great success and helped thousands of young people to earn a productive living in Russia and also proved of inestimable value to the pioneers in Israel. Now ORT has its headquarters in London (the acronym now stands for Organisation for Rehabilitation through Training) and maintains training schools, open to Jews and non-Jews, in many underdeveloped countries.

Anglo-Jewry also stood up for its persecuted brethren. Every year a great protest meeting against the *pogróms* was held in the City of London, attended by the Lord Mayor and many prominent people from all walks of life. It is probably difficult for younger readers to appreciate the extent to which such a formal condemnation in the City of London, before 1914, reverberated around the world. Certainly Petersburg took notice.

In the face of the Kaiser's sabre-rattling and the building of a battle fleet by Admiral Tirpitz, threatening British naval supremacy, British policy in

Europe was completely re-aligned. The *Entente Cordiale* with France was concluded in 1907, and now Britain was endeavouring to mend its fences with Russia. In 1906, King Edward VII, the great royal ambassador, sailed on the royal yacht to Revel (now Tallinn) on the Russian Baltic coast, (wrested by Peter the Great from Sweden in 1710), where he met Czar Nicholas II, on the imperial yacht. Britain and Russia had fought a bitter war fifty years earlier, were almost at war thirty years ago and a King of England had never visited Russia before (though Nicholas I had visited Queen Victoria at Windsor). It was indeed an historic event. Both monarchs and their families were accompanied by ministers, admirals and generals, and in addition to many glittering banquets there were very serious talks. A complete understanding, if not a formal alliance, was achieved, and Britain, France and Russia were now envisaging a common defence against a German attack.

King Edward VII brought with him a memorandum by Lord Rothschild regarding the persecution of the Jews in Russia which the King handed to the Czar personally. On his return to Petersburg the Czar did consent to receive a deputation of Russian Jewry (something that had not happened since 1881), and a small group, including MaseA, the respected Rabbi of Moscow, Wissotzky, Poliakoff (a Petersburg financier) and other leading personalities were indeed granted an audience at the Winter Palace. As Father told me, the Czar received the deputation politely but, wearing the badge of the *progróm*-sponsoring Union of Russian People, did not listen to their very real grievances, and lectured them instead on the 'revolutionary attitude of your youth', which they should control. Now, if a 'revolutionary attitude' meant demands for constitutional government and civil liberties this was certainly the case, because by that time, after the disasters in the Far East, the *entire* educated youth of Russia, and public opinion, demanded these overdue reforms. But if a 'revolutionary attitude' meant the overthrow of the monarchy (as opposed to autocracy) and of the social order, Jewish youth emphatically was not in the forefront of these activities. The Decembrists of 1825, the nihilists, the anarchists and socialists of all hues, the followers of Prince Kropotkin, Bakunin, Plekhanov and assorted ideologists, the secret societies with their political assassinations, all were drawn from the Russian ruling class, the almost unavoidable corollary of a repressive if generally benevolent regime.

One of the last flings of the anti-semites in Petersburg was to engineer a case of ritual murder. Since antiquity, Jews (and early Christians) had sometimes been accused of murdering children and using their blood for some rite, such as the baking of the unleavened bread for Passover (there was probably initially some confusion with the Moloch cult of the Ammonites and Phoenicians, where children were indeed scrificed). A young boy had been murdered in Kiev in 1913 and an unfortunate Jewish carpenter, Mendel (Menachem) Beilis, was accused of having murdered the child and used his blood. The defence produced Russian Orthodox professors of theology who testified that there was no such Jewish rite, and that it would be contrary to all Jewish teaching. The Vatican confirmed this. In any case, the court found the accused not guilty of the murder, and Beilis emigrated to New York where he died in 1934. Kérensky describes in his *Memoirs* how the whole of public opinion in Russia, including the right wing, was indignant at this attempt to sully the good name of Russian justice with this knowingly false accusation. It was in fact an imitation of the Dreyfus case (to the French, espionage in favour of Germany was, no doubt, a worse crime than ritual murder).

The *pogróms* did abate noticeably after the King's personal intervention at Revel, reinforced by the continuous pressure of public opinion in Britain and France, and soon all but ceased.

However, some years earlier, when prime minister Stolypin, the great conservative reformer (who was endeavouring to create a Russian farmer class), had submitted to the Czar a proposal for abolishing some of the more irksome provisions of the Temporary Regulations, Nicholas II personally vetoed it. Whether of his own volition or at the instance of some fanatical adviser we do not know.

All this time, every downtrodden Jew in the Pale was sustained by the knowledge that somewhere beyond the sea there was an island-kingdom, shrouded in mists, where a Jew could become a Lord Mayor of London, a Minister of the Crown or a Lord Chief Justice (the Viceroy of India came later).

The uncles

In spite of being offered every encouragement with their homework, the Schmerling boys progressed quite differently at school. The eldest, my uncle Leo, just managed his matric, and in the total absence of any academic inclinations, decided to become a banker. Russia was, like the United States, a country with small local banks, almost savings banks, and apparently there was a demand for a reliable local bank at Mogilév. Making use of the family name, Uncle Leo opened a bank, and indeed all the traders and shopkeepers entrusted him their meagre savings, particularly as he paid half a per cent above the government stock coupon. The deposits were invested in mortgages granted to the Polish estate-owners for thirty years or so. The spread between borrowing and lending rates was, I believe, one per cent, which on paper should have given Uncle Leo a comfortable income.

Unfortunately, Uncle Leo committed the classic error, in banking terms, of borrowing 'short' and lending 'long'. Obviously, my Uncle had not inherited the financial acumen of his grandfather of the First Guild of Smolénsk. The inevitable happened. Some day, after the Kishinev *pogróm*, I believe, many depositors decided that they would sooner keep their savings at home, albeit without interest, so they could flee the town at a few hours' notice should the need arise (the railway had not reached Mogilév). There was a run on the Schmerling bank, and it would have become insolvent had not Grandfather sacrificed the larger part of the family fortune (almost half a million roubles) to bail out his elder son. The disgrace of a bankruptcy was unthinkable. All depositors were paid in full and the bank was liquidated. Uncle Leo moved into a small flat in the family house, and devoted himself to honorary work for the numerous Jewish charitable and educational institutions that flourished in Mogilév.

Grandfather's elder daughter, my Aunt Maria, had married well and happily, with a dowry of a hundred thousand roubles—that was before the bank crash—to a bank manager in Kharkov, the commercial capital of Malorussia (Ukraine). There was now no money left for a similar dowry for the younger daughter, Aunt Sophie. She was teaching at an infant school, I believe, and met and married, also very happily, a school teacher in Lithuania. In 1941 they were overtaken by the German invasion, and fell victim to the Black Death.

The second boy, Uncle Isaac, passed his matric tolerably well but not well enough to qualify, under the *numerus clausus* system, for a place at a Russian university. As Uncle wanted to study chemistry, Grandfather (this was still before the bank disaster) was able to arrange for Uncle Isaac to study at a German university, like so many Russian–Jewish students denied access to higher learning at home. Before taking up his studies, however, Uncle Isaac was called up under the selective conscription then operating. The family were rather apprehensive: service for a Czar of Temporary Regulations and *pogróms* was, understandably enough, not popular in the Pale. There was the added indignity (or hardship) that grammar-school boys (in Russia as in Germany) normally served as officers but Jewish boys were, under the Temporary Regulations, excluded from this privilege and had to serve in the ranks. This meant, among other discomforts, sleeping on vermin-infested straw palliasses and eating a diet of cabbage soup. However, one had not reckoned with the Russian genius for circumventing inept laws. When Uncle Isaac, always a bit of a dandy and 'von Baron', much to Grandfather's dislike, reported for duty the sergeant-major told him that as Uncle was obviously a *bárin*, or gentleman, he would arrange for a gentleman's bed to be placed for Uncle in the barracks dormitory. 'And this will be fifty roubles', said the sergeant with a tone of finality, making it clear that this was the going rate for such privileges. The good-natured peasant lads with whom Uncle Isaac shared the dormitory seemed to consider it as perfectly natural that the young *bárin*, denied his proper place in the Officer's Quarters, should sleep in a bed, and in fact Uncle Isaac, fortunately a good mixer, got on famously with the other recruits. For the benefit of those interested in the minutiae of Army life in those days I would mention that the wooden legs of the bed were placed, according to time-honoured tradition, in bowls filled with paraffin oil to prevent the bugs from crawling up them. This stratagem was eminently successful: no bug was ever observed crawling up a bed leg. The insects simply crawled up the barrack walls, then along the ceiling and dropped, with precision, into Uncle Isaac's bed. They recognised no privilege. Dichlordiphenyltrichlorethane (DDT), that great boon to suffering humanity (even if it reduces the reproduction rate of some birds of prey) was still some forty years away.

After completion of his military service, which he greatly enjoyed, Uncle Isaac did study chemistry in Germany. With the modest capital Grandfather could spare for him, Uncle opened a small chemical factory in Sarátov on the Volga, where the naphtha from Baku arrived by barge. Sarátov was over five hundred miles east of the Pale, but as Uncle Isaac was a university graduate and, moreover, as the Government favoured industrialisation as the only way of raising the general standard of living, he had no difficulty in obtaining all the required permits and worked and lived in Sarátov unmolested. The factory prospered.

Notes

1   The massacre was commemorated by Bialik, the great Hebrew poet, in his poem *Be-ir ha-Haregah* (In the City of Slaughter).
2   In Auschwitz, of course, fifty people were killed every ten minutes.
3   In Britain the last restrictions on Jewish people were removed by the Jews' Disabilities Act of 1858, and Lionel de Rothschild was able to become the first Jewish Member of Parliament.
4   The Jewish population of Warsaw, Lodz and other main cities was 30–35 per cent, that of Romania about 5 per cent but that of the principal cities 20–50 per cent, making the position of the Jews even more endangered.

4

Father

Grandfather's youngest son, Boris, my father, passed his matric with flying colours. The written examination consisted at the turn of the century of translating a passage in Greek, generally Homer, sent by the Ministry in a sealed envelope, into Latin. Any Russian grammar-school boy could do that, of course; what mattered was the *quality* of the Latin prose. Father did well—all Jewish schoolboys were fluent, of necessity, in Yiddish–German, Hebrew and Russian, and could therefore easily take the three additional languages of the curriculum (Greek, Latin and French) in their stride. Father absorbed a great deal of Greek and Roman culture: at the age of 70 he could quote long passages from Homer in the original Greek. And Father's favourite precept for life—public and private—was the Roman maxim *Si vis pacem, para bellum* (if you want peace, prepare for war). I have no doubt what Father would have thought of the present protagonists of unilateral disarmament.

The Examination Board awarded Father a Six as an overall result of the examination. Actually, the best mark one could have in Russia in any subject was a Five, but there were various voluntary extra subjects, and if these were *all* taken, and Fives awarded in *all*, the total examination result was upgraded to a Six. The magic figure entitled Father to *compete* for a place at a Russian university, under the *numerus clausus*. After various attempts nearer home, Father was accepted at the University of Dorpat, or Derpt (originally belonging to Novgorod) in the Baltic province of Estonia, wrested by Peter the Great from Sweden in 1710. There was a strong German element settled in the Baltic provinces since the days of the Teutonic Knights. The University, although founded by Russia in 1802, was virtually German-speaking, with many of the professors German nationals or

Russian-born Germans. Under Alexander III (or Pobedónostsev's) Russification policy, the University was compelled to make Russian the official language, and many of the German or German-speaking professors left. The original Russian name of the town, Yuriev, was to be exclusively used (at present, in the Soviet Union, the town bears the Estonian name of Tartu: three entirely different names for the same town is nothing unusual in border areas).

Father decided on chemistry, like Uncle Isaac, and was fortunate in studying under Professor Tammann, a Russian-born German renowned to this day in physical chemistry. Yuriev was a working university. No ivory tower, no gilded youth, and Father, like most of the students of whatever background, concentrated on his studies. The rational approach was entirely new to him, as no science had been taught at the grammar school. He completed his studies with a thesis on the equilibrium diagram of some organic binary system and graduated in 1904, just in time before the student strikes of 1905 and later. University graduates in Russia received the title of Candidate, and Father could proudly write Candidate of Chemistry on his visiting cards—a title that, in Russia, conferred many privileges and opened many doors.

The Japanese attack

The years 1904 and 1905 were traumatic for Russia. In the Far East, Russian, Chinese and Japanese interests were clashing in Manchuria and Korea. Having concluded an alliance with Britain in 1902 Japan felt safe to attack Russia and decided that there was little time to lose before the Trans-Siberian Railway was fully completed (the Baikal still had to be crossed by ferry), thus transforming the logistics of the situation.

Russia maintained a powerful fleet in the Far East, divided between Port Arthur and Vladivostok, and equal in strength to the entire Japanese fleet. On 8 February 1904 the Russian battleships were peacefully riding at anchor in the Yellow Sea, at the Port Arthur naval base (Japanese Ryo-Jun, Chinese Lu-shun, now part of Dairen city, with its four million inhabitants, in Manchuria). At the dead of night, the fully illuminated squadron was sunk or crippled by a flotilla of Japanese destroyers, which then vanished into the darkness. War had not been declared. It was a dress-rehearsal for Pearl Harbor (except that in 1941 carrier aircraft were used).

Having gained mastery of the sea—an essential prerequisite—the Japanese were able to land troops, unopposed, at the rear of Port Arthur and besiege it (a rehearsal for the capture of Singapore). They could also land an army in Korea, cross the Yalu river and attack the main Russian army in Manchuria. In the great battle for Mukden alone, the Russians lost a hundred thousand men, and the total Russian war losses were almost half a million dead and a similar number wounded.

The powerful and modern Black Sea Fleet was geographically several thousand miles nearer to the theatre of war than the Baltic Fleet and could probably have reached the Far East in time to save the situation. But, thanks to Disraeli, the Straits were closed to Russian warships. Nicholas II, remembering his grandfather's humiliation in 1878, refused permission for a forced passage attempt (would the British have closed Suez?) and decided to send a modernised and augmented Baltic Fleet instead. The original Baltic Fleet consisted of older and slower ships, many never designed for the high seas—really, a coastal defence force, not a battle fleet. In a frantic effort, mobilising the whole of the Russian engineering industry, the ageing ships were refitted, new engines and new guns installed and some new or bought-in ships added. The Czar (accompanied by the ubiquitous Pobedonóstsev, whose name, ironically, means Harbinger of Victory) reviewed the fleet (now named Second Pacific Squadron) at Revel (now Tallinn) in the Baltic province of Estonia, and personally visited over twenty warships in two days. On 14 October 1904 (eight months after the Japanese attack) the great Armada of forty-five ships (including eight battleships), with over twelve thousand men aboard, sailed from Libava (now Liepaja) in the Baltic province of Latvia. The force was commanded by Admiral Rozhdestvensky (flying his flag in HIMS *Suvorov*), a great sailor in the Nelson mould.

On its voyage of some 20,000 miles (two and half times the distance to the Falklands) round the Cape the Fleet was denied coaling facilities in British-controlled ports (which, at the time, meant most ports); Britain and Russia were still enemies, although the Alliance, concluded in the face of the Kaiser's threat, was only four years away. The Admiralty in St Petersburg had to contract with the German Hamburg America Line to supply the fleet with coal during its epic voyage. A whole flotilla of German freighters was busy for seven months, shipping millions of tons of coal over the oceans, generally to be taken on board by the warships in the open sea, perhaps in the lee of some coast. In January 1905, while the Armada was refitting and restocking in French-controlled Madagascar, one of the few havens open to it, the commander of Port Arthur, General Stoessel, surrendered the heavily fortified and well-stocked base, with a whiff of treachery in the air (he was later court-martialled in Russia). The Black Sea fleet could have been there in time. The Armada, after a rendezvous with some reinforcements at Cam Ranh Bay (then in French-controlled Indochina, now in Soviet-controlled Vietnam, and a Russian naval base), had a choice of either turning back or setting course for Vladivostok, at least a further fifteen hundred miles away than Port Arthur, and far removed from the theatre of war. Moreover, according to their contracts, the German freighters were not supposed to enter the war-zone, deemed to commence beyond Indochina. In order to be able to reach Vladivostok, the Russian ships would have had to take on excessive quantities of coal, weighing them down and reducing their speed even further. No-one in Petersburg dared explain these things to the Czar. Rozhdestvensky was ordered to break through to Vladivostok. He never got there.

On 27 May 1905, seven months after sailing from the Baltic, the battered, overloaded ships with their worn-out engines and weary, sick crews, steamed into the narrow strait separating Japan and Korea, like an Eichmann train entering Auschwitz, all on board doomed to perish. They were intercepted by the Japanese battle fleet, fresh from home base, ships and crews in prime condition, commanded by Admiral Togo (his flagship was built in Barrow-in-Furness). In the greatest naval disaster of modern times the Russian fleet was annihilated off Tsushima Island. Some thirty warships were sunk and the others captured or interned in neutral ports. Only four fast ships (out of some fifty) reached Vladivostok. Over five thousand Russian sailors were drowned. Russia now had no navy at all, except the Black Sea Fleet, powerful but bottled up, its inactivity breeding mutiny.

America was alarmed at the sudden emergence of a new naval power in the Pacific. President Theodore Roosevelt called a peace conference at Portsmouth, New Hampshire. The Czar sent Witté to negotiate a peace treaty (Witté chose Grigory Wilenkin, the financial counsellor in London and the only Russian of Jewish faith in government service, to assist him in financial matters). The terms of the Treaty were not too onerous, considering the crushing defeat: cession of Port Arthur to Japan (now Chinese), evacuation of Southern Manchuria and recognition of Korea as being in the Japanese sphere of interest. What rankled was the humiliation: it was as if Britain had lost the Boer War and had to surrender the Cape Colony to, say, Germany.

Needless to say, once again the 'Jewish conspiracy' was revived by the anti-Jewish camarilla in Petersburg: was it not Disraeli who had wrested control of the Straits from Russia at Berlin? Now the consequences were there for all to see. Russia needed free access to the open seas from all her ports.

One of the heroes of the defence of Port Arthur was a Jewish private, Joseph Trumpeldor, who lost a leg during the siege. He received many commendations, was decorated by the Empress and even commissioned a lieutenant in spite of the Temporary Regulations barring Jews from officer rank. Later, in World War I, Trumpeldor fought as volunteer with the British forces in Palestine, and then with the Jewish self-defence, and died in 1920 defending the Jewish settlement of Tel Hai in Upper Galilee against marauding Arabs. Trumpeldor is now commemorated there by the celebrated statue of a roaring lion, and has become one of the heroes of Israeli youth.

The Franco-Prussian War had been fought with gunpowder. The Russo-Japanese War was the first to be fought with high explosive. It was, of course, molecular high explosive, nitroglycerine, nitrocellulose (e.g. cordite and pyroxilin) and trinitrotoluene (TNT); atomic and nuclear high explosive was beyond the horizon. Even so, traditional fighting valour was being superseded by mass slaughter.

One of the non-combattant participants in the Japanese War was Captain Max Hoffmann, sent by the German (or Prussian) General Staff as an observer with the Japanese Army. Hoffmann's observations of Russian Army methods (and deficiencies) and lack of adaptation to the new type of warfare enabled him, ten years later as staff officer with Hindenburg in East Prussia, to develop the strategy that annihilated the First and Second Russian Armies at the Masurian Lakes and Tannenberg in August and September 1914, with the loss of a quarter of a million men.

The revolution of 1905

While the Japanese War was being fought over five thousand miles away (the distance from London to San Francisco), things came to a head on the home front. In 1904 the general demand for constitutional government and an elected assembly, regularly voiced since 1825 (the 'Decembrists'), became overwhelming. The country was in ferment. On 22 January 1905, three weeks after the fall of Port Arthur, a peaceful and orderly procession of workers from the Putilov munitions factory in Petersburg, led by a priest, Father Gapon, and intent on presenting a petition to the Czar at the Winter Palace (the Czar was not there), was ambushed and fired on by guards and Cossacks, leaving some *thousand* marchers dead in the snow. The disasters in Manchuria did the rest. It was widely believed that some of the grossly incompetent commanders in the Far East owed their appointment to patronage at Court rather than merit, and, of course, the corruption in the supply services leading to badly deficient equipment was common knowledge.

In Moscow everyone was against the Petersburg government that had become, in 25 years, incompetent, corrupt and profligate. Public accountability and a Civil List on the British model were demanded. Universities (professors and students) were on strike. At the Vinogradskaya, the schoolgirls were singing with enthusiasm the popular revolutionary song:

A déspot pirúyet v roskóshnom dvortzé
Svobódu nogóy popiráya.

The despot feasts in the sumptuous palace
Trampling freedom underfoot.

The teachers turned a deaf ear.

There was a mutiny in the bottled-up Black Sea Fleet, led by the crew of
the battle-cruiser *Potémkin*, now of motion-picture fame.

The entire nation—that is, the literate and politically conscious part of
it—was now united against autocratic government. In the end, and under
duress, Nicholas grudgingly and with bad grace made some concessions: in
the Imperial Manifesto of 30 (17) October 1905 constitutional government
was promised. There was going to be an elected assembly, the *Duma*
(*Dumat* means thinking; in other words, a consultative assembly), political
freedom and civil liberties. An Edict of Toleration of the Old Believers, the
Russian Dissenters, was issued. The Imperial Manifesto corresponded,
perhaps, allowing for the quite different constitutional history of Russia and
England, to the Petition of Rights of 1628.

Factory workers' grievances (their condition was as unsatisfactory as
everywhere in Europe) and socialist ideology—in fact any ideology—did
not play a significant part in the Revolution of 1905 (though there was an
abortive attempt to emulate the barricade-building Paris Commune of
1871, considered an heroic epic in Marxist folklore, when a short-lived
soviet, or council, of self-appointed workers, delegates appeared for the first
time on the Russian political scene as a vacuum-filling surrogate for an elected
parliament). And the professional revolutionaries, the secret societies that
carried out the political assassinations and, even less, the emigrés in Zurich,
had little influence, if any, on the 1905 Revolution.

The First *Duma* was elected in 1906. It was a consultative assembly with
no real power, but it was the start of the constitutional process. There was a
Second, Third and Fourth *Duma*—the last provided the lawful Provisional
Government after the Czar's abdication in 1917. But for World War I,
Russia might have developed into a constitutional monarchy on the
British model.

Father's progress

Father graduated, *summa cum laude*, in 1904, missing the university
strikes of 1905 and 1906 which delayed later graduations by two years. As
he was interested in textile chemistry, he decided, with Grandfather's
agreement and support, to specialise in this field by attending for another

two or three years post-graduate courses at the Technical Institute of Mulhouse in Alsace (then German, now French), near Basel, then the leading establishment for textile chemistry in Europe.

On returning to Russia in 1907, armed with his university degree and Mulhouse diploma, Father readily obtained a position as a dye chemist, or colorist, at a textile factory on the outskirts of Moscow, the first Schmerling to set foot in this historic city (also the first to accept salaried employment).

Father's career seemed all set, progressing as a dye-house chemist, and finishing perhaps as Works Manager. But fate decreed otherwise.

5

Mother's People

Vítebsk

The Dvina springs from the watershed of the Valdai Hills, together with the Dnieper and the Volga, but flows westward for seven hundred miles until it reaches the Baltic at Riga. This sluggish and pedestrian river cannot hold a candle to the majestic Dnieper, but it did serve as the last leg of the Great Waterway (there was, however, an alternative, more northerly route from the upper reaches of the Dnieper, leading through some comparatively smaller rivers to the great trading centre of Novgorod and thence to the Gulf of Finland). The Dvina still had a great deal of commercial traffic, particularly the floating of logs.

When coming from the Dnieper, Vítebsk was the first trading-post on the Dvina, and gradually grew into an important town, of some hundred thousand inhabitants at the turn of the last century. Like most of Byelorussia, the town had belonged to the Polish Realm and came to Russia in the First Partition, together with Mogilév, in 1773. As in all towns of the Pale, a third to a half of the population was Jewish. Vítebsk was a much poorer town and more plebeian than Mogilév, and the citizens of Mogilév looked down at Vítebsk with some disdain. After all, *they* were on the Dnieper, in the best part of the great river between Smolénsk and Kiev, *they* now had piped water, every few years *they* had a theatre troupe from Kiev performing Shakespeare.

The history of Russia under the last two Czars shows a strange dichotomy. Whereas in the political sphere there was repression, reaction and revolutionary ferment, in the economic field there was intense development in industry and commerce, forcing liberalisation. The emancipation of the peasants in 1861 has released tremendous energies and provided a huge market for indigenous manufactures, and a reservoir of labour for the indus-

56

trial revolution proceeding apace. Under Alexander III, despite all political oppression, the rate of growth in Russia was, with 8 per cent annually, one of the highest in Europe. The economic development was presided over and nurtured by Sergei (later Count) Witté, of Dutch descent, Minister of Finance 1892–1903, and later briefly Prime Minister. He was one of the great statesmen of the period, and main opponent of Pobedonóstsev and Plehvé. Witté did a great deal to develop Russian industry, and the Trans-Siberian Railway, over five thousand miles long, was his crowning achieve-ment. Witté also introduced the eleven-and-a-half hour working day; this may sound like slave-driving today but it represented a great advance on the working hours customary throughout Europe at the time; only Britain was leading, with ten hours (in biblical Israel, it would seem, twelve hours were worked—Matthew 20, 1–16).

The standard of living was continuously rising and, in step with it, edu-cation and public health. The spread of education and the fight against illiteracy was proceeding with great energy; in the beginning of Nicholas II's reign just over a quarter of the population aged ten or over could read or write; in 1917 half the population was literate. According to the official plan, illiteracy was due to be wiped out by the late 1920s.

Witté was anxious for the Jewish population to contribute its full poten-tial to the economic development of the country, and often successfully opposed, or moderated, anti-Jewish measures which hampered Jewish enterprise. He even saw to it that a Jewish banker from Petersburg, Grigory Wilenkin, was appointed Financial Counsellor at the Russian Embassy in London, an unprecedented step under the Temporary Regulations.

One of the many thousands of Jewish heads of families in Vítebsk earning a precarious living as shopkeepers was Grigory Poverkhovsky,* my maternal grandfather. He owned an exceedingly small draper's and haberdasher's shop near the cattle market. Actually, Grandfather was born at Pskov, a very ancient Russian city indeed, boasting its own *Kremlin*, or walled inner city, and known since pre-Conquest days, when Pskov belonged to Novgorod. Later, with Novgorod, it was absorbed into Muscovy. As Pskov had belonged to Russia before the Partitions it was outside the Pale of Settlement, though only some hundred miles away. Evidently, the Poverkhovsky belonged to the very small number of Jewish families living in Russia before the Partitions and were allowed to continue with their residence. However, when Grandfather married a girl from the Kunin family at Vítebsk, he moved to Vítebsk himself and set up house there. Perhaps the shop was Grandmother's dowry, I really do not know. As Mother died when I was a little boy, and Mother's brother and sisters are now all gone, I know nothing of Grandfather's early days at Pskov, except that *his* father, Saul, lived and died there.

See p. 52 Witté was a close friend and colleague of Gregory Wilenkin. Together they signed the treaty closing the Russo-Japanese war. 1905

Ponizousky

The shop at Vítebsk was, as usual, a single room, with the family living behind it. There were no assistants, and Grandmother took turns with Grandfather to mind the shop. The stock of inexpensive fabrics was small; mainly cotton prints, perhaps a few rolls of cambric, muslin and batiste, some black crepe for mourning and a bolt of silk for the carriage trade that never came. On market days the peasants would come in and buy coloured ribbons, sewing-thread, needles and *English pins* (safety pins). Sometimes, perhaps a length of cotton print for a new petticoat for the wife. Grandfather noticed that the liberated peasants, or their free-born children, were gradually becoming better off, the women more clothes-conscious, and that demand for cotton prints was increasing from year to year. But, for some reason, cotton prints were difficult to come by. The shops were often out of stock. The women had to do with the old petticoat for another year. The local wholesaler blamed the main wholesaler in Moscow or Warsaw. The main wholesaler blamed the manufacturers at Ivánovo Vosnesénsk (northeast of Moscow) or at Lodz. It seemed there was a shortage of raw cotton, or of ginning capacity, or of looms, or of printing colours from England or, later, from Germany. The truth was simply that the manufacturers manufactured what they always had, and did not adjust their production to the changing demand.

Emigration to Moscow

Grandfather recognised that there was a great opportunity for someone with an intimate knowledge of the market to match supply and demand nationwide. He raised two thousand roubles by selling the shop, drawing out his meagre savings and even, I believe, borrowing from relatives, and journeyed to Moscow, some time in the reign of Alexander III. Although Vítebsk had now belonged to Russia for over a century, to its citizens Moscow was quite a strange city, probably much more unfamiliar and forbidding than say, the Lower East Side of Manhattan, or Whitechapel in East London. In fact the move to Moscow was a form of emigration from the Pale. I do not quite know how, under the anti-Jewish Czar, Grandfather managed to obtain the required residential qualifications; he did not seem to fit any of the exempted categories, and I would assume that it was owing to his birth at Pskov, outside the Pale.

Life in Moscow was dominated by the Christian Orthodox faith. The Russian Orthodox Church is a truly national church; the fount and sustenance of Russian culture, its history intertwined with that of the Russian people to a much greater extent than in the relationship of Church and Nation, even in Ireland, Poland or Spain. Of the Christian Churches only perhaps the Maronite and the Armenian occupy a similar central position in the history of their peoples. Throughout the Tartar yoke, the monasteries were the repositories of the national tradition and heritage. The language of the Church was church Slavonic, readily understood by all Russians, and the great figures of Russian history who introduced Christianity and led the nation in its struggle for survival against Teuton and Tartar are all venerated as Saints: St Olga, St Vladimir, St Alexander Nevski, St Sergius.

Lent was a period of public mourning and abstinence: it extended a full seven weeks before Easter, and during this period no Believer is allowed any meat, and most weeks no fish, milk or eggs either. In fact, the last week before Lent is called Butter Week, and for the whole week, not only Shrove Tuesday, people ate pancakes, fried in triple pans without handles, placed with tongs on the glowing embers of the wood-burning kitchen range. A special Lenten diet had evolved over the centuries, consisting mainly of the previous year's dried mushrooms in various forms, nuts (particularly almonds) and sunflower oil, or the cheaper hemp oil, for frying, known as Lenten Oil. There was mushroom soup, mushroom pie, even a mushroom 'caviare' (more expensive than the natural product). During Lent it was then as impossible to order, say, a beef stew in a Moscow restaurant as it is today to order pork in a Kosher or a Muslim restaurant. There were also similar, though less rigorous and shorter, fast periods during Advent, before Assumption and, I believe, even before Saints Peter and Paul.

There was always much less meat eaten than at present in Western Europe, with its vast imports from all continents, let alone in North America. The beef was of poor quality, lamb—in Moscow and Petersburg—a luxury and pork was produced mainly in Malorussia (Ukraine). There was the occasional chicken or goose. Pigeons were not eaten for religious reasons. As yet, there was no refrigerated storage or transport, so that local livestock only was slaughtered and consumed. On the other hand, Russia's rivers and streams, then unpolluted, were teeming with fish, and bass and bream, perch and pike were in Moscow part of everyone's regular diet. There was, naturally, no fresh sea-fish, but herrings in brine, so missing in England, were enjoyed by almost the entire population and are still part of the daily diet in the Soviet Union. Even in the prisons and labour camps, we are told, the guards receive herring flesh, and the prisoners, although enemies of the people, a wholesome soup of ground herring-bones.

In and out of Lent, people ate a lot of cereals, buckwheat (black rice) and millet; buckwheat *kasha*, or gruel, was the standard dish, as nutritious as oatmeal porridge but more tasty, and much cabbage soup, or *shchi*, was eaten, according to the saying *shchi da kásha pishcha násha* (cabbage soup and buckwheat gruel are our food). In winter, when there were no fresh vegetables, sauerkraut was eaten (even more than in Germany). There were, as yet, no refrigerators; for the hot Russian summer everyone had an ice cellar which was filled with ice bars in spring, and the ice just lasted until the autumn, though at the end of the season it was floating on a pool of water. Steps led down to the ice, and every housewife knew what to keep at the very bottom, and what at varying heights on the steps. The system worked quite well; the main problem was that there was no refrigerated transport and food often arrived spoilt. Fish, in summer, could only be safely bought live.

Lent ended with the triumphant Orthodox Midnight Mass, heralding Easter Sunday. Everyone in Moscow was there except, of course, the handful of Tartars, Jews and non-Orthodox Christians. Each member of the congregation stood with a candle and, at the moment the Resurrection was announced at midnight, all the candles were lit. At three in the morning, or later, when the crowds returned home from church, there was the traditional *razgovlenye*, or breakfast, with *paskha* (a cheesecake of pyramid shape) and *kulich* (a tall fruit cake). To this day, Sunday—any Sunday—is called in Russian *voskresenye* meaning resurrection; there is no other word.

This, then, was the great city of Moscow in which Grandfather arrived. He had never been to any school except, of course, like all Jewish boys in the Pale, the *kheder*, or Jewish parochial school, up to the age of thirteen. He could speak a Russian of sorts, though heavily accented, and could sign his name in Russian. In Moscow, Grandfather took a room in a cheap lodging-house in the Taganka—the remote, old-fashioned quarter favoured by the Old Believers which was also the natural place for Jewish people and other Dissenters. The room also served as his office for the first few years.

The history of the firm

G.S. Poverkhovsky
Textile Wholesalers

has not been written, and never will be, as it came to an abrupt end, like all private enterprise, after Lenin's successful coup in November (October) 1917. All I know is that when Grandfather died he left a wholesale business with a turnover of forty million roubles and owning and occupying substantial office and warehouse buildings in Moscow, Petersburg, Kharkov and Warsaw. There were no bank debts, no mortgages. What exactly the secret of Grandfather's success was, I do not know. I think, apart from enterprise, scrupulous integrity and meticulous management, mainly his ability to predict precisely what types of cotton prints would be required throughout the length and breadth of Russia next year, and to have them in stock when required. When the season started, Grandfather could supply all orders from stock, and when it ended, there were no left-overs, and no need for loss-making stock-clearance. Supply and demand—Grandfath have said, demand and supply—were always perfectly matched. C Poverkhovsky's did not restrict themselves to cotton prints, though these always represented the bread and butter. All dress fabrics were supplied, and Grandfather even imported fine worsteds from England, as worn by *gentlemen* in Russia. Naturally, Grandfather rode on the crest of the wave; the prevailing rate of growth of 8 per cent annually meant that in twenty years the national product and standard of living increased fivefold, and the lion's share of the *increase* in the textile field went to G.S. Poverkhovsky as the more efficient firm. The market leader was still the very old-established firm of Morósov (non-Jewish), but Poverkhovsky followed, albeit at some distance, having overtaken all other rivals, the Pikes,* the Fungus* and others.

Like most local boys made good (whether Jewish or non-Jewish) Grandfather did not forget the poverty and hopelessness in the Pale. He was one of the first supporters, I believe even a founder-member, of ORT, the Manual Trades Society, and generously assisted their training courses. He also made a large donation towards the building of the Great Moscow Synagogue (the family were granted hereditary pews), an edifice of architectural distinction and, as far as I know, still a place of worship, having miraculously survived over sixty-five years of militant state atheism.

The Grandparents had four children, all born at Vítebsk; a boy, and three girls. The youngest, Rose, was my mother. The eldest child was my Uncle Matthew, and I recall him remembering the Turkish prisoners being marched through Vítebsk in 1877, when he was four years old. As soon as Grandfather had made some money in Moscow, he bought a small and somewhat dilapidated house in Bolshaya Alexéyevskaya in the Tagánka and brought the family to Moscow. Mother was about fourteen and managed two years or so at the well-known Vinográdskaya Gymnasium, the only school of higher education for girls in Moscow, privately owned, and originally founded by Anna Vinográdskaya for the upbringing of Bulgarian children orphaned by the Turkish massacres of 1875.

Around 1906 Grandfather, now a millionaire, died suddenly and in agony of a neglected and now-strangulated hernia and, as a result of the shock, Grandmother suffered a stroke, which left her with her legs permanently paralysed. She spent the rest of her life in a wheelchair. Fortunately, her brain and energy were quite unimpaired—if anything, enhanced—and she kept business and family affairs on a tight rein.

Uncle Matthew had married the daughter of a Jewish banker in Petersburg (trade was in Moscow, but the banks were in Petersburg); as there were ~~six~~ daughters (and three sons) there was a luxurious trousseau but, I believe, not much in the way of a dowry. However, Grandfather, as an entirely self-made man, was pleased for his son to marry into the Jewish equivalent of aristocracy. Mother's two elder sisters had also married, each with a dowry of half a million roubles; Grandfather did not like the idea of having sons-in-law in the business and saw to it, when the marriages were arranged, that the prospective husbands had their own businesses. One of my uncles was a stockbroker, and the other had his own firm in another trade, both in Moscow. But now, after Grandfather's sudden death, things were different. Grandmother knew her only son's somewhat genial disposition only too well, and realised that, while he could be (and proved to be) of immense benefit in giving the general direction of the firm and maintaining its impetus, he would not cope with the day-to-day running of the business, and could easily overextend and break the firm. The family needed a steady, conscientious and reliable administrator to complement Matthew's vision and prevent it from turning into extravagance.

Mother, now twenty-two, was looking after Grandmother and presiding over the all-female Tagánka household. There were two maids, I believe, and a Jewish kosher cook imported from the Pale. Mother had always been Grandmother's favourite daughter, and now, tied to the wheelchair, Grandmother certainly did not cherish the thought of losing her daughter. But she knew she had a duty to her and to the family business, providing for the entire family, many relatives and dependants, as well as for ORT and the Great Synagogue. In the spring of the following year, Grandmother sent for Mr Kagán.* Eliah Kagán was a university graduate of the legal faculty and had been a successful advocate, specialising in commercial law. He knew all the leading Jewish families had established himself as the recognised matchmaker, giving up his legal practice. It was Mr. Kagán's proud boast that of all the marriages he had arranged not one had broken down.

Grandmother received Mr Kagán in her wheelchair and offered him, as was customary, a glass of lemon tea and a dish of strawberry or raspberry jam. Mr Kagán noticed that the solid silver glass-holder was a trifle heavy, testifying to old Poverkhovsky's somewhat ostentatious inclinations. He had been expecting this call for some time, and was well prepared for it. However, he naturally listened carefully to Grandmother, making occasional notes in his notebook which was, for greater effect, fitted with a padlock. Naturally, the young man would have to be of an old-established family, a university graduate and with an understanding of cotton prints. No gaming, no women. And the dowry would be one million roubles, plus a fifth of the Poverkhovsky shares. And after Mr Kagán had suggested a suitable candidate, Grandmother would employ a private detective to check on the prospective suitor's habits.

Next evening Mr Kagán boarded the second-class sleeper on the Warsaw express, passed through Smolénsk, alighted early morning at

Orsha junction, the last stop before Minsk, and caught the morning train to Mogilév (thanks to the French one could now travel to Mogilév by train). After breakfasting at the station buffet (in Russian provincial towns generally the best restaurant), Mr Kagán presented himself at the Schmerling house (he had sent a telegram announcing his visit). Grandfather was engaged at prayers (as Mr Kagán expected) and Grandmother received the visitor. No, she had *never* heard of the Poverkhovsky family. Did not Vítebsk people eat from the knife, and even drink tea from the saucer, like a *muzhík*? Her father-in-law had been a Merchant of the First Guild of Smolénsk. Mr Kagán reassured Grandmother on these points, mentioned the hereditary pews in the Great Synagogue, and named the dowry. Hard as Grandmother tried, she could not hide the fact that she was impressed. Grandmother promised to place the facts before her husband; Mr Kagán did not doubt the outcome, had a leisurely lunch at the station and returned, again via Orsha, on a first-class sleeper to Moscow. His fee being one per cent of the dowry, there was no need to save money.

A fortnight later (to convey his time-consuming labours) Mr Kagán called at the Tagánka and unveiled his candidate: Solomon Schmerling's grandson, Candidate of Chemistry, and with a German diploma in cotton printing. He seemed made to measure. Grandmother propelled her wheelchair nearer to watch the expression on Mr Kagán's face and barked: 'Personal habits?' Mr Kagán reassured her on that point (quite truthfully). As it happened, Mr Kagán continued, young Schmerling was working not a mile away. He could be introduced at any time. Grandmother would have none of this. The prospective bridegroom would be introduced to her beloved daughter in the style she deserved. This was not Vítebsk. Introductions were properly arranged at a spa. Grandmother would take a furnished villa for the season in Bad Homburg and travel there with her daughter. Boris Schmerling could present himself there, and be introduced. One would then see how the young people were getting on.

Mr Kagán could not help admiring the old woman. Here she was, sitting in her wheelchair, talking of a strenuous two-day journey to the other side of Germany the way healthy people talked of going to their *dácha* an hour's drive away. And how well informed she was, shut up in the sombre house in the Tagánka. No old-fashioned Carlsbad, or Baden-Baden, but the latest favourite of European society, patronised by the English king himself.

A trip to Homburg

Mother, efficient and business-like as always, organised the journey without being told the real reason. She thought it was a question of her mother taking the waters. A furnished villa, the property of a Russian noblewoman in need of a little extra income (as so many were after the liberation of the peasants), was rented. A specially adapted invalid railway coach was ordered from the Wagon-Lit company and, on the appointed day, coupled to the Nord Express, Grandmother was transported in her chair to the Byelorusski Voksál and wheeled up the special ramp into the coach. With Grandmother travelled, in addition to her personal physician, her lady's maid and kosher cook. The great Express sped on its fifteen-hundred-mile journey across the North European plain, through Warsaw, Berlin and Cologne to Paris. However, Grandmother's coach was uncoupled at Berlin, shunted on to the Frankfurt express, and finally reached Bad Homburg after a forty-eight-hour journey. The villa proved to be well furnished and supplied, and soon Mother had everything under control. The wicker trunks had been unpacked and the *mesusahs* (small brass tubes the size of a cigarette, containing, in rolled-up form, the Ten Commandments and other biblical texts) nailed to all doorposts—Grandmother would not stay in a house without them. She had stood the journey remarkably well and was soon soundly asleep. The doctor walked across to the nearby *pension* where a comfortable room had been booked for him. Mother ordered provisions and hired a German maid to help with the household. Even on the next day there was a set-to between Grandmother's Russian maid, who considered herself more or less housekeeper, and the German maid, who considered she knew how things were done in Germany. It would seem that the German maid had used the kitchen tub in which pots and pans and crockery were washed for laundering some of Grandmother's underwear. From the German point of view this was quite in order provided that the tub was cleaned in between. From the Russian point of view—almost as strict as the kosher laws of not mixing meat and milk—this was *pogánno* (pagan), as the Russian maid shouted, and using the same receptacle for washing personal clothing and for food preparation was filthy. The national ideas on cleanliness were simply incompatible. In fact, Russians and Germans always consider one another as dirty.

In the meantime, Boris Schmerling, my father, had been fully briefed by his parents and by Mr Kagán. He gave up his job at the textile factory and prepared for the journey. A few suits, in English worsted, were ordered from a Moscow tailor recommended by Mr Kagán (the Mogilév tailored suits all had a touch of the caftan about them; moreover, they were made of inferior cloth from Lodz and always crumpled up). A *chapeau claque* folding top-hat, white gloves, silver-topped cane and other gentleman's accoutrements were purchased at Muir and Merrylies, the great British-owned store in Moscow (I do not know the correct English spelling). Father had been to Germany quite often, when studying textile printing at Mulhouse, and had no problems travelling to Bad Homburg on a second-class sleeper. In Homburg, as instructed by Mr Kagán, he checked in at the Ritters Park Hotel, the one patronised by King Edward. It was a grand place, very 'von Baron', and Grandfather in Mogilév would certainly have disapproved. The next day, Father armed himself with cane, top hat and white gloves and, with some trepidation, rang the bell at the villa, which was round the corner, all as instructed by Mr Kagán. The Russian maid opened the door and Father placed his visiting-card in the solid silver bowl thoughtfully brought from Moscow for this very purpose. He then returned to the hotel. The next day, Father received a note from Grandmother, inviting him to call, and the samovár would be boiling at four o'clock. In the meantime, Grandmother explained to Mother the real purpose of the long journey; in fact, Mother had divined it long ago. And, of course, Grandmother stressed—and meant it—Mother was fully entitled to reject the suitor if she did not like him.

At four o'clock Father entered the room, announced by the Russian maid, and paid his respects to Grandmother in her wheelchair. He was still carrying the *chapeau claque* and white gloves of which the maid, unaccustomed to such distinguished visitors, had failed to relieve him. Grandmother then sent for Mother, who was quite busy supervising the household arrangements and had had no time to prepare herself in any particular way for the visit. As Mother, with her long black tresses, came in, Father naturally advanced towards her and dropped the gloves and the *chapeau claque* on the floor. The fall released the catch and the contrivance opened up to its full length. Mother burst out laughing. The ice was broken. In fact, it was love at first sight. There were daily tea-parties, walks in the *Kurpark*, with Grandmother joining in her wheelchair (now pushed by Father) and visits to the theatre. On one occasion Grandmother felt that a drive to a nearby beauty-spot was called for; a *landau* open carriage was ordered, and Father was instructed by Mother (who had by now assumed command) to stand in the drawing-room, with his back turned to the windows, while Grandmother was being installed in the *landau*. After half an hour's studying the pictures on the wall, Father was called and found Grandmother sitting in the *landau*, her legs covered with a large tartan rug, and the drive proceeded, with Grandmother chatting amiably all the way. Her willpower was tremendous. After a few weeks at Homburg, Father and Mother became formally engaged, and Father telegraphed the good news to Mogilév. Father then left for Mulhouse, where he wanted to collect some information about the new fast dyes then on the market, and Grandmother and Mother stayed on at Homburg for another fortnight or so, and then travelled back the same way. In Moscow, the marriage contract was signed. Written in Hebrew characters, it was particularly concerned with protecting Mother's financial interests and that of her children as, at the time, in Russia as in most European countries, women had practically no property rights. Mother would be retaining half the dowry in her own name; in the event of Mother's death and Father wishing to remarry, he first had to settle a million roubles on the children, and so forth.

In autumn, Father and Mother were married in the Great Synagogue and there was a family gathering at the Tagánka home. This was after the end of Plehvé's disastrous reign, and the Mogilév parents obtained the necessary permits to travel to Moscow to attend their son's wedding.

My parents left for their honeymoon which was, in fact, a Grand Tour of Europe; more accurately, a semi-Grand Tour paid for by Grandmother. They visited Berlin and Dresden, Paris and Amsterdam, Rome, Naples and Venice. Not England (it was not customary) and not Spain. Father had some interest in visiting Madrid and Seville, Granada and Cordoba (the birthplace of the great Maimonides, whose Bible commentary, under the acronym *Rambam*, was required reading for every Jewish parochial schoolboy of twelve or thirteen). It seemed, however, that the rabbis had cursed Spain when the entire (unconverted) Jewish population and the Moors were expelled in 1492. True, when the persecution of the Jews had commenced in Russia in 1882 the Spanish Government did offer a refuge to Russian Jews, and some availed themselves of this. But for the majority, Spain was still taboo, certainly for a honeymoon visit, and Father told me that before World War I one just did not go to Spain. This attitude has now long been forgotten. During World War II General Franco—said to be himself partly of Jewish descent—steadfastly refused to hand any Jews over to Hitler, and in fact thousands of Jews were smuggled across the Pyrenees from France and survived in Spanish sanctuary.

6

Childhood in Moscow

When Father and Mother returned from honeymoon Grandmother gave them a house to live in as a wedding present. It was a house with a difference, though; in fact, it was a newly built block of flats in the Nóvaya Basmánnaya No. 169. Basmánnaya, in the Old Town, was the street of the Icon-framers, but its new extension, the Nóvaya Basmánnaya, was in a pleasant residential area beyond the Red Gate. In each entrance there were, I believe, a six-room and an eight-room flat on each floor—by the simple expedient of joining two flats on the second floor of the middle entrance, a fourteen-room flat would be produced. Mother was, after all, Grandmother's favourite daughter. The other flats would provide a handsome income. It was a characteristic Poverkhovsky arrangement; Father, in his heart, would have preferred a small house to oneself.

Even Jews with full residential qualifications in Moscow, like Father, were still not allowed to purchase property there; so it was necessary to incorporate a company, *Domovladélets*, owning the property, and Father was presented with the shares. The building alterations, redecorations and so forth took over a year and, in the meantime, my parents took a small flat in Petróvka No. 19, a busy thoroughfare leading from Theatre Square, with the Bolshoi and Maly theatres, and I was born in that flat in 1909.

I was named Grigory after Grandfather Poverkhovsky, though at home for some reason I was always called George. As customary, I had—so I am told—a wetnurse, Russian non-Jewish; some people consider this as of significance, though I fail to see how. My great attachment to Russia is surely due to family tradition and upbringing.

For the new home, Mother chose Adam-style furniture and decoration. The reason was not a particular preference for this so elegant style but simply the fact that Fischer's, the leading reproduction furniture manufacturers in Moscow, at that time only supplied three styles: *Louis Quinze, Empire* and Adam. As Mother's two elder sisters had furnished in *Louis Quinze* (the merchant) and *Empire* (the stockbroker) there was only Adam left for Mother. In the event, the rooms, with their plaster medaillions on the walls, were light and airy, and seemed much more elegant than the Moscow versions of sumptuous *Louis Quinze* or sombre, ebony and gilt *Empire*. In the modern block of flats Father now found himself owning, with oil-fired central heating (but no hot water), each flat had, in addition, two separate servant rooms, so that we had four servant rooms altogether. True, as I remember them (I was not supposed to go there but naturally investigated them often enough) they were more like whitewashed cells, but nevertheless were a great improvement on the custom prevailing at the time in Moscow (as, I believe, in London) of having the servants sleeping in 'areas' in the basement or in the kitchen. Mother had three Russian maids and a kosher cook, all living in, each with her own room centrally heated. The maids were devoted to Mother, who took a personal interest in their welfare, and not only provided free medical attention when required but personally nursed them if they were ill.

By the standards of the period my parents lived rather modestly. Father went to the office in a cab, or sleigh in winter, with one horse only; this mode of transport was quite adequate for town but lacked the glamour of a *troika*. Mother dressed well, I believe, but again without extravagance, using Moscow dressmakers only, no Petersburg-style trips to Paris to order the season's wardrobe. Her furs were modest too: no sables (mink had not yet been discovered), a black Pacific seal coat for daily use, a *karakulchá*, or broadtail, for special occasions, a chinchilla hat and muff, an ermine cape for the Bolshoi.

The continued prosperity of the Poverkhovsky firm depended, of course, on the relationship between Father and Uncle Matthew. Fortunately, being so different in character, they got on extremely well. It was, in effect, the relationship of Chairman and Managing Director. Uncle Matthew had inherited his father's vision, though not, perhaps, his diligence and attention to detail, and was only too glad to leave the day-to-day running of the firm to Father. He travelled a great deal in Europe; being, like all Moscow merchants, a great admirer of the English parliamentary system and of the political climate so friendly to business, he went to England every summer (which was unusual) with his family, and attended the Cowes Regatta on the Isle of Wight—as a spectator only, of course. There, one could see the King and Royal Family almost as easily as one could the Emperor at Bad Ischl.

Uncle Matthew was very good at building and maintaining personal relationships based on natural empathy. Father used to tell me how one day, after a week or two of absence from the office (which was not unusual), Uncle Matthew put in an appearance and remarked casually that he had spent a capital evening with the Smirnóv* brothers at Yar (the leading restaurant), in a private room with gipsy chorus and some charming actresses, and that in future Poverkhovsky's would get Smirnóv's entire production. Father could hardly believe his ears; the Smirnóvs were very old-established manufacturers at Ivánovo-Voznesénsk, who had so far steadfastly refused to supply the upstart and non-believers Poverkhovsky and sold their entire output to Morósov. But a personal, and probably quite unpremeditated, success like this was characteristic of Uncle Matthew. For some reason he was also particularly successful with customers from Siberia and the Far East (Manchuria and Korea), and there were plans for a fourth branch office and warehouse at Irkutsk.

In the meantime, Father was continuing with the administration of Poverkhovsky's, who now employed several thousand people, all men, of course. The company was very progressive in its treatment of employees, almost a pace-setter; there was full sickness pay and widow's pensions and the other benefits nowadays provided by a welfare state. When one of the accountants (like most of them, an Old Believer) developed consumption he was sent to Davos in Switzerland (this was before the discovery of penicillin), where indeed he recovered after a year. His family received his full pay during the period.

There was also a canteen where, for a few kopecks, an excellent meal (shared by the Directors in their dining room) was to be had. More accurately, three canteens, each with its own kitchen, Christian Orthodox, Jewish Kosher and Muslim Halal (the warehousemen were all Tartars, as was customary in Moscow, both because of their strength and their invariable honesty). The Old Believers preferred to bring their own food. There were no Hindus.

Uncle Matthew also arranged for the firm to take part in the famous Nizhni Novgorod (Lower Newtown) Fair. Nizhni Novgorod (quite different from ancient Novgorod the Great on Lake Ilmen off the Baltic shore) was situated at the confluence of the Volga and the Oka, and was an important trade centre, particularly for Eastern Russia and Asia. (Should the reader wish to locate Nizhni on a present-day map the town is now called Gorky, in memory of Maxim Peshkov, the Russian Upton Sinclair, whose pen-name was Gorky, meaning Bitter.) There had been an annual Fair at Nizhni since medieval times, and this was not an exhibition but an annual bazaar; all the wares had to be there in stock and were sold on a cash-and-carry basis for six weeks in midsummer. Merchants came from Eastern Russia, the Caspian, the Caucasus, the Urals, Siberia, Central Asia with

Khiva, Bokhara and Samarkand, Persia, Afghanistan, even North-west India. They sailed up the Volga, or Oka, or Kama, or arrived with their own horse or camel transport, paid cash and collected the goods. In order to sell at the Fair it was necessary to own a store-building there, with office and living quarters, throughout the larger part of the year only inhabited by a watchman or two and their families. Six weeks before the Fair opened a large stock of the precious bales of cloth was sent up, worth several million roubles and a large team of storesmen, sales clerks and accountants followed to ready everything for the Fair. It was said that up to half a million buyers visited the Fair annually, and no-one travelled to Nizhni for sightseeing. Nor were the exhibitors all Russian; there were Persian merchants, for instance, selling their famed carpets, and more than one Moscow household had its carpets from Nizhni.

Tea with the Mother Superior

Back in Moscow, one day in 1913, Father received a visitor from Ivánovo Voznesénsk, the great cotton-manufacturing centre (now Ivánovo). The visitor was an old-established cotton converter, supplier of Poverkhovsky's, an old man and heirless. He had decided to sell his enterprise and retire to the Crimea. Uncle Matthew, when Father told him, was most enthusiastic, and Poverkhovsky's acquired the old-established Pokrovskaya Manufactura, employing four thousand men (with today's high-speed machinery, the same work would probably be done by four hundred men). There was a last-minute hitch; the factory stood on church land, and apparently there was an old church law forbidding the lease of land to non-believers. The land-ownership was, in fact, vested in a convent, and the owner's lawyers held discussions with the Mother Superior. Apparently, the Mother Superior, who was a practical woman, decided that it was left entirely to her discretion whether or not to enquire by whom Poverkhovsky's were actually owned. Perhaps Father would take a glass of tea with her and also present the Convent with one of these new writing machines which she could use to invoice the celebrated patchwork quilts her nuns were making? She would then probably ask no further questions. Father duly called, carrying a Remington, probably the first Jew (if not the first layman) in Russia to visit a Mother Superior in her convent. The raspberry jam served with the tea was very good, and the Reverend Mother satisfied herself that Father apparently had no horns or tail. The deal was signed, and Father greatly enjoyed putting his technical training to practical use, introducing the latest fast dyes from Germany and Switzerland (England, where synthetic dyes had been pioneered with Perkins's synthesis of mauve in 1856, was falling behind in this as in many another industry), and generally modernising the old-fashioned factory, not forgetting urgently required improvements in working conditions.

Mother's private philanthropy

According to the marriage contract Mother had retained half of her portion of the Poverkhovsky shares, the other half being transferred to Father. She thus had a considerable private income, the dividends being paid into her personal account at Junkers Bros, a leading private bank, comparable perhaps with Coutts in London. (Father was banking with the Russian Siberian Bank, a major joint-stock company.) Mother's private means enabled her to lend generous support to ORT, thus continuing the family association, and also to assist, most discreetly, a dozen or so young people to pursue their studies at Russian, or German or even French universities, or at the Conservatoires, and then to establish themselves in their professions (the extent of Mother's private philanthropy Father only discovered after her death).

In the arts, opera dominated our life, as it did that of the whole of Moscow. There was nothing 'elitist', as some sociologists might mistakenly call it, about opera in Moscow. Petersburg might have its Imperial Ballet but Moscow had the Bolshoi (or Grand) Theatre, with Chaliapin, Sobinov (a peer of Caruso) and the divine Nezhdanova. We were brought up on *Carmen* and *The Pearlfishers, Rigoletto* and *Traviata* and *Aida*, Gounod's *Faust*. And *Eugene Onegin* and *Boris Godunov*. And *Pagliacci* . . . the list has no end. Mozart was never performed. Not for the Muscovites the Master's polished elegance. They preferred Verdi's blazing fires, Bizet's leaping flames. Mother's favourite was actually *The Queen of Spades* (in Russian called *The Dame of Spades*). I remember Mother singing the Shepherdess's song, accompanying herself on the harp she had standing in the drawing-room, while I was listening from my favourite hideout underneath the Steinway.

There were also concerts, often with Rachmaninov as conductor and, of course, also drama: *The Seagull, Three Sisters, The Cherry Orchard* were all unveiled at the Arts Theatre. This theatre was subsidised by the Morósovs, and other wealthy patrons (or *maecenas*) and, quite generally, the great Moscow merchants vied with each other in donating to university institutes, lecture halls and art galleries (the Tretyakov!), not to mention hospitals and orphanages. Unfortunately, the great Morósov (a non-Jew, of course), also subsidised the Bolshevik emigrés, and his regular cheques were said to have greatly contributed to the comforts of Lenin's celebrated *ménage à trois* at the Zurich lakeside. My Uncle Matthew had occasion once to remonstrate with Morósov, who apparently defended his actions by saying that, of course, he did not agree with Lenin's aims and would never want to see him in government, but that he was the best man to get the incompetent and corrupt government in Petersburg out. In fact, Lenin did not contribute to the fall of the Czar's government, but more of that later.

A kosher household

Our own household was strictly *kosher*. As is well known, the Pentateuch forbids consumption of pork, various other mammals, certain types of fish and all lower forms of animal life such as snails and seafood (these restrictions make, or made, perfect hygienic sense).[1] There was also complete prohibition of the intake of blood and, in consequence, the ritual-slaughter method in which the animal's blood is drained. The drinking of blood was part of many pagan rites and leads to excesses and orgies. Even today, it is practised in some parts of Africa. The prophet Mohammed, who accepted the Divine Revelation from Sinai, ordained these Mosaic prohibitions and the ritual slaughter for Islam, so that today, as far as I know, Moslems do not eat pork either, and *Halal* meat is obtained by almost the same slaughter method as *kosher* meat. In addition to the prohibition of pork and other animals, and ritual slaughter, the Jewish dietary laws contain a third provision which is not found in Islam. The Bible (Exodus 23, 19 and 34, 26) decrees: 'Thou must not boil a kid in its mother's milk.' Excavations in Israel and Syria have produced evidence that this was a prevalent idolatrous practice of offering a sacrifice to Baal. It would seem that the biblical injunction simply meant, in language then universally understood, a prohibition of engaging in a popular pagan rite. This is also clear from the context in which this provision is included, not in the dietary laws. Apparently, after a thousand years or more, when the centre of Judaism moved to Babylonia after the destruction of Jerusalem by the Romans, the meaning of the injunction was lost, and the rabbis began interpreting it literally. According to Uncle Isaac (the one with the gentleman's bed in the barracks' dormitory and irreverent, as always) the following discussion took place at a meeting of one of the two rabbinical colleges in Babylonia (Sura and Pumbedita), whose deliberations over several centuries constitute the *Talmud* (Teaching):

First Rabbi: There is this worrying matter of the kid's meat. Nowadays, in these pagan cities, our people buy their milk from a shop. They have no means of knowing from what kind of animal the milk was taken. Should we not, in order to prevent an accidental breach of the Law, say that kid's meat must never be cooked in *any* milk?

The other Rabbis: Agreed. [*The scribe makes a note.*]

Second Rabbi: But what about the people buying ready-cut kebabs and suchlike from the butcher's shop? They have no means of knowing whether the meat dish contains some kid's meat. Should we not, in order to prevent an accidental breach of the Law, say that *any* meat must never be cooked in *any* milk?

The other Rabbis: Agreed. [*The scribe makes a note.*]

Third Rabbi: But what about the earthenware cooking pots? My wife spends hours cleaning them with potash and pumice stone, but after some time they always smell of food. So, if a gruel was cooked with milk which happened to contain some goat's milk, and a few drops of that milk are retained in the pot, and if meat, which happened to contain some kid's meat, was subsequently cooked in the same pot, and if the kid's meat contained in the meat happened to be of a kid from whose mother some of the milk used for the gruel was taken, then the Law would be broken. Should we not, in order to prevent an accidental breach of the Law, say that separate cooking and eating utensils must be used for cooking meat and for cooking with milk?

The other Rabbis: Agreed. [*The scribe makes a note.*]

And so, according to irreverent Uncle Isaac, that strange *kosher* restriction unique to Judaism was born, which prohibits the mixing of meat and milk in the same dish or, to be on the safe side, in the same meal, and requires separate pots and pans, plates and cutlery (and, no doubt, separate dishwashers) for a 'meat' meal or a 'milk' meal. 'Theirs not to reason why?' There was something touching in the way a million Jewish households in the Pale, most of them on the breadline, complied without murmur with this strange and irksome regulation which, they were taught, was the Word of the Lord. Foregoing pork and bacon, hare and rabbit was no problem, and seafood or *escargots* were not available anyway. Keeping the *kosher* meat salted for an hour before cooking (to draw out the last remnants of blood) was not difficult. But to the harassed and overworked housewife, trying to feed a large family on a few kopecks, without refrigeration, with the prohibition of cooking or warming up on the Sabbath, to that heroic housewife of the Pale the requirement of not mixing meat and milk in a meal, and the need to have completely separate sets of all kitchen- and tableware, never to be mixed, even when washing up, made life very difficult indeed. As a boy I was, of course, fully familiar with the intricacies of *kosher*; I well remember remonstrating with a new (non-Jewish) maid who, when laying the table for a 'milk' supper, placed the 'meat' salt-cellar on it. In our spacious household in Moscow, with all conveniences (as were available at the time) and several servants, there was, of course, no hardship whatsoever in complying with the *kosher* dietary laws, and Mother did not consider she was making a particular sacrifice. Father disliked the *kosher* regulations because they made it impossible to serve a well-cooked and balanced meal. If there was a meat course, no butter could be used for cooking anything, no cheese served after dinner, no cream with the coffee (unless one waited for six hours). Moreover, *kosher* meat is tasteless.

Mother makes the Rabbi sin

There was a celebrated occasion when my parents gave a small luncheon party for the highly respected Rabbi of Moscow, Dr Masé. Several leading members of the community were coming, including, I believe, the great Wissotzky himself. Our cook (Jewish and well trained in the *kosher* regulations) was suddenly taken ill, and Mother had to borrow the cook from the Poverkhovskys (whose household was not *kosher*, Aunt Amalia favouring French cuisine). Mother had decided on a light 'meat' dinner: smoked salmon and smoked sturgeon, *borsht* (without the customary sour cream, of course), veal cutlets and fruit jelly (most sweets, pastries, etc. were out as they contain milk, butter or cream). Naturally Mother was always served last, and further delayed by some trifle, and only when the guests had almost finished the meat course did she realise that the sauce (which the Rabbi had liked and singled out for praise) was a cream sauce. I believe, sincerely, that Mother was never so embarrassed in her life. However, none of the other guests seemed to notice, and she had to make *bonne mine au mauvais jeu*. Finally, when the guests settled down to black coffee and Chartreuse, Mother went to the kitchen to remonstrate with the cook, who was most anxious to please her and comply with the regulations, but explained in tears that Mother had told her: no milk, no butter, but had not mentioned that cream was prohibited.

The taboo on the idolatrous Baal rite was still as powerful in Moscow after two thousand years as it is today in New York and Chicago, Toronto and Los Angeles, Johannesburg and Melbourne.

Uncle Jacques

Under Alexander II Russia had advanced considerably in Central Asia. The Khanates of Bokhara, with Samarkand (1868), of Chiva (1873) and Kokand, with Tashkent (1876), all singularly ill-ruled even by the standards of the time in Asia, were occupied and the turbulent tribal areas pacified. Russia now controlled the entire vast area between the Pamirs and the Caspian, bordering on Persia (Iran), Afghanistan and China, and traversed by the ancient 'silk route' from China. The appearance of Russian troops at Merv (now Máry) on the border of Afghanistan led to the celeb-rated attack of 'Mervousness' in the British Parliament (although it took Russia a century to take advantage of this geographical proximity). The trans-Caspian railway was built—no mean feat—from the eastern shore of the Caspian to Samarkand (later extended to Tashkent and, in a westward loop, to Orenburg). Kerensky, the socialist and anti-imperialist, knew the area well as his father was headmaster in Tashkent (1890–99). In his book he describes Russian rule in the area as wholly beneficial, providing prosperity and greatly increased standards of living, without interference with the national customs or Islamic religion of the population. This semi-arid area is traversed by the Amu Darýa (the Oxus of the Ancients) and Syr Darýa (the Jaxartes), each about 1500 miles long, and flowing from the Pamirs (the 'Roof of the World') into the Aral Sea. Great irrigation schemes were carried out by Russia, making large-scale cotton-growing possible in vast tracts of hitherto wasted Karakum desert. Russia now had its own cotton. One of our Moscow relatives (we called him Uncle Jacques) became the leading cotton-broker, travelling every year to Merv and the other cotton-producing centres and promoting the sales of home-grown cotton in Russia, and abroad. The authorities were naturally only too pleased with Uncle Jacques's work and placed no obstacles in his way, whatever the Temporary Regulations might or might not have said about the area.

Note

1. Most of the biblical regulations of personal conduct show a remarkable degree of medical understanding. It is now known that male circumcision protects the female partner from cervical cancer, and that the rabbinical prohibition of inter-course for five days *before* the period prevents grossly malformed births (which do not occur among observant Jewish couples). As to the biblical prohibition of homosexual acts, their wisdom has now, with the AIDS epidemic, become apparent.

7

War

In the early summer of 1914 we spent a few days in Vienna *en route* to Switzerland. At the Hotel Sacher (the originators of the Sacher Torte gateau) Mother was putting me to bed while Father was trying to obtain tickets for the Opera, where the great Caruso was due to sing the Duke in *Rigoletto*. I would not go to sleep because in the adjoining room someone was singing at the top of his voice. In desperation Mother complained to the hotel manager, asking him to stop the noise. 'But, *gnädige Frau*', he replied, in horror, 'it is Herr Caruso!'

From Vienna, Father returned to Moscow—the business was never left alone for more than a fortnight—and Mother with us children went to St Moritz, which she favoured in summer and where Father was supposed to join us in August and return home with us two weeks later.

These well-laid plans were rudely shaken. The heir to the Austrian throne, Archduke Francis Ferdinand, was paying a visit to Sarajevo, the capital of Bosnia (ethnically Serbian, now a constituent province of Yugoslavia, but at the time administered (later annexed) by Austria since the days of the Congress of Berlin in 1878). On 28 June the Archduke was assassinated by revolver shots fired by a Serbian nationalist, a member of a Serbian secret society. On 23 July, after some diplomatic skirmishing, Austria presented Serbia with an ultimatum which went far beyond any reasonable claims for compensation and was intentionally so designed that Serbia could not possibly accept it in its entirety. For instance, Austrian officials would in future have the right to act independently on Serbian territory against organisations hostile to Austria. On 28 July Austria declared war on Serbia and on 29 July attacked Belgrade. Austria knew full well that, although the Russian Government did not want war at that time as the Army had not yet fully recovered from the disasters in Manchuria in 1905, Russian public opinion—in foreign policy always more forceful than the Czar—would compel Russia to come to the aid of Serbia. It was said that Marshal von Hötzendorf wanted war with Russia before Russia had regained her strength. On 30 July Russia ordered general mobilisation, hoping that this might force Austria to leave Serbia alone, but it did not, because Austria received full backing and encouragement from the Kaiser. On 31 July, the next day, Germany demanded of Russia that the mobilisation be stopped forthwith. Russia refused, as Germany expected, and *Germany declared war on Russia* on 1 August. It is thought, sometimes, that Germany declared war on Russia not with the main object of helping Austria but in order to expand eastwards, and gain the vast territories which Russia was forced to cede to Germany at Brest-Litovsk in January 1918. This may be correct, but I have never seen published evidence to support this view; personally, I tend to think the dismemberment of Russia by Germany in 1918 was more a case of *L'appetit vient en mangeant.* [1] (With Hitler, the Austrian, it was quite different.) True, in 1890 the Kaiser dismissed Bismarck, who was always in favour of close co-operation with Russia ('never allow the wire to Petersburg to snap'), and dropped the Russian alliance, with Caprivi as Chancellor, but this could have been simply a form of self-assertion. Bismarck himself had in 1887 concluded the alliance with Austria which, unavoidably, had an anti-Russian character. In fact, the Kaiser's Germany was mainly interested in expansion in Africa and in the Middle East (the 'Baghdad railway'), securing a 'Place in the Sun'. Germany's perceived enemy was therefore Britain and, to a lesser degree, France.

It is the duty of all General Staffs to prepare detailed plans for all possible contingencies. The German (or Prussian) General Staff had a contingency plan for the dreaded possibility of a war against France and Russia simultaneously. This had been formulated by Count Schlieffen, Chief of General Staff 1891–1905. The Schlieffen Plan was based on the well-known slowness of mobilisation of the Russian Army, which was believed to require weeks if not months. Consequently, it allowed for token defence of the Eastern Front only, with the entire might of the German armies marching *through Belgium* and overwhelming France from the north, destroying the French army *à la Sédan* and capturing Paris. With France prostrate and suing for peace, the armies would then be switched to the east and take on Russia, who might just have completed mobilisation. On paper, this looked the perfect plan.

The German General Staff were convinced—no doubt, correctly—that France, Russia's ally since 1893, would come to Russia's aid. Consequently, having declared war on Russia (to assist Austria) on 1 August, the German

General Staff felt that there was no time to lose if the Schlieffen Plan was to be carried out before the Russian Army was at full strength. So they prevailed upon the Kaiser to *declare war on France* on 3 August. With this action, Germany transformed an east European war into a world war. Two precious days for Germany had already been lost. German troops, with *Gott mit Uns* (God with us) engraved on every belt-buckle, invaded Belgium, racing to the French frontier. The neutrality of Belgium had, however, been guaranteed in an international Treaty (the Kaiser's celebrated 'Scrap of Paper') co-signed by Britain in order to provide a 'neutral zone' (I almost wrote 'nuclear-free zone') in western Europe. On 4 August Britain issued an ultimatum to Germany to respect the neutrality of Belgium and withdraw its troops. In the absence of any reply, and with the continued invasion of Belgium, Britain and Germany were at war. And now only, Austria, who had initiated the whole chain-reaction by attacking Serbia, belatedly declared war on Russia on 5 August.

A month later, on 5 September, Britain, France and Russia negotiated the Treaty of London, in which they concluded a formal tripartite alliance and undertook not to make a separate peace. No doubt, there must have been secret clauses, protocols or understandings about war aims; France knew that after victory she would regain Alsace-Lorraine and Russia control of the Straits—its absence ten years earlier having cost her dearly.

As events proved, the Schlieffen Plan, which caused Germany to bring France into the war and—because of Belgium—also Britain, was sadly out of date. With the French-inspired and French-financed railway network in Russia's western provinces completed and the general co-operation of the Russian and French staffs, Russia's mobilisation had been remarkably swift, and they were able, to everyone's surprise, to field *eight* fully operational armies by the middle of August.

The First Army, commanded by von Rennenkamp (a German–Russian of Baltic descent), attacking from the east, penetrated into East Prussia, only lightly held, whereas the Second Army (General Samsonov) attacked from the south. In the second half of August von Rennenkamp and his staff were dining in style at Insterburg castle (at present, in the Soviet Union, Chernyakhovsk), on the road to Konigsberg (at present, Kaliningrad), one of the sacred cities of Prussian military tradition. The effect in Berlin was electrifying; it was as if, in June 1940, von Rundstedt had been dining with his staff, say, at Castle Howard. And it was probably adding insult to injury that this blow to Prussian pride had been inflicted by a member of the expatriate Prussian nobility loyal to his adopted homeland.

In a panic, on 25 August, the German High Command withdrew *four* entire divisions from the mighty host advancing on Paris, whilst the French were commandeering taxicabs in Paris to rush reinforcements to the front.

The balance was tilted in favour of the French defence, Gallieni stopped von Kluck thirty miles from Paris and in September the front was stabilised on the River Marne. Paris was saved—only one German gun, monstrous 'Big Bertha' (so named, officially, after Frau Krupp) managed, from time to time, to launch a projectile—half-shell, half-missile—into the capital.

The Schlieffen plan was in tatters and Germany had lost the war—even if it took another four years and ten million dead on both sides, not to mention the Russian collapse, for the German High Command to sue for peace.

Early Russian disasters

The Russian Army had saved France from certain catastrophe but was now itself faced with two major disasters. On 31 August 1914 the Germans, now commanded on the Eastern Front by von Hindenburg, with Ludendorff as Chief of Staff, assisted by General Hoffmann (whom we had met in Manchuria) destroyed the Second Russian Army under General Samsonov in a classic double-envelopment manoeuvre at Tannenberg, when a hundred thousand prisoners were taken. In early September, Rennenkamp's turn came: the First Army, which had drawn those vital four German divisions away from France, was now annihilated, with ten thousand men disappearing in the treacherous bogs of the Masurian Lakes. Samsonov, outmanouevred, shot himself; von Rennenkamp was recalled and remained on active service until 1918, when he died in the Civil War. It was the *disappearance* of an entire army (there were few prisoners taken from the First Army) in the Masurian Lakes which particularly incensed public opinion in Russia. With Rennenkamp being of German descent, accusations of deliberate treachery were rife. Father, who was always well informed, told me that there was no doubt whatsoever that Rennenkamp was intensely loyal to the Czar. Moreover, it was he who had really robbed the Germans of their great prize in the West and, if his name was execrated in Russia, he surely merited a monument in Paris. Most Russian Germans were, in fact, loyal to the country in which their families had lived, in some cases for two centuries. Most, but not all. Father told me that as late as 1914 Germans in Moscow, most of them Russian nationals, were openly collecting money for the German Navy League to present the Kaiser with a warship squadron. And there was the odious arch-traitor Alfred Rosenberg, but more of him later.

We are trapped in Switzerland

Whilst these historic events were taking place and soldiers of all nations were dying in agony in their hundred thousands, a large contingent of

Russian holidaymakers were trapped in Switzerland, their ranks soon to be swollen by fellow nationals escaping from Germany and Austria.

Mother moved with us to Montreux on Lake Geneva, where we spent the winter of 1914. All the Russians trapped in Switzerland were anxious to return home as soon as possible (except, of course, the clique of political emigrés who lived there permanently). With many, the money was running out. We were fortunate in this respect, as Mother was always travelling with a Letter of Credit in favour of Poverkhovskys, which was, apparently, unlimited (I do not know the exact technicalities). In fact, the proprietor of the Hotel Eden, where we spent the winter of 1914/15, and who was aware of Mother's favourable financial position, offered her a third share in the hotel. Mother somehow liked the idea, and had an exchange of telegrams with Father over the investment offer, which Father indignantly vetoed ('I am not an hotelier'). Four years later, he would regret this decision bitterly, but then no-one could foresee the Bolshevik coup. It is also possible that an investment of this kind would have been contrary to the spirit, if not the letter, of the wartime Russian foreign exchange regulations which Father certainly would not want to contravene or evade. However, Mother managed to help various families who were in difficulties.

In summer 1915 the position in the Balkans had stabilised and a precarious route to Russia was (temporarily) established. Turkey, with two German cruisers anchored in the Bosphorus (having stolen a march on the British Mediterranean Fleet), had entered the war on the side of the Central Powers, and attacked Russia at the end of October 1914. In Italy, on the other hand, British diplomacy was most successful in weaning that country from Austria, and in May 1915 Italy threw in her lot with the Allies. It was now possible to travel to the heel of Italy, cross the Ionian from Brindisi to the Piracus in neutral Greece and then travel northwards through Serbia, via Nish, and Romania to Russia (or from Bulgarian Rushchuk on the Danube direct by boat to Odessa). Mother decided on the first route, collected a large amount of Swiss francs from the bank, in gold, and embarked on what was to an unaccompanied woman with two small children a fairly hazardous journey. All went well, and after four or five days' travelling we were met on the Russian–Romanian frontier by Father. Next day we were home in Moscow.

Three years later we had to flee from Moscow in the reverse direction; with hindsight, it would have been better if Father had joined *us* in Switzerland. But Moscow was our home and naturally, like everyone else, we returned there.

In the meantime, German diplomacy promised Bulgaria, at the expense of Serbia and Greece, the whole of Macedonia, with Salonika and Greek Epirus (south of Albania), giving Bulgaria not only a major outlet to the

Aegean but also an Ionian coastline. Although Bulgaria was indebted to Russia for its very existence and liberation from the Turks, the ruler, Ferdinand of Coburg, entered the war on the side of the Central Powers, which included Turkey, Bulgaria's erstwhile tormentor, on 15 October 1915. The narrow gap between the Austrian–German positions and Bulgaria was soon closed, and Germany and her allies ruled over a continuous territory from Ostend to the Persian Gulf. Russia was completely cut off from her Western allies, with devastating consequences. The arctic route to Archangel was very precarious, and closed by ice a large part of the year. In June 1916, when Lord Kitchener sailed to Russia for urgent discussions on military co-ordination, the cruiser *Hampshire* carrying him was torpedoed and sunk with all on board. The route via the Cape to Vladivostok took three to four months and the carrying capacity of the Trans-Siberian railway was still very limited.

In wartime Moscow

To begin with, life in Moscow was not much affected by the terrible war raging over 500 miles to the west, the first high-explosive war in Europe. The Russian Army still had, largely, the traditional composition of peasant lads officered by the gentry. On mobilisation, only reservists were called up, i.e. those that had previously received military training, like Uncle Isaac. Even then, there were numerous exceptions, and many occupations were exempt, including heads of businesses. In practice, I do not believe that a single Moscow merchant, for instance, was on active service, nor did public opinion demand of able-bodied men that they volunteer. Young ladies did not hand out white feathers. There were no posters depicting the Commander-in-Chief, Grand Duke Nicolai Nicolaewitch, proclaiming: 'The Country needs You!' The reason is that in Russia the shortage was not of manpower but of equipment. The Army had lost much equipment in Manchuria, not yet fully replaced. In 1914 there were even not enough army boots to go round (for an army that still had to march a great deal), and, as Father told me, quite a few boots had the flimsiest of soles or even cardboard ones owing to notorious corruption in the supply services. In some regiments, it was said, there was one rifle to three men. If there was in 1914 a country that did not want war, and was not prepared for it, it was Russia. Britain was probably the other.

Father was certainly not liable for military service and was not called up. The Jewish population shared the general sense of outrage at the German attack on Russia. The *pogróms* had ceased completely, but the hated Temporary Regulations remained in force, though with the residential restrictions much relaxed for refugees from the war-zone. Father used to relate a charming anecdote illustrating both the gulf that, after a century and a half, still divided the Pale from Moscow, and the fame of Wissotzky as public benefactor among the Jewish population of the Pale.

An old man from Minsk (or Pinsk), now a refugee in Moscow, was showing his grandson the sights. They were walking along Red Square (which was always so called), looking at the monument to Minin and Pojársky, the great national heroes, who freed Moscow from the Polish invasion in 1612. The following dialogue ensued:

Little boy (pointing at monument): Who are they?
Old man: Must be Wissotzky and his son-in-law.
Little boy: And what does 1612 mean?
Old man: Their telephone number, of course, stupid!

Father continued to run Poverkhovskys but also, at his personal expense, equipped a small factory producing much-wanted field kitchens, said to have been the best in service, for the Army, and supplied these strictly at cost.[2] Father also subscribed much to the War Loan—something which not all Moscow merchants did.

Whilst the war had caught us in Switzerland, Uncle Matthew was in Dresden, at the famous sanatorium of Dr Lahmann at the Weisser Hirsch, where the overweight men of Europe were being fed a diet of toast and lemon juice, at rates double those of the Ritz, and for an extra charge made to chop Dr Lahmann's firewood. However, Uncle Matthew, rejuvenated, managed to catch the last train to Warsaw and returned home to Moscow.

As the war dragged on, Citizen's Committees arose to help the war effort, and they were also supposed to look at the lists of all men of military age in the district who were not with the Colours. The Moscow Committee included young Fungus,* of the old-established non-Jewish competitors of Poverkhovskys (in fact, all competitors were non-Jewish), who were falling behind. When Fungus noticed Uncle Matthew's name of the list he saw red, and made sure Uncle Matthew's name would be recommended for call-up, which the Committee could do. I believe this was the only case which the Committee ever referred to the military authorities. They did not question the name of Alfred Rosenberg, which must have been on the same list.

Uncle Matthew did not have the slightest wish to be called up. He was now over forty, and had never received any military training. Besides, no-one else served. Fungus, though younger than Uncle, had no intention of joining up, although *he* did not have the Temporary Regulations to contend with. *He* would be an Officer travelling by sleeper, and Uncle Matthew a trooper travelling by cattle truck (in Russia cattle trucks are used, to this day, for the transport of troops, rather than goods wagons, because the

former are heated). So Uncle Matthew had to travel to Petersbur,
spend a fortune obtaining a part-time position as technical adviser to the
Admiralty on textiles.

Vodka from the teapot

Generally, the war made little impact in Moscow (I believe this was different in Petersburg, where everyone was in uniform, though not at the
front). Little boys like myself, who used to be dressed in sailor suits, were
now wearing a 'French', a military style khaki suit named after Sir John
French. I found it a great improvement on the sailor suit as it had more and
larger pockets.

Only a few imported luxuries were in short supply, owing to the German
blockade. We had been brought up on Pears soap but now there was none.
Mother used scented soap from Roger & Gallet in Paris, and that, too, had
disappeared. Father liked to offer his guests, after the frugal *kosher* dinner,
some green Chartreuse but now only the yellow variety was obtainable.
Apart from such merest trifles, nothing was as yet in short supply. The
many parties at the Yar restaurant in the Sparrow Hills (at present, Lenin
Hills) continued, and there were ample stocks of burgundies and champagne (German wines were *never* drunk in Russia). Father did not particularly like dining out, even less in wartime, but one evening (Uncle
Matthew was in Petersburg advising the Admiralty) he had to take some
customers from Siberia to the Yar when, to his surprise, the *maître d'hôtel*,
when serving the obligatory *zakúska* of smoked salmon and smoked
sturgeon, started pouring weak tea from a teapot into the vodka glasses on
the table. At least it looked like weak tea. Apparently, some *ukase* had
come down from Petersburg, supposedly by the Czar himself, forbidding for
the duration of the war the serving of vodka with meals, and the teapot
charade was the typical Russian way of complying with the edict. At the
neighbouring table a party of young officers were having a meal, also enjoy-
ing the teapot vodka amidst much mirth. Father was quite shocked at the
spectacle of these young men flouting their sovereign's orders, however ill-
advised, in public—he was still shocked when telling me about it thirty
years later. But perhaps he had not fathomed fully the Russian mind—
perhaps the officers were on the eve of their departure for the Front and
were soon to be sacrificing their lives against the German invader.

Summer at the dácha

Moscow, almost without parks or open spaces, was quite unbearable in the
hot Russian summer, without a refreshing breeze, without rain to lay the

dust and—over sixty years ago—with the deafening clatter of the tyreless iron wheels on the cobblestones. Everyone who could (more than half the population) moved out to a *dácha*, large or small, and office workers commuted daily, generally by train. Our *dácha* was at Sokólniki, then a pleasant wooded area near Moscow (now, I believe, an exhibition area). To say *our dácha* is not quite correct; even Jews like Father, with all residential qualifications in Moscow, could not own property there, and we had, in fact, a very long lease. We spent the whole summer of 1916 there. In May, Mother ordered two *landaus*, and we moved out. The drive took about one hour. At home, the carpets were rolled up, and the furniture covered with dust-sheets. All furs were sent for safe-keeping to a special repository where they were stored in a permanent draught—apparently moths hate draughts and left well alone. The *dácha* was built of timber (like all *dáchas*, and many town-houses too), the walls consisting of logs boarded up on both sides. There was no piped water and no sanitation; the water was brought by a carrier and poured into storage tanks connected to the water taps in the house. There was an outside lavatory with a cess-pool underneath, emptied in autumn by contractors, the *otkhódniki*, specialising in this unpleasant work. (I believe that it was due to similar arrangements at Windsor Castle that, fifty years earlier, Prince Albert contracted the fatal typhoid.) We had a pleasant garden, mainly lawn, used for croquet, and pine trees, with a few flowerbeds in the front garden. It was, of course, not possible to grow roses near Moscow, as they could not survive the winter; there were dahlias (taken out for the winter), hydrangeas and a hardy variety of peonies which seemed to survive the winter under the snow. We also had a huge, amiable St Bernard. The furniture was grandparents' original Tagánka furniture—I only remember the huge and much-carved solid oak dresser.

In winter the *dácha* was only inhabited by the porter with his family, who lived in a separate lodge with a large tiled central stove heating all rooms round it, as was customary in northern Russia.

It was at the *dácha* that I fell ill with diphtheria. I was extremely miserable and my throat so swollen that I was suffocating. The doctor was talking in a low voice, intending that I should not hear, of having to cut an opening in my windpipe and insert a silver tube so that I could breathe. Von Behring had developed the diphtheria serum some twenty years earlier but none was available in wartime Moscow. Fortunately, there was a supply in Petersburg, and Father had to take the night train and bring back the precious preparation. I remember the dramatic improvement a few hours after the injection; the fever subsided and I could breathe again. A week later I was running around in the garden. Undoubtedly, von Behring's discovery (and Father's prompt action) had saved my life, just as Pasteur (and Grandmother) had saved Grandfather's.

Father Gregory calls

Whilst we were at the *dácha* Father was commuting daily to the Poverkhovsky office in Cherkassky Row (which was the correct location for a textile manufacturer or wholesaler). As Sokólniki was nearby, he was generally driven in his small one-horse carriage. One day the doorman burst into the private office, out of breath, announcing that Father Gregory was on his way, and almost immediately the unmistakeable figure of Raspútin entered the room. Father was momentarily speechless but the bogus Holy Man put him at ease and he recovered his composure and sent for tea and strawberry jam (the Russian equivalent of a glass of sherry—drinks at the office were taboo). Raspútin chatted amiably, fixing Father with his celebrated stare. He just happened to be passing and, as he needed money for a special charity, he thought Poverkhovskys might perhaps be willing to contribute five thousand roubles which, he had been advised, they could manage without going bankrupt. Raspútin was the one man in Russia who could destroy Poverkhovskys, Father and our family in five minutes—the autocratic Czar could not. Father sent to the bank round the corner and, in a few minutes, handed the bundle of crisp hundred-rouble notes to the real ruler of Russia. It probably covered the cost of his private court, or harem, for that day. Father never saw him again.

Winter in Moscow

In early September we returned to Moscow. Winter comes early at such distance from the sea and soon the houses were being prepared for the siege by General Frost. The double windows (which were essential) were sealed with tape, leaving only a small top corner-window so that it could be opened for airing. Small beakers with a hygroscopic substance were placed between the window-panes, in our flat at any rate, to prevent misting. Almost all houses were heated with wood-burning stoves, or larger blocks with wood-burning central heating; the oil-fired central heating in our flats was, I believe, comparatively rare. Coal was an unknown commodity in Moscow. The winters were very severe; schools had to close by statute if the temperature fell to 23° below zero, which generally happened several times during the winter. The temperature in Russia was then measured according to the Réaumur scale, devised by the French scientist of that name, with the freezing-point of water as zero, as in the Centigrade scale, but with a boiling-point of 80°. The school-closing temperature of 23° below zero Réaumur was therefore almost 29° below zero Centigrade, or minus 20° Fahrenheit. It always puzzled me why Russia adopted a temperature scale devised by a Frenchman, France and Germany a scale devised by the Swede Celsius and England one devised by the German Fahrenheit.

Our education was not neglected. We received lessons in all elementary subjects and I had to spend the best part of the day on lessons and homework. I also had to darn my socks and sew on buttons—the maids, whilst only too willing, were strictly forbidden to help me with these chores and so was the English governess. The serious business of earning one's living, and being provident and thrifty, was brought home to us at an early age. Krylóv's *Fables* (mostly translated from Aesop or La Fontaine) were required reading for all Russian schoolboys, but one fable had been singled out for us to *perform* in front of an august gathering of aunts and uncles. This was the Fable of the Butterfly and the Ant, the ant living, when winter came, off the food thriftily stored in summer and giving short shrift to the improvident and starving butterfly. I was the ant, with whiskers stuck under my nose. 'You danced all summer, why don't you dance now?' was, in Krylóv's words, my reply, meant to teach me to grow up as an ant not as a butterfly.

After Marie Ivanovna's triumph as theatrical producer (she had joined us as teacher—more of her later) came the English governess's turn, and I had to recite Southey's *Inchcape Bell*, showing that if one sprung a trap for other people one got caught in it oneself. Certainly the twin warning images of Krylóv's starving butterfly and Sir Ralph the Rover drowning haunted my childhood as a fate to be avoided at all costs.

To round off the *soirée* a new record was played which Aunt Amalia had brought us, pronouncing it as educational. It was, in fact, a most enjoyable children's song:

Zhil byl u bábushki sérenkii kózlik.

(Grandmother had a grey goat—which was, sadly, eaten by a wolf.)

I do not quite know the moral of this tale but we enjoyed it.

For our performance the unlucky aunts and uncles had to buy entrance tickets, set by Mother roughly at the rate of a Chaliapin performance at the Bolshoi, and the money was sent in our name to the Russian Red Cross. Thrift and providence, we were taught, had to be tempered by compassion.

Years later, when I read *The Forsyte Saga*, many of the characters, from Old Jolyon to the Aunt of Park Lane, and the entire atmosphere, reminded me of my childhood in Moscow, and so did P. L. Travers's *Mary Poppins*.

Russian children did not have a birthday. Perhaps this ought to be rephrased: in Russia one did not celebrate birthdays but namedays, the feast day of the saint after whom one was named. The little Nicholases had their nameday on 6 December, the Olgas on 11 July, and so forth. This system was actually very convenient for all aunts and uncles, as one did not have to remember the dates of birth. Jewish children did not, of course, have a nameday, nor were their birthdays celebrated, at least not in Moscow. On the other hand, Jewish children were entitled to presents not only at *Hannukáh*, about Christmas-time, but also at *Purim* in spring. But *we* did not receive any presents. When the occasion for presents approached, Mother caused us to write laboriously to the various aunts, asking for cheques in lieu of presents, and the cheques were then sent, in our name, to various self-help charities, generally to ORT, Mother's pet charity, or during the war half to ORT and half to the Russian Red Cross. I remember the Red Cross particularly sending us very impressive Certificates of Donation which we treasured. The foregoing of presents was quite genuine, and we received no substitutes, only the maids were occasionally allowed to give us inexpensive gifts, generally made by themselves.

Our manners were not overlooked either. *Little Lord Fauntleroy*, in Russian, was required reading, and if I dared to point a finger Mother would chide me gently with the words: *sovsem ne po gentlemanski*, not at all gentlemanlike. That settled it: no-one doubted that one had to behave like a gentleman.

That winter I had a severe *oititis*, which required lancing of the eardrum (this was, of course, before the discovery of penicillin). Our family doctor was bringing the leading specialist, a colonel with the Army Medical Corps. In Russia doctors did not send accounts, the polite fiction being that they were entirely altruistic, but the appropriate fee was handed over in an envelope. 'Don't forget he is an *anti-semite*,' I heard Mother cautioning Father, who was getting the envelope ready. I enquired as to the meaning of this long word. 'It means, he charges Jewish people at the double rate,' explained Mother. At any rate, whatever his views or business methods, the Colonel arrived in a much-gold-braided uniform and with incredible skill and speed inserted what looked like a knitting-needle into my ear. The abscess was lanced, and after being flushed with formaline a few times it was healed.

Notes

1 Recent publications have shown, though, that cession of the Baltic provinces up to and including Riga were included in the German war aims.
2 In fact, for this service Father received a decoration (unusual for a Jew)—I believe, the St George's Cross.

8

The Revolution

The Czar at Mogilév

For the Supreme Headquarters, or *stávka*, no other city but Mogilév had
been selected. It now had the best communications with the various parts of
the Front and with Petersburg. It was, in Russian terms, near the Front but
not too near. When the choice of Mogilév was first announced there was
panic among the Jewish population. Would the Jews be expelled? Would
the Cossack guards amuse themselves by pulling rabbis by their beards and
molesting women? Such was the reputation of the Cossacks, possibly undeservedly, in the Pale.[1] Old tales of the (very real) horrors of the Cossack
rebellions under Chmielnicki in 1648, and later in 1768, were revived. That
was before Russian rule, of course. Actually, the Cossack troops were on
their best behaviour, and the location of the *stávka* in Mogilév did not affect
life there in any particularly noticeable way. In 1915 the Czar decided to
personally assume supreme command of the Army, and moved to Mogilév,
leaving the foolish, ignorant and neurotic Empress Alexandra Feodorovna,
née Princess Alice of Hesse, and granddaughter of Queen Victoria, in
charge at Petersburg to rule Russia in the Czar's name. No enemy of Russia
and the dynasty could have given the Czar worse advice. If Marie Antoinette,
the *Autrichienne*, or Austrian woman, as the French called her, had not
apocryphally but plausibly said 'then let them eat cake', the Empress was
fully capable of the same wisdom. But even had she been a Catherine the
Great, it was the height of folly to leave the German-born Empress,
generally known as the *Nemka*, or German woman, speaking very poor,
heavily accented Russian, and suspected of pro-German sympathies, if not
actual treason (certainly not treason, Father told me)—in absolute autocratic control in a life-and-death struggle against her native country. Certainly, the Empress's German-tinged entourage was riddled with spies.

Kérensky relates how the Navy minister, devoted to the Czar, was so beset by suspicions that in reply to persistent and not clearly motivated questions from Czarskoye Selo (where the Empress and her court were in residence) about a planned naval operation, he supplied fictitious information. 'Sure enough, a German naval squadron appeared at the exact hour and at the very spot where the Minister had said the Russian cruisers would be.'

The Factor VIII

The much-wanted heir to the throne, the Cesaréwitch Alexis, was born in 1904. Kérensky hints that he was a love-child. Whether Nicholas was his father or not, the unfortunate young prince was a haemophiliac. Haemophilia, or bleeding-disease, occurs in males to whom it is transmitted through the mother. The blood plasma lacks a clotting agent, so that the slightest cut can result in prolonged, severe bleeding. There is also internal bleeding—even more danagerous. Haemophilia was known to be hereditary, which was the reason why Alexander III opposed the marriage of Nicholas and Alexandra, suspecting her of probably transmitting the disease. In this one case, Nicholas did not heed his father's advice. Today, the Factor VIII missing in haemophiliac blood has been isolated, and since 1968 injections are available which stop the bleeding. Had those injections been available sixty years earlier, the history of Russia and indeed the world might have been different.

Gregory Raspútin (1872–1916), whom we briefly met earlier in these pages, was the ignorant and almost illiterate son of a Siberian farm labourer and horse-dealer. His real family name is, I believe, unknown. Raspútin was his nickname, best translated as Debaucherer. For a while, Raspútin was seized with a quasi-religious mania and became a kind of itinerant preacher—surrounded always by female disciples. Eventually, he reached St Petersburg, where he managed to insinuate himself into the confidence of the Father-Confessor to the Empress. In 1906, 'Father Gregory' was introduced to the Imperial couple. This was the beginning of the end. Like Hitler (who resembled Raspútin in many ways, except that Hitler's perversion was masochism and Raspútin's exhibitionism), Raspútin had a strong personal magnetism and a hypnotic power. Both were basically Asiatic *shaman* types.

The young prince was bleeding and Raspútin managed to stop the bleeding. Perhaps he hypnotised the child. According to Kérensky, Raspútin always managed to arrive at the bedside just before the crisis was over, when the bleeding would have stopped anyway. Perhaps he did not stop the bleeding at all but hypnotised the Empress into believing that he did. He is supposed to have stopped the bleeding by telegram; this might have affected the Empress but could hardly have a direct effect on a ten-year-old boy, except possibly through the newly found confidence emanating from the mother. In any event, with his uncanny magnetism and its strong effect on women, Raspútin completely dominated the Empress, who was at his beck and call for ten years, while at the same time he was leading a private life scandalous by any standard and known all over Russia. During 1915 and 1916, while the Czar was at the Supreme Headquarters at Mogilév, Raspútin practically ruled Russia through the Empress, appointing and dismissing ministers of the Crown and prelates of the Church. Public opinion was scandalised. Raspútin was exposed in the *Duma* and the monarchy was badly discredited. There were even rumours that Raspútin was the lover of the Empress. (Father believed this to be quite untrue.) Kérensky even considers it possible that Raspútin was having the Czar regularly drugged.

Some day, as Father told me, Raspútin summoned some leaders of the Jewish community in Petersburg and told them that he was willing to procure an abolition of the Temporary Regulations, against the payment of an astronomical sum of money. There was no doubt that Raspútin could do it: a scribbled note from the Empress to 'Nicky' at Mogilév would suffice. However, apart from the fact that even if the handful of Jewish millionaires in Russia would have sacrificed their fortunes, this would not have been enough. There was unanimity that an end to the anti-Jewish policy must be obtained by political pressure on the legitimate government, and not by bribery of an usurper and imposter.

At the end of 1916 some patriotic members of the Czar's entourage decided that the only course of action left was to do away with this criminal who was ruining Russia and the dynasty. On 29 December Raspútin was killed by them in the house of Prince Yusupov.

The February Revolution

The general mismanagement and paralysis of government continued. Some Army generals were said to be planning to capture the Czar at *stávka* and force him to abdicate. There was, according to Kérensky, even wild talk of 'another 11 March' (the day on which in 1801 mad Czar Paul was murdered by Guards officers). Even the moderate Progressive Bloc (Cadets, Octobrists and other liberal groups) was planning a coup, with the Czar abdicating in favour of the Czarewitch and the appointment of Grand Duke Michael, the Czar's brother, as Regent. All these plans were really aimed at removing the Empress Alexandra Feodorovna from power. While they were being hatched, matters came to a head, quite spontaneously, in March 1917. There were food riots in Petersburg. Conscript troops were called out to restore order but refused to shoot and joined the rioters. On 12 March (27 February old-style) the Czarist Government simply disintegrated. Ministers were arrested by rioting soldiers, the sailors of the Baltic Fleet mutinied and on 15 March a Provisional Government, representing the major parties in the *Duma*, assumed power. The new Prime Minister was Prince Lvov, highly respected in all quarters, and the Government included Kérensky (1881–1970) of the Trudovik (Labour) as Minister of Justice, the only socialist in the government. No-one had planned or organised the 'February Revolution'. The leaders of the political parties were caught unawares, and the emigré revolutionaries in Switzerland hardly believed the headlines.

In the meantime the Czar at Mogilév, hearing of the events, decided to return to Petersburg (which he should never have deserted). The Imperial train was halted on the way, and the Czar, finding the line to Petersburg barred, went to Northern Command Headquarters at Pskov. There, at the request of the military and naval commanders, who realised what was afoot, Czar Nicholas II abdicated in favour of his brother, Grand Duke Michael, on 15 March 1917. A deputation from the Provisional Government went to see the Grand Duke in Petersburg on 17 March. Milyukóv (the leader of the liberal Cadets) and Guchkóv (leader of the more conservative Octobrists) wanted a constitutional monarchy on the British model, with Royal Prerogatives (as then exercised); the more left-wing, socialist ministers like Kérensky wanted a Republic (in the end, Kérensky, by then Prime Minister, proclaimed Russia, quite illegally, a Republic on 14 September 1917). Seeing that his assumption of the Crown would be controversial, Grand Duke Michael (personally an admirer of the British constitutional system) decided that he would only accept the throne at the request of the Constituent Assembly which the Provisional Government had undertaken to convene. Evidently, the Grand Duke saw himself as a Russian William of Orange.

I well remember the delight, short-lived, of Father and Mother reading the *Rússkiye Védomosti* at breakfast, announcing the abdication of Nicholas II, the autocrat who had tolerated, if not supported, the Black Hundreds, and maintained the hated Temporary Regulations against repeated requests by the *Duma* to have them rescinded. My parents, and most members of the family, supported the liberal Cadet party (with the exception of one uncle, the one with the Empire furniture, who supported the more conservative Octobrists). Now, Father was explaining, Grand Duke Michael, who was known to be a liberal, would become Czar, and Russia would be a constitutional monarchy in the English manner. Under his government, the war would be won, and Constantinople pass into Russian control.

The maids were, inexplicably, in tears. They seemed to have a more accurate foreboding of the long vale of blood and tears Russia was entering.

The end of the dynasty

The Imperial Family were living under guard at the palace in Czárskoye Seló. The Czar wanted to go to England with his family and, like Napoleon III, live out his days in exile there. The British Government had originally agreed to the request. However, when Kérensky, as preparations were advanced, approached the British Ambassador, Sir George Buchanan, to finalise the arrangements the Ambassador averred with considerable embarrassment that the offer of asylum had been withdrawn. Apparently, it has since been revealed, this was on the personal wish of King George V himself, who feared serious complications with the Czar and his haughty and unrepentant Empress residing in wartime England. Naturally, the King was not to know of the tragic fate that awaited the Imperial Family in a year's time. As England was not possible, the Czar wanted to go to the Crimea (where he and his family would probably have survived, as the Dowager Empress did), but Kérensky apparently considered the journey unsafe (or undesirable) at the time and decided on Tobolsk, in comparatively mild Western Siberia (on the Irtysh, the chief tributary of the Ob, altogether 3500 miles long). It is difficult not to resist the thought that Kérensky, who had to look over his shoulder constantly to watch the reactions of the Petersburg Soviet, also had a kind of symbolic banishment in mind.

In 1918, when Siberia fell into the hands of the Bolsheviks, the Imperial Family were transferred to Ekaterinburg (at present, Sverdlovsk) in the same area, where, on Lenin's instructions given to Sverdlov (who was there at the time), the Czar, the Empress, the four princesses and the little Czarewitch were butchered in the cellar of their house on 16 July 1918.

Such, then, was the tragic end of the Románov dynasty that had ruled Russia since 1613; the dynasty of a Peter the Great and of Alexander II, the dynasty that had transformed Muscovy from a landlocked principality into a great empire reaching from the Baltic to the Pacific; all destroyed by the disastrous combination—deadly at a time of ferocious external attack and internal ferment—of a dedicated and conscientious but weak and vacillating absolute monarch, a family man, not a statesman, even less an autocrat, ill-advised by fanatical and sycophantic counsellors—and a neurotic and ignorant consort, dominated by an unscrupulous and scandalous adventurer. This disastrous combination led to the tragedy of Russia that is unfolding before our eyes.

Grand Duke Michael was also murdered by the Bolsheviks, for good measure, in 1918; as his marriage was morganatic, any issue was not eligible for the succession. The present heir to the throne of Russia is Grand Duke Vladimir, born in 1917, descendant of Alexander II. Will the freely elected Constitutent Assembly which, some day, will decide Russia's future, restore to the Grand Duke, or his heir, the Imperial Crown, which the National Assembly bestowed upon Michael Románov in 1613?

The German advance

While the in-fighting and internecine strife were going on in Petersburg, first under the Empress's 'monstrous regiment', and then, more openly, after the February Revolution, the half-forgotten real war was continuing. Owing to their artillery, superior in numbers and explosive power, the German armies were advancing, slowly but continuously, with heavy casualties on the Russian side. The Russian soldiers fought superbly when given a chance, be it by infantry in close combat or by magnificent cavalry charges. But generally they were simply slaughtered without a fight by German high explosive. The Germans had occupied almost the whole of Latvia, Lithuania and Poland, including Liebava, Kovno, Vilna, Grodno, Warsaw, Lodz and Brest-Litovsk, and were advancing on a broad front due south from Dvinsk. They were only 200 miles from the Dnieper. Naturally, the Germans were trying to woo all disaffected minorities in the area, to create an anti-Russian movement, and particularly addressed themselves to the Jews. Ludendorff in person issued his celebrated proclamation 'An meine lieben Juden in Polen' (To my dear Jews in Poland)—that, of course, was twenty-five years before the Black Death—in which he promised full protection and the end to all discrimination. However, the Germans did not succeed in turning the Jews into a fifth column, though they did have some success with Ukrainian and other separatist movements.

The general and the greengrocer

General Hoffmann, in effect the military governor of the occupied Western Provinces, was implementing Ludendorff's policy and decided to visit a Rabbi to demonstrate his respect for Judaism and solicitude for the Jews. The Kaiser had visited a synagogue or two, but in Russia this was an unprecedented move. The General's aide, after making enquiries, suggested a famous Rabbi, somewhere in Poland, believed to work miracles such as healing the sick. It was 'a kind of Jewish Archbishop', the titled aide explained. In the Pale of Settlement Jewish communities were desperately poor; the Rabbis had, of course, no stipends, and were expected to earn their living like everybody else (in practice, it was the Rabbi's wife who was the breadwinner). So, when General Hoffmann drove up to the 'Jewish Archbishop's palace' he found himself entering a humble greengrocer's shop, with Jewish women haggling over the price of cabbages and an old man with a flowing white beard poring over huge tomes in the backroom by candlelight. It is not clear who was more unnerved: the proud Prussian general at finding himself in a dark and dank greengrocer's shop, surrounded by chattering women, or the myopic Rabbi, who probably thought the bespurred and monocled apparition was the Angel of Death come to claim him. At any rate, so it is related, the veteran of Mukden and of Tannenberg turned on his heels, and fled. The unfortunate aide who had organised the visit to the 'Archbishop' without reconnoitring first was sent to the front, where relegated staff officers, unused to front-line conditions, had a very short expectation of life. The Rabbi resumed his studies.

Passover in Moscow

At Easter time we celebrated at home the Eve of the Jewish Passover with the traditional *seder*, the only festive meal in the Jewish religious calendar. A million Jewish households in the Pale celebrated the *seder* at the same time, though under very different circumstances. There was always a certain nervousness when celebrating the deliverance from Egypt because in Russia, as in many other devoutly Christian countries, Lent frequently led to a build-up of anti-Jewish feeling. The illiterate peasants were often simply taught that 'the Jews' murdered Christ; no-one told them that Christ was born into a Jewish family, that all the Apostles (not only Judas Iscariot) were Jews, that the people of Jerusalem welcoming Christ with palm branches were Jews; nor were they told that the soldiers mocking and crucifying Christ were Roman soldiers carrying out their usual method of execution (the Jewish method was stoning). As the Jewish calendar is lunar, Passover is always on the full moon, commemorating the Exodus; Easter, as agreed at the Council of Nicaea in AD 325, is on the Sunday after the very same full moon (I will not worry the reader with the full technicalities of the calculations). The Eve of Passover celebration thus occurred quite often on Maundy Thursday or 'Good' Friday (originally God's Friday), in devoutly and publicly Christian countries (now hardly any left) a day of mourning. The suspicion that, while everyone was fasting, the Jews were feasting to celebrate the death of Christ was always ready to surface. There had been Easter *pogróms* in Germany (as movingly described by Heine in the poem *The Rabbi of Bacharach*), and the celebrated Don Pacifico incident in 1847, which caused Palmerston to send a squadron of the Mediterranean Fleet to Piraeus to seize several Greek ships as compensation for the damage sustained by Don Pacifico, a British subject, was in fact a traditional Easter *pogróm* in Greece, with a mob engaged in burning down Don Pacifico's house. In Moscow and Petersburg there were never any *pogróms* as the authorities did not permit riots of any kind in capital cities.

The nearest approach to an Easter *pogróm* in Moscow was at the end of the century (1891 I believe, but I may be out by a year or two). The Grand Duke Sergei, brother of Alexander III and uncle of Nicholas II, an anachronistic *condottiere* and, at the time, Governor of Moscow, decided there were too many Jews in Moscow, and the best way to catch them would be the Eve of Passover celebration. Consequently, as the Jewish families of Moscow (there were actually very few) sat down to celebrate the Pash, much as Christ and the Apostles celebrated it, the police raided all known Jewish homes, and all Jewish people who could not prove there and then their right of residence in the city were deported, like convicts, under Cossack escort to the Pale. It would be idle to pretend that when the Grand Duke was assassinated by (non-Jewish) revolutionaries in 1905 there were many Jewish tears shed for him.

But all this was past history at the Passover celebrations in 1917. The Temporary Regulations had been abolished by the new Government of Prince Lvov. The Jews now had equal rights.

We children first carried out the traditional symbolic search for any leavened bread, and crumbs 'found' were burned. For the eight days of Passover only the hard-baked, unleavened *mazzoth* were eaten in commemoration of the Exodus. No cakes or pastries were possible, though a kind of unleavened almond macaroon was made. Most of our younger relatives who had no household of their own, the family doctor (who was a bachelor) and a few other friends were invited, so that we had a party of thirty or so sitting down at the enlarged dinner-table. Mother generally planned a meatless dinner, because of the *kosher* problems, and a huge whitefish from the Volga had arrived, a few days earlier, live in a tub of water. Father still had, since before the War, a few bottles of wine from one of the first Russian–Jewish settlements in Israel, from the early 1880s (Rishon le Zion, I believe) and, although not noticeably religious in his daily life, pronounced the prescribed benediction of the Lord over the unleavened bread and the wine. It was then my turn at the dinner-table, as the youngest celebrant present, to ask the famous Four Questions (in Hebrew, naturally, and rehearsed daily for weeks ahead). *Mah nishtanáh* . . . What is the difference between this night and other nights? Why do we eat unleavened bread? Why . . .? Why . . .? The ritual questions gave the head of the household the opportunity to recite the *Haggadáh*, the story of the Exodus. *Avodim hoyinu l'Phárye b'Misráim* . . . Slaves were we to the

Pharaoh in Egypt . . . *Misráim* means Egypt, and each time Father called out, with suitable indignation, the name of that oppressing country, which obviously happened quite often, our English governess, with the homonymous name of Miss Ryan (her name passed for English in Moscow) blushed. The poor soul evidently thought Father was referring to her, and she must have offended him somehow. *Dam, sphardéah* . . . Blood, frogs . . . (both referring to the Nile) Father thundered, evidently warming to the occasion.

And finally came the ritual ending of the *seder* (added after the destruction of Jerusalem by the Romans in AD 70 and the final expulsion of the Jews by Hadrian in AD 135):

Leshonó haboóh b'Jerusholáim

Next Year in Jerusalem! A million Jewish householders in Eastern Europe spoke these words that night.

I do not think that Father, as he spoke this time-hallowed invocation in Moscow, visualised that he himself would be in Jerusalem next Easter. The invocation was a symbol of the eternally burning resolve of the Jews that some day Jerusalem would be liberated and become the centre of Jewish worship again. In 1917, with the Turkish empire breaking up and the Balfour Declaration approaching, the age-old cry of defiance had a new actuality.

Holidays in the sun

Under the Temporary Regulations the Crimean coast and the Caucasus were, without exception, out of bounds to all Jews, even those having rights of residence in Moscow and Petersburg. They might have been Turkish spies. Now in 1917 we could travel anywhere in Russia. We would go to the Crimea *and* the Caucasus. After all, we did not go away in 1916.

I had been receiving lessons in the usual *four* Rs (in Russia they were four because the fourth was religion) for some time, and could read and write in Russian, English and Hebrew, but now my parents decided that it was time for me to be properly prepared for the entrance examination of the prestigious Moscow Imperial Academy of Commercial Sciences (I still remember the full title) where, it was hoped, I would be accepted when eight. Mother therefore asked the head-mistress of her old school, the Vinográdskaya, to recommend one of her young teachers who would join us for the summer and give me daily lessons. The head-mistress recommended Marie Ivanovna M., who accepted Mother's offer. I believe, she liked Mother when interviewed and was particularly attracted by the prospect of travel to the Crimea and the Caucasus—in those days out of the reach of a Moscow teacher.

Marie Ivanovna was twenty-five and an orphan. She had lost both parents at a tender age: her father, an accountant from Zagorsk, died of cancer, and her mother of pernicious anaemia (before 1948, when Vitamin B12 was isolated, fatal). Her mother came from an old Moscow merchant's family who owned woodlands in Vladimir province, and Marie Ivanovna was brought up by two aunts, her mother's sisters. The elder aunt, Nadéshda, a spinster, managed the family woodlands (which included visits to the forest in the depth of winter), and the younger aunt, Catherine, a widow, lived on a small estate not far from Moscow, where she also maintained, in a large room in the manor house, a small silk-spinning workshop. Silk was an indigenous industry in Russia, and Aunt Catherine received the cocoons after they had been harvested, and the thread was unwound (each cocoon yielding about a thousand metres), spun and twisted into yarn, and sold to the silk-weavers in nearby Orékhovo Zúyevo. Women from the village were only too glad to earn a few roubles with this comparatively comfortable work, certainly a rest from the back-breaking labour in the fields, which, moreover, did not clash with the sowing or reaping seasons. As a girl of twelve, Marie Ivanovna was determined to receive a higher education, which was unusual for girls in Russia, and the only way to achieve this was as a boarder at the Vinográdskaya in Moscow. All Russian secondary schools for boys (and the few for girls) had boarding sections for pupils whose parents lived out of town. This was quite expensive, and the family income from the woodlands would not suffice, so entry depended on the silk market that year. Fortunately, the season's yarn fetched a very good price, and the aunts were able to place their ward as a boarder at the privately owned Vinográdskaya, the only secondary school for girls in Moscow. Marie Ivanovna graduated with a Gold Medal and then studied mathematics, which was her chosen discipline, and also attended classes in Russian language and literature, her hobby. Women were not yet admitted to state universities, but Moscow (and Petersburg) boasted women's colleges, thanks to the munificence of the merchants, who duplicated the university courses, with the same professors giving the lectures. After graduating (or, more accurately, gaining her diploma) Marie Ivanovna returned to the Vinográdskaya as teacher, until she came to us. Soon Mother and Marie Ivanovna became great friends, and Mother considered her a younger sister. To Marie Ivanovna, I believe, our home offered her first opportunity of family life. She came for six months, and stayed for sixty-five years, until she passed away in her ninetieth year having shared all our vicissitudes and sorrows.

Mother took us for the summer to Eupatoria, a rather boring seaside resort on the flat south-west coast of the Crimea, renowned for its beaches (the British troops landed there in 1854) and healing mud. The terrible war raging in the Western region seemed to make even less impact in the Crimea than in Moscow. The only reminder of the grim reality was that at night one was not supposed to show lights visible from the sea, as the German warships in the Bosphorus could sally forth in the darkness and bombard us (they had bombarded Odessa). I did not much like Eupatoria, and preferred our *dácha* at Sokolniki. For Marie Ivanovna, Mother organised a three-day sightseeing trip to Yalta, Sebastopol and Bakhchisarai, the ancient capital of the Khans, with its famous palace and dancing dervishes.

From the Crimea we travelled direct to the Caucasus, where Father joined us for a few weeks. The Caucasus has been an object of strife between Russia, Persia (now Iran) and Turkey for centuries, and was finally secured for Russia by Alexander II in 1859, when the leading chieftain, Shamil, a religious fanatic in the manner of the Sudanese Mahdi, who terrorised the tribesmen, was captured and his followers dispersed. We spent the autumn at Kislovódsk, the famous spa situated at a height of about three thousand feet on the northern slopes of the Caucasus (I believe, the most easterly point of the German advance in the direction of the Baku oilfields during World War II). The scenery in the Caucasus is truly magnificent, there is no other word for it, and it certainly surpasses anything I know in the Alps and the Pyrenees. And we only viewed the lower northern slopes, with the main range with the snowcapped Elbrús (at 18,000 feet the highest mountain in Europe) and the slightly lower Kasbék, in good weather just visible on the horizon. The famous military road traversing the main range at 8000 feet from Vladikavkás (at present, Ordzhonikidze, after a Bolshevik) to Tiflis (Georgian, Tbilisi) was said to be infested by insurgent tribesmen armed by the Turks so we did not venture that far. Lermontov, the greatest Russian poet (a descendant of the Scot Learmont), sang the beauties of the Caucasus in his poems.

Food was abundant at Kislovódsk, as in most parts of southern Russia; the extreme food shortage in the northern cities like Moscow and Petersburg was at the time (1917) due mainly to a breakdown of rail transport. Mother bought several large wicker baskets and had them filled with hundredweight bags of flour and cereals as well as some sugar. The provisions travelled with us on the return journey to Moscow and saw us through the hungry winter of 1917/18, without any recourse to the black market that, for many families in Moscow, was from the winter of 1917 onwards the only means of survival.

The German intervention

Our return journey was uneventful. But when we drove through Moscow on 14 November we found the streets deserted, and echoing to the sound of gunfire. I well remember Father asking the cab driver what was happening (this was, of course, before the days of radio, let alone television and instant news). The cab driver explained that there had been, they say, a Bolshevik rising in Petersburg, and that the Officer Cadets in the Kremlin were resisting the conspirators.

In 1916, British, French (and German) soldiers were bleeding to death in their hundreds of thousands on the Somme, at Verdun and along the entire Western Front. Both sides were straining to break the deadlock. Technical innovations were tried: on 22 April 1915 the Germans used gas for the first time, at Ypres. On 15 September 1916 the British introduced the *tank*, an entirely new conception in land warfare, and produced in full secrecy (the very codename 'tank' was designed to make enemy agents believe that the bulky articles produced were fuel tanks). None of the innovations proved decisive. Helped by the unrestricted U-boat warfare unleashed by the German High Command against neutral shipping (including US ships), the British Government was working for the entry of the USA into the war. In February 1917, after the sinking of several of its ships, the USA severed diplomatic relations with Germany, and on 6 April declared war. In Churchill's immortal phrase, the New World was called in to redress the balance of the Old.

The German High Command knew full well that when American manpower and industrial strength entered the fray the war was finally lost. Germany's only hope was to get Russia out of the war before the American war effort had gathered momentum. The Russian 'February Revolution' and introduction of full, unrestricted and sudden political freedom in midwar offered the German High Command undreamt opportunities which it was not slow to exploit. Their excellent intelligence service informed Berlin that there was a group of Russian emigrés in Switzerland, socialists of some kind, headed by one Ulyanov, who wanted Russia to pull out of the war immediately and conclude a separate peace with Germany at any price. The group's reasoning was thought to be that once they had achieved their aims in Russia, likeminded revolutionaries would come into power in Germany and other countries and would form a kind of world government, so that it did not matter at all where the frontiers lay—in fact, frontiers would fade away. All this was, of course, laughable, the intelligence report concluded, but these people could be relied upon to sabotage the war effort in Russia and possibly even, with the chaotic conditions prevailing there, achieve political power and a separate peace.

Chemical warfare having failed, the German High Command decided to resort to bacteriological warfare. In March 1917 a strange train consisting of second-class sleeping cars, a restaurant car and several luggage vans was assembled in a siding on the German–Swiss border. Into this train piled two hundred passengers, Russian emigré socialists with their families. The socialists included two principal groups: the Bolsheviks (*Bolshói* = big, with the big demands) and the Mensheviks (*Ménshiy* = smaller, with the smaller demands). All the carriages of the train were carefully sealed by the German frontier guards (in Churchill's words, like a *pest bacillus*) and the train rushed as military priority traffic through the whole of wartime Germany to Sassnitz on the Baltic and via the ferry to Sweden. The next day, the revolutionaries were let out in Stockholm, all with the co-operation of the Swedish Government which was non-belligerent and pro-German during the *First* World War. The German High Command had thoughtfully placed a large sum of money at the disposal of Ulyanov and his henchmen in a Swedish bank, and the revolutionaries made their way separately or in small groups to Finland (at that time part of Russia with a degree of home rule) and from there to Petersburg and other Russian towns.

Ulyanov, using his alias Lenin, which we shall also use in future, arrived at the Finlándski Voksál in Petersburg on 16 April 1917 (a black day for Russia and Europe), ten days after the USA had declared war on Germany. So both sides had played their trump cards almost simultaneously; the Allies bringing in a fifth ally and the Germans a fifth column.

Vladimir Ulyanov (1870–1924) was born at Simbirsk (at present, Ulyanovsk) on the middle reaches of the Volga, son of a senior civil servant Ilya Ulyanov.[2] Kérensky, whom Lenin was later to destroy, was also born at Simbirsk, where Kérensky's father was Headmaster of the Gymnasium attended by Lenin. Lenin's elder brother, Alexander, had been executed for an (abortive) attempt on the life of Czar Alexander III. Vladimir Ilyitch emigrated shortly after 1905 and lived abroad, mainly in Switzerland, until he returned on The Train.

The total amount of money handed by the Germans to the Bolsheviks was 80 million marks, not a very large sum in terms of the general war expenditure. The despatch of Lenin proved in the short term to be a very cost-effective investment for the Germans, as it took the entire Russian Army out of the war, balancing the arrival of the American Army; the appalling long-term cost of installing this pernicious regime in Russia was hidden in the future.

It would be misleading to describe Lenin as a German *agent*, though he was, undoubtedly, a tool of the German High Command. It is a time-honoured stratagem to cause diversions in the enemy's rear; in 1916 the Germans landed Sir Roger Casement in Ireland from a submarine to organise the Easter Rebellion, and to Germany the insinuation of Lenin and his henchmen into Russia was the counterpart on the Eastern front.

Lenin and his associates wasted no time. Their aim was simply absolute dictatorial power such as no Czar (except possibly Ivan the Terrible in his later years) had ever exercised. Their propaganda concentrated on the soldiers, both at the front and in the Petersburg garrison, as well as on the sailors of the Baltic Fleet at Kronstadt. Lenin promised immediate peace and, seeing that the vast majority of soldiers were peasant lads, immediate expropriation of all landlords and distribution of their lands to the peasants (the expropriation of the peasants, to achieve the collectivisation required by Marxist doctrine, was to come later, when the blockheads had done their work). Soldiers deserted the Army in droves—'voted with their feet', in Lenin's graphic phrase—in order to take part in the share-out of the land-lords' estate.

Soviets, of councils, of self-appointed Worker's and Soldier's delegates were organised on the embryonic 1905 model, and these extra-parliament-ary organisations, dominated by the Bolsheviks, soon developed into an alternative government, manipulated by the Bolsheviks. Lenin's chief agent in the Petersburg soviet was Vyacheslav Scriabin (born 1890), a cousin of the composer, using the alias Molotov (the Hammerer), and the Party organiser was Yakov Sverdlov (1885–1919). Grigory Apfelbaum (1883–1936), using the alias Zinoviev, who had arrived with Lenin on The Train, acted as Lenin's personal assistant and office-boy, whilst Leo Rosenfeld (1883–1936), alias Kamenev (the Rock), the mild-mannered intellectual who had spent the war-years in banishment in Siberia and therefore had some standing with the entire Left, was used by Lenin to maintain liaison with the Mensheviks and other left-wing socialists in order to make sure they would not, with their militias, actively oppose Lenin's planned coup (they did not, hoping to ride the tiger).

On 15 May 1917 the Petersburg soviet, supported by the Mensheviks, forced Professor Milyukóv (1859–1943), the great leader of the Cadets, and Guchkóv, the able leader of the Octobrists, to resign from the Cabinet. Both were outstanding statesmen and patriots. Some Cadets remained in the government and were forced out in early September. The Government, since 20 July 1917 headed by Kérensky, became based on the Mensheviks and other socialist groups only. 15 May 1917, when the Cabinet (some say only too willingly) bowed to pressure of the soviet mobs, was the real birthday of the Soviet Socialist tyranny.

In September 1917 the Bolsheviks felt so strong that they began organ-ising quite openly for a military coup, and an armed militia, soon to become the Red Guard, appeared in public. On 25 October 1917 Lenin set up, in the name of the soviet, a Military Revolutionary Committee. The Kérensky government was paralysed: they still considered the Bolsheviks as fellow-socialists, even if somewhat ill-mannered, and Kérensky could not bring himself to call in the Army, arrest the Bolshevik leaders and disarm and dis-band the Red Guards. He felt that, having introduced the long-demanded freedom of speech and assembly (now being abused by the Bolsheviks), the Government had no mandate for such repressive measures, reverting, as it were, to Czarist methods. He was also apprehensive that calling in the Army would result in a military dictatorship, which Kérensky and his fellow-socialists probably considered the greater evil, at least at the time. In Germany, a year later after *their* revolution and learning from the Russian experience, the parliamentary socialists and the Army co-operated very effectively in crushing the Spartakist (Bolshevik) rebellion.

So Kérensky waited, like a rabbit mesmerised by a cobra, for the Bolsheviks to strike, meaning to call in the Army as a last resort when the coup was actually taking place. Lenin himself as a precaution went into hiding in Finland whence he was directing operations. As his military locum in Petersburg he appointed Leo Bronstein (1879–1940), using, at the time, the alias Trotsky (he had several aliases, Trotsky being presumably derived from the German *Trotz*, defiance). Trotsky was the son of a Jewish farmer (Jews had been permitted to farm in the southern steppes acquired from the Turks). When studying at Odessa he had caught the revolutionary infection then prevalent in Russia and took part in the ephemeral Petersburg soviet of 1905. Banished to Siberia twice, he escaped each time (not an unusual occurrence under the comparatively easy-going Czarist regime) and lived in France, whence he was expelled during World War I, finding his way eventually to New York. At that time, the US immigration authorities apparently admitted self-confessed revolutionaries intent on subverting the country offering them refuge, and Trotsky, as we shall now call him, wasted no time in joining the staff of a scurrilous revolutionary publication engaged in opposing Eduard Bernstein's 'Revisionism'[3] or downgrading Marxism, adopted by German Social Democrats and also by *Forward*, the Yiddish-language daily appearing in New York for Russian immigrants. After the Russian Revolution Trotsky saw an unlimited opportunity for mischief presenting itself there and, within weeks, obtained a passage on a Norwegian boat. Off Halifax, the boat was boarded by the Royal Navy maintaining the worldwide blockade of Germany, and Trotsky and a few other passengers were taken off to Canada, where he was interned. The British authorities were, of course, not only within their rights to arrest Trotsky. It was their duty, at the height of the war with Germany, to detain anyone who intended going to Russia with the self-confessed intention of helping to overthrow the Government and take Russia out of the war. Unfortunately, some sinister backstage influence was brought to bear on the British authorities in London (according to Trotsky, pressure of the Petersburg soviet via the Russian Foreign Ministry), and this pernicious revolutionary was freed within a few weeks (while British soldiers were dying in Flanders) and allowed to sail on a Danish boat to Sweden and thence to Russia. In May 1917 Trotsky reached Petersburg and immediately offered his services to Lenin, who had already been planted there in April by the German High Command.

The Lenin coup (perhaps one should say the Ludendorff–Lenin coup) was prepared with military precision in the Bolshevik headquarters at the commandeered Smolny Institute (formerly a girls' boarding school). On 6 November 1917 (24 October old-style) Lenin emerged from his hideout, like some poisonous reptile from a crevice in the rocks, and returned to Petersburg for a second time (apparently not at the Finlándski Voksál as in April but surreptitiously at some suburban station and thence unglamorously by tram) and gave the go-ahead. As pre-arranged, Red Guards (heavily armed, with Kérensky's impotent knowledge) were occupying Government offices (scarcely defended) and arresting ministers and senior civil servants. Kérensky called for troops to restore order but none arrived. The Post Office, the Telegraph Office, the railway termini, had all been occupied by the Red Guards. Kérensky's SOS messages did not get through, or when they did there were no troop-trains, or if there were trains, they were stopped. The cruiser *Aurora* (one of the few ships to escape at Tsushima), manned by mutinous sailors, had been brought up the Neva, its guns trained on the Winter Palace, the seat of government with Kérensky's offices, which was cut off and without telephones. The Government wireless station at Czarskóye Seló was captured and Bolshevik propaganda beamed at the troops. The next day, 7 November 1917, Kérensky escaped from the beleaguered Winter Palace and went by road to Northern Command Headquarters, two hundred miles away at Pskov (where the Czar had abdicated in March) in order, as he explains in his *Memoirs*, to summon troops to Petersburg. During the night, while Kérensky was at Pskov, the Red Guards occupied the seat of government (in Bolshevik folklore 'the storming of the Winter Palace') and arrested all ministers in session. Victory was complete.

There must have been a smile on the harassed face of General Ludendorff that night as he went to bed at his Supreme Headquarters at Neuwied on the Rhine.

The General Election

Kérensky had been hopelessly outmanoeuvred, a victim of his incredible vanity (matched only by that of Trotsky). The great orator, who could indeed hold crowds spellbound with his rhetoric to which also his great forensic successes were due, thought no doubt that at the last moment he would harangue the revolutionaries, and the lion would lay down with the lamb. Sadly, there were no crowds to be addressed. Unfortunately, he had

not thought of the old Army saying: *kto pálku vzyal tot i kaprál*—he who
has taken the stick is the corporal.

The Bolshevik coup was not immediately reflected in our life in Moscow.
Lenin's first concern was to take Russia out of the war. A Bolshevik ensign
was appointed Commander-in-Chief and despatched to Mogilév to take
over General Headquarters on 3 December. General Dúkhonin, the
'progressive' Commander-in-Chief only appointed by Kérensky in September,
was dragged out of his train and murdered. An armistice was concluded
with the German High Command and peace negotiations opened.

It is often argued whether single men really decisively alter the course of
history. Napoleon, for instance, did not. The world today is much the same
as it would be had he never lived. Had Karl Marx never lived, again the
world today would be much the same, except that 'Marxism' would be
called 'Engelsianism' or dialectical materialism or something else. But
there are men who indeed affect the course of history by what they did or by
what they did not do. Lenin and Kérensky *jointly* did affect the course of
history, by what the one committed and the other omitted. There would
have been no Bolshevik take-over in Russia without Lenin *and* Kérensky;
there would be no Soviet Government today, Father used to say, if
Kérensky had been the leader of the Bolsheviks and Lenin the democratic
Prime Minister.

Election of a Constituent Assembly had been called by the Kérensky
Government for 25 November. Unfortunately, the election date was only
fixed in September, six months after the 'February Revolution'. It was
thought difficult and undesirable, as divisive, to hold elections in wartime.
This was in itself a sound argument but greatly weakened the authority of
the Kérensky Government deriving its legitimacy from a *Duma* elected in
1912 on a somewhat limited franchise and by indirect vote. At the root of it
all was the disaster of the 'February Revolution' occurring in mid-war,
because of the absence of the Czar, and incredible mismanagement of the
government by the Empress and Raspútin.

Although Lenin had been in power for a few weeks (at least in Petersburg
and Northern Russia) there was no serious interference with the election
campagin, or the voting. I well remember the huge party posters on Moscow
walls advising the holding of a *miting*. The election result was, on a perfect
one man–one vote system:

SR Party (Peasants Party)	419
Bolsheviks	175
Cadets, Octobrists, and all other parties	113
	707

Predictably, the SR (Peasants Party), which reminds one of the Ind.....
Congress Party, obtained the absolute majority. *The Bolsheviks received a
quarter of the vote*; even that was more than their real standing in the country
and was due to their programme of immediate peace on any terms and redis-
tribution of the land. It is difficult to see why Lenin allowed the election to
take place at all; possibly he was so conceited, so out of touch with the
reality of Russian life and so intoxicated with the heady revolutionary
atmosphere of Petersburg (very unrepresentative of the country) that he sincerely expected the Bolsheviks to gain a majority, or at least to become the
dominant party (as Hitler did fifteen years later). It also seems that Nicolai
Bukhárin (1880–1938), the chief Marxist theorist of the Bolsheviks, by
whose *placet* Lenin set great store, was in favour of holding the
General Election.

The Russian people's clear vote of no confidence did not cause Lenin any
sleepless nights. Having grabbed the reins of power in a highwayman's bold
coup he was not going to surrender them because of the vote of the ignorant
masses. They needed educating. When the Constituent Assembly, elected
on the one man–one vote principle, met on 18 January 1918 it was allowed
one formal opening session and was then dispersed by the rifle-butts of the
Red Guards. Lenin did not bother to have the building burnt down. The
wheel of history was turned back to pre-1905, and there has been no freely
elected Parliament in Russia ever since.

Kérensky, with the help of the British Government, escaped to England
via Murmansk and the Orkneys. Leaders of the liberal parties (Cadets and
Octobrists) and also of the right-wing socialists (SRs, Mensheviks,
Trudoviks and others) were arrested and shot. Two Cadet leaders, ill in hospital, were bayonetted to death in their sick-beds. Alexander Wilenkin,[4] a
young Jewish lawyer in Petersburg active in the Cadet party, was shot.

The pay-off

Ludendorff was not slow to cash in on his investment. Thirty divisions and
most of the heavy artillery were withdrawn from the Russian Front, where
the German Army was now being reduced to an army of occupation. These
thirty divisions were rested, re-equipped and transferred to the Western
Front. In a last fling, Ludendorff hoped to break the stalemate before
American manpower and firepower would irrevocably tilt the balance.

For his attack Ludendorff chose the British sector, which he considered
the weakest. This proved a misjudgement. On 21 March 1918 the re-
formed German armies from the East were launched against the Arras–St
Quentin line. But the British Army of 1918 were no longer the Kaiser's
'Contemptibles' of 1914. Bapaume was lost and the British line dented, but

not broken. At the end of March it was clear that the German attack had failed. The British casualties of that attack totalled 300,000 (entitling Lenin to a bust in the town hall of one of London's 'Red' Boroughs).

Brest-Litovsk (now Brest) is a fairly important centre on the border between Russia and Poland, on the trunk railway from Warsaw to Moscow. At the end of 1917 the town was a German headquarters and it was there that the armistice had been signed and the Bolsheviks were negotiating a separate peace. Brest's only other claim to fame, or, rather, notoriety, is that the Fourth Partition of Poland between National Socialist Germany and the Soviet Union was negotiated there in September 1939. Incidentally, Menachem Begin was born there in 1913; in 1939 he was serving with the Polish Army and thus, through Russian prison camps, eventually came to the Middle East. His aged parents and parents-in-law, a brother, his sisters-in-law and two nephews, five or six years old, were all murdered by the National Socialists.

The Treaty of Brest-Litovsk was concluded on 3 March 1918. When the terms became known in Russia, public opinion of all colours was stunned. I remember Father being indignant as I seldom saw him. Even the Central Committee of the Bolshevik party only accepted Lenin's motion in favour of signing by a majority of 7:6. Not only Poland and Finland, but the provinces of Estonia, Latvia, Lithuania and even arch-Russian Byelorussia would become 'independent,' with German troops permanently stationed in these countries. Malorussia (Ukraine) with the Crimea would become a separate state too, in a 'special relationship' with Germany, i.e. a German protectorate. South of the Caucasus range, the western areas, including Batum, would be ceded to Turkey, and the eastern part, including the Baku oilfields, would form a puppet state of Azerbaijan under German control. The Russian Army and Navy were to be fully demobilised. Truly a handsome return on the investment made in Lenin and his henchmen.

Russia was to be reduced to the area of landlocked Muscovy before Peter the Great, and would lose a population of some 45 million. No local plebiscites (as granted to disputed German border areas at Versailles a year later). It was as if a victorious Germany had made Wales, Cornwall, Ulster, the Isle of Man and the Channel Islands German dependencies, with German troops permanently stationed there, and Scotland with the Orkneys and the Shetland Islands a separate state protected by Germany. Actually, Brest-Litovsk was worse, because it left Russia with no European coastline (except in the Arctic).

The *diktat* of Brest-Litovsk was, probably, the harshest 'peace' treaty in modern European history; certainly, compared with it, the much-maligned Treaty of Versailles was a vicarage tea-party.

Of course, Lenin was a true Marxist internationalist, not in the least interested in the fate of Russia and her various peoples. Moreover, he had convinced himself that a socialist world revolution was imminent, so that, with a fraternal socialist regime installed in Berlin, it did not really matter where the boundary lay (the Soviet Union has since changed its views on the matter). Perhaps also, with the delusions of grandeur characteristic of the advanced stage of certain diseases, Lenin saw himself ultimately as the President of a United Socialist Europe. Russia became the Union of Soviet Socialist Republics, considered the nucleus of an international socialist superstate. The Russian tricolour (white, blue and red horizontally) was abolished; the flag under which two and a half million Russian soldiers had died, protecting their homeland from invasion (and relieving France from certain defeat) and cheated of the just reward for Russia by Bolshevik treason. Instead, the international Red Flag, with a hammer and sickle (as outdated symbols of worker and peasant) became the standard of the new world state nucleus.

No-one suspected in Moscow or Berlin that the Treaty of Brest-Litovsk, meant to redraw the map of eastern Europe for centuries, would, in fact, last eight months and eight days; the shameful *Diktat* was annulled by the victorious Allies in the Armistice of 11 November 1918, and a few weeks later, as the German troops started pulling out of the occupied territories, the Kremlin also 'repudiated' the Treaty.

Lenin also repudiated all foreign loans and bonds, wiping out the savings of many a French peasant. One sum, however, he had repaid in full and with interest—the loan which a group of London sympathisers, at the instance of George Lansbury, made to Lenin in 1907.

Under Bolshevik rule

We are now talking of Moscow and its Kremlin as the decision-making centre because, on 9 March 1918, the mob rule and anarchy in unruly Petersburg having served its purpose, Lenin transferred the seat of government to Moscow, leaving it to Trotsky to deal with the mutinous Red Sailors of Kronstadt (finally massacred in 1921) and with all others whom Bolshevik propaganda had made into revolutionaries for life. Moreover, while the Treaty of Brest-Litovsk was being negotiated, the German Army advanced steadily into Russia unopposed, and was now only a hundred miles from Petersburg, as well as occupying Byelorussia, Malorussia and all 'independent' territories in the West.

Moscow had been the historic capital of Russia until Peter the Great built St Petersburg (named after St Peter) on Baltic territory wrested from the Swedes, when, in Pushkin's immortal phrase, Moscow gave precedence to Petersburg like the purple-bearing widow to the young queen.

Lenin had all senior civil servants arrested or dismissed, except for some officers who were pressed into serving the new Red Army. He believed that existing officials would obstruct or thwart his plans, and wanted to wipe the slate clean and make a new start.

But Lenin soon found that drunken soldiers, mutinous sailors and a few illiterate peasants make excellent revolutionaries but are less successful as diplomats and heads of trade missions. Casting his eyes round for the new Civil Service, Lenin discovered that there was a large reservoir of educated Jewish people, with a knowledge of languages and often with university degrees, employed in menial occupations in the former Pale of Settlement, because under the Temporary Regulations they could not occupy any position in public life commensurate with their education and skills. It was from this group, uncompromised by any public office, or senior position, under the Czar (and from the Armenian community, also discriminated against) that Lenin recruited so many members of his foreign legations and trade missions until, in a new generation, non-Jewish replacements became available. There was no thought, or claim, or any reverse discrimination (I do not think the term had yet been invented); it was simply a question of speaking foreign languages and having some commercial understanding.

We now found ourselves living in the capital of the new Dictatorship of the Proletariat. Food was getting scarcer and scarcer; fortunately, owing to Mother's foresight in bringing a vast stock of flour and cereals from the Caucasus (where there was an abundance), ours was one of the few homes in Moscow (except those in the Kremlin) where no-one left the dinner-table hungry. Almost daily, we had relatives and friends for dinner (including, quite often, Marie Ivanovna's sister) as most of them were getting undernourished. There was hardly any meat, milk or butter, and only occasionally some fish. For some reason, however, the caviare continued to arrive daily from the Caspian—it was said that the Kremlin saw to it—and, as the special shops for Party members had not yet been established, the caviare was sold freely—if one could pay for it—at Eliséyev (the Moscow equivalent of Fortnum and Mason in London), still open, where Mother, an old customer, bought several pounds daily. We had caviare for breakfast, lunch and dinner—an excellent substitute for hen's eggs, butter and fish. Less fortunate people were starving in their first taste of socialism.

The war with Germany having been terminated, Lenin began with the class war in earnest. The dreaded *Cheká* (later GPU, later yet NKVD, at present KGB) was founded under Felix Dzerzhínsky, a Polish nobleman by birth. For some reason, Letts and other Baltic people and, generally, ethnic non-Russians were prominent in it (somehow, one is reminded of the French using the Vietnamese in Algeria).[5]

Bank accounts were frozen. Fortunately, as so often happened during that turbulent period, Father, like so many others, had an inkling of what was coming and managed to draw an exceedingly large sum of money which was kept in his study under the floorboards. This paid for our living for the next two or three years and financed the various stages of our flight; without it we would have perished, probably still in Moscow, like so many others. Jewellery and foreign currency had to be surrendered. Dividends and interest on Government loans were no longer paid. Commercial life was gradually coming to an end. The Poverkhovsky offices and warehouses were taken over.

There was no personal safety. Official Red Guards, drunken soldier-deserters and common riff-raff, masquerading as revolutionary vigilantes, roamed the streets, entered houses at will any time of day and night, conducted searches, looted and, if resisted, injured and killed. Cigarette-smoking Red Guards lolled in churches during Mass. The Rabbi, as Father told me, was made to clear the snow and denied food, with the suggestion that he should rely on manna from Heaven.

The population of Moscow had increased greatly through the influx of war-refugees and the swollen bureaucracy of the new capital. Lenin solved this problem quite simply by dividing the total area of housing accommodation available by the population number, and decreeing that henceforth every person was entitled to a certain number of square metres and no more. However, in practice, two adults were entitled to one medium-size room; a single person had to find a very small room or to share. Bolshevik officials were, of course, excluded and allocated mansions or large flats that had been confiscated. All were equal, with some more equal than others. This floor space-rationing was called *uplotneniye* (densification).

There was panic at home, and, no doubt, in many homes. Our household consisted of some seven or eight persons occupying fourteen rooms (with the exception of the 'telephone room', all large), plus four small servants' rooms. The decree meant that the new housing commissariat could draft complete strangers into our home, who were possibly verminous, suffered from VD or other contagious diseases, spat on the floor, drank themselves senseless and left the sanitary facilities in a filthy state. Possibly even attacked women. Plehvé or the Grand Duke Sergei had never done anything like this. But Mother was equal to the occasion. She repaired to the small 'telephone room', which was really her private office, and when Father returned home he found the flat transformed. Most rooms had been converted into bed-sitting rooms, some almost into dormitories with three or even four beds or sofas, and were occupied by our various young relatives and their friends. All were only too pleased to receive free board and lodgings in one of the few houses in Moscow where no-one remained hungry. Our housing quota was fulfilled. Most people did not fare so well. One of our relatives—a widow with two young daughters—had a lady of easy virtue quartered on her, who was visited by several clients nightly.

Notes

1   But when Uncle Matthew, a nonagenarian in Paris in the 1960s, was debilitated by a stroke, it was a fellow refugee Cossack who nursed him with great devotion for several years.
2   Lenin's mother was a Russian—German; a fact often made use of in anti-German propaganda.
3   Not to be confused with the right-wing 'Revisionism' of Zionism.
4   Brother of Grigory Wilenkin, the Counsellor at the London Embassy.
5   It would seem that people are more readily prepared to ill-treat persons of different background: according to Keneally, the SS had ordered that in the women's concentration camps Czech women were to be flogged by Slovak women, Slovaks by Czechs, Russians by Poles and vice versa, etc.

9

Flight from the Bolsheviks

Lenin and his gang considered themselves heirs and successors to the French Revolution. Their entire thinking and vocabulary was permeated by words such as *Thermidor* and *Brumaire*, *Gironde* and *Vendée*. They were, well into the twentieth century, nineteenth-century men re-enacting eighteenth-century events. Sadly, there was no Bastille to be stormed; its nearest equivalent, the Peter and Paul Fortress, had fallen into disuse, like the Tower of London, after the abdication of the Czar and the peaceful transfer of power to the parliamentary government in March 1917.

It now became a crime simply to be, or rather to have been, a *burzhúy* (bourgeois) just as it was a crime under Hitler to be a Jew. A *burzhúy* was anyone who had belonged either to the political ruling class, i.e. the aristocracy and high bureaucracy, or who was a landowner or a merchant, or had a business of any kind—in short, every 'capitalist' or 'capitalist's lackey', which included all professional people. Anyone who wore a suit and white collar was suspect. Some people started tucking their trousers into their boots and wearing cloth caps. Father did not; he never believed in mimicry; besides, he would not have passed for a *muzhík* anyway.

Lenin proclaimed his intention of ridding Russia of 'harmful insects'. We were the insects, perhaps the ants of Krylóv's fable, invaded by an echidna.

Baron von Mirbach, the German Ambassador at the Kremlin (yes, after Brest-Litovsk there was, in mid-1918, already a German Ambassador), Protector of the Bolsheviks, and considered as an effective Viceroy by many, was assassinated on 9 July. On 30 August, Fanny Kaplan, a Jewish girl from the Mensheviks, shot at Lenin, considering him a traitor to the universal brotherhood type of socialism in which she and many other starry-

111

eyed young people at the time believed. She saw herself as another Charlotte Corday assassinating Marat. However, she only succeeded in wounding Lenin and he lived for another six long years. By coincidence, on the same day in Petersburg, the chief of the local *Cheká* was also assassinated.[1] The attacks convinced Lenin that a *Thermidor* was imminent and, seeing himself as a second Robespierre, he launched the Red Terror. It was the cue he had been waiting for.

Lenin ordered the taking of hostages from the ranks of the *burzhúy*. Ten hostages would be killed in reprisal for one Bolshevik. (The same ratio was later used by the German National Socialists in the Ardentine Caves massacre and other reprisals.) Often there were more than ten for one; the murder of the *Cheká* chief in Petersburg was said to have been avenged by the killing of five hundred hostages, but, of course, he was a very highly placed person in the new socialist hierarchy. In any case, the pretence of killing the hostages in retaliation was soon dropped, and the *burzhúy* hostages were simply ill-treated for a few weeks and then shot in pursuance of the liquidation of the bourgeoisie.

One morning Mother received a guarded message from one of her former protegés, whom she had helped to study law, and who now had since the Kérensky days, a fairly junior position at the Ministry of the Interior. Apparently, he had seen Father's name on a list of hostages which, on Lenin's instructions, had been prepared. Moreover, Father was fairly near the top and could be arrested anytime, even tonight.

I cannot describe in detail that fateful day in our life because, being a little boy, I was told next to nothing. In fact, just in case I would be questioned, I was told at a late hour that we were going to Mogilév to visit Grandparents. In fact, Father and Mother had decided that we should go to the Crimea next morning, which was outside the Bolshevik grip (Mogilév was not).

Father spent a hectic day in town. Train-reservations had to be obtained, which was very difficult and, I believe cost a lot of money, as most of the seats were allocated to the new Bolshevik bureaucracy. After Brest-Litovsk, Malorussia and, at one time, even the Crimea had been occupied by the unopposed German army, and one actually required a German transit visa to travel from Moscow to the Crimea. Fortunately, we still had a valid foreign passport, and there were no difficulties at the German Embassy, though it all took time. No exit permits or travel documents of any kind were required from the Bolsheviks at that stage; if anything, they were probably only too pleased if people were leaving overcrowded and hungry Moscow. Having obtained the rail reservations and German visa, Father then did something which was completely outside the scope of his usual business affairs and was to safeguard our future for decades to come. He met one of Moscow's leading fur-traders, who had made his peace with

the new regime or at least he thought he had. I believe his son-in-la[w]
obtained a prominent position in the new bureaucracy (some years
still under Lenin, both the furrier and his son-in-law were deported,
perished). The fur-trader had a consignment of valuable Siberian fu[r] —
sable, ermine, blue fox, white fox and others—on the high seas between
Vladivostok and Yokohama. He believed, quite rightly, that with the political situation as it was he had no chance of ever seeing the payment for the
consignment and was willing, and in fact anxious, to sell Father the bill of
lading. Father purchased the document, much to Mother's astonishment
when she heard of it, as it naturally considerably reduced our cash-holding
(bank accounts had been expropriated). I am not familiar with commercial
maritime law but apparently possession of the bill of lading (actually called
in Russian a *connossement*) gave the bearer the indisputed ownership of the
consignment, more or less like the title deeds of a house. Even now, I admire
Father for his foresight and resource under unprecedented circumstances
and when escaping arrest.

In the meantime Mother was making all preparations at home, packing
some trunks (not too many, as excessive luggage was clearly undesirable)
and organising our departure next day. Money-belts were sewn to transport
the large amount of banknotes which now represented our entire disposable
capital. Mother had also managed, when the jewellery had to be surrendered, to retain without Father's knowledge the most compact but valuable
items and these also went into the belts. In all this Mother was helped by
Marie Ivanovna who, in just over a year, had grown into the family and from
whom Mother had no secrets. It was understood that Marie Ivanovna was
coming with us; after all, I had to be coached for the entrance examination
of the Academy which would, surely, re-open as soon as the Bolsheviks had
been put down. Father, as agreed with Mother, did not return home that
night but stayed with our family doctor, who had a small self-contained flat.
Doctors were the one section of the professional classes who did not count
as *burzhúy* for the simple reason that there was a grave shortage of them and
a danger of epidemics (which did materialise very soon) and Lenin considered all doctors as proletarians *honoris causa*. It was agreed that Father
would join us at the station a few minutes before departure, just in case the
Cheká would be looking for him. (I was told that Father had gone to
Mogilév a day ahead of us.)

I doubt whether Father, Mother or even Marie Ivanovna had much sleep
that night; I slept soundly. Next day, we went with Mother, Marie Ivanovna,
my little sister, our comparatively modest luggage and, of course, the invisible money-belts to the Kurski Voksál in two cabs, and waited by the platform entrance of the spacious station, somehow reminiscent of King's
Cross in London. Mother was getting distinctly nervous, and was looking

round in all directions. Suddenly to my surprise Father arrived—I still remember his sudden appearance, in a black coat with astrakhan collar and bowler hat, looking noticeably pale. We immediately boarded the train, which left in a few moments on its thousand-mile journey. Russian long-distance expresses, in addition to ordinary cars, had two kinds of sleeping cars: the Fiscal and the International. The Fiscal sleeper belonged to the Railway; the International to the Wagons-Lit company, or, to give it its complete and (in its heyday) fully justified title: Compagnie Internationale des Wagons-Lit et des Grands Express Européens. The International was somewhat more comfortable than the Fiscal and much more expensive. Mother did not even know whether Father managed to get sleeping-car reservations at all, and was pleasantly surprised when we found ourselves in the International right in front of the train, in two first-class compartments joined by a washroom. Not everyone was fleeing from the Bolsheviks in a first-class Wagon-Lit suite. It was known that there would be no restaurant car and, in any case, it would probably have been unwise to make use of one. However, Mother had prepared adequate provisions in the hand-luggage and even a small spirit heater (probably against railway regulations) for making tea and even porridge. Owing to the condition of the track, inadequate engine fuel and general disorganisation of the railway system, the trip was expected to take up to two days.

The German Army saves our lives

The first day was uneventful. We stopped at Kursk in the evening for a longish period and many passengers had tea or a meal at the station buffet. We did not leave our compartments. The Wagon-Lit attendant who was, strangely, still on duty—the new bureaucracy probably saw to that—then transformed the daytime seats into beds, with immaculate linen, and let down the blinds. My sister and I were put to bed. My parents, in the one compartment and Marie Invanovna with us, also lay down, but in their clothes because some time during the night we would probably be reaching the German occupation-line in Malorussia when, no doubt, papers would be checked. There could also be a Bolshevik exit control (fortunately there was not). We were rather looking forward to reaching German-occupied territory because Father would no longer be in danger of arrest, and generally the Germans treated civilians with all propriety during World War I. Indeed when the train stopped at the German checkpoint about midnight, a German NCO appeared, checked our papers and was quite correct. He also told us, quite politely, that we had to clear the compartments within fifteen minutes, as the International was requisitioned and had to be prepared for a party of *Herren Offiziere* who would be boarding at Kharkov.

My parents and Marie Ivanovna had a very uncomfortable fifteen minutes getting us ready and packed. We then had to squeeze through the crowded corridors of the train until we reached the luggage-van at the rear, where we had been permitted to continue our journey. The train started and I soon fell asleep, lying on some coats Mother had placed on our trunks. Instead of being in a *wagon-lit* we were now in a *wagon-bagage*. My little sister was sleeping on another trunk. Father, Mother and Marie Ivanovna were sitting on the others. Soon I was awakened by a jolt which almost threw me off the trunk. There was a long grinding noise. The train came to a halt. Outside people were shouting and rushing around with lanterns. The Crimea Express had run head-on into another train. The International, as yet unoccupied (except, probably, for the attendant) was pulverised and the three front coaches behind it telescoped or reared up. I believe that there were many dead and injured. By turning us out of the sleeper *the German Army had saved our lives*. As we heard years later, that very night the *Cheká* came to our flat in Moscow. They did not seem to mind particularly that Father had gone and just went to arrest the next one down the list. They only had to fulfil their quota.

After some hours a relief train arrived and the undamaged coaches were coupled to it. We were even given two second-class day-compartments in which we completed our journey. On the third day after leaving Moscow we arrived at Simferopol, the capital of the Crimea, situated in the interior of the peninsula and terminus of the main line. There is now a gap in my memory, presumably I was asleep, and I do not recall how we got to Yalta. There was no branch-line serving Yalta—I believe, there still is none—and, no doubt, we went across the mountains by road.

In the Crimea

The Crimean south-east coast from Sebastopol to Yalta is exceedingly beautiful as the mountain range, rising to five thousand feet, runs along the coast, much more majestic than the *Corniche* in the south of France. We stayed at Yalta at an hotel for a few days where we met, much to our surprise, Aunt Helène and Uncle Jacques, who had just arrived from Petersburg, and gave us the sad news of Aunt Amalia's death from typhus fever.

Father managed to rent a furnished villa at Simeíz, not far from Yalta, and Aunt Helène and Uncle Jacques—they were only two—would be sharing the villa with us. Uncle Jacques was now retired and suffering badly from asthma. Their Moscow mansion had been confiscated (later it was allocated by the Soviets to the British Embassy—this did not assist Aunt

Helène in obtaining a British immigration visa when marooned in France in 1940).

The villa at Simeíz was perched on the mountainside, overlooking, like Amalfi, the azure sea below. The view was enchanting. Here and there were tall cypresses and an occasional pine. There were vineyards on the terraced hillsides and lemon groves. We were in a different world.

No sooner were we installed in the villa than we all fell ill with the severe influenza which then spread over the entire world and which was known in Russia as the *ispánka* in the (erroneous) belief that the disease originated in Spain. We all had a very high fever and felt sick and weak, hardly being able to move. Fortunately, in the balmy climate of the Crimea the illness ended after a week without complications. We had probably caught the virus while still in Moscow; what would have happened if we had been taken ill while still in Moscow one shudders to think. We would have been compelled to postpone our departure and Father would have been arrested—being ill made as little difference to the *Cheká* as it made later to the Gestapo. Worldwide, I believe, the epidemic killed twenty million people, twice as many as the war.

Below us, in a largeish villa with extensive grounds, stayed the Dowager Empress Marie Feodorovna, *née* Princess Dagmar of Denmark, sister of Queen Alexandra of England and thus Aunt of King George V. Like Alexander III, she too had disapproved of her son's marriage and disliked her daughter-in-law. She was also against the Czar's effective abdication in 1915, when he moved to Mogilév, leaving the reins of government in the hands of the young Empress and Raspútin. Now, this universally liked and respected grand old lady was mourning the horrible death of her two sons, her son's entire family and the end of the great dynasty to which she had become devoted.

I do not imagine that my parents enjoyed the stay in this beautiful country any more than the Empress did. It was generally expected that the Bolshevik insurrection would be put down soon and we could return to Moscow. But there was no sign of this happening. In the meantime, we were living in expensive rented accommodation, with light luggage, and the money, though still ample, was diminishing and there was no prospect of any income. Obviously the situation could not have appealed to Father and Mother, even if they must have appreciated the Mediterranean climate and beautiful scenery.

We spent almost a year, I believe, at Simeíz. As far as I was concerned, I was too young to share my parents' worries. Our life in the Crimea was a perfect long holiday. Naturally, I had my daily lessons with Marie Ivanovna—it was still assumed that I would enrol in the Academy in Moscow as soon as conditions were back to normal. Marie Ivanovna also took us on long walks and picnics, and practised horse-riding, in which she became quite proficient. I too trotted around on a pony from time to time.

Uncle Matthew escapes

Just before our flight from Moscow Uncle Matthew and his family went to Petersburg. He reasoned that, not being a resident, he would not be on the local arrest list, and also that with his maritime connections he might obtain a passage to Sweden, as the Baltic was now open, though there was no passenger traffic as yet. And from Sweden, when the Germans were beaten by the Allies, as assuredly they would, he might find a passage to England, where he still had pre-war connections which might facilitate his journey.

Uncle Matthew did secure a passage on a Swedish cargo boat. Unfortunately, on arrival in Petersburg, Aunt Amalia had been infected with typhus, probably in the cab taking them from the station, and she fell ill a fortnight later just when the family were due to sail. The passage had to be cancelled, and there were the greatest difficulties in finding a hospital place as all hospitals were overcrowded. In the end, Uncle Matthew secured a bed in some hospital, where Aunt Amalia died after three weeks. And so one of the best-dressed women of Moscow died in the common ward of a Petersburg hospital from the bite of a typhus-bearing louse.

Uncle Matthew, now a widower, secured a new passage and sailed with the four children to Sweden and thence, after the German surrender, eventually reached England. *Warm welcome by his brother-in-law, H. E. Gregory Wilenkin and family.*

The German surrender

On the Western Front Ludendorff's last fling with the thirty divisions transferred from Russia, with all their heavy guns, had been repulsed, with great loss of life. The German Army which had raised the wind of *Materialkrieg* against the Russian Army was now reaping the whirlwind from Pittsburgh and Detroit, annihilating it under a deluge of steel, while the homeland was being strangled by the British naval blockade. On 5 October 1918 the German High Command sued for peace. On 9 November 1918 the Kaiser abdicated and fled to Holland and General Ludendorff, in mufti and disguised with dark glasses, escaped to Sweden. On 11 November the German surrender was received by three French generals and three British admirals in Marshal Foch's railway salon car in the Forest of Compiègne. Ten million men had died. Twenty million had been wounded, many permanently maimed. Europe had been dealt a crippling blow. Ludendorff's hideous creature, Soviet socialism, lived on.

These events were later described in National Socialist mythology as the *Dolchstoss*, the stab in the back. The Jews were to blame.

Russia's borders

During our enforced holiday in the Crimea Russia's fate was being decided. One of the provisions of the Armistice between the Western Allies and Germany was the cancellation of the infamous Brest-Litovsk *Diktat*, and the withdrawal of German troops from all occupied territories. But the freed territories were not all restored to Russian suzerainty. In 1919, at Versailles, a Polish state was formed from the ethnically Polish territories of Russia, Germany and Austria, thus undoing the Third Partition of 1795, and—in respect of Germany—also the Second Partition of 1793. Finland too was formed into an independent state which was, at any rate, arguable, particularly with the close association with Russia it has now. A Lithuanian state was also formed, although there had been no independent Lithuania since 1387, and the case for an independent Lithuania is weaker than that for an independent Wales. Finally, without any valid justification except that of weakening Russia, Estonia and Latvia were formed into independent Baltic mini-states, although these two provinces had never enjoyed statehood. Estonia and Latvia and Lithuania, with Revel (Tallinn), with Riga and Liebava and Dvinsk, and with Vilna and Kovno, and Klaipeda, are now again incorporated into the Russian Federation and will remain so, possibly confirmed by a plebiscite (as suggested by NTS, the leading Russian underground opposition group), long after Soviet socialism has vanished into the dustbin of history.

All this rearrangement of the map of Eastern Europe at Versailles was decided on without Russia's participation in the Allied councils, simply because Russia had no voice to speak for her. The lives of two and a half million dead and five million wounded which Russia had contributed to the common cause, and without which the Allies would have lost the war, had been squandered by Lenin concluding a separate peace with Germany in 1917, in contravention of all solemn treaty obligations (which the Czar and the following Parliamentary Government had been keeping). In fact, on 15 July 1918 Clemenceau, the French premier, told Kérensky to his face in Paris: 'La Russie est un pays neutre qui a conclu la paix séparée avec nos ennemis. Les amis de nos ennemis sont nos ennemis' (Russia is a neutral country that has concluded a separate peace with our enemies. The friends of our enemies are our enemies).

Of course, France herself was in exactly the same position in 1945, but

General de Gaulle had spent the war years ensuring that, in spite of Pétain's separate peace in 1940, France would still sit at the victor's table. Russia in 1917 unfortunately produced no de Gaulle. Perhaps the time from separate peace to Allied victory was too short.

In the Armistice, the Allies could have imposed on the Germans the obligation to remove the Bolsheviks, whom they had created—the German army of occupation in Russia could probably have done it without a shot being fired—and ensure that the Constituent Assembly was reconvened and a democratically elected government formed. But that government would have claimed, in spite of Clemenceau's dictum, to be represented at the peace conference. It is difficult to resist the impression that this was something the Allied governments preferred to avoid. With Lenin in power, Russia's claims to territorial integrity and for control of the Straits, which were at last within her grasp, could be conveniently ignored.

The Civil War

In early 1918 the Bolsheviks controlled Moscow, Petersburg, and more or less, the old territory of Muscovy. The west and the south were occupied by the Germans. The vast area on and beyond the Volga and the whole of Siberia and Central Asia were free of Bolsheviks. Unfortunately, there was no authoritative successor to the Kérensky Government. In Ufá, east of the Volga and in the foothills of the Urals, a non-Bolshevik Directorate or Provisional Government had been formed in September 1918. Almost a year had been wasted. The Directorate was not particularly representative, however, and consisted of some lesser-known members of the Cadet and SR Peasant and Right-wing socialist parties. The Mensheviks, or Left-wing non-Bolshevik socialists, and other Left-wing parties and groups were not represented as they did not want to fight the Bolsheviks as fellow-socialists whilst disapproving of their methods. Later, the Directorate moved to Omsk. There were no outstanding personalities, no Garibaldi, no de Gaulle, to rally anti-Brest-Litovsk, patriotic anti-Bolshevik Russia, the silent majority of the population.

In the meantime, military anti-Bolshevik forces were being formed in various Bolshevik-free parts of the country. This movement was fairly spontaneous, and there was no political or even strategic central direction and no co-ordination with the parliamentary Directorate at Ufá, or later, Omsk. All these forces were generally organised by army generals who found themselves in a Bolshevik-free region and called for volunteers to fight the Germans, Brest-Litovsk, the dismemberment of Russia, and the Bolshevik government that had capitulated to the Germans.

In the south-east, General Deníkin, assisted by General Wrangel, assembled a fairly substantial volunteer army, and, as the Germans moved out, gained control of the whole south, including the Crimea, where we were at the time, and Odessa. In Siberia, the anti-Bolshevik army was headed by Admiral Kolchák, the former Commander-in-Chief of the Black Sea Fleet. After the Revolution he went to Washington, whence he reached Vladivostok, with British assistance, via Singapore. There were two smaller volunteer armies: General Yudénich, formed in the Baltic provinces, and a very small group in the north, centred on Murmansk and Archangel.

The Volunteer Armies, or White Guards, as they became known were naturally all assisted by Britain and France, as their initial aim had been to fight the Germans and re-open a Second Front in Russia. To achieve that, one had to get rid of the Bolsheviks. Britain primarily supported Kolchák, and also Wrangel and Yudénich, France primarily supported Deníkin. Allied support continued, in varying degrees, throughout 1919. In Britain, Lloyd-George, the Prime Minister, was opposed to continuing support for the Whites once Germany had been beaten. The Bolsheviks had mobilised all their numerous friends and sympathisers in Britain and France to oppose assistance. At the Labour Party Conference at Southport a resolution was passed against further support and strikes were being threatened. Not only socialist but also liberal opinion thought that the Soviet Socialist Government, as the Bolsheviks now were, should be given a chance. At the other end of the political spectrum a section of Conservative opinion too, headed by Lord Curzon, wanted an end to the assistance, in order to keep Russia weak and divided and form a string of anti-Bolshevik, anti-Russian mini-states (the 'Curzon Line') along its Western borders. Churchill alone, then Minister of War, continued the assistance to the Whites in defiance of the Cabinet. With his knowledge and sense of history, and feeling for the common European heritage, Churchill alone understood that Soviet socialism was an international danger and, once established in one country, would be continually striving to spread their system of 'dictatorship of the proletariat' to all other countries. Bolshevism was an infectious disease endangering all its neighbours. Unfortunately, at the end of 1919 Lloyd-George and Clemenceau agreed that all British and French help to their former allies should cease and Churchill had to comply. In the House of Commons he declared: 'Lenin was sent into Russia by the Germans in the same way that you might send a phial containing a culture of typhoid or of cholera to be poured into the water supply of a great city, and it worked with amazing accuracy.'

The White Armies and the Red Army each had at their peak about half a million men under arms. The Whites were all volunteers; in fact, their official style was the Volunteer Army. Naturally, they were largely ex-officers and also ex-Regular Army soldiers. The Reds were mainly conscripted from all areas where Lenin's writ ran, but included professional officers and NCOs pressed into service. The Civil War was real fratricide. Unfortunately, the White Armies, being manned by volunteers, included some detachments of former Black Hundreds and similar extremist elements, who considered the murder of Jews their main occupation rather than fighting the Bolsheviks. Such detachments were particularly found in General Deníkin's armies, constituting a small minority, and Churchill warned Deníkin to enforce discipline and prevent further excesses.[2] Furthermore, part of Malorussia (Ukraine) was, after the Germans had left, controlled by the separatist Petlýura, who, in 1918–20 had allowed some thirty thousand Jewish men, women and children to be murdered (Petlýura himself was assassinated in Paris in 1926 by a young Russian Jew whose parents had been murdered in a Petlýura *pogróm*). Of course, twenty years later, thirty thousand men, women and children were being killed in Russia by the German National Socialists in a single day, but before Hitler Petlýura was considered one of the biggest mass-murderers of Jews of all time.

In addition to the Whites and the Reds there were also local warlords, or glorified bandits, like one Makhnó, also in Malorussia, as far as I know without any particular political allegiance. His bands were known as the Greens, and also specialised in the killing of Jews. Yet others simply got hold of an armoured train (the ultimate weapon in those days in Russia) and careered up and down a railway-line, terrorising the adjacent villages and living off the fat of the land, or whatever was left of it. Anarchy reigned supreme.

One day in 1919 our Uncle Volóvnik (a cousin of Father whom we called by his surname) was travelling in the Ukraine when he saw an old Jew lying on the platform and being beaten up by three black-jacketed thugs (political affiliation, if any, not known). Uncle Volóvnik jumped out of the train to rescue the old man and was himself beaten to death. Passengers and station staff looked the other way.

The entire population of Russia suffered terribly during the Civil War from hunger, disease, and pillaging and ravaging by ill-disciplined soldiery of all political colours and none, but the local Jews were always exposed to an extra hazard.

In early October 1919 it looked as if the anti-Bolsheviks, or Whites, were winning. Deníkin, coming from the south, had entered Kiev, and advanced further to Kursk, and even Orél, and was now 250 miles from Moscow. In the north-west, Yudénich was twelve miles from Petersburg. Kolchák controlled the whole of Siberia and had reached the Urals.

And then, suddenly, all fronts collapsed. At the battle of Zméevka, north of Orél, Deníkin's army was beaten and forced to retreat to the south. The tragic fate of Russia, if not of Europe and indeed the world, for this century was sealed.

In December 1919 Deníkin was being driven towards the Black Sea, Yudénich was pushed back into Estonia where his army was disbanded and Kolchák was driven eastwards over two thousand miles across Siberia. He was finally treacherously surrendered by the French and Czechs to the Bolsheviks, who shot him on 6 February 1920. A great Russian patriot who might have created a strong, free and humane Russia.

Soviet power was now established over the whole of Russia except for the chain of independent mini-states in its Western region. The war had been won against Germany but lost against her surrogate. What were the causes of the Whites' defeat? They were political and military. Politically, the Whites had no charismatic leader who would rally all Russian patriots and freedom-lovers. There was no legal and unifying government. Kolchák did declare himself Supreme Ruler of Russia and might have succeeded in establishing a military regime, as Admiral Horthy did so successfully in Hungary at precisely the same time and in very similar circumstances after overthrowing the Hungarian Bolshevik government of Bela Kun, who had seized power. But Kolchák was not recognised as Supreme Commander by the anti-Bolshevik generals on the other fronts. In fact, there was a good deal of rivalry between the various generals and the Great Powers behind them. The peasants saw, wherever the White armies gained control, the landlords' estates, which they had seized, naturally returned to their rightful owners. Militarily, the Bolsheviks occupied the central core, and were attacked on three or four points of the periphery, with little or no co-ordination. The Bolsheviks could readily transfer troops from one front to another. There was almost no physical contact between the four armies of the Whites. And, of course, the withdrawal of Western help greatly weakened the White armies.

Evacuation

During all these climacteric events we were continuing with our sheltered life in the Crimea. The peninsula is connected with the mainland by the Perekóp, a low-lying, long isthmus only a few miles wide. It was said to be dominated by the guns of two French light cruisers stationed offshore. Even with the Bolsheviks approaching the Black Sea in 1919, we felt quite safe in the Crimea, as the Perekóp could not be crossed under the muzzles of those guns.

One evening, a small fishing boat approached one of the cruisers, made fast and two men boarded the ship through the small trapdoor used for loading stores. The officer of the watch did not pay much attention, if he noticed at all; it was quite normal for local people to board the ship and sell fresh fruit, home-baked cakes and even vodka. Why not? After an hour or so, the boat cast off and proceeded to the second cruiser. All perfectly normal. As the moon rose some hours later, the duty officer thought he discerned some moving shadows on Perekóp. He ordered the searchlight to be trained and could hardly believe his eyes: a long column of men, with some horse-drawn equipment, was advancing southwards. The officer raised the alarm and the captain ordered the guns to be manned. The French sailors refused to a man to carry out his orders. They just stood there in dumb defiance. There was no violence. The visitors—some of the Bolsheviks' best agitators—had harangued the sailors, and sung the *Marseillaise* with them:

> Contre nous de la tyrannie
> L'etandart sanglant est levé

The sailors had been brainwashed to believe that it was the Whites who represented the tyranny with its bloodstained banner! The good Captain had no wish to be locked up, or shot. Perhaps he himself wanted to get home, and failed to see why the fate of the Crimea was any concern of his.

This, at any rate, is the story as I heard it at the time. The incontrovertible fact is that the French did not shoot, as they had undertaken to do, and the Bolsheviks entered the Crimea unopposed.[3] There was panic all along the coast that morning. I do not recall noticing anything unusual, nor was I told anything. My sister and I were playing in the garden as usual. All I do remember is that in the evening, instead of going to bed, we were dressed in warm clothing. An open carriage and a *teléga*, or open van, drew up, the five of us and Aunt Helène and Uncle Jacques took our seats in the carriage, the luggage of the two families was piled on to the van and we left the villa where, as far as I was concerned, we had spent a very pleasant year.

We soon joined an entire procession of carriages and vans, all horse-drawn, of course, and started on the coastal mountain road from Simeíz to Yalta. In front and at the back of the convoy was a *teléga*, with armed White Guards; their commanding officer and his adjutant accompanied us on horseback. In the centre of the convoy was a large coach, drawn by four horses, believed to contain the Dowager Empress. Throughout the journey we were followed by the searchlights of a British destroyer watching over our safety. I had never seen the mountains at night, and they presented a beautiful sight under the star-spangled sky.

Early next morning we reached Yalta and immediately boarded the British destroyer HMS *Montrose*, presumably the same ship that had been following our progress during the night. I had never been on a warship before—in fact, not on any ship (except in 1915 from Brindisi to Piraeus, of which I remember nothing). For me, it was a great adventure. The officers surrendered their cabins to the ladies, so that Mother, Marie Ivanovna and we children stayed in the cabin, whereas Father and all men were on deck. The Dowager Empress was, I believe, not on board; perhaps another warship had been found for her.

A British sailor gave me a bar of chocolate. Now we had chocolates in Moscow from time to time. When one of our aunts came to tea there were generally *langues de chat* from Einém on the table. Naturally, we helped ourselves to these wafer-thin, pale chocolates, supposedly shaped like a cat's tongue, though I always thought rather like a kitten's. I did not think much of them because they melted away as soon as one had tasted them. But the Navy chocolate was something entirely different. This was a big crunchy bar of real dark chocolate, into which one could bite and bite. Even today, after sixty years, my mouth waters when I think of that chocolate. I decided there and then that England must be a very nice country where they made such wonderful chocolates.

There were some White troops in the Crimea under the command of General Wrangel, a gallant soldier, and they were fighting the Reds, but this was unavoidably more of a rearguard action. The bulk of the troops had been fighting under General Deníkin on the mainland.

The Allied Forces in the Crimea, mainly, if not exclusively, naval, were under the command of a British admiral; the forces at Odessa, which included a large contingent of French troops, were commanded by a French general. The British made Sebastopol the evacuation harbour for the Crimea and HMS *Montrose* was taking us to Sebastopol. It was only a few hours' sailing for a fast destroyer and, in Sebastopol, we were all transferred to a huge Russian battleship, the *St George*, which was anchored immobilised in the harbour. I do not know why she was immobilised; perhaps she had been damaged and was undergoing a refit; perhaps the Germans had immobilised her before departing. The *St George* was quite an ageing ship (in 1905 she had joined *Potémkin* in the celebrated mutiny); however, the battleship was still on the active service list, with a maintenance crew, and the Russian naval ensign, the blue saltire St Andrew's Cross in a white field, was hoisted every morning and struck at sunset. There were hardly any other Russian warships; the bulk of the Black Sea Fleet had been moved, after Brest-Litovsk, further east to Novorossísk, to prevent it from falling into German hands (no Russian Darlan attempted to trade it to the Germans). When Novorossísk's turn came to be evacuated many of the warships escaped and joined the French fleet at Bizerta, near Tunis. Finally, when the French government, now recognising the Soviets, intended to return the warships to the Soviet Union the crews, now thoroughly disillusioned, scuttled them.

Various parties of refugees, presumably from other parts of the coast, were also disembarked on the *St George*, which obviously served as a reception centre for would-be evacuees. We stayed on the ship for two days, sitting and sleeping on our luggage on one of the lower decks. There was nothing to eat except what people had brought with them. The quayside was crowded with people all desperate to get away. It was said that the whole of the Crimea had, by now, been occupied by the Bolsheviks except Sebastopol, its perimeter being defended by British marines with machine guns facing *landwards*. Behind the arc of the mountains lay the Alma river, the Inkerman Heights, the little harbour of Balaclava. Sixty-five years earlier the Russians were defending Sebastopol heroically for eleven months, under Admirals Nachímov and Kornílov, and the British and the French, the Turks and the Sardinians were attacking; now the roles were reversed. The White Guards, grossly outnumbered, were falling back on Sebastopol, and naturally given first priority for evacuation by the British; the Dowager Empress had been embarked on a British cruiser the same day and was, by now, probably sailing through the Dardanelles, out of reach of her sons' and grandchildren's murderers. I believe that she disembarked at Malta, and later returned to her native Denmark, where she lived in seclusion in a modest red-brick villa overlooking the Sund until the grand old lady passed away in 1928. The Grand Duke Nikolai Nikolaevich, erstwhile Commander-in-Chief of the Czar's armies, was also evacuated, and so were the numerous generals, ministers and members of the aristocracy who, like us, had found refuge in the Crimea.

Suddenly, the rumour spread on the *St George* that no more space could be found on the few merchant ships that had been requisitioned and assembled at Sebastopol by the British command. After all, Sebastopol was not a commercial port. So the civilians on the *St George* would have to be left behind. There is no doubt that we would all have been lynched by the Red Guards, infuriated at all the prize catches having escaped.

It was decided that a deputation of ladies from the *St George* would go and see the British admiral and implore him to save us. They were mostly elegant Petersburg ladies, all English-speaking and included Aunt Helène, as it was thought they were better equipped to handle a British admiral. I remember the ladies leaving in an open motor-launch, all white gloves, and diamonds sparkling. The deputation returned elated: the Admiral had promised to see what he could do.

A few hours later the good ship *Ocamo* drew up alongside the *St George* and we were all transferred aboard together with our luggage. According to Lloyds Register of Shipping, to whom I am much obliged, the SS *Ocamo* was built in 1877 in Glasgow and was originally called *Taymouth Castle*. The ship's gross tonnage was 1910 tons (the size of a small cross-Channel ferry) and she was broken up in 1922. In 1919 the *Ocamo* (presumably so renamed after the river of that name in Venezuela) had been delivering a cargo of cheese to the British forces in the area and, when requisitioned, still had quite a lot of cheese in her hold. We were all quartered in the hold amid the maturing cheese and I am sure that the ladies found the smell sweeter than that of the finest French perfume. Many of them, and some men too, found the steep iron ladders leading into the hold difficult to negotiate but were assisted by the crew.

In the meantime the British evacuation had been completed to the extent possible, all British personnel and White Russian troops embarked and the last flotilla of warships and merchantmen steamed slowly into the evening sun. *The Royal Navy had saved us.* As we were leaving the doomed port one could see the dense throng on the quayside—Lenin's insects—waving arms and shouting. One mother held out her baby in dumb entreaty. Improvised Services of Supplication were held. Everyone was butchered when the vodka-crazed Red hordes burst into the port.

Similar tragedies were enacted at Odessa, somewhat earlier (there the French were in charge) and at Novorossísk (British evacuation) later. Compared with other evacuations of civilians in Europe, not to mention the catastrophe of the Vietnam evacuations, and considering the shortage of merchant shipping and the sudden onrush, the British in the Black Sea did as well as can be, under the circumstances. Certainly, we owe Britain our lives, and so do tens of thousands, possibly hundreds of thousands, saved from the Bolsheviks.

Notes

1   Moses Uritzky—of Jewish birth, one is ashamed to admit.

2   Typical of colourful characters on the fringe of the White Armies was the Kubán Cossack Andrei Shkuro, leader of the Circassian horsemen, who conducted daring advance raids into enemy territory. In fact, Shkuro's raids were so effective that at the recommendation of British liaison officers on General Deníkin's staff, he was honoured by the Order of the Bath. Unfortunately, Shkuro and his 'Wolves' spent their rest days pillaging and raping, and murdering all local Jews on sight, and Deníkin is reported as having said that he needed Shkuro at present but would have him court-martialled when the war was won. So when, in 1945, the emigré Shkuro was handed over to the Soviets, in contravention of all international law, by the British authorities in Austria, and in 1947 executed in Lefortovo prison one must admit that not many Jewish tears were shed for this particular Circassian.

It must be said that, as opposed to Deníkin's reluctant sufferance of Shkuro, General Wrangel in the Crimea rigorously enforced full order and discipline. In fact, when the daily *Russkaya Pravda* published an incitement to *pogróms*, Wrangel dismissed the military censor and ordered the paper to be closed down (N. Ross, *Wrangel v. Krimu*, Possev, Frankfurt, 1982).

3   According to another version, the Bolsheviks entered through the Sivash flats east of Perekóp, which were traversed by the railway causeway.

PART TWO

In Exile

10

In Czargrad

The Black Sea is, I believe, some four thousand feet deep and can be very stormy. We were very lucky with the weather; the sea was calm and after some forty-eight hours we had crossed the Black Sea, quite uneventfully, and anchored in the Bosphorus (sixty-five years earlier, the towed troop barges sailed *twelve* days from Varna to Eupatoria).

In front of us unfolded the panorama of Constantinople, with all its domes and minarets. Like Naples, Constantinople presents a breathtaking sight when viewed from the sea; when in the city, one sees mainly the squalor and filth. Actually, we could enjoy the view from the Bosphorus for another full three weeks. Although Constantinople was occupied by the Allies, the Turkish civil authorities still had some part to play, and were in no hurry whatsoever to issue landing permits to the uninvited guests. Probably, they were really waiting for a *baksheesh* but there was no-one on shore to give it. The now-numerous refugee-help organisations then did not exist, and we were no-one's responsibility. I do not know who the owners of the *Ocamo* were; presumably she was technically on charter to the British Admiralty, who was paying the owners. So they had nothing to lose.

Forty years ago, the Russians stood at the gates of Constantinople as conquerors, thwarted in their age-old ambition by the British fleet. Now the very same fleet had brought us here as fugitives, craving admission. So we were all left in the hold of the *Ocamo*, where the subtle aroma of the now fully matured cheese mingled with the delicate slum fragrance wafted across from the Golden Horn. And, of course, we had all not been able to wash for a month, were sleeping in our clothes on the luggage, some people had been seasick, and the sanitary facilities of a small antiquated cargo ship were quite inadequate, not to mention the ship's rats and their deposits.

129

Incredibly, there was no infection of any kind. Yet, how infinitely lucky and privileged we were, compared with the unfortunates left behind on the quaysides of Sebastopol, Odessa, Novorossísk and, later, Baku. We had almost shared their fate had the British admiral not sent, at the last moment, the *Ocamo* which he probably had kept in reserve.

Fortunately, the traders of Constantinople saw to it that we did not starve. The *Ocamo* was all the time surrounded by small boats offering bread, hard-boiled eggs and cooked chickens (in less than immaculate condition). No-one was allowed on board or ashore, but a brisk trade was going on, with baskets being lowered on ropes with the money, and the food coming up, sometimes with the change. Father, without experience of this type of commerce, generally managed to bring us some food. People who had no money (and there were some) stayed hungry.

After three weeks some officials came on board and stamped our passports. We had received the *visa*, that twentieth-century achievement that was to plague us for the rest of our lives. We took leave of the good ship *Ocamo* that had brought us to safety, and were disembarked with our luggage miraculously still complete and deposited with us on the quayside. I have no knowledge as to what happened to the cheese.

We *had* been evacuated and it was now every man for himself. Constantinople was, naturally, overcrowded, but Father managed to find two rooms at the Grand Hotel, or a Grand Hotel (I believe, there were several), with *ormolu* clocks on the mantelpiece and bugs in the bed. He also found the branch of a major French bank that was still changing 'Kérensky money', and acquired a bank account with a small capital of French francs, the principal currency in use in Constantinople at the time. Unfortunately, as the bank was changing the money with a considerable discount Father only changed part of it, and was later left with a quantity of worthless Russian currency. He also discovered that the best place to stay at were the Princes Islands (now Kizil Adalar) in the Sea of Marmara; a paddle steamer was going out there every morning and returning in the evening. Mother was by now quite ill—the last month did not do her much good—so Father went alone and, most successfully, hired a villa on Prinkipo, the principal island (now Büyükada). Again, Aunt Helène and Uncle Jacques joined us.

The villa had belonged to a Greek professor (Constantinople and the whole area had still, at the time, the character of a Greek country occupied by the Turks until the one and a half million Greeks were all expelled in 1923), and his widow was only too glad to let the house and earn some money. So we all took the next steamer and moved into the villa, leaving the squalor of Constantinople behind. It was quite a handsome building, smaller than the one in the Crimea but of classical proportions, standing on high ground in an extensive garden overgrown with poppies (I do not think they were opium poppies as they were red, and opium poppies are, I believe, white). The raised ground floor of the villa, with a terrace with superb views in front, was one vast marble-floored and marble-pillared hall, with a many-tiered chandelier with real candles (there was no electricity, of course, no piped water and no sewerage). There were five or six bedrooms on the first floor. No bed bugs, to our pleasant surprise, though vicious mosquitoes.

From the terrace one could see, in the distance, the powerful squadron of the Mediterranean Fleet, riding at anchor in the Marmara Sea, headed by the dreadnought *The Iron Duke*, with its characteristic twin, or tripod, mast. Perhaps the squadron was at the same anchorage off San Stefano whence the victorious Russian army had been stopped at the gates of Constantinople in 1877. But now they had saved us. Although I was only ten, it was clear to me that the man who commanded those grey ships with their menacing guns was the real ruler of this area.

The garden contained a separate kitchen building, a lavatory with holes in the ground, Turkish baths that required heating, and—unusually—a library into which the widow moved (the books had been sold). She spoke, like all educated people in Turkey (and that meant, at the time, Greeks, Armenians and Jews), fluent French, so that there were no language difficulties, and she also helped us finding a Greek cook and a Turkish maid, and, generally, starting a household. Prinkipo had a small sephardic[1] synagogue, built and decorated in the Moorish style, which we occasionally visited for the Friday evening service.

Mother had to lie down a lot, and Marie Ivanovna did most of the organising, helped by Aunt Helène. Perhaps, from her frequent childhood stays on her aunt's estate, Marie Ivanovna was more used to this style of country living. The boiler in the bath-house was lit, and we all had hot Turkish baths and cleaned ourselves up.

Before leaving Constantinople we had bought, with some difficulty, various items from the shops to set up a household: blankets, bed- and table-linen, pots and pans, cutlery, as well as tins of condensed milk and bully beef, and biscuits. Everything, from blankets to biscuits, had curious markings, a broad arrow or letters such as WD or RN. Only twenty years later, when working on government contracts in London, did I understand the meaning of these symbols: everything we had bought at exorbitant prices, originated from British government stocks, there being no other sources of supply in Constantinople at the time.

Mother was now very ill and clearly needed the attention of a reliable gynaecologist, but none was available. There was a rather good British military hospital, as it happened, on our island, but it was for men only.

Father went to town once or twice a week on the steamer to find out what was happening in Russia and to try to bring our affairs into some order. His main concern was to obtain a *visa* for us to go to Western Europe, France or England. Before the war one just bought tickets and went wherever one wanted to, but now a visa was required. We were no longer welcome visitors but unwanted refugees, and had to get used to our new status.

Visas for the West were issued by the *Bureau Interaillié des Passeports*, on which, as I recall, Britain, France and Italy were represented. There were now several hundred thousand Russian refugees in Constantinople, with no foreseeable prospect of a return to their homeland. On the other hand, the Western Powers were trying to rebuild their shattered economies and were conscious of the need for employment opportunities to the servicemen returning to 'civvy street'. And all had elections to contend with. True, quite a proportion of the refugees were actual combatants who had fought with the Allies, and in 1914 the Russian Army undoubtedly saved France, at an appalling cost to itself. But, as the Russian saying goes: *svoyá rubáshka bleezhe k télu*—one's own shirt is nearer to one's skin. So the principal brief of the Bureau seemed to be to *deny* the refugees access to the West. In fairness, I believe former combatants did receive some priority for entry into France, and many others were accepted by Yugoslavia, Serbia's successor, remembering 1914. Civilian refugees like us were just told we had to wait. Mother's need for medical treatment did not interest the Bureau at all. If only she had, five years earlier, bought that hotel share at Montreux we would have had a visa for Switzerland in no time. There was, of course, not the slightest possibility of earning one's living in Constantinople (although, I believe, one Russian refugee opened a successful restaurant which, now at Ankara, is still going strong), and everybody's money was running out.

Father was sending frantic cables to the shipping agents, fortunately a British firm in London, regarding the Siberian furs, and in the end it transpired that the consignment was, miraculously, undamaged, had crossed the Pacific and was in a warehouse in San Francisco, awaiting cargo space for London. As Father would know, merchant shipping was in very short supply, and it might take a very long time. The furs could not be sold in San Francisco as there were no inspection facilities and no-one would buy such a cargo unseen.

Sad news from home

In the meantime, out of the blue, Uncle Isaac appeared at Prinkipo. He, the former private, had been a volunteer with General Deníkin and was evacuated by the British from Novorossísk. By chance, he found out our whereabouts in Constantinople. He had a sad tale to tell; while he was with

the White Army his wife and child were staying somewhere in Kiev, with
his parents-in-law, when, after the Germans had left, all were murdered in
an anti-Jewish *pogróm*, by Black Hundreds, or similar thugs, either
nominally under General Deníkin, or, more likely, under Petlýura, or under
no-one in particular. The news from Mogilév was also very bad: Uncle Leo
had been arrested by the Bolsheviks as a 'banker' and sent to forced labour,
building a canal in the frozen North, one of Lenin's pet projects. True,
Uncle Leo's excursion into banking was as short-lived as it was disastrous,
but that made no difference: bankers were right at the top of Lenin's list of
'insects'. Reports filtered back that Uncle Leo, mercifully, had died after a
few weeks in the Arctic forced-labour camp. The faithful Alexei had been
shot by the Chekists when protesting against Uncle Leo's arrest. Alexei's
widow had returned to her native village, and the other servants had to do
the same. Grandparents had been left alone in the vast house, so far
unmolested. Grandfather's bank account had been confiscated, of course,
and the Czarist loans in which Grandfather kept most of his capital
were worthless.

Father was very sad, particularly about the fate of his elder brother, also
because he could do nothing to help his parents.

Uncle Isaac, now a widower, had no money, the flourishing factory at
Saratov which he had founded had been expropriated and he had had no
chance of salvaging anything. Whatever money he had, naturally he gave to
his wife before volunteering. Uncle Isaac stayed with us, of course, pump-
ing the water from the well, churning the meagre milk to butter, filling the
bath-house boiler with buckets of water from the well, lugging the logs to the
bath-house, lighting the boiler and doing similar household chores. I myself
was not privy to our worries, though I could see that Mother was ill. Marie
Ivanovna continued to give me regular tuition in all subjects, in spite of her
preoccupation with the household arrangements. My sister, who was growing up, was learning to read and write.

In order to teach us how to put pen to paper and express our thoughts
coherently, Marie Ivanovna, who had very advanced pedagogical ideas,
also started a periodical to which I, as well as our two Moscow cousins
Grisha and Luba (who were also at Prinkipo) and even my sister, had to
contribute essays depicting our life in the Crimea, the adventurous flight,
and now life on Prinkipo. There were, of course, no duplicating facilities,
and the periodical was assiduously copied by hand by Mother, Uncle Isaac
and Aunt Helène, and copies sent to Uncle Matthew in London, and other
relatives who had managed to escape from the Bolsheviks. Altogether, I
seem to remember, some seven issues were produced, though none
have survived.

I had a complete set of Russian school textbooks for the lower forms, and these included a *chrestomathy* with passages every schoolboy was expected to know. There was a short story by Nemirovich-Danchenko, 'The Red Lantern', a true story, I believe. A ganger, finding the track damaged by a landslide, stops the approaching Trans-Siberian Express by slashing his wrists, soaking his shirt with the blood and draping the red cloth round his lantern placed on the track. The express was stopped. The ganger died.

It always seemed to me that the type of quiet, undramatic heroism praised in this story was a very Russian one (similar to Ivan Susanin's self-sacrifice in 'A Life for the Czar'). In France, the ganger would have rushed to meet the train and thrown himself dramatically into its path. In England, the ganger would have improvised something which would make an English train driver (but no other) understand that something was very wrong and stop to investigate. In Germany, the Reichsbahnoberbezirksgleisüberwachungsdirektor would have been taken to court for criminal negligence in not issuing the ganger with a signalling lamp. In quite a few other countries the ganger would panic and run away, leaving the express to crash.

Aunt Olga, Mother's elder sister (with the *Empire* furniture) also appeared in Constantinople. She and her little son, my cousin Simon, had stayed on in the Caucasus after Lenin's coup, and spent the winter there. Next year, when the Bolsheviks broke through, she had to cross the Red Army lines sitting on top of a haycart disguised as a peasant woman, with her boy, and they were finally evacuated from Novorossísk by the British. My Uncle, the stockbroker, managed to escape from Moscow, via Kiev, with a lot of money to Berlin (which was quite unusual and generally impossible), where Aunt Olga and my cousin would be joining him. One of Mother's cousins in Moscow, however, fell a victim of the Bolsheviks; on the occasion of a house-search Red Guards arrested her when she was ill in bed with pneumonia and transported her for interrogation in an open van in deep winter; although she was returned home soon, she died shortly afterwards. In the meantime, further grim news had come from Mogilév. Rationing had been introduced, and Lenin decreed that only those who 'worked' or, if over a certain age, had 'worked', were entitled to ration cards. *Burzhúys* were therefore not entitled to ration cards. Most people thus condemned to starvation were selling their furniture or bartering it against food. The peasants were quite willing to give half a dozen eggs for a chair, or a chicken for a dining-room table. To Grandfather it was inconceivable for a Schmerling to stand in the marketplace selling sticks of his own furniture. And he refused to eat anything which he suspected the former servants had brought Grandmother (they did). In the end he died of starvation. Schmerling House had been confiscated and some Bolshevik office was established there. Grandmother went to live with her relations at Chernígov. What thirty-five years of Temporary Regulations and *pogróms* had failed to achieve, the Bolsheviks had attained in two years. The Schmerlings of Mogilév had been destroyed. Only the gravestones of past generations remained in the Jewish cemetery (*they* would be destroyed in the carcharinid frenzy of the National Socialists some twenty years later).

Uncle Isaac

In the meantime Uncle Isaac received a *visa* from the French under some scheme for ex combattants and, I believe, even an assisted passage, and found himself in Paris, still without money. He wanted to start a chemical factory, as he had done so successfully at Sarátov, but no bank would give a stranger a totally unsecured loan. There were new plastics now—the best place would be where the oil arrived, as it did at Sarátov. Le Havre, perhaps, or Marseilles. Marseilles would be better, as the oil came from Mesopotamia and he could go to Nics for the weekends. Nice . . .. Uncle Issac had now no family to look after, and life was not worth living as a newspaper-seller or night-club pianist, strumming *Black Eyes* for the entertainment of *nouveaux riche* patrons and their ladies. Uncle Isaac pawned, or sold, his gold watch and chain, gold cigarette case, the famed *cabochon* emerald cufflinks, and took the *Train Bleu* overnight to Nice, as he had done so often before the war. At Nice he checked in at the Negresco on the Promenade des Anglais. The manager recognised him but seemed none too pleased; Russian refugees now often stayed on credit, waiting for some money that never came, and then found that they could not pay the bill. However, Uncle Isaac paid for one day in advance, had a rest and a meal, and strolled in the Park until opening time. He entered the Casino as soon as the doors opened. It had not changed at all. *Faites vos jeux*, exclaimed the Levantine croupier, and Uncle Isaac took a note from the wad of hundred-franc notes which were all he had in this world and placed it by a black number on the green table. *Rien ne va plus* declared the Levantine. The roulette spun. A red number had won. Uncle Isaac repeated the process according to a system he had tried before. But it was not his day, and the red seemed to win all the time. After some hours, Uncle Isaac was a pauper. He bowed, walked out into the park and took out his service revolver. A shot rang out.

Suffering in Russia

The Russian people, ordinary people, suffered terribly from the Bolshevik terror, the Civil War and its aftermath. In the Civil War towns and villages changed hands several times, often with house-to-house fighting. There was a complete breakdown of agriculture, of transport, of all essential services.

There was no food and no fuel. Lenin's town-bred commissars requisitioned the seedcorn. In Moscow's winter, people lived in their totally unheated houses or flats, huddling together for warmth in one room or even a tent of carpets in the room. Ink froze in the ink pots. In most districts, there was no fresh water, no sewerage; garbage was thrown into the street. The bath-houses were unheated and people could not have the weekly Turkish bath, obligatory in Russia since times immemorial. It was impossible to keep oneself clean. Everybody in Russia, even the most fastidious, became infected with lice. The lice spread typhus (as the rats had spread the plague in times gone by). There was a terrible typhus epidemic, a much more serious disease than typhoid, and often fatal.

In 1921, mainly at the initiative of Russian–Jewish groups in America, humanitarian relief work was organised under Herbert Hoover (later US president, 1928–33), himself a Quaker and supported by the Quakers and a large section of the American nation. Large shipments of grain, dried milk and tinned meat were sent to Russia and, with Lenin's grudging consent, an American organisation was built up in Russia to feed the hungry and, with volunteer American doctors, provide medical treatment for the starving. The centre of the relief work was the Volga region, where conditions were particularly bad. I believe that altogether ten million people were fed, medically treated and, when required, clothed. It has been estimated that in 1918–22 altogether twenty-five million people died in Russia from unnatural causes. Of these less than one million died in the actual fighting, and probably another million from the *Cheká* terror, massacres of civilians by the Red Guards, *pogróms*, and other forms of mass murder. The remaining twenty-three million, a staggering figure, died of famine, cold, and disease. One wonders whether General Ludendorff who, like a present-day Khan Janibeg, organised the *infection* of Russia, slept soundly. But he, an old hand at coups, was now busy masterminding the (unsuccessful) Hitler 'Munich Beer Cellar' coup of 1923.

A letter from Barclay's Bank

In the meantime we were living on our island, with its equable climate, in perfect safety, with enough to eat, in the marble-floored and marble-pillared villa. But Father was getting desperate about Mother's health, and the money was running out. Uncle Jacques and Aunt Helène, who had contributed to the household expenses, were no longer with us. Aunt Helène had a brother who had lived in London since before the war and he procured a visa for her and Uncle Jacques.   H.E. Gregory Wilenkin.

The summer of 1920 was drawing to a close when Father received a brief letter from Barclay's Bank, DCO, in London. It notified him that a sum of just over £20,000 had been placed to the credit of his account by the shipping agents. The furs had arrived in London and been sold at the auctions. For Britain and Western Europe the war was over (or so it was thought). People replenished their wardrobes and, as owing to the Civil War no furs had been exported from Siberia for some years, prices were very good: £20,000 was, in those days, quite a tidy sum—worth, perhaps, half a million pounds today.

Father wasted no time and the next morning saw him in Constantinople. The Bureau Intcrallié said, yes, now that Father had visible means of support in London a visa to the West could be granted. But, of course, a visa could only be granted to the holder of a valid passport, on which it could be stamped. As Father no doubt knew, the Czarist passports had been declared invalid by the Soviets, who were now the legal government of Russia. Father did not know. We were now stateless persons, a new development in the history of Europe; hitherto, one always had a sovereign, good or bad, and was his subject. Somehow, Father found out that the Dutch, always humanitarian, were generally prepared to help in such cases and he called at the Netherlands Consulate.

LE CONSULAT DES PAYS BAS
à
Constantinople
prie et requiest au nom de SA MAJESTE LA REINE DES
PAYS BAS toutes les autorités tant civiles que militaires
des Princes & Etats, Amis & Alliés de Sa Majesté non
seulement de laisser passer
le sujet russe Schmerling, Boris, fils de Moise, negotiant,
se rendant en France et Angleterre par voie de mer,
avec ses bagages, mais aussi de lui donner ou faire donner,
au besoin, toute aide et secours.

It was the temporary passport, couched in French, the international diplomatic language, issued to Father. Armed with this impressive foolscap document, surmounted by the Netherlands coat of arms, Father just managed to makc the Bureau before closing-time and received the precious visa, stamped on the Royal Netherlands passport.

Father then called at the French Line, which had restarted a weekly service to Marseilles, and booked second-class passages for us on the next steamer, sailing in two days' time. In the evening, he returned triumphant to Prinkipo.

The next day must have been as hurried as when we were leaving Moscow, or the Crimea, but no-one threatened our life.

In 1929 the abominable Bronstein, as Father used to call him, himself arrived at Prinkipo, now a stateless exile. Someone told us, he thought Trotsky had settled in our villa. But *his* wife was not dying.

I do not remember much about the 2500-mile trip through the length of the Mediterranean. The boat was of a few thousand tons; similar to those crossing the North Sea from Harwich to the Hook. I was by now used to destroyers with chocolates, immobilised battleships, ageing tramps and antique paddle steamers and do not even recall the name of the French boat. The voyage was no more exciting than a tram ride. I suppose my parents were most grateful for that. We sailed in the evening, so that I missed seeing the Dardanelles, that most historic of all straits. We ran into a storm off Crete, and sailed through the Straits of Messina, though I do not recall seeing the Scylla rock. Probably no-one pointed it out to me; this was not a sightseeing cruise.

Note

1   The Sephardim were largely the descendants of the Jews expelled from Spain (together with the Muslims), for reasons of religious intolerance, in 1492 (and a few years later from Portugal), who found refuge in the Ottoman Empire from North Africa and the Balkans to Mesopotamia.

11

With the Victors

On the eighth day of our voyage, in the morning, we docked at Marseilles. I remember Father, in the PLM Railway Company's Gare Maritime, buying, in his best French, second-class tickets to Paris. In the evening we were in the metropolis and checked in at a comparatively modest hotel in the rue Mont Thabor.

The fratricidal and suicidal war had been won, at a cost of ten million dead and twenty million wounded, on both sides. The statues of Alsace and Lorraine at the Place de la Concorde were undraped; sixteen German battleships and battle cruisers, eight cruisers and fifty destroyers lay, surrendered and scuttled, at the bottom of Scapa Flow. The German colonies were surrendered and distributed among Great Britain, France, South Africa, Australia, New Zealand, and Japan. Brest-Litovsk, which would have made Germany, even in defeat, the greatest power in Europe, was dead and the German troops had pulled out of their would-be East European empire. Peace treaties had been concluded with Germany (at the Palace of Versailles, where the Reich had been founded by Bismarck in 1871), Austria (at St Germain-en-Laye), Hungary (at the Trianon in Versailles), Turkey (at SeAvres), and Bulgaria (at Neuilly). The map of Europe had been redrawn, Poland re-created and new states created: Czechoslovakia, Yugoslavia, as well as, carved from prostrate Russia, Finland and the three Baltic mini-states. The eastern and northern provinces of France were in ruins. The French people were exhausted.

Death of Mother

Within a few days of our arrival Mother was examined by a leading gynaecologist who diagnosed cancer, as suspected. The tumour was quite

139

advanced and the operation was at least six months overdue. The gynaecologist could not predict the outcome. Mother moved into the professor's clinic at Neuilly where the operation was carried out. She died shortly afterwards, thirty-six years of age, one more of Lenin's twenty-five million victims. I was eleven, and my sister eight. Father was shattered. In a year he had lost his father, his two brothers, two sisters-in-law and now our Mother.

Uncle Matthew, a widower too, came over from London and managed to see his favourite sister before the operation. He also completed all formalities and made the funeral arrangements; Father was too stricken. The clinic's death certificate, Uncle Matthew noticed, gave cardiac arrest as the cause of death: technically, no doubt, correct. Uncle Matthew checked with the professor. The professor was astounded. 'In France,' he said, 'we always give cardiac arrest as the cause in *such cases*, otherwise, the little girl's marriage prospects would be damaged.'

The funeral was at Montparnasse Cemetery, in the Jewish section, where Uncle Matthew had purchased a *concession perpetuelle*. He also placed a notice in the *Poslédniya Novósti*, the Russian emigrés' daily newspaper then appearing in Paris. No-one was expected at the funeral except us. But over twenty strangers came to pay their last respects—they were all people whom Mother had helped, at one time or another.

While Mother was at the clinic, where Father also spent his days with her, Marie Ivanovna, at Father's request, found a furnished flat for us in the freshly renamed Avenue du President Wilson, near the Pont de l'Alma. The flat was actually the town apartment of a French count who had married a Russian noblewoman (of somewhat plain appearance, I believe). As the remittances from her estates no longer came, they moved permanently to the Count's chateau, and were glad to let the apartment. Marie Ivanovna took charge of the household with her usual efficiency, and a French maid, Blanche, was engaged (who often mitigated Marie Ivanovna's loving but strict approach to our education).

On Mother's death, according to Jewish custom, the satin-lined, gilded chairs were removed from the Countess's salon, cushions placed on the floor for a week, and everybody sat on them for the best part of the day, Father almost continuously, others frequently. Some of the unknown mourners also came. Not a word was ever spoken. The memorial candle had been lit and would be kept burning for a year. After that, it would be my duty as the eldest (and only) son to light it every year on the anniversary of Mother's death (also, of course, of Father's death when it would occur). After a few weeks of shock, Father recovered sufficiently to start thinking about the future. He had to see to our upbringing and education and to earn money for it. Father decided to go to London and to organise a business exporting textiles to the old Poverkhovsky customers in the string of states carved out of the former western region of Russia. London was the centre of textile trading, Father's money was there, and he expected some co-operation and introduction, if not participation, from Uncle Matthew. In London, Father took a small room at the De Vere Hotel in Kensington, then, as now, a good-class medium-priced family hotel. From time to time Father came over to see us in Paris, and I remember him complaining how ruinously expensive London was: his room at the De Vere was costing one pound a day. He also had a small two-room office in an old office building at Moorgate, and travelled to the various centres in the former Russian western region, from Riga to Warsaw, to re-establish contacts with former customers. All these countries were reconstructing, urgently requiring manufactured goods, and for a year or two the business developed quite well.

Whilst in London Father never forgot us in Paris, sent a postcard every week and came over every few months. He knew, of course, that he could fully trust Marie Ivanovna with us. To save having to go out and buy the weekly picture postcard for us Father bought a series of twenty-four—if I remember rightly—postcards depicting all the details of the Albert Memorial, and so, after half a year, I was fully conversant with all the features of this Gothic monument.

In London, Father also found time, with the help of some business associates in the City, to put my name down for Harrow School. I have the greatest admiration for this school—the *alma mater* of Winston Churchill and of so many famous personages from Palmerston to Leo Amery, from the murdered King Faisal II of Iraq to King Hussein of Jordan. But somehow I feel I personally would not have fitted in, and quite possibly have grown up there hating all established order—a revolutionary. So it is, perhaps, just as well, that my enrolment never came about.

At the Lycée

I had, however, been accepted by the Lycée Janson de Sailly, near our flat in Paris, and was going there daily. This was the first time I had gone to school and was quite happy there. There were no games (which I always disliked) and very good tuition. Particular attention was paid to mastery of the French language, and the subtle shades of meaning of words. As homework we were given a word, say *gourmet*, and had to find all its approximate synonyms (I believe there are ten) and explain in writing the slight differences between *glouton and gourmand*. Marie Ivanovna, and even Blanche, helped and I spent hours at the public library consulting dictionaries and encyclopedias. This training in vocabulary helped me a great deal later when learning other languages, particularly as the tuition I received in Russian letters was directed mainly towards composition, as demanded by the Russian curriculum at the time.

The Lycée gave us quite a lot of summer-holiday homework, and this included the drawing of some object of a classical character, a vase, perhaps, or a bust. I chose a punchbowl from the Countess's silver plate, which had the Count's initials BM engraved in a huge monogram. When I unveiled my *chef d'oeuvre* at the Lycée there was a roar of laughter: it transpired that BM was the well-known cypher of that popular store, the Bon Marché.

Perfect discipline was maintained at the Lycée. The boys knew that their careers with the Civil Service and in private enterprise depended on the marks and assessments they would receive on their school-leaving certificate, and no-one wanted to finish his life as a clerk or navvy. Any kind of corporal punishment was, of course, entirely out of question, as it was in Russia. Characteristically, in my class only the son of a French millionaire once caused a minor disturbance, knowing that Papa would find him an agreeable job anyway—he was ·expelled. Another incentive to good behaviour and scholastic achievement was the *Tableau d'Honneur*, on which the names of the best pupils were entered and a special certificate issued (I still have mine); here again, the certificates greatly improved career prospects and all boys vied with each other to get on the *Tableau*. At the end of term-book prizes were given to the best pupil in a subject of each class: the prize-giving was a public ceremony in the town hall or similar building, in the presence of the Mayor and various academic dignitaries, and, of course, all parents. The lists of prize-winners were published in the press, and I still hold the copy of the august *Le Temps* with my name included in it. The Lycée's prize-giving, incidentally, was in the Trocadero, the original Trocadero, a public building (since demolished) so named in honour of the French victory in Spain, near Cadiz, in 1823.

The Russian refugees

There were now over a million Russian refugees scattered around the globe, homeless and stateless, from western Europe to the Argentine and Chile; from North America to Harbin in Manchuria and the caves of Dunhuang in Chinese Turkestan. Broadly speaking, the refugees represented the cream of the Russian nation.

Over a hundred thousand 'insects' were still trapped in Constantinople. Their position was desperate; they had no money, no possibility of earning a living and were being harassed by the Turkish authorities. People lived in the open, in streets and under bridges, begging and stealing. Constantinople was the kind of city, like so many in Asia today, where people died in the street and the police collected the dead every morning. *Ad hoc* committees were formed in London and New York to do something about it. Uncle Matthew was asked by one of the London committees to go to Constantinople and report on the situation. He travelled on the Orient Express, now re-established, at his own expense, second class, and met representatives of various refugee groups there. One of the first callers at the hotel was Fungus, down-at-heel and shabby, representing no-one but himself. He hoped that the minor misunderstanding over Uncle Matthew's call-up had been forgotten. From Moscow he had brought a completely worthless cinema film which he wanted Uncle Matthew to buy. Uncle Matthew declined the film, but 'loaned' Fungus a hundred francs, I believe. But for the furs, *we* would have been in the same position as *he*.

The immediate problem was that all refugees were now 'stateless' and could not move anywhere without travel documents. In the end the various help committees achieved the calling of an intergovernmental conference in Geneva, under the chairmanship of Fridtjof Nansen, the great Norwegian polar explorer and humanitarian. The conference agreed that all the participating governments would issue the stateless Russian refugees with an identity document (known as the 'Nansen Passport') which did not provide an automatic right of abode but made it possible for the owner to travel, and use the document on the innumerable occasions when proof of identity was required in daily life. We too received our 'Nansen Passports' some time, I believe, in 1923. In Russian refugee circles Nansen was revered almost as a saint. An International Nansen Office was permanently installed in Geneva to deal with refugee questions.

Uncle Matthew's family

Uncle Matthew managed to bring with him Aunt Amalia's fabulous jewellery. This was many times more valuable than Mother's and, moreover, none of it had been surrendered to the Bolsheviks. Although worth a fortune, the jewellery was not ostentatious, as Aunt Amalia was always perfectly dressed and her jewellery was in keeping with her style of clothing—*chic*, in great taste, and never vulgar. On arrival in London, after Aunt Amalia's death from typhus in Petersburg, Uncle Matthew unwisely pawned the jewellery, rather than selling it, because at that time it was generally thought that the Bolsheviks would be beaten, as they very nearly were (and would have been had not Britain and France abandoned Russia), and he would return to Moscow and redeem the jewellery for his daughters. Even by pawning, Uncle Matthew obtained a large sum of money, certainly more than Father's £20,000, Father used to say.

Expecting to return to Moscow soon, Uncle Matthew set up a comfortable household with his four children in Kensington Gore, in a large furnished flat in the Mansions past the Albert Hall, and tried to organise some business. Father used to say that Uncle Matthew gave several luncheon parties at the Piccadilly Hotel, at that time apparently fashionable, to various businessmen and financiers in the City; the luncheons always ended with Crème Poverkhovsky, a special ice cream desert created in Moscow by Aunt Amalia's cook. The City men came, some titled, some non-titled, some Jewish, some non-Jewish, and consumed Uncle Matthew's smoked salmon and Crème Poverkhovsky, but in the end no business materialised. In the meantime, the Soviets had opened a trading office in London—I seem to remember that it was called Arcos or something similar. As they met with much political resistance—Sir Henry Deterding of Shell quite correctly proclaimed the oil the Soviets were trying to sell as 'stolen'—the Soviets offered Uncle Matthew an agency, or directorship, to obtain respectability, but he indignantly refused, although financially near the end of his tether.

The money was going at an alarming rate. However, Uncle Matthew did manage to give his two sons a good education: one of my cousins graduated at Imperial College as an engineer; the other a BA at Cambridge. Then the money all but ran out. Uncle Matthew closed the Kensington establishment and went to Warsaw where he gained possession of the Poverkhovsky branch-office building and warehouse and tried to revive the firm. However, nothing came of it. The family name meant something to the older generation but did not generate business. Warsaw was not a congenial place for Uncle Matthew, and in the end—this saved his life—he retired to Paris, whereto most Russian refugees finally gravitated, and settled down in a tiny flat in greatly reduced circumstances, like most Russian refugees, devoting his time to various Russian emigré charitable causes. He had not managed, like Father, to cut his coat according to his cloth in time, and preserve his small capital.

My two cousins did reasonably well but both came to a tragic end. James, the engineer, thanks to one of Uncle Matthew's pre-war connections obtained a very responsible, though onerous, position as European technical representative of a major US manufacturer. Unfortunately, cousin James contracted meningitis and died of this disease, fatal before the age of antibiotics. Alexander, the Cambridge BA, settled down as a stockbroker in Paris, specialising in 'Anglo-Saxon' securities. He had a great personal admiration for the murdered Czar, Nicholas II, whom he considered ill-used by the Empress and ill-advised by misguided or inept or self-seeking courtiers. A large portrait of the Czar hung in his room, and my cousin also supported a Russian emigré monarchist organisation. He was later murdered by the Gestapo. The two plucky girls also soon earned their living: my elder cousin by travelling twice a year to New York and selling Paris *haute couture* models to a very exclusive clientele—this was before the jet age—and as a journalist; and my younger cousin (after staying with Aunt Helène at Nice and finishing at the lycée there) as a ~~quadrilingual~~ interpreter and translator.

bilingual!

12

In Defeated Germany

For a year or two Father's export business in London went quite well, but then he found that Germany started manufacturing again and owing to the German inflation and depreciation of the mark, their goods were considerably cheaper and it was no longer possible to export from Britain to the Baltic. The Poles too had resumed their manufacture at Lodz, and could supply goods very cheaply. For a while, Father ran the business in a triangular way, going to places like Chemnitz (at present, for some reason, Karl Marx Stadt) in Saxony for buying, then to the mini-states for selling and returning to London via Paris. These arrangements were quite expensive and could not be sustained by the modest size of the operation. Father was determined not to live on capital, which he now knew to be irreplaceable, as the Bolsheviks would obviously rule the unfortunate Russian people for a while. So he decided that we should all move to Germany, where he also knew the language better, and he would conduct his business from there. Exports were much desired in Germany, as the Reich was desperately short of foreign currency to buy much-needed food, cereals, meat, edible oil and raw materials for re-starting German industry. Father was therefore granted an entry visa and temporary residence permit in Berlin, which for stateless persons was very difficult to obtain, as there was nowhere a civilised country could deport a stateless person to in case of need. So at the end of 1922 we moved to Berlin. This city, never a Paris, or London, or Vienna, was now at its most depressing. The Germans, who had been told by General Ludendorff as late as 1918 that their Army was invincible, were now bewildered and demoralised. The great victory in the east that was to have secured grain, meat and edible oil from the Ukraine and mineral oil from Baku vanished like a mirage. Hyperinflation was rampant,

146

and the value of the mark sometimes halved overnight. On pay-day, people *ran* with their pay-packets to the baker and butcher to buy food before the price went up, which was often twice a day. People's savings were wiped out. As always in such situations, 'spivs' appeared, known as *Schieber*, who made fortunes. Most were non-Jewish. Some were Jews. Some even foreign Jews. These attracted attention. The *nouveaux riche* (personified by the fictional Frau Raffke) were strident and offensive, particularly when viewed against the background of general misery.

There was a great shortage of housing, and all vacant accommodation (mostly apartments: in Berlin there were hardly any family houses) was requisitioned by a special authority of the socialist-dominated city council, the *Wohnungsamt*, that allocated the flats only to persons on their housing list. Ex-service men naturally came first; foreigners, including stateless persons, were not entitled to be placed on the housing list. People not on the housing list were permitted, if they were wealthy enough, to build themselves new accommodation (for instance, a penthouse suite), and a handful of refugees who had managed to salvage a larger share of their former wealth did just that. Naturally, it put them even more in the public eye. Most people probably thought the money for the penthouse suite had not been brought into Germany but earned in Germany by illicit activities.

There was, not unnaturally, a lot of xenophobia about. People were starving, and blamed the foreigners. Few understood that they were paying for the war. Russian refugees—especially, but not exclusively, Jews—were particularly disliked. The authorities were rather hostile; whilst one did not expect the German Government to admit publicly that the refugees were there because of the upheaval caused by the German High Command in Russia, the authorities might have been more sympathetic. I remember how nervous Father was every year when our strictly annual residence permit had to be extended on a personal visit to the *Polizeipräsidium* at the Alexander Platz (presumably named in honour of Alexander I). Although Father was always and everywhere scrupulously law-abiding one never quite knew what the outcome would be. Fortunately, an agent sprung up (they always do), an ex-policeman, who for a modest fee prepared the ground for the interview, filled in all the forms and was permitted to accompany his clients to the interview in the rather forbidding surroundings; it was generally thought among refugees that if one had not blotted one's copybook in any way the agent's assistance more or less guaranteed extension of the residence permit. What exactly the arrangements were between the agent and the underpaid clerks at the *Polizeipräsidium*, with their white celluloid collars, I do not know; Father thought that the clerks had no more than a box of cheap Sumatra cigars at Christmas, and mainly appreciated the fact that the agent ensured a correctly completed form.

Father had secured for us three furnished rooms in Wilmersdorf, sublet by a now impoverished widow, *mit Küchenbenutzung*, which meant that the maid engaged by Marie Ivanovna would share the kitchen with the widow. The *Wohnungsamt* did not permit the subletting of self-contained apartments. This arrangement invariably led to friction; however, owing to Marie Ivanovna's tactful firmness we managed tolerably well, and Marie Ivanovna even saved the widow from a suicide attempt.

I was accepted by the Hohenzollern *Oberrealschule*, a secondary modern school in Schöneberg. The school fees in Germany were as high as in France (or in Russia), but Father naturally found them. The school, government-owned as were all schools in Germany (and in France, and all boy's schools in Russia) was very instructive, and in style and curriculum broadly similar to the French lycée. However, whereas in language teaching in Russia the accent was on imaginative essays, and in France on vocabulary, in Germany it was on narrative. Here again, perfect discipline was maintained without any corporal punishment, though one or two more temperamental teachers permitted themselves an occasional and immediate cuff on the ear (something entirely ruled out in Russia or France— in both countries it would have led to dismissal of the teacher) in cases of wanton insolence. Here too, the boys were motivated in their good behaviour by career prospects, and also, perhaps because the school was in a lower middle-class area, they appreciated their parents' sacrifice in paying for the school (the Lycée in Paris was in the wealthy XVIth *arrondissement*). It was quite difficult for a foreigner to be accepted, and the school, Father found, was some distance from our rooms, so I went by tram each day, taking a packet of sandwiches with me (school meals had not yet been invented). I also carried a cardboard shoebox stuffed with bank notes—my tram fare, towards the end of 1923 fifty thousand million marks. In the end, the German government succeeded in stabilising the currency, one new mark (initially Rentenmark, later Reichsmark) being one million million old marks. The tramfare became again five pfennigs. The traditional middle class, backbone of the established liberal order, had been wiped out. I well understand why, even today, the inflation rate in Germany, although not negligible, is so low. The horror of hyperinflation (worse even than unemployment), into which 'ordinary' inflation slides very easily, has not been forgotten.

With the end of inflation Father's export business to the East came to an end. German manufacturers could no longer compete with Lodz, which was also geographically better placed. We now seemed to be settled in Germany (or so Father thought) and Father transferred the £18,000 or so which he had kept in London to Germany, and invested in real estate and securities. Had he invested a year earlier he would have become a millionaire, but he had been caught with worthless Kérensky currency before and was very careful. Even after the currency reform, though, real estate prices were depressed, because there was very little income—if any—from real estate, owing to the punitive 40 per cent *Hauszinssteuer* rate, based on *gross* rent income (this in addition to income tax).

The German recovery

After the currency-stabilisation and the realistic settlement of the reparations question with the Dawes Plan at the London Conference of 1924 German industry recovered and expanded and the German economy flourished. Under the guidance of Gustav Stresemann, as Foreign Minister, Germany became a prosperous country again, admitted into the League of Nations and, because of its strong economy, of increasing influence in world affairs.

Our own position improved gradually too. The requisitioning of accommodation had been eased and was finally abolished, and we moved first to a part of a larger flat where we had our own kitchen and then to a self-contained furnished flat in Friedenau. The return on Father's investments also improved, and we lived tolerably well for refugees. Father managed to pay for our education, though holidays were, of course, out of the question. Perhaps I should have said, holiday travel: naturally, we had our school holidays which we spent at home. And, of course, we never went to the theatre, or opera, or a concert, or smoked, or even bought books (except second-hand school textbooks; there was no free issue), as we knew that every pfennig had to be saved in order to afford our own home some day. This attitude is, even today in this country, typical of European refugees (and Asian immigrants). The authorities were also less hostile, and Father received the much-desired residence permit *bis auf weiteres* (until further notice). No longer had we to undergo the humiliating experience of annual extensions. Naturally, the authorities retained the right to withdraw our residence permit at any time; this seemed natural, and the penalty of being refugees. After all, Germany was not an underpopulated country, though Russian refugees could have expected some consideration by way of atonement for the crime committed by General Ludendorff and the German High Command against the Russian nation.

In spite of the general prosperity and *joie de vivre* there was a certain malaise in the air. The *panem* was now plentiful, but where were the *circenses*? The Republic had been consciously designed at Weimar, in reaction to Prussian militarism, as sober, drab and eschewing all pomp and circumstance. It was modelled on the French (Third) Republic constitution, but there were no trappings of power, no *Garde Nationale*, no *Quatorze*

Juillet parades, no *spahis*, no *zouaves*. No colour of any kind. The loss of the German colonies in Africa and the Pacific rankled—the approaching general decolonisation, accelerated by World War II, had not yet dawned. Although other countries in Europe were more densely populated than Germany there was an irrational feeling of being hemmed in, of national claustrophobia. Hans Grimm caught this mood in his novels, particularly in *Volk ohne Raum*, Nation without Space.

It was, as everywhere, a period of gay abandon after the regimentation, rigours and privations of the war period (in Germany extended another five years by the post-war collapse and inflation). The savings habit had been lost. People tried to enjoy life while the going was good. The new generation sang the worldwide popular *Schlager*, or hits, 'Yes, we have no bananas', 'Tutankhamen', 'The Girls of Java'. 'Valencia' swept the board, but when the opening bars were struck up:

> In the Hafenbar von Rio, by Laternenlicht
> Sah der rote Jim zum ersten Mal ihr Gesicht

the young men were thinking not only of that 'most beautiful of all roses to be caressed' but also of the tropical night skies with the Southern Cross they were fated never to see.

To the seekers of glamour and adventure the only opportunity was political extremism. But in 1923 the Ludendorff–Hitler Munich Beer Cellar coup had been foiled and, at the same time, a Left-wing provincial government in Saxony, of the Kerénsky (or Allende) type, allowing the Communists to prepare for the seizure of power, was forcibly deposed by the Army, on orders from central government. There remained the flourishing *Kulturbolshevismus*, Cultural Bolshevism, a coterie of journalists and literati who lampooned all traditional values and denigrated everything German. In England, such activities would be considered as belonging to the lunatic fringe, and ignored. In a Germany that had—inexplicably to its people—been defeated in war, been ravaged by hyperinflation, had lost the monarchy and had to come to terms with its new position in the world as a vanquished and impoverished Republic—in such a Germany these literary activities were a potent poison, political pornography of the worst kind. Erich Kästner (a non-Jew, who also wrote attractive children's books) sang:

> Wenn wir den Krieg gewonnen hätten
> Dann wäre Deutschland nicht zu retten
> Und gliche einem Irrenhaus
> Zum Glück gewannen wir ihn nicht.

(Should we have won the War
Germany could not have been saved
And would have become like a lunatic asylum,
Fortunately, we did not win.)

Kurt Tucholsky (a lapsed Jew) poured out from Paris an incessant stream of slow-acting poison, cleverly camouflaged, like brandy laced with arsenic. There were other Kästners and other Tucholskys, all best forgotten.

The human heart has a built-in compartment for hero-worship: with most Germans this compartment is congenitally of large size. A small section of German youth found a sublimation of their yearnings in the noteworthy poets of the period, Rainer Maria Rilke, Stefan George, Agnes Miegel, and the great epic novelists, Thomas Mann, Franz Werfel, Stefan Zweig, and many others. And particularly in the writers of heroic cast: Ernst Jünger, Werner Beumelburg, Ernst von Salomon, Walter Flex, Arnolt Bronnen. But the majority of German youth lacked a lodestar; only a few saw it in the Church, others in *erstaz* religions like Communism or Racialism.

The pornography industry had not yet appeared on the scene. There was, however, one book that cleverly combined the most virulent pseudo-scientific anti-semitism with fairly explicit—by the standards of the day—erotic passages. It was *Die Sünde wider das Blut*, The Sin against the Blood, by one Artur Dinter. Avidly read by all sixteen-year-olds, edition after edition came out (the copy I read in the 1920s was the 15th edition, I seem to remember, and there must have been many more after that), poisoning not the blood but the mind of German youth. Unlike Tucholsky, the poison here was camouflaged as an aphrodisiac.

In the meantime, Germany's unheroic but highly successful reconstruction and political rehabilitation continued. In 1927 the Allied Control Commission was withdrawn and in 1930 the Allied occupation troops left the Rhineland, and in the Young Plan reparations were further reduced and finally ended at Lausanne in 1932. What was now left of Versailles was the restriction of the army to a hundred thousand men, without tanks and heavy artillery, i.e. to a militia for maintenance of internal order, and the prohibition of warships over ten thousand tons (hence the building of the four 'pocket battleships'), and the demilitarisation of the Rhineland. And, of course, the loss of the colonies and of European territories, particularly those restored to Poland, resulting, as East Prussia remained German, in the Polish Corridor, of necessity an inelegant construction but the best one could think of. (The Soviet Union in 1945 cut the Gordian knot by incorporating East Prussia into the Soviet Union, in fact, into the Russian Federal Republic, expelling all Germans who had lived there for centuries, renaming Königsberg Kaliningrad, Insterburg Chernyakhovsk, and Tilsit

Sovietsk[1].) In 1932 the limit for the Army was increased by international agreement to two hundred and fifty thousand men.

Unfortunately, the German non-socialist Right became more and more anti-Jewish (a tendency which started with Eugen Dühring and Adolf Stöcker). Of course, they did not advocate, or intend, persecution or even legal impediments, but practised social discrimination, and Jewish members were forced out of the National Party, student fraternities, mountaineering clubs and similar organisations. The elected president of the Stahlhelm Ex-Servicemens' organisation, Dusterberg, had to resign because it was discovered that he had a Jewish grandmother. The social anti-semitism sometimes took ridiculous forms. Germany, before Hitler, never had the equivalent of America's restricted Hotels, where Jews (and other lower forms of humanity) were not welcome. But there was an entire island, Borkum, of the East Frisian chain in the North Sea, whose hoteliers decided that they wanted no Jewish visitors. This policy was well advertised and commercially quite astute, and every day the *Borkum Lied* was sung on the beach (I am quoting from memory):

> Doch wer sich naht mit flachen Fussen
> Mit schwarzem Haar und krummer Nas'
> Der soll nicht Borkum's Strand geniessen
> Der soll hinaus, hinaus, hinaus!

or

> He who approaches with flat feet[2]
> With black hair, and crooked nose
> He shall not enjoy Borkum's beach
> He should get out, out, out!

Personally, I found these antics hilarious, and used to suggest to my German–Jewish friends to let the islanders stew in their own juice—particularly as neighbouring Norderney, where Jews were welcome, was the better island. However, my friends were so thoroughly assimilated that they had acquired the somewhat tiresome German trait of pedantic *Prinzipienreiterei*, and spent an incongruous amount of time debating how to force the islanders to accept Jewish holiday guests.

The catastrophe that was to engulf German Jewry was only a dozen years away.

Germany had at that time a rather complicated, and mathematically perfect, proportional representation voting system. The candidate with most votes in a parliamentary division was elected, as in Britain; the votes of the other candidates, however, were transferred to a *Reichsliste*, or central list, of their party, where the prescribed number of votes elected the candidates on the central list, in descending order. But even for each parliamentary division, a party nominated not one candidate but a list of candidates, so that if something happened to the top candidate during the election the next on the list automatically became the candidate, and so forth rather like a proxy nomination for a shareholder's meeting. Whereas, however, the proxy nominations usually have three names it was customary for the divisional lists in Germany to carry *ten* names, just in case. It was also a way of showing appreciation to the various groups from whom support was drawn.

I remember an election at this time when the Catholic Centre Party decided to take advantage of the fact that so many Jewish people had conservative leanings, but would not vote for parties who were, at least, inimical to the Jews. So, in the Berlin division, the Centre Party placed Herr Kareski, the President of the Jewish community, as number ten on their divisional list. As the Centre Party had no chance whatsoever of winning a Berlin seat, because there were hardly any Catholics in Berlin, there was not the slightest possibility of Herr Kareski being elected to the Reichstag, even if the nine candidates in front of him had all been struck down by lightning. It was a gesture, and understood as such. But it was estimated that a third of the German Jews, most of them in Berlin, voted for the Centre Party in that election. Their votes were all transferred to the central list.

Personally, I had a happy time in Germany. As a young boy, I would not understand Father's problems and worries. I never experienced any anti-semitism on a personal level. We did not go on holidays so it made little difference to me if one particular island was out of bounds. Of course, it is possible that many of the inconveniences to which we were subjected as foreigners by the authorities were really anti-Jewish; certainly they were often waived in the case of Russian Germans.

We often went for walks in the surroundings of Berlin; a flat, sandy countryside, punctuated by numerous lakes, and fir woods here and there. It was remarkable how the names of the lakes and streams betrayed the original Slavonic settlement of the area: the Griebnitz Lake was still re-nowned for the mushrooms on its shores (in Russian *grib* means mushroom), the Liepnitz Lake was surrounded by lime trees (in Russian *lipa* means lime tree), the delightful Briese stream had birch trees on its banks (in Russian *beresa* means birch tree), and so forth. Of the place-names, however, only the oldest were Slavonic, such as Brandenburg (originally Branibor) and Potsdam (originally Poddubam, Under the Oaks). Most towns were, however, founded and named by the German Margraves (March counts) who crossed the Elbe in the twelfth century, inaugurating the German *Drang nach Osten*, or colonisation eastwards. The original March, westwards of the Elbe, became the *Altmark* (familiar as the name of the German prison-ship in World War II), and the new Marches beyond the Elbe, the *Neumark* and Mark Brandenburg. The entire area from the Elbe to the Odra had originally been inhabited by the Slavonic Sorbs (or Serbs); small linguistic islands of this submerged race were still in existence in the *Spreewald*, a fenn country east of Berlin, and in a few other areas such as Lusatia, where the Wends, as they were called, were left unmolested. It is a remarkable twist of history that the present effective border between Eastern and Western Europe corresponds to the pre-twelfth-century ethnic boundary.

In the meantime we were continuing with our very modest way of life in a furnished flat, but now self-contained. About 1930, Father's net income improved owing to more equitable taxation under a non-socialist government.

I had passed my matric, and was at that time particularly interested in heavy organic industry, particularly oils, vegetable and mineral, and saw myself as a future manager of an oil refinery, or edible-oil and margarine works. I knew, of course, that as a stateless person I had no chance of obtaining a job in German industry, and would have to emigrate to the USA or to some underdeveloped country. In fact, I had entered my name on the waiting list for a US immigration visa. Immigration into the USA was, at that time, governed by the Johnson–Lodge Act of 1924, which aimed at maintaining the ethnic composition of the population as it was then. Immigration entitlement was based on the place of birth, and each region was given a fixed quota of the total applications. For persons born in Eastern Europe the waiting time was very long indeed; I was told that it could be ten years. It depended on how many Britons and others applied, as the ratio had to be maintained. Emma Lazarus's proud words, 'Send these, the homeless, tempest-tost to me' no longer applied unrestricted to Russian refugees.

Some readers may ask whether we had thought of taking out German nationality. For Father, and Marie Ivanovna, it would have been inconceivable. We all considered nationally not simply a question of passports but of loyalty, and the insinuation of Lenin and his henchmen into Russia and the *Diktat* of Brest-Litovsk were still fresh in memory. Incidentally, I seem to remember that naturalisation in Germany required a residence time of twenty years (which for a European overcrowded non-immigration country seems quite fair); it was also known that the proposed naturalisation lists of any state government (for example, Prussia) had to be passed unanimously by the *Reichsrat*. This was not the elected *Reichstag*, but the supreme administrative council of the German Federation, on which all state governments were represented, and by that time there were one or two minor state governments which were very right-wing (in Germany automatically meaning anti-Jewish) and they always vetoed applications by Jewish persons. It was also in the Reichsrat, as I recall, where Hitler's first abortive attempt to gain German citizenship came to nought. Around 1930, a National Socialist Government came into power in Thuringia, and the National Socialist minister Frick (after 1933 Reichsminister of the Interior) appointed Hitler nightwatchman–this is no joke–because all civil servants were entitled automatically to German nationality. However, Hitler's name was spotted and it had to be withdrawn. Jewish people, incidentally, could be comparatively easily identified in German documents sometimes by their surname (change of surname was always all but impossible in Germany, as it is today in the Soviet Union), and always by their religion, which was officially shown because in Germany churches (and, before Hitler, synagogues) were supported by the *Kirchensteuer*, or church tax, which was collected by the Inland Revenue as a 10 per cent surcharge (at present, I believe, 8 per cent) on the amount of income tax payable and passed on to the taxpayer's denomination.

In the groves of academe

Enrolment at the famed Technical High School in Berlin Charlottenburg was extremely difficult for a foreigner, particularly a stateless person who could generate no orders for German industry. I had almost given up hope when Father happened to meet one of his former professors of Dorpat, who later moved to Germany and now exerted his influence on my behalf. The Chemical Engineering division was overcrowded. Teaching methods seemed rather old-fashioned and the equipment inadequate and obsolete. Articles of value were guarded like the Crown Jewels; there was, for instance but one small platinum dish, and when a student had to carry out a practice electrolysis which required a platinum vessel he or she was locked into the (windowless) room with the platinum (weighing an ounce or two) for four or five hours until the electrolysis was completed. However, I learnt what I know of chemical engineering science at Charlottenburg, and it stood me in good stead later. The Technical High School fees were quite high; there were few bursaries and grants, and certainly not for foreigners. Fortunately, Father's financial position was now better, and he was able to pay the fees.

Students were very much the future engineers and managers of industry; one dressed very formally, with white starched collar, and spats. For examinations, a cutaway morning dress was *de rigueur*, mostly hired. I was fortunate in having the same figure as Father and was thus able to wear his 'cut' which, by pure chance, Mother had packed when leaving Moscow. On works visits there was a very noticeable atmosphere of class antagonism;

the students were very superior, and the 'proles' looked at their future masters with hatred in their eyes. I do not recall a single student of working-class background. This was probably quite different at university.

Student life at the Tech. was dominated by fraternities: *Burschenschaften*, *Landsmannschaften*, etc. In some, practice duelling with sabres was obligatory; in others, only in response—*unbedingte satisfaktion*—to a challenge (or provocation). In German society, duelling scars on the cheeks conferred similar social advantages as a Brigade of Guards tie in Britain; some people, supposedly, had them inflicted by their barber. The student fraternities played a similar role as the old school tie is said to have done in Britain; in Germany, of course, there were no 'public schools', so the fraternities evolved as a ruling-class defence mechanism. Personnel managers in heavy industry belonged to this or that fraternity, and many students with whom I had friendly relations told me quite frankly that they had joined a particular *Burschenschaft* or *Landsmannschaft* because they intended to join Krupp, or Stinnes, or some other major group, where it was essential for promotion, often even for engagement, to belong to the right fraternity.

Twice a week the fraternities mounted a *Stehkonvent*; members of each fraternity stood, in peaked caps, wearing coloured sashes and grim expressions, completely motionless, in a circle on the appointed spot in the great entrance hall for ten minutes. I imagine that this was meant as showing the flag, though to me—will any *alte Herren* reading this please forgive—it always looked faintly ridiculous. On certain evenings the Fraternities had a *Kommers*, at which beer was drunk by order with military precision, and the freshmen, or *Füchse*, were taught beer-drinking as an art by the *Fuchsmajor*. In between the organised drinking student songs were sung with gusto: *Gaudeamus Igitur, Filia Hospitalis, Gold und Silber, Das Band ist Zerrissen*. The latter was actually a student song of the abortive Liberal Revolution of 1848:

> Das Band ist zerrissen
> War schwarz rot und gold
> Und Gott hat es gelitten
> Wer weiss was er gewollt.

> (The band is torn
> It was black, red and gold
> And God has allowed it
> Who knows what He had willed.)

However, the song was sung substituting *schwarz, weiss und rot* (black, white and red) for black, red and gold; the former being the old colours of

Imperial Germany, and after 1918 the Party colours of the Right, and black, red and bold the re-adopted colours of the Weimar Republic. Germany was indeed two nations, each with its own national flag.

I found most subjects of chemical engineering fascinating and spent much time at the fractionating columns of the pilot plant on the nearby Moabit embankment, attached to the Tech.

I had passed by intermediate examination and was preparing for my thesis and final examination, and did not take part in any political or student activities except for a brief spell in 1932. At that time, owing to the rise of the National Socialists, the Jewish students of the Tech. (almost all foreigners) felt that there ought to be a 'Jewish delegate' on the Student's Committee which represented the students in discussions with the Administration on various comparitively trivial matters. I was not particularly interested, mainly because of the time involved, as I work fairly slowly, and required all my time for my studies, and, before Hitler's rise, would have seen no justification for a sectional Jewish representative. But now there was a special case and, in the end, I agreed to stand as the 'Jewish Candidate'. There were actually very few Jewish students at the Tech. as compared with the University, where in some faculties (law and medicine) I believe that about a third of the students were Jews, reflecting the different distribution of specific abilities between Jewish and non-Jewish German students. So I did not see how I could be elected in any case, even allowing for the votes of a few personal non-Jewish friends. However, I was elected with a largeish and seemingly quite inexplicable number of votes. Until a squat, black-haired, studious-looking fellow student introduced himself to me. His surname ended with . . .ian, so that he was obviously an Armenian. He congratulated me on my election and explained that all Armenian students, of which there were many, had voted for me because Armenians always voted for Jewish candidates if they had none of their own. The Armenians would never forget how Theodor Herzl and the 'Jewish press' refused to condone the Turkish attempt at genocide of the Armenians (he did not use the word 'genocide' which had not yet been invented). The Committee was overtaken by political events and soon went out of existence like all elected bodies of any kind and size.

A few days after my unexpected election I saw, on entering the Inorganic Laboratory, a new face. Clearly a Jew, very markedly so, probably meeting a lot of anti-semitism. Being now the 'Jewish delegate' I felt it my duty to introduce myself, offered by assistance, explained laboratory routine, where reagents were purchased, how to obtain better Bunsen burners, and so forth. I also made remarks about the sad times in which we were living, which seemed to puzzle the new arrival. He thanked me profusely and gave me his card. He was an Arabian prince.

Father now felt that our financial position had improved sufficiently to enable him to lease a spacious six-room flat, off the Halensee end of the Kurfurstendamm, and to furnish it with rather nice, second-hand reproduction furniture.

Only then did I begin to understand Father's strength of character in living out of suitcases in mean furnished rooms, wearing ill-fitting off-the-peg suits, without touching our capital, and investing it all to secure the future. Of course, he could have no knowledge of the cataclysm that was coming, duplicating Soviet socialism. Just before Christmas 1932 we moved in; fourteen years after being driven out of Moscow we had once again our own home. I remember now triumphant Father was at having brought the family ship into harbour, as we all thought. Father's enjoyment did not last long. Six weeks, in fact. On 30 January 1933 (like 7 November 1917, a black day in Europe's history) we stood on our balcony and watched the torchlight procession which the inventive Dr Joseph Goebbels (Hitler's Director of Marketing) had organised to mark Hitler's appointment as Reichschancellor.

Germans are, or (let us hope) were, very credulous. Some time around 1930 a German businessman (non-Jewish) who owed Father some money left hurredly abroad, leaving his creditors unpaid. One of his assets consisted of an apartment block and Father's solicitor obtained an attachment from the Court giving Father the right to collect one month's rent from the property, which would amost cover the debt. Father sent me to collect the rent. Actually I was a very shy young man, and never collected a kopeck, or centime, or pfennig from anyone. However, I knew we needed the money—Father had himself a major tax payment to make—and so I went to the apartments, the impressive document from the Court, taped and sealed, in my briefcase. No doubt, I had an honest face, but so has every confidence-trickster. After this experience, I was not surprised by the Germans being taken in by Hitler's fraudulent prospectus.

Notes

1   In view of the repeated German aggression against Russia throughout this century, and the planting of Bolshevism, one can only hope that the frontier settlement in Eastern Europe is final, and accepted as such by the German nation.
2   Flat feet, or dropped arches; an affliction believed to be frequent among Jews (and Arabs, I am told).

13

Madness

Verderblich ist des Feuers wüten,
Gefährlich ist des Tigers Zahn,
Jedoch das Schrecklichste der Schrecken
Das ist der Mensch in seinem Wahn.

It is over fifty years since I last read this prologue from Schiller's 'Glocke' (The Bell) and I am quoting from memory, but it also seems a suitable prologue for the period we now entered:

Perilous is the raging fire
Dangerous the tiger's tooth
But the most terrible of all terrors
Is man in his madness.

In 1929, only ten years after the new order of Versailles, the overblown share prices on the New York Stock Exchange collapsed. It is not for me to hazard an opinion whether the Wall Street crash triggered off the Great Depression or was its first manifestation. Business executives, professional men, fathers of families, who all speculated on the margin, were bankrupted, many turned out of their homes and camping in Central Park. 'Bears', speculators, including some prominent personages (non-Jewish) added fuel to the flames. Soon the entire free-enterprise world was in the grip of a ferocious crisis. In the Argentine grain was being burned whilst other countries were starving. The proponents of a planned world economy were winning the intellectual argument. Socialists of all hues were gleefully rubbing their hands. In Germany alone there were *six million* unemployed,

159

receiving only a pittance from the *Wohlfahrtsamt* state charity, and no
F. D. Roosevelt to bring a New Deal. A new deal of sorts was offered by
Adolf Hitler, who saw his opportunity. In the elections of 1930, the
National Socialist German Workers Party[1] (to give it its full name) gained a
substantial number of seats, making it overnight the second largest party,
and the non-socialist minority government of Dr Brüning had to govern by
presidential decree (a possibility foreseen in the Weimar Constitution). In
the April election of 1932 Hitler's share grew even larger and the National
Socialists became the leading party. The National Socialists and the Communists (who also flourished) now jointly commanded a majority in the
Reichstag, making parliamentary government impossible. The President,
Marshal von Hindenburg of World War I fame, first appointed von Papen
Chancellor and then General von Schleicher (later murdered by the
National Socialists). In the November 1932 election the National Socialist
vote *fell* from 230 seats to 196, and it looked as if the tide was now receding,
and General von Schleicher seemed to be heading towards a successful
military dictatorship which would have saved Germany and the world from
the horrors of National Socialism and World War II. Unfortunately, von
Papen, Hugenberg and others with access to the 86-year-old President and
his entourage persuaded Hindenburg to drop Schleicher as Chancellor and,
on 30 January 1933, to appoint Hitler as Reichschancellor, with von Papen
as Vice-Chancellor and various other non-socialist ministers. Evidently,
Papen, Hugenberg and their backers thought they could ride the tiger, as the
Mensheviks and other Left-wing socialists in Russia thought fifteen
years earlier.

In March 1933 a new general election was held. In spite of all pressure
and intimidation, breaking up of meetings, and so forth, the National
Socialists secured only 45 per cent of the vote, and fell short of an absolute
majority. The German people thus proved politically less mature than the
Russians, who in similar circumstances gave Lenin only 25 per cent.
However, the National Socialists did have a majority together with their
allies, the right-wing National Party led by Hugenberg. Hitler, determined
to the last to achieve absolute power by formally legal means (the Soviets'
status as usurpers rankled with him) prevailed upon the National Party to
commit political suicide by voting for an expulsion of the Communist
deputies from the Reichstag, thus giving Hitler an absolute majority in the
rump Reichstag. In an Enabling Act he was given unlimited power and was
now absolute dictator of Germany. The Gestapo, with its torture-centres
and concentration camps, was formed, all other political parties and
organisations suppressed (including the National Party and the *Stahlhelm*
(ex-Servicemens' organisation) who were, so far, represented in the
Government).

The brown-shirted stormtroopers, led by Ernst Röhm, a noted sexual pervert, terrorised the population, and sang:

> Wenn's Judenblut vom Messer spritzt
> Dann geht's nochmal so gut.
> (When the Jew's blood from the knife spurts
> We'll be much better off.)

And when dismissed at public parades, they had to bawl:

> Deutschland erwache, Juda verrecke.
> (Germany awaken; Judah perish.)

The Hitler Youth—practically obligatory for all boys—also had an official marching song (considered by Dr Goebbels as essential as an attractive uniform):

> Und wenn das Reich erstanden
> Trägt deutsche Jugendkraft
> Hinein nach welschen Landen
> Den schlanken Fahnenschaft.
> (And when the Reich is risen
> The strength of German youth
> Into welsh² countries carries
> The slim flagstaff.)

Unofficially, these boys of twelve or fourteen sang:

> A ... an die Wand
> Röhm geht durch's Land.
> (A ... to the wall
> Röhm is on the prowl.)

How many thousands, perhaps tens of thousands, of German boys were corrupted by Röhm's depraved example will never be known.

The anti-Jewish campaign

As soon as he had his Enabling Act from the Reichstag Hitler immediately proceeded to give effect to his pathological hatred of the Jews. Jewish people—at that stage euphemistically described as 'non-Aryans'—had to leave all public activities, the professions, press and radio. Civil servants and university professors were thrown out at a day's notice without any compensation or pension.

On 1 April 1933 a boycott of all Jewish-owned places of business was ordered. All shops, professional offices and other places of business owned by or maintained by Jewish people were peacefully picketed by storm-troopers, generally two at each entrance, with a placard. Apart from a hand-ful of exceptions (I had heard that the Prussian Crown Princess was one of them) no-one dared to cross the picket lines. The Jewish owners stayed at home. If the boycott had gone on any length of time it would have made it impossible for Jews to live in Germany. However, owing to pressure from Hindenburg (who received a deputation from the Association of Jewish ex-Servicemen) and from Hitler's non-socialist partners, at that time still hold-ing some residual influence, the boycott was called off after two days and Jewish commercial activity, particularly in the field of sorely needed exports, was allowed to continue.

One of Hitler's first discriminatory laws prohibited 'mixed marriages' between 'Aryans' and 'non-Aryans'. I remember an incident revealing the nonsensical nature of these pseudo-scientific euphemisms: a registrar refused to marry a German man and a Hungarian woman because he had discovered in conscientious consultation of an encyclopedia that the Hungarians were non-Aryans (they are indeed, as are the Finns and the Estonians, because the Hungarian language is not of Indo-European origin). The Minister of the Interior, Frick, of the National Socialist Old Guard, had to issue a circular hurriedly declaring the Hungarians to be Aryans (I was later reminded of the episode when the South African government declared the Japanese to be Europeans).

Another early law prohibited 'non-Aryans' from employing female 'Aryan' servants under the age of 45. This law probably reveals the real origin of Hitler's irrational hatred, as there were persistent rumours that one of Hitler's female forebears, possibly his grandmother, had been disgraced while in domestic service with the Vienna Rothschilds, and, repudiated by her own parents, had to live in shame and misery, as decreed by the custom of the period. I believe the story is told in the book by August Thyssen, the steel industrialist, *I paid Hitler*. At any rate, it is known that when Hitler marched into Austria a special Gestapo squad had been detailed in advance, to make sure that members of the Rothschild family did not escape, and in fact they were arrested at the airport and, I believe, beaten to death.

Another early anti-Jewish move was the prohibition of Jews acting as pawnbrokers and moneylenders; they had to sell their business to 'Aryans', who soon became even more unpopular than their Jewish predecessors, and were generally known as the 'white Jews'. I have never heard an expla-nation as to why this particular occupation was singled out in advance of the general anti-Jewish legislation: could it be that Hitler, in his down-at-heel days at Vienna, had some unfortunate encounters with moneylenders? Did he, perhaps, think that 'Aryan' moneylenders would wipe out debts and return the unredeemed pledges in deserving cases?

The general discrimination came in 1935 when the 'Nurnberg Laws' officially created two classes of citizens, 'Aryans' and 'Non-Aryans', with Jews belonging to the second class.

Many Jewish people, as well as non-Jews, thought that with these laws the National Socialists had achieved their objective, and the Jews would now be allowed to live on the new, circumscribed basis. How wrong they were. In the meantime, I had to break off my studies in mid-thesis.

At the Hohenzollern modern secondary our Headmaster had been Geheimrat Müller. *Geheimrat* (Counsellor) was an honour given to distinguished civil servants, corresponding perhaps to a British OBE. The German system of titles had the advantage that the recipient's wife was also honoured, and became, for instance, Frau Geheimrat. There was therefore no need for knighthoods. Geheimrat Müller retired a year or two after our matriculation, and as he was going blind, and was also widowed, a roster of Old Boys was organised who would come and read to him. I would visit him every second Saturday morning, reading from a book of his choice. For various reasons all the other boys slowly fell away, and in the end I was the only reader left. One Saturday morning, when I had just finished a chapter from the life of Thucydides, I think, and the housekeeper came in and brought me the customary cup of cocoa, the Geheimrat, now almost blind, told me, visibly shaken, that we would have to discontinue our reading sessions. The National Socialist block-warden, otherwise his greengrocer, had told him that he would have to stop seeing 'enemies of the people', probably reading subversive books to him, otherwise he would lose his pension. As I took leave, I noticed on the hall-table the latest edition (in the 250s) of *Mein Kampf*, obviously for the greengrocer's benefit. I never saw the Geheimrat again, and he probably never heard the end of Thucydides. Enquiries I made after the war informed me that he had died, a German in the mould of Kant.

My sister, who by now was at university, reading law—Father had found the money for her studies as well as mine—also had to give up. In fact, Jewish people were no longer admitted to places of higher learning. She married a Jewish ex-fellow student who had also read law, and was now training as a welder for emigration (training for manual skills, known as *Berufsumschichtung* and organised by Jewish relief organisations, became quite customary for young people). However, my sister and brother-in-law became involved in clandestine anti-National Socialist activities and were arrested by the Gestapo, accused of harbouring the *Brown Book*, a collection of documents relating, I believe, to National Socialist complicity in the Reichstag fire and other crimes, and therefore anathema to the Party. As this was a specific illegal act, and their other activities remained undetected, my sister and brother-in-law were fortunately not sent to a concentration camp but handed over to the Prussian judiciary, and in due course given three years' hard labour, expiring 15 August 1939. The Prussian gaols were, at that time, extremely harsh, but not inhumane, and I felt that my sister and her husband were most fortunate that the prison sentence had saved them, for the time being, from the concentration camp.

Having disenfranchised the Jews politically in 1935 and removed them from public life, the National Socialists concentrated in 1938 on making it impossible for Jewish people to earn their living. As a first step, Jews had to submit to the Inland Revenue authorities a complete list of all their assets. The purpose became clear later. Father submitted his list: by coincidence the total value of all his assets was the exact equivalent of the £18,000 he had brought into Germany in 1924. So during these fourteen years in Germany we had neither increased nor decreased our nominal capital, but had, of course, lived modestly on its earnings. Moreover, even if inflation was quite low, there must have been some, so that in real terms we had lost part of our capital, probably 10 or 15 per cent, to the German economy.

By a sheer miracle—there is no other word for it—I had obtained employment in my profession as a chemist in the Berlin laboratory of an industrial group founded, and still owned, by a distinguished German–Jewish family, the Schwenden*. They had been allowed to carry on their business, which was of considerable national importance, and included materials for the synthetic fuel programme, until early 1938. Then unsurmountable difficulties were placed in their way. The Reichsbank had been instructed to deny them allocations of foreign exchange for the purchase of essential raw materials and the Schwenden had to sell. Dr Schwenden, the founder, who started the business in 1906, had died in 1937. He would not have survived the shock. The enterprise had been inherited by his two sons; the elder was now the managing director and the younger had been reading chemistry. In a poignant head-office ceremony on 15 July 1938 which must have been heartrending to the brothers, young Schwenden, the managing director, handed over the great enterprise to the new owners, a major industrial group who were one of Schwenden's main customers.

Naturally, all employees of Jewish or part-Jewish descent had to leave; by that time, all 'part-Jews' up to and including one Jewish grandparent were proscribed. The Schwenden were generally model employers—not necessarily the rule in the Germany of those days—and they made individual provisions for each person whose employment was being terminated. In 1938 this meant assistance towards emigration—the possibility of Jewish people earning their living in Germany, even manually, was coming to an end.

For several Jewish employees the Schwenden managed to purchase a share in a farm in a British East African colony, which entitled them to a visa; this was one escape route still open at the time, though, of course, it required foreign exchange not generally available to German Jews; the Schwenden were one of the very few people who could legally effect such a transaction through their foreign holdings. The 'National Home' in Palestine was firmly barred. The world was closed.

The Schwenden themselves had prepared their emigration to England, under the New Industries scheme—more of that later. By a further miracle I was offered employment as a chemist with them in a subsidiary company in England. The Schwenden left in August 1938 while I remained in Berlin waiting for *my* visa.

The November attack

The day of 9 November 1938 was the twentieth anniversary of the German Revolution and the abdication of the Kaiser. Although the German High Command had sued for an armistice on 5 October, Hitler, Ludendorff and their followers had persuaded themselves that it was the revolution of 9 November (which actually started with a mutiny of the sailors at Kiel)—the *Dolchstoss*, or stab in the back—which had caused the German collapse (Ludendorff was probably thinking of his nefarious activities in Russia in 1917). Moreover, the *Dolchstoss* had been clearly perpetrated by the Jews, who wanted the Allies to win and implement the Balfour Declaration (actually the German Jews at the time included practically no Zionists and probably did not even know of the Balfour Declaration, which was directed at American Jewry). So 9 November 1938 was deliberately chosen by Hitler as the day of revenge against the German Jews. Some 25,000 Jewish men, many quite old, were arrested and transported to concentration camps. This was the first time that Jews had been arrested in any numbers simply because they were Jews. The journal of the SS, *Das Schwarze Korps*, came out, as I recall, proclaiming with gloating hatred:

> Juden, jetzt haben wir euch!
> (Jews, now we've got you!)

It seemed that the SS had been working towards this end for some years, probably since 1935, when the Nurnberg Laws appeared to allow the Jews a ghetto existence. The physical attack of 9 November 1938 on German

Jewry has been described as a *pogróm*. Reprehensible as the *pogróms* were, they were not on a comparable scale, and not meant to end Jewish existence in Russia. The events of November are also sometimes described as *Kristallnacht*, or Night of the Broken Glass, which is a gross and objectionable understatement. Synagogues throughout Germany had been set aflame. Altogether over a hundred were burnt down, and I believe that there were no synagogues left. I remember passing the great Synagogue in the Fasanenstrasse, an imposing white-domed building, the pride of German Jewry, erected about 1912 and inaugurated by the Kaiser in person (a photograph of this event was to be seen in the entrance hall until 1938). Now, I remember, a horrified bystander saying: 'Wenn Gotteshauser in Flammen aufgehen, das nimmt kein gutes Ende' (When Houses of God go up in flames this will come to a bad end), a premonition, perhaps, of Berlin being a heap of rubble seven years later.

The night of 9 November 1938 marked the end of the toleration of any kind of Jewish life in Germany. We were once again Lenin's insects, with no right to exist. After 9 November 1938 all Jewish persons in Germany were, in effect, outlaws: there was no longer any recourse to the courts of law; anyone could have attacked me in the street, beaten me unconscious, robbed me, and neither the police nor passers-by, indoctrinated or intimidated, could have intervened. The German people could have made life impossible for Jews. But the public did not attack the Jews or take advantage of their plight. The old anti-semitism, which had been considerable in Germany before Hitler, had totally evaporated in five years of National Socialist rule; in fact there was considerable sympathy and clandestine help, even more so during the war.

The next morning I received, by coincidence, a postcard from the British consulate asking me to call. Perhaps my visa was ready? The consulate (or, at least the visa section) was situated in the fashionable Tiergarten district, Berlin's Belgravia. The street running alongside the park—I think it was called Von der Heydt strasse—had been laid out by some Prussian Cubitt in such a manner that there were identical plots between the street and the park, each plot containing a house facing the street and a largeish garden, or courtyard, facing the park. One such building housed the British visa section and the neighbouring building belonged to the German War Ministry.

On 10 November 1938 the contrast between both sites could not have been greater; the yard—originally, I imagine, a lawn—of the visa section was crammed with a disorderly throng of Jewish people, many of them women, all clamouring for visas. Most were probably relatives of those arrested, desperate to save their fathers, sons and husbands from the horrors of the concentration camp. From time to time a bewildered clerk would come out and shout: 'Three young men for Bechuanaland, no family' (this is an actual example I heard). Immediately there would be some jostling, and three young men with the strongest elbows would come forward. None probably knew where exactly Bechuanaland lay, but it did not matter.

The neighbouring yard, separated by a low fence only, contained a solitary figure: a high-ranking German staff officer, with monocle and red tabs, immaculately turned out, sitting erect on a perfectly groomed bay gelding, obviously about to take his morning canter in the park. The rider was surveying the scene next door with an attentive gaze, and I was trying to read his impassive features. Did he show any compassion for these desperate, trapped people? None at all. Was he, perhaps, on the contrary, gloating over the misfortune of these strangers, in appearance so far removed from his idea of an officer and a gentleman? Certainly not. He was evaluating the situation with the cold, calculating eye of a general surveying a battlefield, and I imagined his thoughts ran, apprehensively, something like this: 'Here we have this Austrian corporal fellow telling us all the time that we cannot afford a two-front war again, and that he will dispose of France first and then turn on Russia. And now he is busy creating a third, civilian front against us. These people may not be much to look at on the parade-ground, but they do have brains. In the last war, we could not have lasted four years without their technical and economic skills. And now they will all work for the enemy, and re-awaken all anti-German sentiments abroad.'

My visa had indeed arrived.

But now I was worried about Father and Marie Ivanovna. And what would happen to my sister and brother-in-law when they came out of prison next year?

After 9 November 1938 all Jewish persons left in Germany (including those classed as Jews because they had even one Jewish grandparent) were trying to emigrate. That was precisely Hitler's intention. Almost all were trying to emigrate, but not all. I knew a young German Jewish lawyer, Kurt Machol, who actually had the opportunity of emigrating to the USA and refused. '*This* is the land of my forefathers,' he said, 'and no one will drive me from it.' After the outbreak of war—more accurately, after Hitler started the war—the Machols shared the fate of all Jews left in Berlin. Jewish families were turned out of their apartments and concentrated in a slum area; Jewish persons had to wear the Yellow Star; they were forbidden to listen to the radio or read newspapers, and World War I ex-servicemen were not allowed to wear military decorations like the cherished Iron Cross. In the end, all were deported to Auschwitz or the other extermination camps, including the inmates of the Jewish Old Age Home (this actually led to protests by the local residents—unprecedented in wartime SS Germany). Machol, together with his young wife and little daughter, perished at Auschwitz, that crowning achievement of National Socialism.[3]

Trapped

Emigration was very difficult. The world was closed to Jewish people, and obtaining a visa was the sole topic of conversation in those days. 'They say that visas for Guateragua can be bought for 5000 marks.' 'They say, that the Falkland Islands in the South Pacific will admit a veterinary surgeon.' In March 1939 the *St Louis*, with 900 Jewish men, women and children aboard, their passports stamped with what was thought to be valid visas for a Central American State, returned from the Caribbean and disembarked her cargo of wretched humanity in Germany, as the visas were declared invalid, and no other country in the Western hemisphere would admit the Jewish passengers.

American-based Jewish relief organisations were combing the world for havens of refuge. Japan was approached, and the Emperor's brother advised that after careful consideration they could not accept any immigrants in their overcrowded islands, and certainly not non-Asiatics. The one natural place of refuge for Jewish people, Israel (or Palestine, as it was officially called since Hadrian's Edict) was all but closed. In a letter addressed to Lord Rothschild, dated 2 November 1917, and made public, I believe, at the Conservative Committee Rooms at the Queen's Hotel in Manchester, Lord Balfour,[4] the Foreign Secretary, declared that 'His Majesty's Government viewed with favour the establishment in Palestine of a national home for the Jewish people.' This undertaking was written by the League of Nations into the Mandate for the administration of Palestine issued to Britain. 'Palestine' embraced the territories of today's Israel and today's Jordan, and the Balfour Declaration consequently referred to the whole of Palestine. But in 1922 Churchill, whilst standing up most emphatically for continued Jewish settlement in what is now Israel, detached the entire territory east of the River Jordan (in biblical times the tribal territories of Manasseh, Gad and Reuben), in fact three-quarters of the total area of Palestine, and created the new Arab state of Transjordan, under the Emir Abdullah of the Hashemite dynasty. Thus Palestine had already once been divided, and in the larger part, the new state of Transjordan, not a single Jew would be allowed to settle.

But even in cis-jordanian rump Palestine, the west bank of the Jordan, now somewhat misleadingly simply called 'Palestine', and reserved for Jewish settlement, the British Colonial Office was allowing only a trickle of

Jewish immigrants. In 1937 the Royal Commission, known as the Peel Commission, recommended a second Partition of 'Palestine', and an ending of the Mandate. Had that advice been followed, millions of Jewish people from Poland, the Baltic States, the Balkans, Italy, France, the Low Countries and, of course, those still trapped in Germany could have been saved from National Socialist extermination. A state of Israel in existence at the outbreak of the war would also have materially assisted the British war effort in the Middle East.

Having so spectacularly failed to stop Hitler by appeasement the Chamberlain Government was now endeavouring to appease the Mufti.

In the infamous White Paper of May 1939 (bitterly condemned by Churchill and Amery), issued at the time of European Jewry's greatest need, a quota of fifteen thousand (!) immigrants annually was to be allowed into cis-jordanian Palestine during the next five years. In fact, a quota of fifteen thousand *weekly* would have been required for a year to make some impact. Further land purchases by Jews were to be prohibited.

In 1938, an inter-governmental conference on the Jewish refugees was called at Evian-les-Bains. The British Government's precondition for taking part was that emigration into Palestine—the only solution to the problem—should not be on the agenda.

The entire British diplomatic and intelligence services were mobilised to prevent the entry of Jewish 'illegal immigrants' into Palestine. The co-operation of the governments and various authorities of Bulgaria, Greece, Romania, Turkey, Yugoslavia, and even Nazi Germany was enlisted. All the escape routes were being sealed at the behest of the Colonial Office. Moreover, upon the outbreak of war the principle was enunciated that no refugees from Germany or from German-occupied territory were henceforth to be admitted to Palestine.[5]

Even during the first years of the war it was possible for Jewish people to flee from various parts of Europe, including even Germany, provided there was somewhere to go. Only in October 1941 did Himmler issue an order banning all Jewish emigration *from the Reich*. Jews could still flee from many occupied countries, from Hungary, from Italy, from Vichy France (soon to be occupied by the Germans), but only if armed with an entry visa for some country of the world. But the world was closed (as it is to the Vietnamese 'boat-people' these days), and the door to the 'National Home' firmly shut and barred.

In December 1941 769 refugees fleeing from German-occupied Romania managed to sail from Constanza on the Greek-owned 240-ton river steamer *Struma*, bound for the National Home (in their home town, the Nazi-controlled 'Iron Guard' had commandeered an abattoir, in which Jewish men, women and children were slaughtered and their bodies stamped 'unfit for human consumption'). The *Struma* did arrive off Istanbul after a three-day voyage when her engine broke down. The Turkish authorities, fearful of being landed with the unwanted Jews, refused to allow the passengers to land while repairs were being effected. The engine proved beyond repair and for two months the passengers remained cooped up on the overcrowded and unseaworthy hulk, with only some food being smuggled aboard by Istanbul's Jewish community, while negotiations about their fate were being conducted. The Jewish Agency was pleading with the British Government to allow the wretched passengers into Palestine, but the British High Commissioner, Sir Harold MacMichael, and the Colonial Secretary, Lord Moyne,[6] remained unmoved. In February, all attempts at rescuing the passengers having failed, the Turkish Government ordered the *Struma* out of territorial waters and towed her into the Black Sea, where she sunk with all on board. There was one solitary survivor, a refugee, rescued by a Turkish boat, put in prison and finally admitted into Palestine.

In Tel-Aviv, however, a few desperate young men, their families still in the jaws of the tyrannosaurus, met in the backroom of a dingy café off Dizengoff Square and decided, in spite of Britain's leading the fight against the deadly enemy, that the Mandatory Authority had to be forced by acts of terrorism to open Palestine to the refugees fleeing for their lives. (It did not help during the war. The Jewish people, who could have been rescued had all been murdered by the time the war was over.)

In British policy towards the Jewish refugee problem there was a strange dichotomy: the Colonial Office, in collusion with the Eastern Department of the Foreign Office, was doing its best to effectively annul the Balfour Declaration and the Mandate, and to keep the Jews out of Israel. The reason (need it be spelled out?): oil and the Suez Canal. The Arab leadership reciprocated: the Grand Mufti of Jerusalem went to Germany and spent the war in Hitler's entourage, inciting the Arabs to rise against Britain, raising a Muslim Legion in the Balkans to fight for Germany and organising the highly dangerous pro-German Rashid Ali rebellion in Iraq.

Immigration into Britain

Whereas the British Government had mandatory and moral obligations regarding Jewish emigration to Palestine, it had *no obligations whatsoever* regarding the admittance of refugees to Britain, or indeed the Colonies, except on general humanitarian grounds. Nor did any other government of the world have such obligations. Britain herself was an overcrowded island, housing was in short supply and unemployment heavy.

The Home Office, in co-operation with the Board of Trade, was pursuing an imaginative and humanitarian policy of enlightened self-interest. Britain at that time had some three million unemployed; heavy industry, having originated here, was antiquated and the trade balance was negative. The British authorities therefore devised a scheme to cream off the economically most useful layer of German Jewry and attract it to Britain. German Jews desiring to settle in Britain would have to produce a viable commercial project, showing the type of business they would be starting, how many people they would employ, what foreign exchange they would earn, and so forth. The products to be manufactured had to be, in the main, imported ones, so that there was genuine job-creation not transfer of work from existing manufacturers. There had to be no objections from existing British manufacturers, and the entire scheme was very thoroughly vetted by the Board of Trade, whose approval was required. There were also very humane provisions for immediate dependants.

Apart from these economically useful Jews and their dependants (and a handful of world-famous scientists, now mostly knighted, who proved of great benefit to the war-effort) no other Jewish immigration was permitted at all. As far as I know, Britain was the only country to apply such an economically selective scheme; for a saturated and overcrowded country the only sensible solution; thus, in a sense, partly offsetting the anti-Jewish stance over Israel.

The Schwenden, when they found in 1938 that they were forced to sell their great enterprise, decided to apply for immigration to Britain. Many of the products they manufactured in Germany and were required by a wide range of industries (none were consumer products) were imported into Britain. The Schwenden therefore submitted a project for setting up manufacture of these products in Britain and the scheme was approved by the Board of Trade. The manufacture of one intended product had to be foregone as an existing British manufacturer objected, as he was preparing to manufacture it himself. In addition to the prospective employment of several hundred people the Schwenden would also bring a considerable income in foreign exchange from their overseas investments, which they managed to retain (against payment of a 'ransom' in foreign exchange to the Reichsbank).

In the case of refugee-industries it was the prerogative of the Board of Trade to decide on the location of the new enterprise, generally in a particularly depressed area which was designated as a Special Area. For the Schwenden project Sheffield was nominated; other refugee entrepreneurs were directed to the North-east, the North-west, South Wales and other Special Areas in Scotland. Because of the anticipated size and importance of the Schwenden project and the large number of people to be employed, an exceptionally long list of some thirty people was approved for immigration. These included the Schwenden family with two or three elderly aunts, and some Jewish key personnel, again with their families, particularly Dr Preuss*, one of the leading technical experts in the industry, and Dr Lilienblatt*, who knew all about the chemistry of the Schwenden products there was to know. I learned much from both.

Today, some six hundred people are employed by the Schwenden in Britain.

The Schwenden enterprise in Britain was comparatively large, commensurate with their position in Germany, and I personally only know of perhaps a dozen or so refugee-industries of this magnitude. In most cases a single family of three or four persons would be permitted to immigrate, in order to start a small engineering or chemical manufacture, employing forty or fifty people. In the North-east of England, for example, seventy-six refugee-firms were founded by approximately a hundred immigrant families, and these firms now employ 16,500 people. Similar ratios probably apply to all other Special Areas.

The total number of refugees admitted into Britain from Germany was about 75,000, most of them under Board of Trade auspices. In addition, some 20,000 were admitted in 1938 and 1939 from Austria and Czechoslovakia, mainly on humanitarian grounds, without economic criteria.

There is no official figure as to the total number of jobs created by the refugees; personally, I would estimate it at somewhat above half a million.

In August 1938 the Schwenden family left their native country and moved to London. The money they had in Germany remained there in blocked accounts, including the proceeds of the forced sale of the paternal business. Fortunately, quite exceptionally, the Schwenden had some overseas investments.

On his last day at the Head Office, young Schwenden, the managing director, had a farewell meal, in a somewhat subdued vein, with a few close business associates, at the nearby K. restaurant in the Kurfurstendamm, which he usually patronised. The National Socialists had for some time been putting pressure on the owners of restaurants and cafés to display notices refusing admittance to Jews. Most restaurants had had these notices for years; they were only temporarily removed, on instructions, for the period of the Olympic Games. After the meal, the owner saw Schwenden to the door, wished him God-speed and received the expected 100-mark note. He watched the car round the corner and gave a sign to his assistant. Two workmen appeared with ladders and put up a large sign, prepared some time earlier. It read, in six-inch letters:

DOGS AND JEWS NOT ADMITTED

The National Socialist catering group official called in the afternoon and expressed his satisfaction. Now that the K. had shown its loyalty to the Führer he would drop in for a beer from time to time. The owner actually preferred clientele who dropped in for an apéritif and a meal. But in times like these one could not be too squeamish.

I was, once again, undeservedly fortunate. In addition to their main project described earlier, the Schwenden also submitted a scheme for an additional more modest venture, manufacturing certain specialised chemicals and equipment for the engineering industry, and this project, planned to provide initial employment for some thirty people, was put forward as basis for my immigration as well as of another, more elderly refugee, also a bachelor, and highly recommended to the Schwenden family. He had considerable commercial experience in this field. I would add that this smaller enterprise, which ultimately allowed the immigration of four persons, is also doing well and is now employing sixty people. This additional project was also approved by the Board of Trade and, as mentioned previously, I received my visa in November 1938. And so, a few days before Christmas, I took leave from Father and Marie Ivanovna and boarded the plane for London at Tempelhof Airport.

Father himself did not make any move towards emigration. He was in his sixties, in poor health, in fact semi-invalid. He had lost the sight of one eye owing to detachment of the retina, and saw just enough with the other to move about freely. Like the Geheimrat, he could no longer read. Father believed, or professed to believe, that as he was a Russian refugee from the Bolsheviks, as documented by his 'Nansen Passport', no harm would come to him. He also thought, as others did, that the National Socialists would allow old and retired people to live out their days in peace. Moreover, after inflation had ended, he had transferred all his capital into Germany, and was now not allowed to take any money out nor, of course, any jewellery or valuables. The amount permitted to emigrants was 10 marks, less than one pound sterling at that time.

In any event, the world was now all but closed to Jewish people and Father had nowhere to go, nor had he the wish to find himself without any means of support in a strange country. He knew the fate of the Russian refugees trapped in Constantinople who did not manage to get out. So Father, when he blessed me before my departure, clearly did not think he would ever see me again.

For myself, I considered Father as being in mortal peril, and had resolved to apply for a visa for him and Marie Ivanovna under the dependants' scheme as soon as I was in England.

From Berlin, I sent a trunk with clothes and other personal belongings as unaccompanied luggage and, when in London, went to Victoria Station to collect it. The porter took me into an outsize vault underneath the station, stacked to the top with trunks, and suitcases, several rows deep. 'Trouble abroad,' he said. 'We can always tell by the amount of unaccompanied luggage coming in. We have not had such a lot since 1919. Most are never claimed.'

For our small enterprise the Board of Trade also designated Sheffield, and in January 1939 I moved there, and so did the fellow refugee who had been nominated as managing director. On a personal level we found little in common, as he was a distinctly non-academic type, coming from the sales side, whereas I had no commercial experience, except helping Father in a small way. Furthermore, I soon noticed that he always tried to compromise me, for instance by suggesting defrauding the new company, on a small scale, with fictitious expenses claims. I had the feeling he was trying to place himself in the position of exercising some leverage over me. Fortunately, although young and green, I instinctively refused all his unethical propositions. We were quite busy hiring premises, buying equipment and materials, and engaging staff. My particular responsibility was the equipment of a small laboratory where I would be acting as the Works Chemist cum Works Manager. My knowledge of the English way of life was then mainly based on *The Forsyte Saga* and I assumed that everyone dressed for dinner. So when I took the train to Sheffield and, not having been able to eat the whole day, entered the dining car I stopped in my tracks because the carriage windows bore the ominous inscription 'Smoking'. And in German and Russian *smoking* meant a dinner jacket. So I turned back, and remained hungry.

In Sheffield I lodged in a small and pleasant residential hotel. After some weeks, the manageress told me one evening that the C.I.D. wanted me to call the next day, and she also gave me 24 hours notice to quit, her establishment being a respectable one and not offering accommodation to people wanted by the C.I.D. (in fact, the Aliens Department, who merely wanted to check on my whereabouts, was in those days a branch of the C.I.D.).

The starting capital which the Schwenden had allocated to the new venture was being consumed, and we had to be most careful. Every penny mattered.

The managing director reserved the purchase of machinery to himself, although I thought I could have been of some limited assistance there, having learned about machine tools at the Technische Hochschule. However, on one occasion, when negotiating for the purchase of an expensive machine—in fact, the most valuable of all—I was asked to take part, and we visited the agent, a typical Englishman, jointly. The machine was not to be seen, not even a leaflet, but the managing director referred to the quoted price, and asked for a discount. At this moment I noticed that both men exchanged curious glances and when the agent refused a discount, with synthetic indignation and a suppressed smile, it suddenly became quite clear to me that this was an *abgekartetes Spiel*, a charade, and that the managing director had pocketed the discount long ago. I had been brought there to be available as a witness, just in case, to testify that he did demand a discount, and had been refused. There were other incidents of this kind, and I found working under a man of such low standards rather distasteful, particularly as the Schwenden themselves were of the highest integrity and their business methods most ethical, like those of the vast majority of the refugee immigrants. As to Father and Uncle Matthew, both would have resigned in my position. However, I considered it a lifebelt.

Before moving to Sheffield I had called at the Jewish Refugees' Committee in Bloomsbury and filed an application for immigration visas for Father and Marie Ivanovna. The Committee was organised and financed by British Jews who had rallied to the succour of their persecuted brethren. It was staffed by a number of clerks, engaged and paid by the Committee, and presided over by two or three senior civil servants on loan from the Home Office. The clerks processed all the applications and conducted routine correspondence. When an application was complete, they submitted it to the civil servants for decision. The Committee was located at Woburn House, Russell Square—as the names convey, in the Duke of Bedford's domain in Bloombsbury.

Preparing for attack

In Germany, the odious Heinrich Himmler (1900–45), Reichsführer of the SS and head of the Gestapo, the German Dzerzhínsky, was becoming the most powerful man under Hitler. On 30 June 1934 some hundred National Socialist leaders (including the notorious Röhm), who were politically deviationists or Himmler's personal rivals, were arrested and killed. Also murdered were General von Schleicher, the last Chancellor before Hitler, who had tried to stop the National Socialists, and his wife.[7] On 2 August 1934 President Hindenburg died. He was laid at rest in a mausoleum at Tannenberg, the scene of his World War I triumph (until the remains were hastily evacuated ten years later before the advancing Red Army). Hitler became Führer and Reichschancellor. The maniac was now the untrammelled dictator of Germany. In 1936 control of the police force was officially handed over to Himmler. Germany was becoming the SS state.

German re-armament was proceding apace. There was no arms *race*, as there were no other participants. Armoured divisions, the *Panzer*, were being equipped and, under Goering's aegis, bombers and fighter planes, Junkers and Messerschmidt, were built in large quantities. In 1935 Hitler introduced conscription—one year in the National Labour corps, one year in the Army—thus at a stroke reducing unemployment by some millions. Jews were excluded, which was ominous for their future. In 1936 Hitler felt sufficiently secure, politically, to re-occupy the demilitarised Rhineland, on the French border, in contravention of Versailles, without risking the Anglo-French military action so feared by the generals.

In his aggressive foreign policy Hitler was much encouraged by the pacifist and disarmament movement in Britain, the notorious Peace Pledge Union, and the Oxford Union vote, declaring that the students would not fight for King and Country. I well remember the jubilation in Germany that Hitler was being given the green light. The 'peace movement' was effectively preventing British rearmament and forcing the Government to a policy of appeasement. In France, the pacifist stranglehold was even worse.

On 13 March 1938 Hitler invaded Austria and joined his native country to Germany in the *Anschluss*,[8] thus placing Czechoslovakia in a vice which only needed closing. And he was now poised on the borders of Italy, imposing his will on that country which he disliked and distrusted.

I was still in Germany when, on 30 September 1938, Neville Chamberlain, Daladier, Mussolini, and Hitler—the Big Four of the vanished pre-war world destroyed by Hitler's unchecked insane ambition—met at Munich (in Nazi Germany!) and concluded an agreement which forced Czechoslovakia to cede to Germany its strategically vital (though German majority) Sudeten area (which also happened to contain the Skoda armament works). Hitler promised that this was 'his last territorial demand' and Britain and France *guaranteed* the new, indefensible frontiers of Czechoslovakia. Chamberlain landed at Heston airfield waving the celebrated document signed by Hitler, and announced 'Peace in our time'. Churchill alone foresaw the consequences. 'They want peace and will get war', he proclaimed. No-one paid attention to the old man. The German press, on instructions from Dr Goebbels, described Churchill as senile.

One of the effects of the Munich agreement was that it ended, *de facto*, the Franco-Soviet Pact of 1935 which had dominated the strategic situation in Europe. Czechoslovakia, having lost its protective 'Golan Heights', as it were, now lay wide open at Hitler's feet and on 15 March 1939 Germany marched into Czechoslovakia, as Hitler, with his usual duplicity, had obviously planned at Munich. I was in England by then, and remember the Prime Minister, Neville Chamberlain, chiding Herr Hitler on the radio for having broken his pledge of no further territorial gains, and adding that, of course, the British guarantee given to Czechoslovakia no longer applied because Czechoslovakia no longer existed. I remember the embarassed tone in which Chamberlain read this cheap lawyer's excuse and felt sorry for the Prime Minister of what was still considered the most powerful nation on earth. This inglorious end of the British guarantee given to Czechoslovakia at Munich is, I believe, still remembered in Israel whenever Great Power guarantees are offered in return for the surrender of strategic positions, and Chamberlain's rolled umbrella has become around the world the symbol of well-meaning but futile appeasement.

After 15 March 1939 no wishful thinking could obscure the unpalatable fact that Hitler could not be stopped by appeasement, and, having occupied all strategic positions, obtained armament superiority, and holding all the trump cards, was set on the conquest of Europe, and eventually world domination (initially shared with Japan). The only question was whether Britain and France would surrender, or make a stand, and if so, when and on what issue.

In the meantime, the screw was being tightened in Germany, and now Austria and Czechoslovakia. In November 1938 a young Polish Jew whose parents had been ill-treated and forcibly expelled by the National Socialists in Germany shot a member of the German legation staff in Paris. This murder served as a convenient pretext for the National Socialists to levy a penal contribution on all Jews in Germany of 20 per cent of their total assets (later increased, I believe, to 25 per cent), payable in 5 per cent rates monthly. The declaration of assets by Jews had already been decreed in April 1938, when the National Socialists were evidently planning these confiscations. As no businessman can afford to keep 20 or 25 per cent of his total assets in cash, it meant, and was intended to mean, that all Jewish people still owning a business or property had to sell it in order to pay the contribution. Naturally, the market became very depressed, and people had to sell at artificially low prices to raise the cash. Many lost half their wealth. A few months later, in early 1939, when the contribution had been paid, bank accounts of Jewish persons were placed under supervision, and people were only allowed, as Father told me, to use their bank accounts for paying their current living expenditure on the existing scale, but all extraordinary expenses and capital movements were forbidden. Passports of Jewish people were stamped with a 'J', and Jewish people had, from 1 January 1939, to use the first names Israel or Sarah, in addition to their proper first names, so that any civil servant or other person dealing with them would know at once that he was dealing with a Jew. Jewish doctors were no longer allowed to practise, except to treat Jews; solicitors were struck off, and could only advise Jews as consultants. Jewish children were expelled from schools. Life was becoming impossible for Jewish people.

I called at the Jewish Refugees' Committee every month or so regarding the visas for Father and Marie Ivanovna but there was no progress.

Father is expelled

In early 1939 Father received a mimeographed notice from the *Polizeipräsident* advising him that he was being expelled from the German Reich. If within four weeks he had not left the Reich territory he would be 'removed by physical force'. Marie Ivanovna sent me a copy by express mail, and I asked for an urgent appointment with the Committee in Bloomsbury. The more junior of the civil servants on loan from the Home Office, a harassed middle-aged man, told me that they had taken note of the position, and added with some asperity that apparently all cases were urgent. So, no doubt, they all were. But for me, Father's case was more urgent than the others. I did not think Father had escaped Lenin in order to fall into the clutches of his Berlin imitators.

The pile of the processed case folders on the civil servant's desk was five or six inches high. As I was descending the stairs, in great distress, the clerk, who had been present at the interview, overtook me. He understood the predicament in which Father found himself only too well, he said. At the rate the applications were being procesed, in strict rotation, Father's case would never be considered in time. If I wished, he could move Father's application further up the pile. I would have to send a £10 note (in those days worth, perhaps, £200) to his private address, and he gave me his card with an Irish name, with the typewritten code-word I would have to use. The clerk added that he was not, of course, a civil servant but an employee of the Committee, also that he had no influence whatsoever on the decision of the Home Office; all he could do was to move the application further up the pile. I was stunned. My first impulse was to refuse indignantly, but fortunately second thoughts prevailed, and I said I would consider his proposition. The clerk emphasised again, all he could do was to move the folder so that the application would be considered within the next few days. He had no influence on the outcome.

On my return to Sheffield I spent a sleepless night. From Father I had inherited an almost physical revulsion against all forms of bribery and corruption, and knew that the last thing he would want was a visa for Britain accelerated by bribery. But I could not allow him to be 'removed by physical force'. There were only three weeks left. Yes, I would send the £10 note. I borrowed £10 (it was more than I possessed at the time) and posted the note to the Irish clerk. Three days later I received a request to call at Woburn House. I was interviewed by the senior Home Office official—a fussy but benevolent old gentleman with a hearing-aid on his desk (in those pre-electronic days the size of a biscuit tin). The application met the humane criteria of the Home Office and an instruction for visas for Father and Marie Ivanovna would be posted to the British visa section in Berlin. A week later Father and Marie Ivanovna received their visas. I never told Father how the priority treatment was obtained; I almost felt he might have refused the visa. This is the first time that I have told the story.

On Marie Ivanovna's wise insistence Father left the very next day, while she stayed behind to do the packing, dissolve the household and wind up Father's affairs as far as possible. In spring 1939 Father arrived, unmolested, at Croydon Airport (his first air trip), beating the 'expulsion' date by about a week. The Irish clerk had saved him from great suffering; to this day I am grateful to him. Marie Ivanovna arrived some weeks later.

Two university friends of Father, one a doctor, the other an accountant, had been forcibly 'repatriated' to Latvia, at that time one of the independent mini-states, on the grounds that they were born at Riga and at Liebava. The same happened to thousands of other Russian refugees. They all fell victim to the Black Death after the German invasion.

Even in November 1938 over ten thousand stateless persons, many of them elderly Russian refugees with 'Nansen Passports', whose birthplace was now in Poland, had been deported 'by physical force' and driven by the SS with whips across the Polish border. The Polish Government refused to accept most of them, as they were not of Polish nationality, and large groups of the unfortunates were left in no-man's land to die of exposure and hunger. Fortunately, someone managed to alert one of the neutral delegations that had time for humanitarian issues (I believe, the Swedes) and, with the co-operation of the United States Government, those that were still alive were somehow evacuated by American–Jewish relief agencies. In 1940, when Germany and the Soviet Union had a common frontier in partitioned Poland, similar scenes were enacted there.

Father never talked to me how he felt during those three weeks, waiting for a visa which he must have considered almost hopeless. I imagine my grandparents must have felt like that on that sleigh ride to the life-saving railway, pursued by howling wolves. But Grandparents knew that there was a good chance of the horses making it—my chance of obtaining the entry visa for Father in time was slim. Also death at the hands of the Gestapo was slower and more frightening than being crunched in the jaws of a pack of wolves.

While waiting for his arrest and 'removal by physical force', or the miracle of a visa for Britain, Father had not forgotten that my sister was due to be released from gaol in August. He had strongly disapproved of her becoming entangled in illegal political activities and endangering us all but, of course, she had to be saved. The world was now closed. Palestine, the

'National Home', as the Mandate declared it, was barred. There was one possibility left.

Shanghai

Shanghai was a Treaty Port, an international settlement administered by a Council drawn from representatives of the various European powers. Although the Japanese had occupied Shanghai in 1938, after they had started the war with China, they did not, so far, interfere with the international administration. After all, they were still at peace with Europe and America. Shanghai had no diplomatic representation, and issued no visas; they quite simply refused landing permission to anyone who had no visible means of support. In effect, only people working for one of the many European firms operating in Shanghai, or people with an impeccable bank reference, were allowed to land. There was one exception, though: if one arrived first class on the steamer from Europe, no questions were asked. First-class passengers were obviously wealthy.[9]

So Father decided on Shanghai for my sister and her husband. And the first-class passage would be a useful convalescence after three years of harsh Prussian gaol. So two first-class passages for my sister and brother-in-law had to be secured. Father then consulted his lawyer who, being non-Jewish, continued in practice, and had been Father's adviser for fifteen years. Like most professional men in Germany, he detested the National Socialists but had outwardly made his peace with the regime. Father's lawyer advised that it was necessary to retain one of the solicitors who had access to the Gestapo—he himself had not—in order to obtain passports, exit-permits, tax-release certificates, transit visas for Italy, and so forth, in readiness for 15 August. The solicitor waived his fee and wished Father all the best; he clearly thought he would never see Father again (actually, we were showing him round the Inner Temple in London after the war).

Father went to see the lawyer with access. Before 1933, he had defended some Right-wing terrorists, and this gave him some standing with the National Socialists. The lawyer undertook to make preliminary enquiries and in a few days asked Father to call again. Actually, in the meantime, Jews had been forbidden to enter certain roads around the Wilhelmstrasse, the Berlin equivalent of Whitehall, and the lawyer's office happened to be there, but he received Father in an auxiliary office he had thoughtfully available in a permitted area. The lawyer explained, to Father's horror, that the Gestapo had issued an *Uberfuhrungsbefehl* (transfer order) to the State Prison Service in respect of my sister and brother-in-law. This meant that on expiration of the sentence they were not to be released but handed over to the Gestapo. He could try to get the *Uberfuhrungsbefehl* rescinded but it would cost a lot of money. Father must have at least 5000 marks available (in today's money worth, perhaps, £5000), in addition to the usual fees for his time and expenses. Father said he would, not knowing where from. In the meantime, he had ascertained that two first-class passages to Shanghai would cost 3000 marks. So clearly he required 10,000 marks. Now on paper, even after payment of the 25 per cent penal contribution, Father still owned assets worth, perhaps, twenty times that figure. But, at the end of 1938, administrators had to be appointed for all Jewish-owned assets, and Jews were only allowed to draw money to cover their current household expenditure on the usual scale (clearly a temporary stage in the National Socialists' overall plan of despoliation and total destruction). Fortunately, Father had appointed an administrator recommended to him by his solicitor when it was still possible to do so (later, administrators were appointed by the authorities). And now Father had one of his brilliant inspirations he had in a crisis, on a par with the buying of the furs in Moscow. He went to the administrator and *borrowed* 10,000 marks on account of the revenue from his estate. Now the administrator knew he ran no financial risk whatsoever, because the sum advanced would be covered by some six months' revenue from the estate. But he ran a very considerable political risk because this advance certainly ran counter to the intention, if not even the wording, of the regulations, whose entire purpose was to prevent Jewish people of disposing of any capital sums in cash.

By advancing Father the 10,000 marks the administrator saved two young people, who had already been judicially punished for their folly, from the horrors of the concentration camp. The name of this brave man was von Schlippe and should he, or a descendant, read these lines, I should like him to know of our eternal gratitude.

The lawyer with access obtained the cancellation of the *Uberfuhrungsbefehl*. I could think of nothing more cruel than for my sister, looking forward to the day of her release, to find that instead of being reunited with her husband, and met by relatives, she is being pushed into a Gestapo van and taken to an unknown destination. I think that my sister would have died of shock, under these circumstances probably the best fate. Fortunately, it did not come to it. Father purchased the two first-class passages, departing on 16 August by train to Genoa, and thence by the Italian liner *Conte Biancamano* (if I remember the spelling rightly) to Shanghai. The lawyer charged just under 7000 marks and promised to have my sister met on 15 August and to hand her and her husband passports and all completed travel documents. Father never saw the lawyer with access again. He was deported to Auschwitz around 1942—he had a Jewish grandmother.

Reunited

On his arrival at Croydon, Father was most anxious to tell me what he had done to save my sister and I had the greatest difficulty in restraining him, as it was well known that the Gestapo employed agents travelling on the Imperial Airways coaches meeting Berlin flights and listening for indiscreet remarks.

A few weeks later Marie Ivanovna landed at Croydon, having arranged Father's affairs as far as possible. We were all three reunited, and we settled in a furnished flat in Sheffield.

Father had arrived with the ten marks and a small suitcase, Marie Ivanovna also with ten marks and a larger suitcase, but she also managed to bring two or three of Mother's most valuable pieces of jewellery, simply by wearing them; non-Jewish women were allowed to travel with some jewellery corresponding to their mode of clothing. The bulk of Mother's jewellery—that not surrendered to the Bolsheviks—Marie Ivanovna gave for safe-keeping to a trusted German associate of Father in Berlin (non-Jewish, of course), who preserved it through the war, the air raids, the artillery bombardment and, above all, through the terror reign of the Gestapo, and returned it intact to Father as soon as this became possible after the war.

In Sheffield, Father sold one of Mother's rings, with a three- or four-carat *solitaire*, for £250—from inexperience not too well—worth, perhaps, £5000 in today's money, and this enabled us to buy some furniture and other necessities and to set up a modest household in an unfurnished, self-contained flat in a rather nice part of Sheffield, with a view of the Derbyshire hills.

The crunch

In the meantime, events in Europe moved fast. Hitler had achieved arms superiority and was now by far the strongest power in Europe, and in an unassailable strategic position. After the rape of Czechoslovakia it was clear that his next victim would be Poland. Britain decided to draw the line as British and Commonwealth public opinion was now ready. The territorial integrity of Poland was guaranteed by the Prime Minister, Neville Chamberlain, on 31 March 1939.

Hitler was plagued all his career by the spectre of another two-front war. He knew full well that it was the two-front war and not the imaginary *Dolchstoss*, or stab in the back, which made Germany lose World War I, as Ludendorff's intervention in Russia, though successful, came too late. Hitler sent von Papen, the arch-intriguer, in secret to Odessa, where he would not be seen, to negotiate with the hated Bolsehviks. Their turn would come later. The previous year, as a precaution, Hitler had taken great care to weaken the Soviet Union, then France's ally, by playing on Stalin's obsession with *brumaire*. The Gestapo managed to plant extremely well-produced fake documents which purported to show that Marshal Tukhachevsky and other senior officers were planning a military coup; they were arrested and executed, leaving the Red Army almost leaderless.

Stalin thought it a good idea for the 'capitalists' to cut each other's throats. He dismissed Litvinov, the Foreign Secretary, who was a lapsed Jew, and a few other high-ranking Jewish officials, in order to provide a negotiating team free from personal animosities. On 23 August 1939 the chancelleries of the world were surprised by the announcement of the German–Soviet 'non-agression pact', signed by Ribbentrop (the former champagne sales-man and now National Socialist Foreign Minister) and Mólotov, the organiser of the 1917 pro-German coup in Petersburg and now the new Foreign Minister. In the Yad Vashem museum in Jerusalem hangs a large photograph of the Pact being signed by an arrogant Ribbentrop, an embarassed Mólotov, with Stalin looking on benignly. In secret clauses, a demarcation line was agreed (the 'Fourth Partition of Poland') up to which Germany would enter Poland, whereas the Soviet Union would also attack Poland and occupy its Eastern part.

The Soviet Union further undertook to deliver vast quantities of oil, grain and various raw materials to Germany, thus stultifying the very effective British naval blockade. The Luftwaffe that destroyed the French Army and almost brought England to her knees was fuelled by Soviet oil, and so was the armour that subdued the whole of western Europe.

The Soviet people were being re-educated. Anti-Hitler literature was withdrawn overnight from public libraries; the film *Alexander Nevski* (made in 1938 and extolling the repulsion of the Teutonic attack in 1240) was withdrawn from Soviet cinemas, and Eisenstein commissioned to make a film of Wagner's *Valkyrie* (the premiere actually took place in November 1940). It was the period of intersocialist honeymoon. Hitler had out-manoeuvred all his adversaries. War was now imminent.

On 16 August we received in Sheffield a telegram from my sister sent from the Italian side of the Brenner Pass. She and her husband were safe now in Fascist Italy and on the way to Genoa. The lawyer with access had kept his bargain. If the German court of law that had sentenced my sister had passed judgment a fortnight later, they would not have got out in time, and would have perished in agony.

On 30 August 1939 the Schwenden brothers' elderly cousin—a retired electrical engineer and his (non-Jewish) wife—arrived in London, having caught the last boat train from Germany. They had just received their immigrant visa, for which the Schwenden had applied at the beginning of the year!

Owing to military traffic the boat train was diverted to Blackfriars Station, in Victorian times a cross-Channel terminus, with the names of all the capital cities of the various German principalities engraved on the facing stones, from Brunswick and Coburg to Zerbst. This was a vanished world.

On 1 September 1939 German troops entered Poland.

On 3 September the Prime Minister, Neville Chamberlain, announced that if Germany did not withdraw her troops within the next few hours, a state of war would exist between both countries. France followed suit in the late afternoon. Germany was by now holding all the trumps.

I remember Chamberlain's broken voice on the radio; this man, who knew personally the horrors of World War I, had striven so hard to prevent the new conflict. 'The balloon barrage is ready,' he added, almost as an afterthought and without much conviction. One had the feeling that this soporific had been written into the draft of the broadcast by the Home Office.

Sheffield also had its balloon barrage. Balloon barrages could not, of course, protect cities and were never meant to; their height was limited and enemy bombers flew over them. The purpose of the barrage was to prevent dive-bombing (a German speciality with their *Sturzkampfflugzeuge*, or Stukas) of vital targets, such as munitions factories. In this, the balloon barrage proved quite effective.

In Sheffield we employed, part-time, a young accountant working a few hours a week on the books of our fledgling company. Our office happened to be opposite the recruiting office of the balloon barrage. The young accountant had an elder brother in the civil service in London who apparently would know shortly *before* the Prime Minister's broadcast whether it was war or another surrender. The brother would phone him in our office. The phone rang shortly after 10 a.m., the young accountant received the information he was waiting for, and rushed out, sprinting across to the recruiting office. He managed to get into the balloon barrage before the lists were closed. I learned a little more how such things were done with decorum.

We were at war.

Notes

1   For the origins of National Socialism see Hayek, *The Socialist Roots of Nazism* and *The Road to Serfdom*, Chapter XII.
2   'Welsch' has in German the original meaning of 'foreign'.

3   More about the plight of the thousands of Jewish men, women and children left
     in Berlin during the war (and the heroic efforts of many non-Jews to save them)
     in the remarkable book by Leonard Gross, *The Last Jews in Berlin*, 1982.
4   Balfour had actually visited the Pale of Settlement in about 1905 and came to
     the conclusion that the millions of Jews trapped there had no future in Eastern
     Europe and required their ancestral home.
5   During most of the war years the pitiful immigration quota of 15,000 was
     therefore not even taken up.
6   Lord Moyne was later assassinated by Jewish extremists of the 'Stern Gang',
     arrogating to themselves the right to avenge; Sir Harold MacMichael
     fortunately escaped the assasination attempt. Weizmann and Ben-Gurion con-
     demned the murder unreservedly and the Jewish Agency co-operated fully with
     the British authorities in rooting out the terrorists. Lord Moyne's murderers
     were caught and executed by the Egyptian authorities.
7   This Night of the Long Knives is said to have impressed Stalin greatly and
     inspired the 1936 purges.
8   The fate of Austrian Jewry is graphically described by George Clare in his
     autobiography *Last Waltz in Vienna*, London, 1981.
9   Shanghai, too, was closed after Japan's entry into the war in 1941. Altogether,
     about 20,000 Jewish refugees survived the war in Shanghai and were then
     evacuated by UNRRA to various countries of the free world.

14

In Wartime England

The crowded troop-train stopped on the overloaded Dover–Victoria line. In the mean backyards of Battersea, facing the railway, little girls immediately appeared from nowhere as if summoned by a magic wand. They welcomed the soldiers rescued from Dunkirk with little songs. 'There's a boy coming home on leave.' 'Roll out the barrel.' Sometimes even 'There'll always be an England,' but not too often. The English do not wear their patriotism— which should not be underestimated—on their sleeves. Then the troop-train moved on to the next section of the track. Only in England, I thought, were such entirely spontaneous manifestations possible.

The new partition of Poland

Hitler's *Panzers* had entered Poland on 1 September 1939 without declaration of war. The fine Polish cavalry had been destroyed. On 17 September, the Polish resistance broken, the Soviet Union attacked from the east, as agreed in the German–Soviet Pact. In October, Poland was crushed by the two socialist powers and Hitler held a victory parade in Warsaw. According to Leonard Shapiro: 'In the Soviet zone of Poland Jewish religious and political organisations were crushed and their leaders gaoled, sent to labour camps, or murdered. From early 1940 the Soviet authorities began the mass deportation to the east of "suspect" elements from Soviet-occupied Poland, and later from Bessarabia, the Bukovina and the Baltic states; Jews, though only 10 per cent of the population, numbered about 20 per cent of an estimated 350,000 deportees; large numbers perished of cold, hunger, or harsh labour conditions.'

186

The fall of France

During the winter not much happened in the West. It was the period of the 'phoney war'. The French felt protected by the Maginot Line, the formidable line of fortifications built after World War I and covering the entire Franco-German frontier. But not the Franco–Belgian one.

On 10 May 1940, Hitler unleashed the *Blitzkrieg*, the lightning war. The Netherlands and Belgium (which were both scrupulously neutral and had refused Britain and France any military facilities for fear of provoking the Germans) were attacked in force without declaration of war. The port of Rotterdam, undefended, was destroyed without warning, in a savage air raid when twenty thousand civilians perished in an hour. The British Expeditionary Force (BEF) moved into Belgium. German superiority in tanks was overwhelming.

This would have been the time for a 'Second Front'—in the *East*. Probably Hitler could have been crushed there and then, and tens of millions saved from death and suffering. But in the Kremlin, the bloody tyrant was rubbing his hands with glee. *He* had concluded a non-aggression pact, and, when all was said and done, socialists had a lot in common. And the Jews were all too argumentative, like that fellow Trotsky, soon to be disposed of. Just as well to teach the rest of them a lesson.

Soon the whole of Belgium was occupied. The Germans were breaking through to the Channel, cutting off the BEF and the French units in Belgium from France. Holland was conquered. On 28 May Belgium capitulated. The BEF and French units were driven to the coast at Dunkirk. And now came the famous evacuation, when over 300,000 troops, British, French and Belgian, were embarked from the beaches in small civilian craft, hurriedly mobilised in England and directed by the Navy, and ferried across the Channel.

Most troops had had no food and sleep, sometimes for days (at Dover each was given an apple before boarding the trains), and had to wade to the boats, but now they were safe and welcomed home by those touching little serenades.

Having turned the Maginot Line, the German armour from Belgium cut into France on a broad front. Civilians were bombed and machinegunned from low-flying aircraft as deliberate policy in order to create panic and havoc on the roads and prevent French reinforcements getting through. This fiendish plan succeeded only too well. Paris fell on 14 June 1940, five weeks after the launching of the *Blitzkrieg*. The first part of the Schlieffen legacy and thinking had been brilliantly executed. On 11 June Mussolini declared war on France and Britain. He so wanted Nice, and Tunis, and *Corsica* other African territories. In France Marshall PeAtain became Head of Government and sued for peace. On 21 June 1940 France signed the Armistice. Hitler insisted, in revealing schoolboy-fashion, that Marshall Foch's railway carriage, preserved at the Invalides in Paris, should be transported to the Forest of Compiègne, where Germany signed an Armistice in 1918, and it was at the same spot, in the same carriage, that France had to sign now (I do not know whether the inkpot was the same).

The revenge was complete and Hitler must have felt good. There is, in fact, some film footage, shot on the occasion, of his apparently doing a jig!

Britain stands alone

Britain, with Churchill now at the helm, sood alone, facing Hitler's formidable war-machine across the Channel. She had, though, the active and indispensable support of the Dominions and Colonies, and the benevolent encouragement of Roosevelt's America.

On the outbreak of the war the Schwenden enterprise received important contracts from the Ministry of Supply for the reclamation of scarce materials, in which the company had considerable experience. On the other hand, the small subsidiary firm with whom I was employed was put largely into cold storage for the duration of the war, and I joined the Schwenden laboratory which had been established in a disused carpet factory at Battersea. The laboratory, conducted by Dr Lilienblatt*, was wedged between dwelling-houses and facing the Dover main line, and it was from our laboratory yard, washing out some carboys, that I witnessed the return of the troops miraculously saved from the beaches at Dunkirk.

Britain was now a beleaguered fortress threatened with invasion. Churchill stirred the nation with his famous speeches. The spirit of the population was remarkable; general genuine fraternity linked with grim determination. After all, Britain had not been invaded by a foreign power since the Norman Conquest, though most dangerously threatened by the Spaniards and by Napoleon.

Energetic preparations were being made to meet an invasion. Ten thousand huge, reinforced concrete anti-tank obstacles, cubic in shape, were produced *in situ* and placed in-depth in the path of any tanks that could possibly be landed. Some are so indestructible that they are still in position today. A part-time Home Guard of civilians was formed to deal locally with any sabotage attempts by Fifth Columnists which had helped Hitler so much on the Continent. An Observer Corps watched for unidentified aircraft or parachute landings. Two tunnels were secretly dug under the

Solent, connecting the Isle of Wight with the mainland, so that tanks could be rushed in were the Germans to attempt a landing there as a base for operations against the mainland.

The Germans could not cross the Channel without mastery of the air, as otherwise their transports would have been sunk by the Royal Navy and Royal Air Force. So the German High Command concentrated on wearing down Fighter Command (with only about one thousand fighters) with its three thousand aircraft. In August and September 1940 the German daylight attacks were repulsed by the RAF. Two squadrons of Polish fighter pilots, transferred from France, fought valiantly with their British comrades. The fledgling British radar (or radiolocation, as it was then called), developed hastily during the year's grace granted by Munich, proved of immense benefit in giving a few minutes' advance warning of approaching aircraft, so that the Spitfires and Hurricanes could 'scramble' and meet the enemy in the air. The German losses were generally in the 2:1 ratio, and on 17 September, as we now know, Hitler postponed 'Operation Sealion', the invasion, that year, and commenced the siege of the island. The Royal Air Force had won the Battle of Britain, the 'Aerial Trafalgar'. The battle was won by a very small margin; at times, all the fighters were in the air at once. Had the invasion suceeded, Hitler and the Japanese warlords would have been the rulers of Europe, Africa and Asia.

The siege of the island

The German plan was now to prevent food and war materials reaching Britain, to cause the maximum damage in the country and to sap civilian morale.

There was indeed a small but vociferous anti-war party, agitating for capitulation to Hitler; this consisted of such disparate elements as adherents of Sir Oswald Mosley (whom Churchill had to intern) and the communists, who declared the war against Hitler as 'imperialist', fomented strikes in war industries, and sponsored the pacifist 'People's Convention'.[1] I well remember seeing leaflets signed by Dimitrov, General Secretary of the Communist International, exhorting workers to sabotage the British war effort. The *Daily Worker* had to be suppressed in early 1941 for several months because of its vicious anti-war agitation.

The Germans could now use the entire French Atlantic coast and a principal U-boat base was established at Lorient, in Britanny. Even a year earlier, in October 1939, Scapa Flow itself, Britain's Pearl Harbour, had been penetrated by a U-boat and the battleship *Royal Oak* sunk with over eight hundred men aboard. The out-of-date defences had been modernised and Scapa was now impenetrable. But the U-boats were threatening the

Atlantic lifeline. In the defence cuts between the wars the Navy had been reduced to such an extent that Britain was desperately short of destroyers to protect the convoys of food, materials and munitions from America. Providentially, the US Navy had fifty destroyers built towards the end of World War I which had not been scrapped but laid up in Brooklyn Navy Yard. After the 'Aerial Trafalgar' Roosevelt offered them to Britain in exchange for the grant of naval-base facilities in various Caribbean islands, then undisputed British territory. The destroyers, although old and slow, were supplied fitted out as fully as possible, complete with ammunition, binoculars and well-stocked galleys, and proved indispensable for convoy duties. Some naval experts consider that without those destroyers Britain would have been starved into submission. Whilst attacking the convoys with their U-boats the Germans concentrated their Soviet-fuelled bomber fleet on night raids on London and other cities to terrorise the civilian population. During darkness, fighter planes could not operate efficiently, and enemy bombers could only be engaged by holding them in a searchlight beam and directing anti-aircraft fire at them. The 'Ack-Ack' guns were Oerlikon (Swiss) or sometimes Bofors (Swedish). The target-finding, a piece of precision mechanism, was operated by a mechanical predictor— electronics had not yet been invented—which had to be set by hand according to the present location of the aircraft, its estimated speed and direction, wind direction and strength, and so forth. Some enemy aircraft were actually brought down by anti-aircraft fire, or set alight, or severely damaged, but the losses were insufficiently high to deter the bombers, and they returned to London every night during the last months of 1940. As soon as dusk fell, the sirens sounded their piercing air-raid warning and most inhabitants who had no duties went to the shelters. Civil Defence in Britain had been excellently prepared. Corrugated-steel outdoor Anderson shelters for families had been installed everywhere, window-panes were very effectively protected from splintering by sheets of plastic pasted over them and there was an effective blackout. The entire male population not on active service was organised for civil defence with local air-raid wardens, firewatchers, and so forth. Buckets of water and stirrup pumps, operated by foot, were in readiness everywhere, as the mains water supply could easily be damaged.

I personally had no more onerous duty than to patrol our laboratory building on some two or three nights a week, together with other colleagues, to watch for any incendiary bombs. We were busy on the Ministry of Supply work, so one could only get an hour or two of sleep after the 'all-clear', or sometimes none, and then the laboratory work began. In the residential areas the Germans used more incendiaries than high-explosive, although sometimes they would drop a land-mine, demolishing several houses and leaving a large crater, which soon became waterlogged. But their real aim was to start fires and render the population homeless, hoping for a 'peace revolt' as they so successfully procured in Russia, by bacteriological means, in 1917. They completely misjudged the British people, Oxford Union and all.

The incendiaries were generally of magnesium, which burnt up, with a steel-finned tail, and I still hold the tail-piece of the one incendiary I extinguished during, perhaps, some five hundred night patrols. Still, if the bomb had not been extinguished the laboratory would have caught fire and burnt down. I remember one night when I returned from a brief visit to Sheffield, where Father had just had an operation. A particularly heavy raid on the City of London had taken place and as I walked from St Pancras Station to Clapham Common (there was, of course, no public transport) one could see from Waterloo Bridge St Paul's Cathedral apparently on fire, with Wren's magnificent dome surrounded by leaping flames. Fortunately, owing to the devotion of the firemen, the noble building was saved. I remembered the blazing synagogue in the Fasanenstrasse, also domed, but there, of course, no-one was allowed to extinguish the fire.

There was food rationing, which functioned remarkably smoothly under Lord Woolton;[2] no-one was hungry, or undernourished, and the rations were always honoured, except very occasionally fresh meat, which sometimes could not be met in a particular area when due, but it was always honoured a week or so later.

Eggs required much precious shipping-space, greatly curtailed by the German U-boat warfare, and were therefore distributed with the rations when a consignment came in, mostly one egg per person every few weeks. People were allowed to keep hens but feeding-grain was virtually unobtainable. Naturally those living in the countryside were better off in this respect, as in many other ways.

The food ration depended largely on the American Lend–Lease supplies, which were introduced in March 1941 (later extended to the Soviet Union) and which sustained Britain throughout the war.

Dried eggs, requiring little shipping-space, represented a useful supplement to shell-eggs; their nutritional value was unimpaired, though a dried-egg omelette never tasted as good as a shell-egg one, and dried eggs were withdrawn from the market, owing to lack of demand, in 1950. Condensed milk, tinned ham, 'spam' and corned beef were vital additions to the British diet.[3] Sugar, of little or no nutritional value, was heavily rationed, speaking from memory to one pound monthly, and for people with a 'sweet tooth' like myself, the low sugar allocation represented the greatest 'hardship' of war-time rationing.

There were also restrictions on what one was allowed to spend for a meal in a restaurant (speaking from memory, five shillings, in today's currency worth, perhaps, four or five pounds) so that no-one could obtain an opulent or gargantuan meal. In practice, one could only have a three-course meal of soup, a meat or fish course and a sweet. There were also the 'British Restaurants', operated by the municipal authorities, in order to ensure that full rations were available to those dependent on catering; generally speaking, they were unpopular, being run on canteen lines, and came to an end after the war.

An expatriate Irishman named Joyce and known derisively as Lord Haw-Haw, was regularly broadcasting defeatist propaganda from Germany. According to him, the war was engineered by the Jews. In fact, Jewish people were the last to want a war, because there were still hundreds of thousands of them in Germany, Austria and Czechoslovakia, not to mention three million in Poland, one million in Romania and three hundred thousand in the Baltic mini-states. And it was well understood that in the event of war Hitler would vent his fury on the Jews within his grasp. They were, in effect, hostages.

Nevertheless, as always, some of the mud stuck. There were also questions asked why the foreign Jews were not in the Army. The reason, that the British Army, unlike the American, did not accept foreigners, was not generally understood. Later in the war, the Pioneer Corps accepted Jewish refugees, and many joined up.

As a chemist working on Ministry of Supply contracts I was in a 'reserved occupation' and would have been exempt from military service even had I been a British citizen. But I must confess that I did not even try to volunteer for some form of service, perhaps Special Operations, where foreigners were sometimes accepted, because I knew that without my earnings Father and Marie Ivanovna would have literally starved to death (as Grandfather did). Father would never had accepted any charity, and, moreover, I had obtained their immigration visa with the undertaking that they would never fall a charge to public funds.

There was talk of 'the Jews' operating a black market in food, and Jewish families always eating better than their gentile neighbours. The *Evening Standard* arranged for a distinguished journalist, Rebecca West, to investigate. She visited quite a number of households up and down the country. Her findings were: Yes, Jewish families, on the whole, ate better. No, there is no black market. The better meals of many Jewish families were due to the fact that the typical Jewish housewife, whose grandparents were immigrants from Eastern Europe, would go to considerably more trouble procuring and preparing food. She will spend hours in the kitchen preparing tasty dishes from left-overs. After all, in the Pale everyone was rationed by money. If, for instance, pickled herrings were sold, off the ration, in

London's dockside, which happened and was legal, the Jewish housewife in Golders Green would think nothing of walking two hours there and two hours back in order to secure a herring for the family. She would then skin it, debone it and prepare a nice and wholesome herring salad, the traditional family dish of Eastern Europe. Most non-Jewish housewifes would eschew the long trudge and nail-splitting chore.

The internment episode

In May 1940, when Hitler invaded the Low Countries, there was panic in Britain, quite understandably, because the National Socialists had used a Fifth Column to a surprising extent. False orders were transmitted and installations sabotaged. It was thought in Whitehall that the Jewish refugees included some National Socialist agents, and no doubt, there must have been a few of Hitler's agents masquerading as refugees—though, on the whole, spies and enemy agents are obviously most effective when recruited from the indigenous population, and there are potential traitors in all countries. At any rate, quite a number of Jewish refugees, mainly men of military age, were arrested and deported to Canada and Australia, where they were considered enemy civilians and interned. The deportation conditions were, almost unavoidably (and only sometimes intentionally), unpleasant, and one of the deportation ships, the *Arandora Star*, was sunk by a German U-boat. In Canada the refugees were, in the beginning, interned with German prisoners of war and terrorised by the SS. The younger of the Schwenden brothers was arrested and shipped to Canada; fortunately, his transport just missed the *Arandora Star* and sailed on the next boat. There were representations in London and, in spite of the threatened invasion, time was found for a debate in Parliament. Very soon, however, precious shipping space was in the easterly direction, and most of the internees were gradually brought back to England and found opportunities of helping the war effort.

The home front

It was remarkable how, in spite of the life-and-death struggle she was waging, Britain managed to maintain her traditional standards of a civilised and Christian country. Some day, the Germans, for some reason, put fifty British prisoners-of-war in chains. When this became known there was naturally great indignation in Britain. Churchill, characteristically, ordered fifty—the same number—German prisoners to be put in chains in reprisal. The Archbishop of Canterbury rose in the House of Lords (of which he is an *ex-officio* member) and said that reprisals were un-Christian. Churchill, virtually the wartime dictator, had to give way. The German prisoners were freed from their chains.

Another incident, minor but in the same vein. A German prisoner-of-war was working in a field in the West Country watched over by two old men from the Home Guard. A young lad of sixteen cycled past and, seeing the German prisoner, stopped and shouted abuse at him, calling him, I believe, Jerry,[4] and possibly making some rude gestures. Proceedings were taken against the lad for insulting behaviour and I remember his being fined £50, quite a largeish sum in those days, to be paid in £1 instalments weekly. I believe this was, in fact, his weekly pocket money that he had to do without for a year.

I remember thinking that a country maintaining such standards in the middle of a murderous war deserved to win, was bound to win.

At the outbreak of the war, when I was transferred to war work for the Ministry of Supply at the Schwenden Laboratory, I had to take a salary cut, quite fairly, and was now being paid £5 a week, an appropriate rate for a junior chemist. But we found it very difficult for three people to live on this. The first thing was for Father and Marie Ivanovna to move to London, in spite of the bombing (which had actually eased, and, after the attack on Russia all but ceased, but we were not to know this). I found quite a nice flat, within the new budget, of two rooms only, near Clapham Common, within half an hour's walking distance from the laboratory and in 1941 we moved in, and were all together again. The larger room served as Father's and my bedroom by night (if I was not fire-watching at the laboratory) and dining-room by day; the smaller but lighter room was Marie Ivanovna's bedroom and sitting-room by day. We were on the first floor; we still regularly meet the very nice couple, a policeman (now retired in Hampshire) and his wife, who lived on the ground floor. There was a little garden in which Marie Ivanovna grew tomatoes and perpetual spinach.

Unfortunately I had spent all my money on the move from Sheffield and we had a financial crisis when it transpired that the Gas Light and Coke Company required a deposit of six pounds in order to instal a gas cooker in our flat. Fortunately, Dr Lilienblatt advanced me the money.

Slowly, I got used to the laconic British ways.

Standing on the up-platform at Sheffield LMS Station I asked whether the train to London would be late and the reply came: Fog in Scotland. Slowly, the underlying meaning sunk in.

Incidentally, Sheffield was served by two railway companies, the London Midland and Scottish (LMS), and the London and North-Eastern Railway (LNER) (*their* stations were all called Victoria). There was fierce competition between the two companies, much to the benefit of the customer. Both companies had parcel vans making the rounds of *all* streets in the business district, and if one had a parcel to go all that was needed was to place an LMS and an LNER card in the front office window, and whichever company called first received the parcel and *delivered* it in London or Manchester or other cities the next day.

I remember, in wartime London when working at the Schwenden Laboratory, how Dr Lilienblatt suddenly required ice urgently when working on an experiment for the Ministry of Supply that was unexpectedly overheating. As the junior, I was sent out to procure some ice. I had no idea where to get it and when I saw a policeman on his beat the thought occurred to me to ask *him*. Now in Germany (even pre-Hitler) or Czarist Russia one did not approach the Arm of the Law with any questions, but the London 'Bobby', I had always heard, was the Friend of the People. So I approached the great man with some trepidation and asked where I could get some ice, please. The officer smiled kindly and replied instantly: 'From the North Pole.' I froze. So, after all, English policemen were no better than their Continental counterparts. Dejectedly, I continued to walk down the road, when I saw a public house. The inn sign showed an arctic bear in a polar landscape, and read 'The North Pole'. I went in (my first visit to a public house) and obtained a bucket of ice, in time to save the experiment.

My next contact with the London police was a few years later. We received a phone call advising us that a carrier had dropped and spilt a carboy of hydrochloric acid, bearing our label, in Vauxhall Bridge Road, near Victoria Station. Would we please urgently remove the acid? I had to set out on a salvage expedition, loading our van with some 2-cwt bags of soda ash, with which I then neutralised the spilt acid in the road, which the police had closed to traffic, and swept what was now a sodium chloride lye into the gutter.

Owing to the highly selective immigration procedure most German refugees in Britain were by now economically well integrated and helping the war effort, sometimes with a vital contribution. One family, who had founded an aluminium plant in Germany, built before the war at Slough the only installation in the country which proved capable of forging Spitfire propellers. It was guarded by sentries day and night and in 1940, the owner, as an 'enemy alien', was denied access. He might have been a German saboteur. Another immigrant firm in south London, specialising in plywood fabrications, produced the all-wooden Mosquito aircraft, specially valuable because its production made no demand at all on the overtaxed metal engineering facilities of the country. The Schwenden produced vital and scarce raw materials by reclamation.

Naturally there was occasional friction here and there, simply because English and Continental habits were so different. Tram conductors (even London still had its trams) were, to a man, anti-refugee, considering them 'stuck-up' and rude. Enquiries were made. The reason was simple. In Berlin, when paying the fare to the Potsdamer Platz one says 'Potsdamer Platz!' and hands over the money, silently and unsmilingly. The conductor then hands over the ticket, silently and unsmilingly. One acts as a robot. In England, one says 'Please' and 'Thank you'. By 1940, the refugees had learnt the island's manners and the tram-conductors became more friendly.

There were some exceptions to economic enterprise. I remember an elderly gentleman who had led a comfortable life at Munich as the owner of a textile business. About to be taken to Dachau, he had to flee in the clothes he had on and with nothing more. He was admitted to Britain on humanitarian grounds because he was fortunate in having a wealthy and knighted cousin settled here who guaranteed that his relative would not fall a charge on public funds. However, the cousin from Munich had no wish to accept charity. He could not speak a word of English—fellow-refugees from Berlin not familiar with Bavarian accents considered that he could not even speak German—and applied to the Hampstead Borough Council for the job of road-sweeper. As far as I know, he swept the roads of 'British West Hampstead', as the area with its high refugee quota was known, in weather foul and fine, and it was said that his 'beat' had the best-swept roads in London. On Sundays he put on his one Munich suit and walked all the way from Hampstead to Marble Arch, where he had a cup of coffee in the great domed lounge of the Cumberland Hotel, supposedly the only place where one could have a cup of Continental-style coffee in Continental-style surroundings, including newspapers for reading.

There were few 'Beiunskys'[5] among the refugees; most tried to understand and acquire British ways. Of course, the 'English' did have some apparently strange habits: they washed *out of* plugged washbasins, even in hotels, rather than with running water *over* a plugless washbasin, as Germans (and Russians) do, and did not fear contracting skin infections.

There were remarkably few suicides: I only know of an elderly small town schoolmaster from Swabia who could not get used to London at all. He did not like the gas fires (which were unknown in Germany) nor the professional landladies. He spent his days desperately homesick in the small bed-sitting room at Kilburn, rereading Berthold Auerbach, his favourite writer, and playing German tunes on the old-fashioned gramophone he had brought with him. It was truly his master's voice that emanated from the horn. His favourite record was (I am qoting from memory), I believe, by Schubert,

Am Brunnen vor dem Tore da steht ein Lindenbaum
Ich hatt' in seinem Schatten manch' schönen süssen Traum

Und seine Zweige rauschten als riefen sie mir zu
Komm her zu mir, Geselle, hier find'st Du Deine Ruh!

At the well by the gate a lime tree grows
In its shade I had many a pleasant dream
And its branches rustled as if calling to me
Come to me, Friend, here you find your rest!

He had no job and was living on a remittance from a well-to-do, not much-loved relative, who had procured his immigration visa. Above all, he was homesick. One day he took an overdose of sleeping tablets. When the land-lady found him, the gramophone was still repeating the last word of the Lied: 'Ruh, Ruh, Ruh.'

Something like a third of the German Jews had non-Jewish wives. On emigration the National Socialists tried hard to persuade the wives to separate and remain in Germany. I do not know of a single case where the non-Jewish wife abandoned her husband, in spite of all blandishments and threats. On the contrary, in emigration there were many cases, for instance, of professional men admitted to Britain where the husband could not at once earn money. Doctors, for instance, even world-famous specialists, generally had to re-study medicine for several years at a British university, and sit for examination, before they would practice again; quite different from the present position for Commonwealth and European doctors, who do not even, I believe, have to master the English language before practis-ing. In all such cases it was often the non-Jewish wife, who provided for the household by working as a launderess or sewing machinist until the husband could start earning again.

The Battle of the Atlantic

The main war activity was now in the Atlantic. It was vital to keep the supply route open. With the help of the fifty American destroyers, the U-boats were just about being contained and most convoys got through with smaller losses. But there was the threat from the German surface fleet, rebuilt by Hitler. Even in December 1939 the pocket battleship *Graf Spee* had been run to ground at Montevideo by the cruisers *Exeter, Ajax* and *Achilles*. She was scuttled in the River Plate, providing a useful tonic to the British people. But now, in 1941, the newly completed *Bismarck*, at 43,000 tons the most powerful ship afloat and carrying eight 15-inch guns, sallied into the Atlantic. It could have destroyed entire convoys and blockaded Britain into submission. For four days nineteen British warships, including five battleships and battlecruisers and two aircraft-carriers, chased the

Bismarck across the Atlantic and finally first crippled and then sunk her on 27 May 1941. Unfortunately, the ageing battlecruiser *Hood*, which played a crucial role in the engagement and which was of similar displacement and armament to the *Bismarck* but completed in 1920 (the Royal Navy still had largely a defence-cut Fleet), was lost in battle with 1,300 men. The sinking of the *Bismarck* put paid to Hitler's hope of starving Britain into surrender, and was one of the major turning-points of the war.

A secret weapon, the magnetic mine, was soon overcome by the brilliant device of degaussing all ships—neutralising the magnetism of the iron hull by an opposing electromagnetic field generated by an electric motor. This worked perfectly. I remember a tragic incident when a Free French merchantman, safely arrived in a British harbour, switched of the degaussing motor and immediately blew up—German aircraft had dropped magnetic mines there the previous night.

The knife in the nosegay

Hitler was now consolidating his empire in Europe, and preparing for the onslaught on the Soviet Union, lulling it into a false sense of security. On 13 November 1940 Molotov visited Berlin, at Ribbentrop's invitation. He congratulated his hosts on their great victory over France (whom the Soviets had not yet forgiven for Munich) and promised to step up Soviet deliveries of grain, oil and raw materials to the Reich. *Gott strafe England* was, one imagines, the toast.

On 22 June 1941 Hitler reached what to him was the zenith of his career, the day for which he had been striving for twenty years. The entire military machine of the Reich, refurbished and strengthened, was launched against the Soviet Union. Schlieffen Plan Part II was being put into operation. But not quite. The old Count had presupposed a neutral Britain, not an armed camp and unsinkable aircraft-carrier in the rear.

It seems that Stalin, so suspicious by nature, was completely taken by surprise. He had, apparently, quite underestimated Hitler's perfidy, at least matching his own.[6] British and American intelligence reports and decoding of diplomatic messages had clearly been pointing to an invasion for some weeks. Britain and America had warned Stalin but the dictator obviously thought that the capitalists were merely trying to make mischief. Obviously, the British did not like being bombed by planes fuelled with Russian oil.

Churchill, with his understanding of history, was all his life an implacable enemy of Bolshevism, the larva of Soviet socialism. Perhaps Hitler had miscalculated, and thought that Britain would now be willing to make peace. Possibly Britain would have been had a civilised government been in power in Germany. With Hitler and Himmler at the top, Churchill decided that, at the moment, National Socialism was by far the more immediate danger. In a famous speech, Churchill pledged unstinted support against Hitler to the Soviet Union. The Communist Party of Great Britain, declared that the war, now overnight no longer 'imperialist', should be given maximum support, and Party members volunteer for the forces. On the Left, only the Trotskyites continued to sabotage the war effort.

Nor did Chirchill confine himself to words. The Arctic convoys via the Barents Sea to the Northern coast of Russia were organised, and British ships delivered throughout the war British, and later, via Iceland, American munitions and lend–lease food to the Soviet Union, with very considerable loss of life from German surface ships, U-boats, and aircraft stationed in the north of occupied Norway. Altogether, the British Arctic convoys delivered to the Soviet Union 5,000 tanks, 7,000 aircraft and a total of 4 million tons of supplies of all kinds.

Russia had been downtrodden under the iron heel of Soviet socialism for over twenty years. In the despoliation of the peasants alone, the so-called 'Collectivisation' which had been completed a few years earlier, some ten million died. In the great purges, just ended, a further three million perished. Naturally, the Russian people initially looked upon the Germans as liberators. The older generation remembered them as an orderly and well-behaved army of occupation. The Russians surrendered in entire units, like the Czech regiments of the old Austrian Army of World War I. Moreover, the military staffs of the Red Army had been decimated and demoralised in the Gestapo-engineered purge, obviously in preparation for the war, when Marshal Tukhachevsky and seven generals were shot, alleged to have been plotting a coup.

In the first six weeks, 600,000 prisoners surrendered; by the end of 1941, in six months, a total of over one and a half million. And then the Russians, even the simplest peasant, discovered that they were driving out the devil by Beelzebub. The occupied territory was being transformed into a vast slave-labour camp. The slightest insubordination led to the SS whip or the hang-man's rope. Not only Party officials and Jews but teachers, professors and all intellectuals were being arrested and symbols of Russian culture sys-tematicaly destroyed. The National Socialists were transforming Russia into a nation of coolies.

They ruled with calculated frightfulness, trying to break the spirit of the people. When the Germans entered Kharkov in the autumn several hun-dred people were hanged from the balconies of the main thoroughfares and left there for a week to remind the population of what happens to the enemies of the Reich. Some observers believe that if, at the end of 1941, there had been a change of government in Germany and an end to National

Socialism, and the German occupation authorities had behaved in a civilised manner as they did during World War I, Germany would have won the war against Russia, and probably could have reimposed Brest–Litovsk. But Hitler's aims in Russia were so stupendous that they even dwarfed the Brest–Litovsk *Diktat*.

Generalplan Ost

Alfred Rosenberg (1893–1946) was a Russian German, born at Revel (Tallinn) in the Baltic provinces. This odious character (of entirely non-Jewish stock, one hastens to add) spent World War I in Moscow, sheltered by the Russian Army. After the Boshevik seizure of power, engineered by Ludendorff, he fled, as we all did, and turned up in Munich in 1919. Whereas most Russian Germans were quite loyal to Russia, this traitor then spent the remainder of his life developing an anti-Slavonic and anti-Russian ideology paralleling anti-semitism. In *Der Zukunftsweg einer deutschen Aussenpolitik* (The Future Direction of a German Foreign Policy), 1927, as well as in *The Myths of the Twentieth Century* (a pseudo-scientific dialectic materialism based on race instead of class and even less readable than *Das Kapital*) the Germans were featured as the master race destined to conquer and colonise Poland and Russia as the Slavs were *Untermenschen*, unfit to govern themselves. After the invasion of the Soviet Union Hitler commissioned Rosenberg to produce a master plan according to which Russia and Poland should be administered by a victorious Germany. He was appointed Minister of Occupied Eastern Territories, and produced his *Generalplan Ost*. According to this infamous document the *Ostraum*, i.e. Eastern Europe, would be permanently divided into four *Reichskommissariat*. However, the *Crimea* and the *Kola* peninsula (with Murmansk) would be direct territories of the Grossdeutsches Reich, which would also include large parts of Poland.

The four Kommissariats, administered by German Commissars, would be *Ostland* (Eastern Poland and the western provinces of Russia, including Byelorussia, Lithuania and the Baltic area), Ukraine, Muscovy and the Caucasus.

These four *Reichskommissariat* would be considered a German *colonial area*, 75 per cent of the Slav population would be removed to Siberia and the rest would work as labourers for the Germanic settlers. There would be no Jews. If Versailles was a tea-party compared with Brest–Litovsk, then Brest–Litovsk was itself a tea-party compared with the *Generalplan Ost*.

It is recorded how Hitler, on one of his visits to Vinnitsa, his eastern head-quarters in the Ukraine (Malorussia), was pointing to the rich black-earth country around him, and visualising all this area settled by German farmers.

This monstrous plan of displacing the entire Russian nation was, of course, not published by the Germans during the war, but the National Socialist rulers were already treating the Russians in the occupied territory as slave-labourers, with no other future. Not surprisingly, the Russians, having discovered the true nature of the 'liberators', rallied in defence of their very existence as a nation, and the Soviet government astutely changed its tune, placed socialism and all its works in cold storage and met the mood of the people by using patriotic language. Stalin himself, in his heavily accented Russian, spoke of 'The Motherland'. A national anthem superseded the *International*. The Church was given a little more freedom. The Comintern, whose function was to propagate Soviet socialism (or communism) around the world, was officially dissolved, this mainly to placate America.

The Eastern Front

Soon the German advance was slowed down and halted. A large part of European Russia was in German hands, in Rosenberg terms two out of four Kommissariat. Moscow was saved, it is said because the Russians had an excellent spy in Japan, a German named Sorge. Apparently he held a position of trust in Japan, officially representing the National Socialists, and had access to Cabinet secrets. Stalin maintained several crack divisions in the Far East in case the Japanese attacked. But Sorge found out unequivocally that the Japanese had decided to attack south and not east. So four crack divisions were withdrawn from the Far East and transferred to Moscow via the Trans-Siberian railway. When the Germans, who had reached Mozhaysk, west of Moscow, regrouped for the final assault on the capital, fortified by a personal message from the FuFhrer, they found fresh and fully equipped troops facing them and the attack was repulsed. Once again, good intelligence proved the most important munition of war.

Tsaritsyn—turning-point of the war in the east

A ferocious battle raged for the entire winter of 1942–3 at Tsaritsyn. We followed its course with intense interest. Here the Germans were trying to cross the Volga. Hitler's strategy had been to reach the desperately needed Grozny and Baku oilfields and then to break through to the Persian Gulf (then firmly controlled by Britain), cut off the oil supply and link up with the Japanese in the Indian Ocean. His position would have been impregnable.

Hitler's grand design was thwarted at Tsaritsyn. The German Army was encircled (due, according to German military historians, to Hitler's incompetent interference) and on 2 February 1943 some 250,000 troops surrendered with their commander Field-Marshal von Paulus. American tanks delivered by British Arctic convoy were said to have played a vital role. The Battle of Tsaritsyn (or Stalingrad, as it was then called, or Volgograd at present) was the turning-point of the war on the Eastern Front.

The British chemical warfare deterrent

Another indelible memory. The Germans, feeling alarmed, were making preparations for forcing the issue by the use of poison gas against the Russians. I remember Churchill, on the radio, issuing a solemn warning that if the Germans used poison gas so would the British. Fortunately, the threat of retaliation was entirely credible; the Germans knew that Britain had ample stocks of the gas and, at that time, the willpower to use them in retaliation. Nothing more was heard of the German project, and the long-suffering Russian people were spared untold horrors.

Pearl Harbor

A few years ago, I went to see, at a London cinema, the Japanese documentary film *Tora . . . Tora . . . Tora . . .* (Victory . . .) showing, from actual Japanese and American newsreels and photographs, the careful preparations, the diplomatic feints, with the Japanese emissaries negotiating with the Secretary of State, Cordell Hull, knowing full well that the carriers were on the way to Hawaii for the brilliant execution of the treacherous Japanese attack on Pearl Harbor. At the end of the film a party of young Asian people (they did not look like Japanese but I am not quite sure), led by a girl, applauded loudly and demonstratively. No-one could care less, and I marvelled at the tolerance (or is it indifference?) of the British people. I cannot imagine anyone daring to applaud a film on the bombing of Hiroshima in Japan.

On 7 December 1941 Port Arthur 1904 was repeated at the American naval anchorage of Pearl Harbor in the Hawaii Islands. Serious damage was inflicted on the American Pacific Fleet, with four battleships sunk and others damaged. All British, American and Dutch bases in the East were attacked.

The fall of Singapore

Singapore had been built as a fortified naval base, with considerable financial assistance from Malaya, Australia and all British territories for whom the security of the Indian Ocean and South Pacific was vital. A British fleet would be stationed there, as in the Mediterranean, and maintain naval supremacy in the defence of the area. To protect a battle fleet in operation from air attacks carriers became essential, as land-based fighter aircraft have a very short range. In British defence-cut naval planning one (!) carrier was earmarked for the Singapore station. When the crisis with Japan came in 1941 the *Indomitable*, the solitary carrier that should have sailed for Singapore (actually it should have been there) ran aground on a reef, which does happen, and required extensive repairs. Britain, the great naval power, had no spare carrier to fulfil its defence obligations. The *Ark Royal* was required in the Mediterranean, the *Victorious* and other carriers were required for the Home Fleet and in the Atlantic. The *Bismarck* could not have been sunk without carrier-borne aircraft. So the *Prince of Wales*, the Navy's latest battleship, which had played a vital role in sinking the *Bismarck* but could now be spared, and the *Repulse* had to be sent to Singapore without carrier escort to almost certain death. Japanese troop transports had been sighted on the way to Malaya, and the *Prince of Wales* and the *Repulse* sailed to intercept them. Both ships were sunk by Mitsubishi aircraft on 10 December 1941 with the loss, I seem to remember, of eighteen hundred men. Only in tolerant (indifferent?) Britain is it possible to sell cars and television sets under the same Mitsubishi trade-name while the widows and orphans of the drowned crews are still alive.

The Japanese landed unopposed (as they did in Manchuria after sinking the Russian battleships at Port Arthur in 1904), occupied Malaya and attacked Singapore from the land side with superior forces. The city, with its half a million inhabitants (they also count) and the naval base, fell on 14 February 1942, and with it, irretrievably, British prestige and standing in the East. Some 130,000 British troops were taken prisoner and used as slave labour for strategic road-building. Hong Kong, with a million inhabitants, fell on 25 December 1941.

America in the war

The USA was now at war with Japan. Hitler, for reasons of his own, possibly hoping to induce Japan to attack Russia (they did not), declared war on the USA. Britain, the USA and the Soviet Union were now at war with Germany and Italy; Britain and the USA at war with Japan. There was no war between the Soviet Union and Japan; both wanted to avoid a two-front war (Stalin declared war on Japan in August 1945, two days after Hiroshima). It was agreed between Roosevelt and Churchill, who had several meetings, that Allied resources should at first be concentrated on beating Germany—the Schlieffen Plan in reverse, as it were. This was sound strategy, if only because Germany would have to divide its forces between east and west and pressure on the Soviet Union would ease.

Soon American reinforcements began to arrive in Britain. The two great liners—*Queen Mary* and *Queen Elizabeth* (the latter the predecessor of the present liner of that name)—laid up at the beginning of the war, were reactivated and ferried altogether two million American troops safely and speedily across the Atlantic. According to Churchill, this shortened the war by a year, and saved London from obliteration by the V1 and V2 weapons.

The troops, the GIs, did not sing 'Over there' as in World War I but 'Mares eat Oats . . .' (I do not remember the rest, but it was more original), and, above all, 'Cut the balloons and let the island sink', with the humorous pretence that Britain would sink into the sea were it not supported by the barrage balloons. The American forces were stationed in various rural areas and, on the whole, got on remarkably well with the local population. There were many mixed marriages. GIs on leave came to London, where they congregated at the 'Rainbow Corner' American Forces Café at Piccadilly Circus and sat around the Lord Shaftesbury memorial known as 'Eros'.

The aerial second front

Britain had in the meantime, in spite of wartime conditions, built some 500 heavy four-engined Lancaster bombers—I well remember them flying westwards over London at dusk—and the Royal Air Force carried out almost nightly raids on railway junctions and munitions centres in Germany. Some raids, like the destruction of the Peenemünde secret research establishment and of the Mohne and Eder dams in the Ruhr, were of crucial importance.

After America's enforced entry into the war the US Air Force with its Boeing Flying Fortresses soon joined in ever-increasing strength, ultimately over a thousand, from bases in Britain, greatly damaging the German war effort. With the introduction of the revolutionary Mustang long-distance fighter, the US Air Force carried out regular daytime raids, so that Germany, from 1943 onwards, was being bombed continuously round the clock. The various reports compiled by British and American missions after the war testify to the horrendous damage inflicted on German industry.

The Aerial Second Front diverted a large part of Germany's fighter aircraft and anti-aircraft installations to the west, thus substantially relieving the hard-pressed Russian forces in the east, until the seaborne landing in France became possible.

In the meantime, the iron ring of the British naval blockade, never broken, continued to deny the German war industries vital raw materials, and above all, oil, now no longer supplied by the Soviet Union. Tanks had to be transported by rail to save fuel.

The desert war

In the meantime the British Eighth Army under General Montgomery had an important success in North Africa against the Afrika Korps under Rommel in the twelve-day battle of El Alamein, in the desert west of Cairo, in November/December 1942. This was the first British victory over the Germans on land and represented the turn of the tide in the west. Montgomery was not only a skilful general but a great leader of men; in his headquarters caravan he was said to have a large portrait of Rommel, his adversary, and before each move he would consider for hours how Rommel would react to it. At the same time an Anglo-American Force under Eisenhower landed in Algeria and Morocco, defeated a German army under von Arnim and joined with the victorious British Eighth Army from Egypt and Libya. In spring 1943 the whole of North Africa had been freed from German and Italian forces and was controlled by the Allies.

Victory in Italy

Having secured North Africa, the Allies were able to land in Sicily, and from there on the mainland of Italy. In July 1943 Mussolini fell from power, and in September 1943 an armistice was signed with Italy. The German line was broken at Monte Cassino (where Polish troops particularly distinguished themselves) and on 4 June 1944 the Allies entered Rome.

My sister in Shanghai

My sister and brother-in-law had safely arrived in Shanghai after the long and relaxing sea voyage—owing to the outbreak of war the Italian liner on which they travelled took avoiding action and the passage lasted something like six weeks. Of course, they had no money whatsoever. During 1940 and 1941 we had several letters. There were in Shanghai something like twenty thousand Jewish refugees from Germany, Austria and Czechoslovakia plus a still-large but diminishing number of Russian emigrés, mostly non-Jewish, who had found refuge there some twenty years earlier. It was very difficult to find work, but my sister was able to earn a little money thanks to her knowledge of languages. Manual work was not available to Europeans, so my brother-in-law had little opportunity of putting his newly acquired welding skills to much practical use and had to undertake a variety of occasional jobs. As the Japanese had been in occupation of Shanghai since 1938 there were no hostilities after Pearl Harbor and the fall of Singapore, but British and American nationals were interned. German refugees (and my sister was a German national by marriage) were not molested by the Japanese, who simply considered them as Germans. In 1943, although the Germans must have had quite a few problems on their mind, the Gestapo found time to despatch two emissaries to Shanghai—I have no idea how; presumably there were occasional neutral ships sailing from Europe to Shanghai, perhaps in stages. The Gestapo men explained to their opposite numbers that the Germans in Shanghai were all troublemakers and fugitives (the 'Aryan' aspect would hardly have found much favour with the Japanese) and together they concocted a scheme to load the German refugees onto boats, on some pretext, and then let the boats sink accidentally. Fortunately, a Japanese naval officer whose co-operation was required did not like the idea as non-Bushido and leaked it, so that the Japanese secret police had to disown the plan and the Gestapo emissaries returned home empty-handed. On such accidents, and the decency of one man, did the fate of ten thousand depend in those days (a very similar case occurred about that time in Denmark, as we shall see later).

The Russian prisoners of war

There were now over two million Russian prisoners of war in German hands. The Soviet Union had not been a signatory to the Geneva Convention of 1929, and the prisoners were completely and knowingly abandoned by Stalin. When the International Red Cross offered to organise a parcel service to them Stalin refused to co-operate, reputedly saying: *Pust ne sdayútsa*—let them not surrender. It seems that Stalin's cynical reasoning was that the majority of the prisoners, at any rate those who surrendered in 1941, were his opponents and would do no good if they returned home alive after the war. To Hitler, the Slavonic (Russian and Polish) prisoners of war were little more than sub-human beasts of burden; a few were induced to join an anti-Bolshevik division which was being formed under General Vlasov. I do not believe that this division was ever involved in actual fighting (Vlasov was captured by the Americans in 1945, and, together with many of the volunteers, handed over to the Soviets for the reckoning). The large majority of the Russian (and Polish) prisoners, however, was divided into those who were physically fit and those who were not. The fit prisoners were employed as slave labour, at Krupp's and elsewhere, under the most atrocious conditions, worse than slaves on any plantation; the unfit, or the fit that rapidly became unfit, were given starvation rations and intended for an early death. Soon, the sub-human accommodation of the unfit was required for relegated forced-labour prisoners, and gassing experiments were carried out on the infirm Russian prisoners of war at Auschwitz. A small gas chamber was built,[7] and Zyklon B gas, developed by a Hamburg firm as insecticide, was found clean, efficient and convenient to use on man. It suffocated humans in fifteen minutes. Ten thousand Russian prisoners of war were suffocated at Auschwitz alone. No carefully tended war graves for them, no requiem mass.

The extermination of European Jewry

The treatment of the Russian prisoners was crying to Heaven. I know of no words to describe that of Europe's ancient Jewish population at the hands of the National Socialists. In Hitler's plans for Europe (and Africa and, ultimately, America) there was no room, however humble and depressed, for the Jews. They were the hereditary carriers of all evil, the anti-race. Destroy them and all will be fine, and the master race will reign for a millennium.

After the invasion of Poland some fifty walled ghettos were created in Warsaw, Lodz[8] and all other towns. All Jewish people, about three million, had to move into the ghettos and wear a large six-pointed star to identify them instantly as Jews.[9] To begin with, the Jews were allowed to leave the ghetto during daytime and go about their business; soon, they were forbidden to leave at all, and the ghettos became vast prison camps. The Jewish inmates were subjected to deliberate starvation; in the end, the total *monthly* ration in Warsaw consisted of 2 lb of bread, 9 oz. sugar, 3½ oz. jam, and 1¾ oz. fats. Often, damaged or spoilt condemned food was delivered. People risked their lives for a turnip. The inhabitants died like flies, as they were meant to.

In 1941–3 such Jewish men, women and children as were left in Germany, Austria and Czechoslovakia were deported to the Polish ghettos, overcrowded even before their arrival, or to a special ghetto provided in Terezin (Teresienstadt), in Bohemia, or direct to Auschwitz. In 1941 some were still allowed to leave but there was nowhere to go; the world was closed, the 'National Home' locked.

Black Death over Russia

By the end of 1941 the entire former Pale of Settlement was in German hands and a large part of the Russian Jews still lived there. In Russia the National Socialists did not bother about camps and ghettos. As the German Army entered an area the Gestapo followed and immediately arrested all

Jewish persons. They were driven with whips into a forest-clearing, or any other uninhabited area, made to dig their own mass grave and undress in the freezing weather, and the completely naked men, women and children, all together, bereft of any last vestige of dignity, were forced to enter the pit and were shot by submachine-gun fire. The pit was generally filled with up to five or six layers of dead or dying people, the new batch being forced to step onto the corpses or dying bodies of the previous one. This was a more economical method than that of the Soviets, who in the mass grave of Polish officers in Katyn forest near Smolensk, used only one layer and murdered their victims in their uniforms, whereas the National Socialists sent the clothes of their victims to Germany.

The mass executions were carried out by four *Einsatzgruppen* of the SS of 3000 trained killers each, formed in May 1941 in preparation of the June invasion. The SS murderers were aided with enthusiasm by Ukrainian, Lithuanian and Lettish separatist auxiliaries (but never Russians, Byelorussians or Poles) as well as by some volunteer (or punishment-drafted) German soldiers who received triple pay, triple leave and five cigarettes a day. And there was gin for all.

Kovno 3800 . . . Lvov 17,000 . . . Zhitomir 18,000 . . . Dniepropetrovsk 11,000 . . . Rovno 15,000 . . . Riga 27,000 . . . Vilna 32,000 . . . Simferopol[10] 10,000 . . . Kharkov 14,000 . . . Pinsk 16,000 . . . These are only some of *a day*'s scores of mass executions of men, women and children carried out by the SS Black Death in Russia from the summer of 1941 until the end of 1942. And finally, Babi Yar,[11] the apogee of frightfulness, where 34,000 old men and women, and children were herded into a ravine near Kiev and murdered by grenades, rockets and flamethrowers. This particular crime is remembered by Evgeniy Yevtushénko – a non-Jew – in his famous poem *Nad Bàb'yim Yàrom pámiatnika net* (There is no monument at Babi Yar) (the Soviets, for reasons of their own, do not permit any memorials or services of remembrance at Babi Yar).

There is no parallel in European history to the mass executions by the SS, and few in world history; one can only think of the Aztecs of Mexico, who, before the Spanish conquest of 1520, sacrificed up to 50,000 prisoners of subjugated tribes at once to propitiate the Sun God. It must be admitted, however, that whereas the Aztecs tore the living heart out of each prisoner, who were all men, the SS confined itself to breaking any dental gold out of the mouths of the dead and dying men and women, to be sent under escort to the Reichsbank. Altogether, over one million Russian Jews—men, women and children—were murdered by the SS in the mass executions (more later in the gas chambers). They included Father's sister, Aunt Sophie and her schoolteacher husband, and probably Grandmother, though that is not quite certain.

The death camps

Heinrich Himmler, Reichsführer SS, had a tender stomach and was prone to psychosomatic disorders. His masseur, Kersten, was regularly in attendance.[12] One day in 1941, it is related, Himmler, on an inspection tour in Russia with his entourage, was shown one of the pits near Minsk where a mass murder had just taken place. There was blood everywhere and some of the dying were still moaning. Himmler was violently sick in front of the cream of the master race. He never forgave the Jews for this public humiliation and ordered that a less gory method of mass extermination be found. It was decided to expand the suffocation facilities at Auschwitz, which had proved so practicable on the Russians, and build a few more camps with gas chambers, all in Poland, of course. The mass murders by shooting subsided, and the surviving Jews in Russia were taken to the Polish extermination camps, together with their Central- and West European fellow-sufferers and other non-Jewish 'undesirables' and 'sub-humans'. To the unfortunate victims of the Black Death it hardly made a difference: the suffocation in the gas chambers was over in a fifteen-minute agony, whereas in the mass executions not everyone was killed outright at once; some, particularly children, lay dying in the heap of corpses for hours or days. On the other hand there was the terrible transport to Auschwitz or the other Polish extermination camps—there were six altogether—and the horrible conditions in the camps while waiting for the suffocation.

Only in some areas of Russia, where the Germans required local labour urgently, were the Jews herded into ghettoes, worked to the bone on some local project, like cutting down a forest with hand tools only, and then all murdered.[13]

The Wannsee Conference

On 20 January 1942 Himmler's deputy, Heydrich, convened a Conference at Wannsee near Berlin (in a police-owned building Am Grossen Wannsee 56/58). The complete annihilation of the entire Jewish population of Europe, estimated at 11 million, was now made official policy of the Reich. It was already well on the way in Poland and Russia.[14]

A young SS *apparatchik*, Karl Eichmann (1906–62) was placed in command of a special Gestapo office charged with the identification, arrest, imprisonment and finally extermination of all 'Jewish' (including 'partly Jewish') men, women and children in German-controlled territory. Eichmann carried out his task with enthusiasm and enterprise—no simple order-obeying civil servant he—but, of course, he was the key link in a chain of command that stretched from Hitler to Himmler to Heydrich (or, after

Heydrich's assassination by Czech patriots, to Kaltenbrunner), and so forth, with Goering getting in on the act somewhere. Eichmann built up a large office, with members of his staff, all SS men, travelling the length and breadth of National Socialist controlled Europe, from the Pyrenees and, soon, to the Volga, receiving priority for scarce sleeping-car accommodation, organising local offices with the Gestapo and the police, and, of course, exempt from military service. Wherever his emissaries travelled, they brought misery and death. In all countries occupied by Germany the Jewish population was being hounded, arrested and deported.

Eichmann arranged for special trains, mostly boxcars, generally carrying thousands of persons in each, tightly packed, like a rush-hour suburban train. The Eichmann trains of misery departed from Paris and Amsterdam, from Zagreb and Athens, crawling along the overloaded lines, unheated in deep winter, unventilated in summer, until they reached Auschwitz, often with half the prisoners dead or dying, ready for the crematoria. This relieved the strain on the gas chambers. At the height of the extermination season six Eichmann trains reached Auschwitz daily. There, Hitler's neo-Leninists used the insecticide gas for the extermination of the human insects.

There were no exceptions; no money or influence could buy a reprieve. The King of Sweden did ask Hitler once or twice for a particular person of part-Jewish descent to be freed and the Fuнhrer obliged. Sweden was important. Himmler's masseur could procure the liberation of a few. No consideration of any kind was shown to the very young or the very old, the sick or the dying. The only case of a flicker of consideration I have heard, out of six million murders, was that of a retired Jewish field-marshal in Austria (the Emperor Francis-Joseph did appoint Jewish officers to the highest ranks); when two SS men came to arrest him for deportation, they placed a revolver on his desk, looked at the time, and said they would return in five minutes. The field-marshal took the hint.

Eichmann's operations took place in all German-occupied countries, from Norway to Greece. Only in Denmark were his designs thwarted: a German diplomat, Dr Duckwitz, thus retrieving the honour of his profession, alerted the Jewish community on the eve of the ordered deportation and six thousand men, women and children were ferried during the night across the narrow Sund to the safety of Sweden, which offered them refuge risking very serious consequences.

Only in the few unoccupied countries of Europe—Sweden, Portugal, Franco's Spain and Switzerland (and Turkey)—was the Jewish population safe so far (no doubt, Hitler had plans to seize them after a German victory).

The two combattant[15] Fascist countries, Italy and Hungary, respected by Hitler as allies, refused to surrender their Jewish citizens and so did Field-

Marshal Mannerheim of Finland. Fascism had never been racialist or anti-Jewish; before Hitler, Mussolini even had a Jewish Minister of Justice (Jung), and anti-Jewish *legislation* was only introduced, under heavy pressure from Hitler, on 15 August 1938 and was largely ignored.

As to Spain, it not only sheltered many Jews from France, particularly children but, when Hitler occupied Greece, General Franco had several thousand 'sephardi' Jews rescued from Salonika, still speaking the medieval 'ladino' Spanish of their ancestors expelled in 1492. And a large number of Jewish refugees survived the war, unmolested in Spanish-controlled Tangier.

In September 1943 German troops occupied northern Italy and in 1944 Admiral Horthy, the Fascist Regent of Hungary, was deposed by the Germans and the country taken over. In both countries Eichmann soon appeared on the scene with arrests and deportations. Because of Admiral Horthy's stand—he should be given a monument in Jerusalem—the deportations from Hungary were so delayed that 80,000 Jewish people were still alive in Budapest when the city was entered by Soviet troops in January 1945. In occupied Italy, thousands of Jews had been hidden, particularly by the clergy, and, of course, Jews are hardly noticeable in Italy.

The Warsaw ghetto uprising

In 1942 the 'liquidation' of the Polish ghettoes began, by deportation to the death camps. There was some futile resistance in the various gettoes. However, in April 1943, when the remaining inhabitants of the Warsaw ghetto were about to be deported to Auschwitz, an organised uprising occurred. The ghetto was so extensive that resistance was possible. Of course, the Jews had no arms, so the outcome was a foregone conclusion. As the SS did not like street-fighting, the Waffen SS had to be called in to subdue the ghetto with tanks, artillery and flame-throwers. The uprising continued for 28 days and over 40,000 Jewish men, women and children perished. They knew that they had no chance but preferred to go down fighting rather than being suffocated at Auschwitz. And the Germans lost the lives of a number of SS men as well as the dental gold, the hair and the soap. And the clothing of the victims, which was usually cleaned, the Jewish Star carefully removed, and sent to Germany for the *Winterhilfe*. We followed the uprising with admiration and trepidation.

Our relatives in France

By the outbreak of the war most Russian refugees (non-Jewish) had congregated in France and settled down there, generally in very reduced circumstances. There were also German Jews who had taken refuge in France, and they were joined in 1938/9 by Austrian and Czech Jews. During the rapid German advance some managed to escape southwards to unoccupied France, and many were there all the time. A few even obtained transport from Bordeaux to the USA. But the vast majority were trapped, including many who had already escaped from the Soviet- or National Socialists or from both. The hateful Red Flag had again caught up with them. The different symbols on it seemed to make little difference: it was the colour of blood.

In 1940 many German Jews still thought that Hitler's final objective had been to drive the Jews out of Germany. Most were allowed to plan their emigration and leave the country, without their money, quite officially. So why should they be molested now? The Russian Jewish emigrés thought that, being anti-Bolshevik, they had nothing to fear. How wrong they were.

We know now that the extermination of the entire Jewish population of Europe (to begin with) was in Hitler's mind. But the Führer was biding his time, and there seemed no urgency—after all, the Jews were in his grasp. Perhaps he still hoped to lure Britain into a 'peace', and did not want to antagonise British public opinion with mass murders. After his attack on the Soviet Union and the Japanese atack on the USA Hitler evidently gave up hope of a separate peace with Britain, and Eichmann was given free rein. The first deportation train for Auschwitz left Paris in March 1942. The Gestapo began with the 'stateless' Jews, i.e. the Russian and other refugees. On 23 June 1942 Himmler issued a secret order that all Jews in France should be deported as soon as possible. During the night of 15/16 July 1942 some 12,000 Jewish men, women and children were arrested; of these, 6900 (including 4051 children) were herded into the infamous Velodrome d'Hiver sports arena for five days, and then the children separated and sent alone to Auschwitz, with their parents soon to follow. Altogether, 80,000 Jewish people were deported from France and murdered; over half of these were 'stateless', i.e. largely Russian refugees.

Most of our relatives were in Paris, except Aunt Helène, who lived with one of her sisters in Nice. Uncle Matthew, who was in his late sixties and had little money, and his younger daughter managed to escape from Paris to the unoccupied south. His elder daughter, with her baby son, also escaped to the south, but her husband Paul, also a Russian refugee, was deported and perished at Auschwitz. Uncle Jacob, Aunt Helène's brother from Petersburg, a widowed septuagenarian, was arrested and deported. According to reports, he died, mercifully, on the Eichmann. One of Father's fellow students, a few years older than Father, who had been a doctor with the White volunteer Army and, having been born in Riga was now a Latvian national, was deported, and perished.

Marshal Pétain refused to surrender any Jews from unoccupied France, but in the end was forced to agree to the arrest and handing over of Jewish men, women and children, who were not French citizens, and also of men of military age even if they were French nationals. In November 1942, after the Allies had landed in North Africa, first the harmless Italians but then the Germans occupied the rest of France, and in 1943 the deportations started there too. With Laval as Prime Minister, the French Police, now Hitlerised and spurred on by the newly appointed Commissar for Jewish Affairs, the infamous Pellepoix, co-operated fully but the French people emphatically did not, and many Jewish people escaped arrest and deportation. Uncle Matthew and his two daughters and the baby survived in hiding. Aunt Helène and her sister were warned by a Catholic priest that they were about to be arrested, and sent into hiding in the French countryside.[16] After the war, Aunt Helène, in spite of her age, worked voluntarily in a much-needed soup kitchen at Nice. In 1947, I believe, she caught a bad chill, but refused to miss her work, and in the end developed pneumonia and, being undernourished like most people in France at the time, died. She was buried at Nice, soon to be followed by her sister *in 1959.*

My cousin Alexander also escaped to the south where he was working for the Resistance. He was, however, caught in 1944 helping escaping British airmen over the underground route to Spain; apparently an escaped RAF man was observed by a detective giving my cousin the thumbs-up sign from the train at Nice railway station which led to the airman's re-arrest and my cousin's interrogation by the Gestapo, at whose hands he died. Shortly before the war, Alexander Poverkhovsky had married, in Paris, a charming German (non-Jewish) girl and they had two baby daughters. Both have, in the meantime, married Frenchmen, and have children of their own, altogether eight, who therefore have two French, one German and one Russian grandparent, perhaps a symbol of Europe's future.

My cousin Simon, Aunt Olga's son from Moscow (Aunt Olga died in Berlin), had been thrown into Oranienburg concentration camp in 1933 for some weeks, but was then freed (that still happened at the time) and fled to Paris. Fortunately he settled in the end at Monte Carlo where he ran a small boutique. During the war he managed to assist a number of hunted people to go underground, with considerable danger to himself. From 1943 onwards, the Gestapo did enter Monaco frequently and arrested people they were looking for, but for some reason they had not yet got round to having all Jewish people there systematically arrested and deported, as in France, and cousin Simon and several hundred Jewish people survived the war in Monaco, unscathed. The position of Monaco was, apparently, somewhat analogous to that of the Vatican, where some Jews (including the Chief Rabbi of Rome, Zolli) also survived the war unharmed. After the war,

[handwritten marginalia: schoolboy! · no · Capt. Chadwick's network · Wrong! Airmen all escaped. Long before Alec's arrest: He was denounced. · No. Only on the border.]

cousin Simon received a high French decoration for acting as guardian and [looking after 8 families] paying for the education of four orphaned children (two Jewish, two non-Jewish), and was elected president of the Russian Refugee organisation on the Riviera. The highlight of his career came when it was his privilege to receive Prince Philip, who was commanding a small British flotilla on a goodwill visit, at a gala organised by the Russian emigré colony for the ship's officers. The framed letter of thanks from Buckingham Palace hangs on cousin Simon's wall in Monaco, and he is immensely proud of being the *No* only member of our family to have shaken hands with royalty.

The Eichmann trains from France continued regularly for two and a half years; the last train for Auschwitz left in September 1944.

A new attack on London

After a respite of three years the civilian population of London had again come under attack, this time by the *flying bombs* (German codename, V1). These were light unmanned aircraft launched from the French coast on a fixed course and 'programmed' for the fuel to be used up and the engine to cut out over London. The plane then crashed and the explosives in it blew up.

The Polish underground operating in Hitler's slave-labour camps discovered that this weapon was being developed at a secret research station at Peenemünde in the Baltic, the very existence of which was unknown in London. Peenemünde was then bombed by the RAF, operating at the limit of its range. The raid delayed production by a year, thus sparing us in London severe hardship and loss of life.

Having experienced 'conventional' bombing at the beginning of the war, and now the flying bombs or *doodlebugs*, I had no doubt that the flying bombs were potentially more dangerous. There was little defence against them, although a line of barrage balloons had been set up in the Surrey Hills, south of London, and some of the flying bombs hit the cables and crashed. In London, one usually heard the loud drone overhead, then the engine suddenly cut out, and one knew that the bomb was gliding downwards and would soon explode. Had this attack gone on for any length of time, London would have become uninhabitable. And, as opposed to the night raids of 1940, the flying-bomb attack went on without respite, day and night, seven days a week. Fortunately, this was 1944, shortly after the Allied landing in Normandy, and in August the launching-pads were captured and the destruction of London ceased.

Our own luck continued to hold, and, though some of the infernal machines fell in our road, we were not injured and sustained no damage. Quite nearby, a number of residents were killed in an old age home.

8 September 1944: England ceases to be an island

An even more sinister weapon, and one heralding a new military and political epoch, was the rocket (German codename, V2), a ballistic missile developed by Germany and the forerunner of all the missiles that at present threaten the world. This weapon travelled faster than the speed of sound, so that one could not hear it approaching; suddenly the ground shook, as I vividly remember, and there was a terrific explosion literally out of the blue, and only several seconds after the explosion did one hear the roar of the approaching missile. I found this experience quite terrifying.

England was now within artillery range of Europe and, militarily, no longer an island, requiring a complete rethinking of traditional foreign policy and an adjustment in the national outlook attuned to living on an island.

The liberation of Europe

With the Mediterranean flank secured, the British, Americans and Canadians were now ready for a landing in France, and total victory over National Socialism. It was well understood that there could be only one invasion. Were it to fail, Hitler would remain master of Europe for decades and, ultimately, probably of America and Africa. It was the greatest military undertaking of all time; according to all military theory, an opposed landing on a fully fortified coast could not succeed. Completely new tactical methods had to be developed; notably the portable Mulberry Harbour (like the tank, a great British invention), of which two were prefabricated, towed across the Channel and anchored in position at the beach-head, making the landing of heavy equipment possible. Complete mastery of the air was maintained over the Channel and the beach-head with 9,000 aircraft, so that the Luftwaffe could not drop a single bomb.

On 6 June 1944, 'D-Day', two days after the liberation of Rome, in a brilliant military operation, meticulously planned, British troops breached Hitler's impregnable 'Atlantic Wall' and landed in Normandy. By the end of the year the Allies had freed the whole of northern France, Belgium and the Low countries and were approaching the heavily fortified German border.

On 20 July 1944 the Allied bridgehead was successfully established and expanding, and the Luftwaffe reduced to total impotence. German staff officers, led by Colonel Count Stauffenberg and realising that the war was lost carried out an unsuccessful attempt on Hitler's life, hoping to form a civilised government and conclude peace on reasonable terms. The conspirators were arrested, interrogated by the SS and, as Hitler had forbidden the torture of German officers, were simply strangled by hanging with telephone wire, cut down, revived and strangled again. One imagines the sarcastic smiles of the SS torturers.

The advance continued through Germany, and on 25 April 1945 US and Soviet troops met at Torgau on the River Elbe, cutting Germany in two. Over one million German prisoners of war had been taken. On 30 April Hitler, always a coward, committed suicide in his Berlin bunker, clutching the original score of a Wagner opera. The Germans tried to surrender to the Western Allies only, but this was refused, and on 7 May 1945 Germany capitulated at Reims, not far from Compiègne, to the British, American, Free French and Russian Forces. The jubilation in London and, no doubt, around the world was memorable. In Paris there was dancing in the streets. Moscow radio was broadcasting 'It's a long way to Tipperary' (of World War I fame).

The war in Europe was over. There remained the war in Asia against that other aggressor Japan. This war was expected to require on the part of Britain and America an even greater and more sustained effort than that against Germany (in which the Soviet Union, owing to its criminal folly in 1939–41, bore the brunt of the German attack from 1941 onwards), and to prove much more costly in terms of human life than the war of the Western Front.

For the population of London and other cities it was relief from the fear of death and destruction and, it was hoped, from wartime shortages and privations. The Services were apprehensive. They knew they would soon face an enemy more ruthless, treacherous and fanatical than the Germans.

German war crimes and National Socialist mass murder

As the Allied and the Soviet armies advanced towards each other concentration camps and extermination camps were liberated.[17] Auschwitz was freed by the Russians, Belsen by the British, Dacau and Buchenwald by the Americans. All the other places of misery and death were freed. The indescribable conditions in these camps, the corpses of the dead and dying, sent a wave of horror and revulsion around the world, including Germany, as the full extent of the National Socialist crime became exposed. Altogether some twelve million men, women and children, civilians and prisoners of war were murdered in cold blood: six million Jews and six million non-Jews. The non-Jews included political opponents of National Socialism from all over Europe, Russian and Polish prisoners of war and slave labourers, because they were unfit, or became unfit, for work, and 400,000 gipsies because they were gipsies. Of the six million Jews (4.5 million men and women, and 1.5 million children) slightly over a half were suffocated at Auschwitz and the other extermination camps in Poland; the remainder were murdered by starvation, disease and conventional means, including over a million in the mass executions in Russia.

It is a measure of the escalation of inhumanity and the fall in ethical standards and respect for human life this calamitous century, of the dechristianisation of Europe, that victims of man's inhumanity to man are now counted or rather estimated in millions.

The expulsion of a group of people from a state has happened often enough in European history—everyone knows about the French Huguenots, and there were several other groups, apart from the Jews. In the St Bartholomew massacre in France in 1572 some 25,000 people were murdered. But an attempt to *exterminate* an entire group, including all women and children, had never occurred before in Europe. It did happen in Asia Minor when the Turks attempted to exterminate all Armenians, the last time in 1915 (when the Western powers could not intervene), and on that occasion succeeded in murdering over a million men, women and children.[18] In Lebanon in 1860, the Druze began exterminating the Maronite Christians but were stopped by the French landing-troops (probably against all international law). 'Only' 15,000 Lebanese were slaughtered.

It is misleading, and obscuring the truth, to describe the National Socialist destruction and annihilation of European Jewry and mass murder of six million people as a *war* crime. The Germans (and here it is right to say the Germans, rather than the National Socialists) did commit terrible war crimes, sometimes by the Wehrmacht, mostly by the Gestapo and the Waffen SS (the thirty-five fully equipped SS divisions that were serving with the Army at the same time guarding against a military coup). British prisoners of war *were* shot in France in 1940 on several occasions. On Hitler's orders, 50 British airmen who had tied to escape in 1944 were shot. Three hundred Italian civilians were massacred in the Ardentine Caves and 1830 civilians, many women and children, at Marzabotto in 1944. In Oradour in France, on 10 June 1944, the Waffen SS murdered the entire village population of 642 (the wrong one) in reprisal for the disappearance of one SS major. The men were shot and the women and children burnt alive in the church. All these—and a long list of outrages in the East, commencing with the destruction of the village of Lidice in Czechoslovakia in 1942 and the murder of its inhabitants—were indeed *war crimes*, committed by the *Germans* in connection with the prosecution of the war.

The mass murder of Jewish (and gipsy) men, women and children by the National Socialists had no connection with the prosecution of the war; on the contrary, Jews on forced labour in war industries (or sewing uniforms for German officers) were removed and deported, and so were gipsies who were actually taken out of the front line. If Germany had won the war (which, but for Britain's lone stand in 1940/41 it would have done), the National Socialist extermination programme would have continued, probably extended to neutral countries, Africa, the Middle East, until not a single person of Jewish or partly Jewish descent or gipsy was alive. It is therefore quite wrong to call the National Socialist extermination of the Jews (and gipsies) German war crimes; they were not exclusively German, and certainly not *war* crimes. This crime should be called what it was: mass murder by the SS, a criminal organisation which accepted all the scum of Northern and Eastern Europe and by the end of the war included *one third* non-Germans. If preferred, the crime can be called *genocide* (mass murder of a hereditary group). Personally, I do not use the term 'Holocaust' because it appears to dignify plain mass murder with an aura of mythology.

At the Allied Tribunal convened at Nuremburg in 1945 the National Socialist leaders, and some politicians and generals, were accused of 'war crimes' *and* of 'crimes against humanity'. Unfortunately, on Soviet and, possibly, US assistance, the 'waging of aggressive war' was also included as a 'crime against peace', a new and controversial, and certainly retroactive, concept. However, the accused were sentenced separately on these various counts. Twelve leading National Socialist leaders were sentenced to death (including Goering and Streicher; unfortunately Hitler, Himmler and Goebbels had committed suicide at the end of the war), seven were given prison sentences (only Hess is now left, and he was not involved in mass murder and should be released), and three were acquitted (von Papen, Schacht and Fritsche), none of whom were indeed National Socialists or implicated in criminal activities.

Perhaps the most important achievement of the tribunal was the painstaking establishment of the facts by examination of witnesses, sworn affidavits, exhibits of captured documents and photographs, which fill forty-two volumes. This led to many prosecutions in Germany and other countries against the criminals from the ranks of the SS and other National Socialist organisations. In Germany alone over 6500 criminals have been convicted to this day, and as the Statue of Limitations was suspended for National Socialist crimes, prosecutions still take place as new evidence of crimes comes to light. The work done by the Federal German State Prosecution Service as well as by Simon Wiesenthal, himself a concentration-camp victim, and his associates in Vienna continue to bring the mass murderers and torturers to justice.

Twelve million people murdered means, taken over the six years 1939–45, on average *four* human beings murdered in cold blood every *minute*: two Jews and two non-Jews.

In Jerusalem, the stark Yad Vashem memorial is consecrated to the memory of the six million Jewish men, women, and children murdered by the National Socialists. There is a special Garden of Remembrance for the one and a half million murdered children, with a moving memorial to Janusz Korczak, the Head of the Warsaw orphanage, who voluntarily accompanied his wards to Auschwitz and entered the gas chambers with them (schools in the Federal Republic of Germany are named after him) There is the Avenue of the Righteous Gentiles, with a carob tree planted in memory of each non-Jew (including several Germans, and also Muslims) who personally saved Jewish lives under Hitler.[19]

In Paris the dungeon-like memorial adjoining Notre Dame Cathedral is dedicated to the memory of all, Jews and non-Jews, who were deported from France under Hitler and murdered. There is a memorial stone to the murdered six million in London's Hyde Park.

There is no monument to the murdered four hundred thousand gipsies, hunted down from the whole of Europe; perhaps Germany will some day feel impelled to erect one, at Nuremburg perhaps.

And some day, a new Nuremburg Tribunal, perhaps convened at Kiev, will establish all the evidence of the crimes of Soviet socialism since 1917, no doubt matching those of German National Socialism. Between them, they have made this century the most calamitous in Europe's history at least since the Black Death in the fourteenth century.

Notes

1   K. W. Watkins, *Political Strikes*, p.148.
2   In peacetime, a retail trade executive.
3   For Jewish people, prohibited from eating bacon and ham (Leviticus 11, 7; Deuteronomy 14, 8) a small extra allowance of an alternative rationed food was granted (mostly cheese), intentionally of a smaller nutritional value, so that observant Jews would be making a sacrifice for their beliefs and could be seen making it.
4   German soldiers had the nickname 'Jerry' during the war as the shape of their steel helmet (the British 'tin hats' were flat) reminded English people of a chamber-pot, which colloquially is called a jerry.
5   An American expression for immigrants who keep on carping that at home—*bei uns*—everything was better.
6   Obviously neither Stalin nor his advisers had ever read *Mein Kampf*, written by Hitler during his enforced but comfortable stay at Landsberg Castle following the abortive Munich Beer Cellar coup. In Chapter 14 the maniac makes it quite clear that it was the mission of Germany to take advantage of Bolshevik rule to destroy the Russian state and acquire land for German settlement from that 'inferior race'.
7   The first gas chamber in the world was actually erected in 1938 at Vorkuta in the Soviet Far East.
8   During the German occupation Lodz was renamed Litzmannstadt after the

general who entered Lodz during World War I, and was after the war an early supporter of Hitler.

9 The Jewish star was initially blue, at least 3 inches wide, on a white background: later, everywhere in Europe, black on yellow, worn on the left breast. In medieval Europe Jews generally had to wear a yellow spot on their cloak and a pointed hat. In Muslim countries they had to wear yellow clothes, a black turban and a heavy ball hanging round the neck; Christians had to wear dark-blue clothes, a black turban and a wooden cross weighing 5½ lb round the neck. Jews and Christians had to pay a special tax, but were tolerated, though despised; other religions or cults were not allowed.

10 In the Crimea, in addition, several thousand Tartars were murdered by the SS who mistook them for Jews on account of their 'non-Aryan' appearance and the fact that, being Muslims, they were circumcised.

11 One of the more horrifying descriptions of the massacre will be found in D. M. Thomas, *The White Hotel*, London, 1981, Chapter V.

12 The fascinating story of Felix Kersten is told by Joseph Kessel (*Les Mains du Miracle*, Paris, 1960). He was born 1898 at Yuriev (where Father studied), of Dutch–German stock.

13 The story of one such Russian Jewish community in Byelorussia is movingly related in A. Rybakov's *Heavy Sand*.

14 Extracts from the Protocol of the Wannsee Conference may be read in Chapter 17 of Martin Gilbert's monumental work *The Holocaust* (London, 1986).

15 Calling the National Socialists fascists is playing the Communist game. The pre-war so-called British Union of Fascists, which was anti-Jewish, was aping Hitler not Mussolini.

16 The Catholic Church in France (as in Italy and several other countries) did a lot to help Jewish people escape from the Gestapo. So did the Orthodox Church in Greece. In Lvov, after the German occupation, the Head of the Ukrainian Catholic Church, Metropolitan Sheptitsky, issued a proclamation against the killing of Jews by the Nazi-controlled Ukrainian militia. The emigré Russian Orthodox authorities in Paris were protecting Russian Jewish refugees even to the extent of issuing false baptismal certificates (Sergei Hackel, *Pearl of Great Price*, St Vladimir's Seminary Press, New York, 1981), and a Russian nun, Mother Maria Skobtsova, died at Ravensbruck concentration camp for helping Jews in hiding. Her name has been put forward for the planting of a memorial tree in the Avenue of the Righteous Gentiles at the Yad Vashem Memorial in Jerusalem.

17 The total number of Jewish soldiers that fought in World War II is estimated at 1.5 million.

18 The *genocide* (mass murder of a hereditary group) of the Armenians by the Turks is described in Franz Werfel's immortal novel, *The Forty Days of Musil Dagh*.

19 The story of how one German, Oskar Schindler, saved fifteen hundred Polish Jews from extermination is told by the Australian writer Thomas Keneally in *Schindler's Ark*.

15

The Aftermath

In post-war Britain

Exceedingly slowly, life was returning to normal in Britain. But not to pre-war normality; there had been profound and permanent changes in the British way of life. The General Election of 1945, to most people's surprise, put a Labour government under Attlee into office and Winston Churchill, the architect of victory, found himself on the Opposition benches once again. Rationing continued for years, there was an austerity programme under Sir Stafford Cripps, regulating such things as the number of breast pockets permitted in a man's suit (one). Britain obtained a loan from the USA of one thousand million pounds—in those days an unprecedented amount; I assumed it would be spent for re-equipment of British industry, which was badly run down but, as I recall, the largest item on the expenditure list was the purchase of Virginia tobacco. Eggs were still rationed to one weekly. The younger of the Schwenden brothers travelled to Canada (he had been impressed by the country's economic potential during his internment there) in order to inaugurate export business for the British firm and sent us three dozen eggs by air. This was by far the most appreciated gift we had ever received, and Marie Ivanovna and I were talking of it thirty years later. For twelve glorious days each of us had a boiled egg for breakfast and it tasted better than Beluga caviare. The Schwenden enterprise was converting to peacetime requirements, and organising worldwide exports from Britain: at present, more than half of their production is exported, and the company received the 1986 Queen's Award for export achievement.

I myself reverted to the subsidiary company taken out of wartime storage and was looking after the chemical side, developing it to the new peacetime requirements for which American industry had become the pace-setter.

In 1952 I visited the USA for the first time (the visitor's visa procedure still included fingerprinting) and was greatly impressed by this vast country and its enterprise and energy, achieving a high standard of living for 200 million people from what a few centuries ago was a wilderness. I found Americans very generous, easy to do business with and profoundly ignorant of European affairs.

In World War II as in World War I, the USA was the only belligerent who was able largely to build a new war industry from scratch rather than converting existing plants. Civilian production was, therefore, by and large, continued and developed, and I wanted to familiarise myself with new processes in our field, and build up connections within our industry. As a result of this trip, followed up by regular visits, we sold the American patents for one of *our* developments to a leading US manufacturer, and also obtained licences for various American processes which we successfully introduced in Britain and a number of other countries. At that time, Britain was one of the 'Big Three', and, having stood alone against Hitler for a year, and marshalled the anti-Hitler alliance, had a tremendous prestige abroad, and it was possible to obtain from the USA overall licences for the territory of Britain, non-Communist Europe, and the British Commonwealth, excluding Canada (which the Americans naturally always handled direct). It became an important part of our activities to grant sub-licences in these various countries, thus receiving considerable royalty income.

As a sad reflection of the decline of the standing of Britain during the following two decades the territory which Americans thought could best be handled from London shrunk continuously, until in the end it was confined to the UK only, and, in many cases, British firms now have to obtain licences for US processes from the European overall licencees in Switzerland, Belgium or even West Germany.

Naturalisation

'I, ... swear by Almighty God that I will be faithful and bear true allegiance to His Majesty, King George the Sixth, His Heirs and Successors, according to law.' This was the wording of the oath of allegiance I swore in 1947 before our local Commissioner for Oaths at Clapham. After having been for thirty years—three quarters of my life— a 'stateless' person I was now a British citizen. I always took my oath of allegiance very seriously and it affected my subsequent thought and deeds quite often. The Commissioner for Oaths (in his main occupation a solicitor, as customary) was in a hurry; he had been delayed by a bit of conveyancing, and was due for a court appearance. He treated my oath as the merest formality, not of the slightest consequence. I sometimes thought that an adaptation of the American Naturalisation ceremony, with the oath administered in the town hall, by the town clerk, under a portrait of the Queen, with banners flying and a band playing, would be more appropriate, as it would etch itself deeper on the minds of impressionable young people and may govern their future behaviour to a larger extent than it sometimes appears to do at present. The wording of the oath should also be strengthened to include loyalty to the Sovereign's government and institutions and observance of the country's laws and customs. Intentional breaking of the oath should result in revocation of naturalisation.

A summons from the Sheriff

'By Virtue of a Precept to me, the SHERIFF of the County of London directed, I SUMMON you to be and appear before HER MAJESTY'S Justices of the Peace AT THE SESSIONS HOUSE . . . on . . . at 9.30 of the clock in the Forenoon PRECISELY, and so on from day to day, to be of a Jury to try between our Sovereign Lady the Queen and the several Defendants and Prisoners to be at the Bar. Whereof fail not as you will answer the contrary at your peril.' Whereof I failed not, and found jury service a unique experience. Fortunately, I had been allocated by the Clerk to a reserve jury, so that I never actually sat on one and did not have to adjudicate on an accused. I had to be present in court all the time, available for jury service if suddenly needed, and was listening to all the sad tales of human frailty, temptation and, occasionally, cruelty. One gained a much better insight into the real life of the country than by reading a dozen treatises or pamphlets. And I do not recall a single petty crime committed as a result of 'underprivilege', deprivation, hunger or of anything that legislation or government policy could put right. All I saw, seemed the result of inadequate moral education, a failing of family life, of the churches or of schools, not of society.

In the witness-box

Another experience of the English legal system I would not like to have missed was being a witness. Our company had supplied a particular chemical process to a customer, and that firm's own customer refused payment for the goods treated by our process on the grounds that the process had not been carried out in accordance with our operating instructions. So our customer, the defendant, requested me to testify in the High Court that they were carrying out the process in accordance with our instructions. In the witness-box I was cross-examined by counsel for the plaintiffs. The process consisted of some fourteen steps, if I remember rightly, two of which consisted of first rinsing in cold water and then in hot water. There are sound technical reasons for this sequence. Counsel was apparently trying to cast doubts on my credibility as a specialist, and read out at high speed the official instructions, intentionally reversing the order of the rinses. He then asked me, in a routine voice, to confirm that these were the correct instructions. I remember considering, would I be wasting the High Court's time by correcting such an eminent person? After all, *he* would never be rinsing the work. Fortunately, I decided, at the risk of being a nuisance, to correct counsel, in spite of his overawing presence, with deference but firmly. From the shadow of disappointment that flickered across the great man's face, and just a hint of satisfaction in the judge's features, I realised that I did the right thing. The defendants, our customers, won the case.

Hitler's legacy

Some six hundred thousand Jewish men, women and children had been rescued by the Allies from National Socialist extermination. Had the war lasted a few months longer, a large part of them would have been dead. Tens of thousands had survived in hiding in France, Italy, Holland and other countries, sustained by the non-Jewish population. Many small children, whose parents were being deported and who were due for deportation too, were hidden away and brought up by French families. The present Archbishop of Paris, Cardinal Lustiger, is one of these children; he hardly knew his parents, who were suffocated at Auschwitz.

Even in Germany, the SS state, several thousand Jews survived, hidden and fed by non-Jews at the peril of their lives.[1] And in all the stories one hears, one thing always stands out: unavoidably, dozens of ordinary Germans, including soldiers and officials, often got to know of a Jew being sheltered but never denounced him, and pretended not to notice.

The vast majority of the survivors rescued by the Allies were, however, inmates of the concentration camps. Of these, most were Polish Jews, because most of the Jews seized by the National Socialists were Polish or Russian, but the Russian Jews had been mainly killed there and then in the mass executions by the Black Death. For the time being, the rescued were housed in the best accommodation available in war-shattered Germany, generally former German Army or SS barracks. But where were the survivors to go? Almost all of them were exhausted and bruised in body and mind, and needed a place where they could recuperate, and rehabilitate themselves through work, in a sympathetic, caring and affined environment. For the Polish Jews, there was only one such community in existence where they could convalesce and rehabilitate: the Jewish settlement in Palestine, which could provide a new home re-creating the old. Most of the survivors did not feel they could now integrate into a foreign and non-Jewish community, where they would be an alien burden, and would themselves suspect every non-Jew of being hostile, perhaps a secret National Socialist, a clandestine SS man. And why should any country accept half a million exhausted and ill-used people, of a different culture and habits, and requiring the special consideration and loving care one extends, at best, to one's own sick and disabled? Probably, with human nature being as it is, an anti-Jewish backlash would have developed in the host community had these Polish–Jewish survivors of Belsen and Buchenwald, Auschwitz and Maidanek, been imposed on any non-Jewish country.

But the British administration of 'Palestine' (more accurately, of the cisjordanian quarter of Palestine that was administered direct by Britain) still obstinately refused to allow the rescued Jews into the 'National Home', the basis of the Mandate. The Jewish community in Palestine had made all preparations for receiving the victims, with camps, clinics and hospital beds, as well as for moral rehabilitation with lectures and courses, and kindred fellowship. American Jewish relief organisations chartered ships to transport the rescued from the various European camps to Eretz Israel, the Land of Israel—these wretched survivors were prevented from landing in the 'National Home' by the armed might of the victorious British Empire, the very power that had just saved them. A large fixed-wing aircraft carrier (of the type now maintained by the navies of the USA, the Soviet Union and France, but no longer Britain), the *Triumph*, with the laurels of gallant victory still crowning her bow, was stationed in Haifa Harbour, and was prostituted by having to fly patrols spotting the immigrant 'boat people' so that the barely seaworthy and overcrowded ships could be intercepted by the Royal Navy and chased away. Fortunately, there were many in the forces who sympathised with the elemental rush of the survivors homewards and looked the other way, so that many 'illegal immigrants' (sic) did manage to reach the 'National Home'. Others were intercepted and forcibly transported to Cyprus and housed in *camps* there, though, of course, humane camps. But the survivors wanted to lead normal lives. In one shameful case, Ernest Bevin, the then Labour Foreign Secretary (who had little sympathy, if not antipathy, for the rescued Jews) ordered one boatload of Jewish survivors, who had arrived on the 'Exodus' and had been intercepted, to be sent to *Germany*, the country of their torment. And—a minor matter this, but characteristic—I remember the film *Oliver Twist* being permitted to be publicly shown in the British Zone of Germany, with Fagin looking like a caricature from the 'Stürmer'. The film was actually of some artistic merit, and quite successful in Britain, but to the Germans, conditioned by twelve years of National Socialist propaganda, it seemed as if the British were endorsing anti-semitism, and it betrayed insensitivity, or worse, to allow the film to be screened to German audiences; I seem to remember that the film was, in the end, withdrawn in Germany owing to American pressure.

To me, British policy in the Middle East seemed incomprehensible. The legitimate (and pro-British) rulers of Iraq and Libya were deposed and murdered while British garrisons, on instructions from 'decolonising' Whitehall, looked on. Aden, vacated by the British, has become a Soviet naval base. The Israelis, though, differentiate between the England of Balfour and Allenby and that of the White Paper betrayal of 1939 and Ernest Bevin. The main thoroughfare in West Jerusalem is still called after King George V (Melech George) and Allenby and Plumer Squares have retained their names.

I remember the United Nations recommending, in 1947, a (second) partition of (rump) Palestine, now meaning cis-jordanian Palestine on the western bank of the Jordan, with economic union of the Arab and the Jewish states, and Jerusalen an international city. This seemed a fair and just proposal and its acceptance would have saved much bloodshed. The Jewish community, while disappointed in its aspirations for Jerusalem as an historic capital, accepted the proposal. The Arab states rejected it. Britain declined to implement the resolution against the wishes of the Arab states, and surrendered the Mandate on 14 May 1948, leaving the Arabs and the Jews to fight it out. On the same day, the Jewish community declared *Israel* a sovereign state, thus abolishing the hated, intentionally genocidal term 'Palestine' imposed by Hadrian after the revolt of AD 135. Professor Weizmann became the first President of Israel, and surrendered his British passport to a British consul, declaring its possession to have been a privilege.

Father was quite thrilled by this development, to which so many members of his family had contributed so much since the 1880s, some even giving their lives. He had been driven from his country of residence twice (the first time losing most of his possessions, the second time penniless) and he knew of the hundreds of thousands that had perished in Hitler's Europe, because there was no country of refuge for them. So he was enthusiastic that at last the Jews had regained their ancestral home to which all had the right to return.

The War of Independence

All the neighbouring states—Lebanon, Syria, Iraq, Transjordan and Egypt, in those far-gone days all client states of Britain—were encouraged by the Foreign Office under Ernest Bevin to attack the fledgling state. The Israelis believe, rightly or wrongly, that the British forces, on instructions from Whitehall, when retiring, loaded all the dice in favour of the Arabs, handing them currency, stores and strongpoints. The British-officered Arab Legion of Transjordan (now hastily renamed Jordan to entitle it to occupy territory on the West Bank), under the command of General Glubb, crossed the Jordan and occupied large areas of Judaea and Samaria (thus creating the 'West Bank'), and prevented the Israelis, with heavy weapons not available to them, from gaining control of the Old City of Jerusalem, which also passed under the control of Jordan. The old-established Jewish community in the Old City was expelled, the Jewish quarters systematically destroyed and the famous ancient synagogues dynamited. (The Jewish Quarter is now being rebuilt in the old style.) From 1948 to 1967 (the liberation of Jerusalem in the Six-Day War) Jews were denied access to the Western Wall ('Wailing Wall'), their holiest shrine, and latrines were built against it. No act of Jewish worship was permitted during the nineteen years of Arab rule, and today every Israeli would lay down his life to prevent control of the Wall passing into Arab hands again. The Jordanians also excluded Jews from the Tombs of the patriarchs at Hebron and other holy places.[2]

The net result of the (quite unnecessary) war of 1948 was that Israel was left with the impossible, indefensible 'pre-1967' frontiers, passions were inflamed on all sides, another four wars have taken place, with much bloodshed, and the Arab states have so far refused any kind of peace negotiations (with the historic exception of Egypt). National Socialist Iraq even refused to sign an armistice and is still formally at war with Israel (which gave the Israelis the legal right to bomb their French-supplied nuclear reactor before it went critical; one shudders to think of the shape of the war in the Gulf today had the Iraqis been allowed to produce plutonium). King Abdullah of Jordan (the grandfather of the present King Hussein) was in 1951 sacrilegiously murdered at prayers in Al Aqsa mosque in Jerusalem, the third holiest shrine of Islam (it is said, on instructions from the Grand Mufti) because he was prepared to *negotiate* with the fledgling state of Israel. The place where he was shot is still pointed out to visitors.

A population exchange

After the formation of the State of Israel and the unwanted war 590,000 Palestinian Arabs left the new state. A very few were—inexcusably—driven away by Jewish extremists who perpetrated the massacre of 254 Arabs at Deir Yassin in retaliation for the murder of Jews (a shameful blot on the otherwise unblemished record of the Israeli independence struggle), some left because they did not want to live as a minority under Israeli rule, but the vast majority of the Arabs left *against* their will because they were forced by their pan-Arabic leaders in Cairo and Damascus to do so, and assured that they would soon, after crippling the fledgling state by withdrawing their labour, return as conquerors. Golda Meir describes in her autobiography how, as a Minister in Ben-Gurion's government, she stood on the beach at Haifa imploring, in vain, the departing Arabs to stay, and promising them full protection and civil rights. Neither the Government nor the vast majority of the Jews wanted the Arabs to leave; there was room and work for both.

The Arab Governments' quite irrational and counterproductive reply to the formation of Israel was the expulsion of their own Jewish populations (who were mostly there long before the Arab conquest): the ancient Jewish communities of Damascus and Baghdad, and other Syrian and Iraqi cities, of the Yemen, Libya and Algeria, were all driven out, leaving their possessions behind. Naturally, all fled to Israel (only Algerian Jews could enter France, and form today the bulk of the French Jews, the original European Jews having been almost exterminated by Hitler). Morocco (and, to a small extent, Egypt) is the only Arab country where indigenous Jews, some 20,000, have been allowed to remain. The number of Arabic Jews forced to leave their homelands was somewhat larger than that of the Arabs who left Israel in 1948, so that, in effect, a population exchange has taken place.

When India was partitioned, also in 1947, six million Moslems moved to the new state of Pakistan, and six million Hindus left what became Pakistan and returned to India. Half a million people died in 'communal' disorders. The partition is accepted by both sides. The Hindus do not strive to destroy the 'Muslim entity' and to return to their old homes beyond the new border. The Federal Republic of Germany has resettled and integrated *ten million* ethnic Germans who were driven out of Eastern Europe after the war.

The expelled Arabic Jews—religiously, generally 'Sephardi'—have been integrated into Israel and now represent almost half of the Jewish population, with a birth rate exceeding that of the Jews of European stock. Unfortunately, of the Palestinian Arabs who left Israel, only about half have been resettled and integrated into Arab, or Arabised, countries (e.g. Kuwait). The remaining half was forced to live a miserable life in 'refugee camps' in the Lebanon and Jordan, unable to earn their living and supported by United Nations charity; a pawn on the political chessboard. These 'refugee camps' form the base (and were intended to do so) of the 'Palestine Liberation Organisation' (PLO), with the declared statutory object of destroying the State of Israel and each family regaining possession of its pre-1948 home in Israel. This, of course, is not possible because the former Arab homes have been, in effect, occupied by the Arabic Jews expelled from *their* homelands, and *they* do not want to return to their birthplace. The Palestinian Arabs, or their descendants, are now the only displaced persons from World War II and its aftermath still living in camps, because the Arab states will not resettle and integrate them.

The Jews of Israel in mortal peril: The Six-Day War

In 1967—and the 'West Bank' was then firmly in Jordanian hands—Egypt, Syria and (breaking its solemn assurances) Jordan attacked Israel, with the declared objective, proclaimed by pan-Arabic Gamal Abdel Nasser, the Egyptian dictator, of destroying the Jewish state and 'driving the Jews into the sea'. Egypt and Syria, both armed by the Soviet Union to the teeth, had considerable military superiority over Israel, and I remember our anguish when it looked as if Israel would be destroyed and the Jewish population (including so many relatives and friends of ours) massacred, as is customary in the Middle East (where human life is rated lower than that of a camel). However, the Israeli forces, though heavily outnumbered and outgunned, knew they were fighting for their families' survival; the Egyptian peasant conscripts were not interested in Nasser's pan-Arabic aspirations and wanted to go home. And they were inadequately trained and exceedingly badly led. In six days, the Israelis repulsed the attack, destroyed the Egyptian and Syrian Soviet-supplied armour, liberated the Old City of Jerusalem and expelled the Jordanian Arab Legion from Judaea and Samaria (the 'West Bank') which they had illegally occupied in 1948. There were emotional scenes at the West Wall when Divine Services were held after a gap of nineteen years, and seasoned military commanders were in tears.[3]

Israel wanted peace negotiations, and might have well surrendered the 'West Bank' (except the Old City), but at the meeting of all Arab governments in Khartoum, the 'Summit of the Three Noes', the Arab states unanimously agreed: 'No recognition, no negotiations, no peace.'

Three million Jewish people of all origins, nearly half of them Arabic, now live in Israel in dignity, wringing their keep with honour from an arid soil, by a combination of hard manual work and ingenuity. The hills grow more and more verdant every year, the Carmel, bare thirty years ago, is now covered with woods and deserts really bloom, and this is, perhaps, an even more valid title deed than the Scriptures, history, League of Nations mandates or United Nations resolutions. The famous Scroll of Fire hilltop monument by Nathan Rapaport, an Italian sculptor, with two great bible scrolls soaring into the sky and bas-reliefs depicting the history of the Jewish people, symbolises the rebirth and rebuilding of Israel.

In addition to being a homeland for three million Jewish people Israel is a protector for Jewish minorities persecuted and endangered anywhere around the globe and an ever-open patrial refuge for Jewish people driven out of their country of birth. A National Socialist revolution, Libyan or Iraqi style, could overthrow the monarchy in Morocco, when twenty thousand Jewish people would have to flee to escape massacre. Where would they go but to Israel? The Soviet-orchestrated crisis in South Africa could, if leading to civil war resulting in either black or white racialist dictatorship, drive the 120,000 South African Jews out. No-one would admit them, as during Hitlerism, but they will be welcomed in Israel and integrated there. The world is in turmoil and will be for decades to come; it does not require much imagination to think of similar catastrophes in other countries, East or West, And the Vietnamese 'boat people' are still drowning . . . .

Israel, living in a state of perpetual mobilisation, with the entire Jewish population (and, voluntarily, Druze, Negev Bedouins and Circassians) subject to military service up to two years and then several weeks annually, with a crushing armament burden, badly needs peace. When will she get it?

The Arabs are realists, and, once the descendants of the Palestinian Arabs at present imprisoned in the 'refugee camps' in the Lebanon and Jordan are resettled in the vast lands of the Arab conquest, reaching from the Atlantic to the Indian Ocean, the great Arab nation will relinquish its claim to the cis-Jordanian outpost (which means little to them but is a matter of life and death to the Jewish people), just as it no longer claims Andalusia, that *Western* high-water mark of the Arab conquest, with Granada, Cordoba and Seville, with the rock of Jebel al Tarik and the swift-flowing Wadi al Kebir.

The 'Soviet repatriation' crime

Another post-war development which greatly stirred us was the forced handing over of displaced people to the Soviet Union. In addition to the liberated concentration-camp survivors, mainly Jewish who in the end found a new home in Israel, there were also millions of non-Jewish 'displaced persons' in Europe, removed by the National Socialists from their home countries by coercion of one kind or another or outright conscription, and employed as slave labour in German factories. A small minority had been recruited for military formations from the starving and ill-treated Russian prisoners of war, abandoned totally by Stalin, or from the occupied territories, or even from Russian emigrés. Few had seen active service. After the war these millions of unfortunate, homeless people were given food and shelter and medical treatment by the British and Americans, and then the majority 'repatriated' to their countries of origin. Unfortunately, on orders from Whitehall and the State Department, some *two million* men, women and children were 'repatriated' to the Soviet Union (and other East

European Communist countries) *against their will*, many at the po
bayonet, on the grounds that this had been agreed at the Conference
'Big Three' at Yalta (and the British and American authorities wante
them off their hands). Many of those forcibly handed over were even
emigrés and no longer Russian nationals, some had 'Nansen Passports',
like us. The majority of all those forcibly 'repatriated' were summarily
executed or perished in Gulag labour camps. In 1982 a modest memorial in
London (opposite the Victoria and Albert Museum) was dedicated to the
victims of this crime, and, after organised destruction at dead of night, was
rebuilt and rededicated in 1986.

The intellectual argument

I remember vividly the fierce debate raging in the 1950s over the political
future of Europe and the merits of Marxism and communism and the
underlying historical and dialectical materialism. Personally, I always
found the materialistic view of history repelling and blinkered, and did not
believe in the class struggle (nor in the race struggle); it did not seem to me
that Hitler had started World War II over markets and in order to provide
the Krupps and the Stinnes with huge profits. In *The Road to Serfdom*, the
most important book written this century, Hayek showed conclusively that
socialism and, generally, collectivism, can only lead to the enslavement of
mankind and I still treasure the first edition (1944) of this remarkable work.
In the economic sphere, James Burnham, in *The Managerial Revolution*,
caused a great stir by refuting Marx's theory that economic power would be
concentrated in increasingly fewer hands, and that nationalisation (so-
called 'public ownership') of all means of production, distribution and
exchange was the universal panacea. In fact, Burnham showed that
ownership of industry was irrelevant, as in advanced industrial societies
industry was being run by an autocratic managerial class, and share-holders
had little influence on policies. Finally, in *The God that Failed* leading
former Communists such as Arthur Koestler, André Gide and Stephen
Spender renounced the false gods. The Communists had finally lost the
intellectual argument, and their spectacular advance over the globe since
then is only due to the military power of the Soviet Union dedicated to the
spread of Communism.

I become a Catholic

Shortly after the war I became a Catholic. I did not think the reader of these
memoirs would be particularly interested in my religious beliefs and I
generally keep them to myself, but a distinguished and learned friend

thought otherwise and suggested I should 'explain my reasons', and I bow to his great experience and judgement. Even so, I write these lines with some reticence. The short answer is: there were no rational 'reasons'. Nor did I undergo a traumatic religious experience. There was no Road to Damascus for me, not even a road to Clapham Common.

I do not think there was ever a single day in my life since my boyhood when I had not prayed, short or long (mostly short), in various languages and none. As a boy, I had, of course, been brought up in the Orthodox Jewish faith (our household in Moscow was *kosher*), but it seemed to me that traditional Judaism of the post-Roman conquest Babylonian Talmud was sterile and formalistic. I found it difficult to believe that it offended God to eat a piece of cheese after a leg of chicken, though I knew that millions, whom I highly respected for this, were making real sacrifices to comply with the Mosaic Law as interpreted by the orthodox rabbis. At the same time, after the horrors of Stalin and Hitler, I felt the need for communal worship. The feeling grew in me that the calamities of this disastrous century were due to the nations of the Western world having, some time last century, taken the wrong turning and returned to paganism in its various materialistic manifestations, worshipping the false gods of a class- or race-war. Hermann Cohen said, I believe, that Man is born with a God-shaped vacuum in his soul and it seemed to me that if religion did not enter this vacuum, as has been natural since the beginning of time, then surrogate secular faiths took its place. And the basis of Western civilisation, the conviction grew in me, was Christianity, itself based on the pre-Talmudic Judaism of Moses and the Prophets. I never doubted that there was only one God who had revealed Himself to the Hebrew Patriarchs, to Moses, the Jewish prophets, Jesus, Mohammed, and many saints and sages, and I was increasingly attracted to the Catholic Church, who seemed to be *nearest* to that Revelation.

It so happened that at that time I was reading James Joyce's *Ulysses*, and few books ever repelled me so much. I felt that this was the spirit of amoral paganism, and that if the author reviled the Church so much, then there must be something good about her. Up to then my knowledge of the Catholic Church was derived from a combination of Jewish resentment (the Inquisition, Crusader's massacres, ghettoes and various persecutions and oppressions), German Protestant school-teaching about Church scandals (the Borgias, sale of indulgences, the Vatican eunuch choir) and secular Berlin's sheer ignorance (as a student, having passed my matric 'with distinction', I thought that the Virgin Mary and Mary Magdalene were one and the same person, to give one example only). But all this was in the past; now, everywhere in the world, the Church seemed in the forefront of the worldwide spiritual struggle against pagan materialism, and for a return to religion as a basis of society. With its social teaching, embodied in the great encyclicals *De Rerum Novarum* and *Quadragesimo Anno*, the Church seemed well placed to provide a spiritual basis for the rebuilding of war-shattered Europe. To me the Gulag and Auschwitz were the result of the dechristianisation of Europe: neither would have been possible during the nineteenth century as they would have been regarded as contrary to Christian teaching. As to dogma, I was never interested in its finer points and was content to leave it to the theologians. It was always my view that God, though omnipotent, abides by the Laws of His creation, and that many things, such as infinity and eternity, surpass human comprehension, so that it is futile to try to define what are and always will be mysteries in precise scientific or legalistic terms.

I had also read Matthew Arnold and was impressed by *Dover Beach*, prophesying a renascence of religion, and was stirred by Father Raphael Simon's *The Glory of Thy People, the Story of a Conversion* (1948). No person, however, ever tried to interest me in the Church, and any missionary approach would probably have been counterproductive, as I have an ingrained resistance to being talked into anything. On impulse, I contacted Father Martindale, SJ, one of whose publications I had seen, and asked for more information on the Church, and in the end had religious instruction and was received into the Church. One of the many positive and non-formalistic features of Judaism is the honouring of one's parents, as ordained in the Fifth Commandment, and a memorial candle is lit and the *Kaddish* prayer recited on the anniversary of a parent's death. This was, in fact, the only Jewish rite I had been observing annually on the anniversary of my mother's death, and naturally I told the good Father, who gave me religious instruction that I intended to continue remembering my mother in this time-honoured way, and, when the time came, also my father. The good Father told me that he would have to consult his superiors, and informed me next time that the *Kaddish* ('Magnify and hallow the name of the Lord . . .') was fully compatible with the Christian religion and, in fact, was the precursor of Christian prayers, but to make quite sure for myself that there was no conflict of loyalties I should always recite the Lord's Prayer after the *Kaddish*. This seemed an excellent suggestion, and I have honoured Father's and Mother's memory in this syncretic way ever since. One could only wish that the two sister-religions of Christianity would adopt this greatest prayer of all times.

My reception into the Church was, of course, before the Vatican II reforms, when the Mass was said in Latin and the priest faced the altar, and I remember feeling that the Latin language was somewhat young and upstart for the great and time-hallowed Sacrament of the Mass, the sublimation of the Temple sacrifice, and would have preferred the priest to celebrate Mass in Hebrew or Greek (and, of course, Latin was the language of the Roman aggressor, the destroyer of Israel). At that time, however, the *Kyrie* was still said in Greek, which meant much to me as a symbol, and I would have liked the *Sanctus* to be said in the original Hebrew. At least, I would have liked the Old Testament and the Gospels to be read in the original languages, as symbols of the continuity of Revealed Religion. So much has been lost in the graecised translations; how many worshippers know, for instance, that Jesus's name was Joshúa, meaning God Helps,[4] and St John the Baptist's name was JochanaАn, meaning God is Merciful? And this list can be continued with so many sacred names and placenames. Of course, the Russian Orthodox Church, the Anglican Church (as she was then) and many Eastern Churches are an essential part of the Catholic Church, but it seemed to me that they had departed a little further from the original Revelation and pre-Roman conquest Judaic tradition, and had largely regional or ethnic validity, whereas the Catholic Church was universal. I was attracted, though, by some features of the Orthodox Church, such as the consecration being carried out by the priest behind closed altar doors, undistracted by the gaze of the congregation and by the prohibition of statues in Orthodox churches which I found, and still find, most disturbing (statues are, of course, also prohibited in synagogues and mosques as objects of idolatry).

Of course, I was somewhat worried over Vatican temporal policies and long-term objectives, not always sympathetic to British, or Israeli, or Russian (as opposed to Soviet) just aims. In fact, the State of Israel is, at present, not yet recognised by the Vatican, and the last pilgrimage of a Pope to Jerusalem took place when this was under illegal and anti-Jewish Jordanian occupation. I now pray for a visit of the Pope to Israel and diplomatic recognition. I also found the Catholic Church's often-expressed claims of supremacy over the Orthodox and Anglican Churches disturbing. 'In thy Father's House are many Mansions.' There were also opportunist tendencies to play down, or conceal, the Church's Jewish roots, and to downgrade the Old Testament, including the Prophets with their great contemporary validity. On the other hand, the fact that the Catholic Church was a *minority* denomination in England made it much easier for me to enter; I would have found it much more difficult to become a Catholic in Ireland or Spain, as I would always have the nagging suspicion that *subconsciously* I had wanted to join the majority, and that is something against which I have a built-in resistance, probably as part of my post-exile Jewish heritage.

Since my reception into the Church I have always felt, with moderate devotion and diverse mental reservations in matters of dogma and teaching, let alone some Vatican policies, at home there, and have coped with life's problems and vicissitudes more easily than had I not found the way to the Church.

Some years after I became a Catholic (not so much a conversion as a natural progression from lifelong belief in the Divine Revelation, but a purely nominal Judaism, to recognition of the need for communal worship and the associated priestly function) I learnt in a practical experience the force of prayer (which I never doubted). The small subsidiary company I was at the time managing had a bad financial year; the accountant was walking around with a glum face, and warned me that there would be a loss. I knew that our shareholders were at the time in a crisis themselves, and that a loss would probably mean liquidation of our company and I would lose my job. Generally, there was full employment, so I had no great worry over the staff, but as a foreigner, without British qualifications, I would have found it extremely difficult to find suitable employment. My first impulse, as always, was to pray that there should not be a loss, but I said to myself that even God, whilst omnipotent, cannot change what *has* happened—this was after the end of the financial year—and 'cook the books'. On second thoughts, though, I walked to our Catholic church, lit a candle and prayed for a miracle that there should be no loss. A few days later we received a cheque for an amount written off as a bad debt of a bankrupt limited company, as *entirely voluntary* repayment from the former owner who had come into some money. The loss was wiped out and soon afterwards we did extremely well. A miracle?

Restitution of Father's stolen property

After this world war there were no reparations. They had caused enough problems after the first one. In any case, Germany was so ruined that it simply did not have the physical means of repairing the material damage she had caused in other countries. The USA, with the Marshal Plan, laid out exceptionally large sums of money for the reconstruction of Western Europe. In effect, it was the USA who paid for the war damage. This proved a farsighted policy (unless now defeated by the new overt or covert neutralist tendencies in Europe and even Britain). However, after some first-aid, currency-stabilisation and so forth, Germany (meaning Western Germany, now the Federal Republic) approached the problem of returning the assets expropriated from the Jewish population. A German–Jewish Claims Conference was established at The Hague, and as a result of an agreed basis the required legislation was passed in Germany. To prevent misunderstanding: the enormous National Socialist crime of the mass murder of six million people was not even mentioned. Murder cannot be expiated by money. No-one spoke of the dental gold in the Reichsbank vaults either. This was an economic conference dealing with the return of stolen property. Here is not the place to elaborate on the details of this complex legislation on which bulky commentaries have been written. The restitution and compensation legislation passed in Germany naturally only referred to assets that had been located in what was now Western Germany (incuding West Berlin). Other countries such as France, Italy, Belgium and Holland passed their own legislation. The Eastern bloc countries (including Eastern Germany with East Berlin) passed no legislation, as far as I know, and have no restitution or compensation for stolen property. In Western Germany (including West Berlin) where Father had most of his assets (a few were in East Berlin) there was a difference between identifiable assets, confiscated by the National Socialists but still in existence physically which were returned to the rightful owner, and confiscated non-identifiable assets, for which compensation was paid. When assets had been not confiscated but sold under pressure at cut prices in 1939, the original owner could either claim return from the present owner and refund the original purchase price to him or the new owner could retain the asset but make up the purchase price to a fair level to the original owner. The present owners were therefore fully protected, and the arrangement worked smoothly. The Schwenden had their factories in Western Germany returned to them but not, of course, in Communist Eastern Germany.

Shares in quoted companies were considered identifiable, and, if they had been confiscated, the post-war value repaid. This could be, naturally, more or less than the pre-war value. On non-identifiable assets—for example, bank accounts, debentures, commercial debts, etc.—confiscated by the National Socialists, and even on discriminatory taxes such as the 25 per cent penal wealth tax, and the emigration tax, the compensation payable by the Federal Republic was 20 per cent of the nominal value. It is often thought that the full value of all expropriated assets was refunded, but that was not the case, nor could it be reasonably expected. Father considered the compensation terms fair. The only exception from the 20 per cent rule on non-identifiable assets was confiscated furniture and household effects, for which the full insurance value was refunded.

The total value of all compensation payments by the Federal Republic of Germany was £17,000 million which works out at just under £30,000 per pre-war Jewish inhabitant. This sum included, of course, in addition to compensation for expropriated assets, compensation for wrongful imprisonment, personal injury, interruption of education, loss of office, etc. Moreover, pensions are paid to German refugees abroad on the Federal Republic scale; in the case of public servants (which in Germany include all school teachers, university professors, etc.) at the rate to which they would have been entitled had they been able to continue with their careers in

Germany. One of my old school friends, for instance, who taught biology in Berlin for a year and was thrown out of the profession by Hitler in 1933 and managed to gain access to Israel, now receives from the Federal Republic a pension of a *Studienrat*, the highest rank of a teacher at a state school, and his pension makes it possible for him to travel regularly to West Germany and other European countries.

Much of the confiscated Jewish property was heirless, because entire families had been murdered and there was no identifiable next of kin. It was agreed at The Hague that restitution proceeds for this heirless property would go to the State of Israel to assist towards the resettlement of the survivors.

Father still had no means of his own (except Mother's jewellery, brought out from Moscow, which, as mentioned, was returned to him by a loyal German after the war) and he took the greatest interest in the restitution proceedings. Not only were we living in very cramped conditions but, having been a man of substance all his life, Father suffered greatly from having now, in his old age, no property and no income. To him it was a moral issue that stolen property must be returned. Father's pre-war solicitor in Berlin, an eminent lawyer, agreed to take on his restitution claims with his fees payable from the restitution proceeds only. I had not lost anything. And, thank Heaven, none of us had been wrongfully imprisoned or permanently disabled: this also entitled to compensation. In fact, compared with the millions that died and the millions—Jews and non-Jews—that survived as human wrecks we suffered nothing worse than the loss of Father's property, and even so were never hungry and always had a roof above our head. Among the victims of socialism—Soviet and National— we were the privileged minority, though Father felt it very strongly that he had suffered despoliation and expulsion twice.

My work with the Schwenden company

The subsidiary Schwenden company, where I was in charge of the chemical business, developed very nicely. I produced a few developments which brought not-inconsiderable profits, and the Schwenden, always generous in rewarding success (though impatient of failure), increased my income, so matters were a little easier. My career with the company had its ups and downs and was somewhat stormy, mainly due to the fact that I associated myself so closely with my work that I behaved as if the company was owned by me, and, when sure of the right course of action, omitted to establish a consensus and to protect myself. Fortunately, the company were very patient with me, and gave me plenty of rope. Certainly I was no yes-man; normally I kept my temper under control but on one celebrated occasion I have never been allowed to forget that I threw a telephone directory *in the direction of* (not at) the Chairman. However, business developed favourably, and with it my financial position.

The elder of the Schwenden brothers, who had so successfully steered the company through the wartime and post-war period died in 1977, after heroically bearing a kidney disease, and the now worldwide enterprise, including the restituted German works, has been presided over and greatly expanded by the younger brother, now nearing retirement.

We purchase a house

Sometime in the 1950s Father told me, to my great sorrow, that he felt he did not have long to live, and it was usual for Schmerlings to die in their own property. Could we manage to buy a house? We calculated and calculated—purely financially a house purchase was somewhat premature. However, the main Schwenden company generously lent me a thousand pounds, interest-free, for a year; this amount was at the time sufficient as a deposit, and we purchased a pleasant, semi-detached three-bedroom house in a quiet, residential road in Streatham. Having spent a dozen years in two rooms, this was a tremendous improvement. Each of us now had a bedroom upstairs, and there were two living-rooms downstairs, with a pleasant garden.

A post-war visit to Germany

The subsidiary company with whom I was working was licensing several processes for which we held the patent rights to companies abroad against royalty payments, and it became necessary for me to travel to Germany to call on a would-be licensee. All Germans professed at the time, to have been anti-Hitler—the SS had obviously been a Foreign Legion—but I knew that the people I went to see had genuinely been against National Socialism all the time; in fact a member of the family (non-Jewish, of course) perished at Dachau. But I was haunted by the ghosts of the past all the time. Naturally, I had brought my own soap—one knew that soap had been made from human fats at Auschwitz. I could not sleep at the hotel because hair was coming out of my mattress, and I fancied it was woman's hair from the stocks produced at Auschwitz and sold to German industry. I had a cup of coffee in the restaurant-car, and persuaded myself that the middle-aged man opposite, of Neanderthal appearance, with receding forehead and brutal jaw, was a former member of the SS Death's Head ('Skull and Cross-bones') formations that provided the concentration-camp guards, and I felt nausea. In vain, I told myself, he could also have been a concentration-camp victim, even a Righteous Gentile, and I left the coffee undrunk and fled. The licence agreement having been concluded, I was glad to return to England. In later years, particularly after the many convictions of National Socialist criminals which, I felt, had cleansed Germany, my reactions wore off, and I travelled to that country without difficulty. Also I was much impressed by the 'moral restitution' practised in Germany: mayors of small provincial towns in the Federal Republic would get in touch with former Jewish residents overseas and invite them for a visit to their home town. This gesture was always much appreciated. As to the German people, the larger part are now under fifty, and were under ten, or not yet born, when the war ended. I do not believe in the heredity of guilt or in racialism. And many of today's Germans' parents suffered in concentration camps too. To me, aggressive virulent socialism is an international plague which can break out from the sewers anywhere.

Father's death

In November 1956 Father received the first compensation payment from Germany, 20,000 marks (at the time, about £1,600), the full value (100 per cent) of his confiscated furniture and household effects. This was seventeen years after the confiscation and no interest was payable, but I still remember Father's jubilant face. At long last, justice had been done, and he had again some money of his own. Father was discussing the best way of investing the money, and was even talking of spending a small part for a holiday for us the next summer, perhaps two or three days at Eastbourne (which we had visited on day-trips and Father rather liked). His last holiday was 1917, in the Caucasus.

In December 1956 Father died, in our own house, and a happy man, from a sudden and instantaneous heart failure at the age of 76. According to his wishes, he was cremated at Streatham Crematorium and the ashes buried there.

Uncle Matthew

Uncle Matthew, though older, and in spite of having had to spend the last years of war in hiding in hungry France, survived Father by several years. His small flat in Paris, which had been confiscated, was returned to him; when I visited him, a nonagenarian, after the war, his sight and hearing were impaired but his mind was completely alert, and he gave me a perfectly lucid exposition of Europe's economic problems, enumerating quite correctly the six countries of the EEC, the seven countries of EFTA, etc. Uncle Matthew was quite fond of France; what he was missing were the birch forests of his native Byelorussia, which he would have loved to see once again.

At the age of 95, Uncle Matthew died and was buried at the Russian Cemetery which, in the meantime, had been consecrated near Paris.

At the German Embassy

Some months after Father's sad death I had an appointment at the German Embassy in Belgrave Square to complete formalities, as I had inherited Father's outstanding compensation claims (all but the household compensation). I would mention now that in the meantime they have all been settled, on the 100 per cent or 20 per cent basis, as appropriate. Overall, the compensation worked out at about 29 per cent in our case.

At the embassy the Legal Counsellor, Botschaftsrat von . . . asked me, with great courtesy, the usual questions of place of birth, date of birth, nationality, residence, etc. Suddenly his face twitched, as if in great pain. There was an expression of anguish, as if he was about to be hit in the face by an SS whip.

'And where did your *Herr Vater* die?' he asked in a low whisper.

'At our home in Streatham,' I replied innocently.

The pain was gone. The Botschaftsrat was again the courteous and self-possessed civil servant. And then only did I understand that the dreaded answer that he expected, the answer he had heard from nine out of ten refugee callers, was 'In Auschwitz, on the Eichmann, deported—place of death unknown'.

Acclimatisation in England

In the course of my employment, working with the staff, visiting British industry first as service chemist then as technical director, I naturally became familiar with the British way of life, so different from the various Continental countries I knew. Also I developed an appreciation of the British national character, slowly moulded over a thousand years from an unusually harmonious and well-proportioned blend of races and cultures in the security of an island-home. I also admired the stability of the British political system, whilst realising that it had gradually evolved in tune with the British national character, and was consequently unlikely to be suitable for transplant to countries of non-British stock.

I joined the Chemical Club, initially having its own fine premises in Whitehall Court, later, after the conversion of that great building to an hotel, using by arrangement the premises of the National Liberal Club in Whitehall Place, and in the end I was elected a member of the National

Liberal Club—a highly valued privilege, and I often use it as *pied-à-terre* in town—whilst being a committed member of the Conservative Party.

Slowly, I began to identify myself with Britain, as I noticed clearly during the Falklands War, and I remember how relieved I was when the *General Belgrano* Argentinian heavy cruiser was sunk and that highly dangerous threat to the British Task Force removed. And there was no doubt in my mind that the responsibility for the loss of life lay clearly with the Argentinian agressor. I also rejoiced at Britain's reputation abroad, somewhat tarnished during the post-war years, being again raised high by demonstrating her will and ability to resist aggression.

At the age of 70 I retired from whole-time duties,[5] retaining a consultancy only, and was able to devote some thought and time to other interests: reading periodicals, history and historical novels, physiology (particularly endocrinology), but not crime and science fiction; writing (long letters to friends, short letters to the press, this book . . .), gardening.

I was fortunate to be able to travel to Israel, Greece and Egypt, the cradles of civilisation, with some preparation (though not too thorough), and am attempting to get to know Britain, its architecture and landscapes. And I started a small record collection, mainly operatic and vocal. With all this I seem to have even less time than before.

Notes

1   The story of some of these Jews has been researched and described by Leonard Gross in *The Last Jews in Berlin*, 1982. A memorial tree is due to be planted in The Avenue of the Righteous Gentiles for the Countess Maria von Maltzan, who sheltered many Jews in Berlin and saved their lives.

2   Our cousin Grisba, born like myself in Moscow, fought with the *Hagana*, the Jewish defence force, in the Tel Aviv area; our cousin Luba's husband commanded the small detachment that crossed the Negev and occupied Eilat (where the Queen of Sheba landed on her visit to King Solomon), thus securing this vital outlet to the Red Sea for the new state. Eilat was then a tiny fishing village, now it is one of the three ports of Israel, serving the Far Eastern and Indian Ocean trade.

3   Daniel, my cousin Luba's younger son, was severely wounded in the Sinai campaign, lay in hospital for a year and still suffers from a partial disability. He is now a shipping manager in Haifa. His elder brother, Raphael, fought with distinction but escaped serious injury. Gideon, my cousin Grisba's only son, fought on the Syrian front, was wounded and narrowly missed death, and is now elected manager of a Kibbutz in Galilee. Raphael now has two boys, Uri and Oded, and Gideon three children; they will all be ready to defend their country.

4   The Orthodox Church acknowledges this by calling Joshua, the successor of Moses, Jesus of Nun.

5   Actually, I was called back for a few months the following summer, as my successor did not find the work congenial, and a new man had to be found, this time of outstanding ability, under whom the work flourishes.

16

$$E = m.c^2$$

Princeton

As early as 1905 a young man of 26, Albert Einstein, advanced the frontiers of human knowledge by formulating, in his Special Relativity Theory, the theoretical convertibility of mass (m), i.e. matter, into energy (E), according to the supremely simple equation

$$E = m.c^2$$

c being the speed of light (or radio waves), 300,000 kilometres per second. Nineteenth-century physics and chemistry were based on the twin laws of the conservation of energy and the conservation of matter. It was axiomatic that total energy in a system was constant and total mass constant. None could appear or disappear. But it had never been thought that mass could be changed into energy. When coal burns and produces energy, the weight of the coal plus the weight of the oxygen consumed equals the weight of the carbon dioxide produced.

In 1896 the French physicist Becquerel discovered radioactivity: a photographic plate wrapped in black paper and exposed to a uranium salt showed an impression of the uranium, whose invisible rays penetrated the paper. Obviously, energy of a sort was produced by the uranium atom. But this was considered a freak.

Rutherford at Cambridge (1911) and Niels Bohr at Copenhagen (1913) began to unravel the mysteries of the atom. In 1938 Einstein, now a professor at Princeton University, heard from Niels Bohr in Copenhagen that the uranium atom had been successfully split in Berlin with neutron bombardment. In a celebrated letter to Roosevelt Einstein advised the President

243

of the implications of this development. The professor explained that it had been known since the beginning of the century that, in theory, atoms of matter could be split, releasing unprecedented amounts of energy. About one hundred pounds of uranium-235 would have, under the right conditions, the explosive power of 20,000 tons of TNT molecular explosive. The Germans had found the key to splitting the uranium. If they pursued this line of research and developed an atomic explosive they could subdue the USA and Hitler would be master of the world. A crash programme of research and develoment was needed for the USA to have its own atomic explosive to counter any German threats. But the resources required for this development were not to be underestimated.

'Project Manhattan' was born. Thousands, later tens of thousands, of scientists, including many driven away by Hitler, were working at the University of Chicago under Fermi, at Berkeley, at the new research centre at Los Alamos under Oppenheimer, soon joined by Niels Bohr, smuggled out of Copenhagen in a small boat to Sweden and thence, with the assistance of the British Government, brought to the USA. They worked on the separation, or enrichment, of U-235, on the splitting of it and finally on the design of a bomb. The largest chemical factory in the world was built at Oak Ridge, Tennessee, for the separation of the hexafluorides of the two isotopes. The only difference between both forms of uranium was that the U-235 was marginally lighter than the U-238, having three neutrons less in the nucleus, so it was necessary for each lot to be processed five thousand times in a diffuser to enrich the U-235 sufficiently.

On 16 July 1945 the first atom bomb was exploded at Alamogordo in the desert of New Mexico. National Socialist Germany had capitulated in May. It is known from the archives that Germany had considered the development of atmonic explosive very seriously. The route they envisaged would require 'heavy water', enriched with the oxides of the hydrogen isotopes deuterium (one proton, one neutron) and tritium (one proton, two ncutrons), and the manufacture of the heavy water required quite prodigious quantities of electricity over several years such as was only available to Germany in Norway with its hydroelectric power. Informed by the Norwegian resistance that heavy water was being manufactured by the Germans at Norsk Hydro and well briefed by his scientific advisers, Churchill ordered the daring raid in 1943 in which the plant and entire stock of heavy water was destroyed. In the end, Germany decided to concentrate on the development of new weapons that could be ready in time for use against Britain and the USA, and so the V1 and V2 were developed. The V2 was the prototype of the long-distance ballistic missile. If completed a year earlier, it could have destroyed London with conventional explosive warheads.

The Soviets too were developing atomic weapons. In 1939 the 'Uranium Commission' was formed, and development began in 1942 by a special organisation under the auspices of the Secret Police chief, Beria, himself, and headed by Academician Kurchatov. The Soviet atomic weapon was exploded in 1949. Solzhenitsyn describes how he and thousands of other physicists and mathematicians were released from the 'Gulag' camps and drafted into the atom-bomb development. Most of them would not have survived otherwise.

The other war

Germany had capitulated on 7 May 1945. Hitler was dead. The Thousand-Year Reich was destroyed after twelve years. For Russia, which since 1941 had borne the brunt of the attack and had lost eleven million dead, it was peace at last. For Britain and the USA, the European war had only been a dress-rehearsal for a sea-borne invasion. Britain had lost 265,000 dead, the USA 300,000. Both countries were bracing themselves for the war against Japan, deferred, at Churchill's insistence, until Hitler was beaten.

The Japanese had conquered Manchuria, Korea, a large part of China including the entire seaboard, Indochina, Burma, Malaya, the Philippines, Indonesia, New Guinea and countless Pacific islands, some of the utmost strategic importance. Now they were threatening India and Australia, and were ensconced in an almost impregnable position, much more difficult to assail than Germany. The distances were vast; they had all the raw materials, including Indonesian oil, and there was no second front. Britain, the USA and Australia were prepared for a war lasting several years with millions of casualties on each side.

Several hundred thousand British and American prisoners of war and civilian internees were in Japanese camps in the conquered territories, and it was known that the Japanese commanders had written orders to murder all inmates of any camp that had to be surrendered.

British and American marines, and special units, were training, great aircraft carriers were being built, squadrons of assault vessels and ocean-going tank-landing craft. The landing in Normandy would have to be repeated dozens of times and thousands of miles away. And the Japanese, one knew, would defend each island to the last man. At Harbin, in Manchuria, in the secret 'Devil's Gluttony' establishment, the Japanese were testing chemical and germ warfare weapons on Chinese and Korean prisoners of war.

Japan had five million men under arms. Each would fight rather than surrender, and in the process kill at least one enemy soldier, probably several. There would have been casualties on the Russian scale.

On 6 August 1945 the atomic bomb was exploded over Hiroshima; as there was no reaction from the Japanese Government, a second bomb was exploded over Nagasaki on 9 August. The third bomb was ready. I was thrilled by these developments and considered the unlocking of the secrets of the atom and the harnessing of nuclear energy for potential military and peaceful use as one of the finest achievements of mankind. Had I been associated with the development of the atomic bomb, or with its delivery, I would have been proud of it to this day.

The Japanese now realised that the USA had developed an entirely new weapon, and had the power, *and the will*, to destroy their entire cities in a few months. On instructions from the Emperor, Japan surrendered unconditionally on 14 August 1945. The 'Co-prosperity Sphere' had lasted four years. The Japanese armies were recalled and disbanded, the prisoners of war and civilian internees freed without massacres. The Soviet Government immediately recognised that Japan had lost the war and on 8 August, two days *after* Hiroshima, declared war on defeated Japan (as it had entered defeated Poland in 1939) to claim a seat at the victor's table.

At Portsmouth, British naval ratings, all ready to sail with the Fleet to the Far East to fight the Rising Sun, set the town alight for three days. Their Lordships turned a blind eye. No doubt, they were themselves celebrating.

The power of the atomic bombs used was 20,000 tons TNT equivalent. The total weight of conventional bombs dropped on Berlin during the last year of the war was 50,000 tons. But that required thousands of aircraft to drop that load; with the atomic bomb, one aircraft sufficed. The war against Japan, expected to last years and claim millions of casualties[1] on each side, was won in *eight days*. During this period there were no casualties on the Allied side. Of the Japanese, 140,000 died at Hiroshima (including those that died in the aftermath) and 70,000 (less, owing to the hilly terrain) at Nagasaki, all victims of their country's aggression which rebounded on them. Before that, more Japanese had died from the 'conventional' air raids on Tokyo than from the two atomic bombs.

The hydrogen bomb

The availability of atomic or fission explosive has led, on the one hand, to the development of uranium-based atomic energy producing electric power for peaceful purposes and, on the other, dangerously, to the development of thermonuclear or fusion reaction. In this, two hydrogen isotopes, deuterium (with one neutron) and tritium (with two neutrons, produced by neutron absorption and the splitting of lithium) are made to combine with helium, as in the sun, by igniting the isotope mixture with an atom bomb, thus obtaining the required minimum temperature of 10 million degrees Centigrade.

The USA began development of the hydrogen bomb in 1950 under the impact of the Berlin blockade and the acute threat of a Soviet take-over of Western Europe; I do not know whether Russia began development of its hydrogen bomb, by Professor Sakharov, a little earlier or about the same time; at any rate, the Soviet bomb was ready in 1953 and the American one in 1954. Today, in addition, China, France and Britain have the hydrogen bomb officially. At least another seven countries (some ruled by vicious dictators) have or are developing the atomic bomb; once this is available for ignition the development of the hydrogen bomb is, it seems, comparatively easy. Hydrogen bombs have a much greater power than atomic or fission bombs, and their use in a war would be a major disaster. The only way to stop this use is for the peace-loving nations with freely elected governments to deter any would-be aggressor by fear of retaliation in kind. Nuclear weapons have kept the peace in Europe so far for forty years.

The application of the *fusion* reaction to the peaceful production of energy will require many generations, as the engineering problems of working at 10 million degrees Centigrade are almost unsurmountable.

The peaceful use of atomic energy

In the meantime, peaceful use of atomic fission energy offers mankind for the first time the opportunity of providing civilised life for *all* nations of the earth; without atomic energy this just is not possible. It is the safest and cleanest form of energy. People die in coal pits and on oil rigs with monotonous regularity (not to mention chemical factories and the hundreds of 'Bhopals' around the world); as yet not a single human being has died from the peaceful application of atomic energy. And the general rising of material standards of living around the globe made possible by atomic energy is one of the best insurances against war.[2]

Notes

1 According to Group-Captain Leonard Cheshire, VC, 3–4 million.
2 These lines were written before the Chernobyl disaster in 1986. This Soviet atomic power station was built to an unsafe design and badly executed, cutting corners to comply with the unrealistic demands of the current Five-Year Plan. The *highest* estimate (American) of the number of people likely to die eventually from the radiation received is about 48,000. In Britain alone, over 100,000 people have died in the past twenty years from road accidents, yet no-one suggests the abolition of road transport. In Southern England, we all live in the shadow of the French atomic fuel-reprocessing plant (the equivalent of Sellafield) at Cape La Hague on the Channel coast, and the French, who obtain 50 per cent of their energy from nuclear power, are certainly not reducing their nuclear programmes, and both the Soviet and the Japanese governments are increasing theirs.

17

The Shadows Lengthen

Some time after Father's death Marie Ivanovna told me that she would soon find it difficult to cope with our house, now unnecessarily large, old-fashioned and coal-heated. We looked around and bought a small, modern and very labour-saving house, fully detached, on the very outskirts of London and on high ground, and in a quiet cul-de-sac. In fact, we are in the County of Surrey, though on the wrong side of the Brighton Road. There are two bedrooms upstairs and a large sitting room, with dining annexe, on the ground floor. The garden, however, is much larger than at Streatham and even boasts an apple tree. We installed electric storage heating and found the house very comfortable. One could not wish for more.

Marie Ivanovna died here, fortified by the Last Rites of her church, in her ninetieth year. According to her wish, she was cremated, and the ashes buried at Mortlake Cemetery, which is regularly visited by Russian Orthodox priests.

Now I sit alone writing these lines, and looking at the garden—my eighth of an acre Surrey freehold, a cherished possession, for which many people around the world would fight and die. Most British people do not know how extremely fortunate they are; no knock on the door at 2 a.m., no closed van waiting. And how much better it is to be unemployed, with the necessities of life and even a modicum of comfort provided, rather than being employed in a labour camp.

I am deeply grateful to Britain for saving us twice from the horrors of the two Red Flags. In over forty years of life in England I have become quite attached to the country and its people. But often I am in despair about the complete lack of understanding of the world surrounding this fortunate isle. Sometimes I feel like going to Speaker's Corner and shouting: 'You do not know how fortunate you are! Defend your liberty! Do not provoke aggression. Site the missiles. Build five Trident submarines, not four. Prepare Civil Defence. The world is a jungle. It is futile to give a good example to a tiger.'

Our *immediate* family has come through the twin horrors of Soviet socialism and National Socialism almost unscathed, though Mother's death was really caused by the Bolshevik Revolution. Of our near-relatives we have lost Father's two brothers and two sisters-in-law, as well as Grandfather (withdrawal of ration cards) as victims of Soviet socialism, and Father's sister in Lithuania and her schoolmaster husband, and possibly, but not certainly, Grandmother, and in France my cousin Alexander, his sister's husband, Paul, and Uncle Jacob, the septuagenarian from Petersburg, as victims of National Socialism. The score is even.

Between them, Lenin and Hitler have achieved their object: a dozen 'human insects' of our family have been exterminated. There are no more Schmerlings of Mogilév in Europe, nor are there Poverkhovskys. There are, however, distant relatives of ours bearing the family-name in the USA, in Canada, in Australia, in Israel, all good citizens, serving their countries with distinction or fallen in their defence. May they flourish, and the countries that offered their fathers a new home. And may the long-suffering Russian people soon regain their freedom and Israel win peace.

Epilogue

For ten years Mary had been my secretary at the subsidiary company I was then managing. She was most efficient and understanding, with creative ideas, more a personal assistant, *but I did not notice her.* And, of course, since settling in England with my Father and Marie Ivanovna I had always known that marriage was out of the question for me for the first twenty years or so because I could not have supported two households. Later, my financial position improved greatly, but we had lost Father, I could not contemplate leaving Marie Ivanovna, who had devoted her life to us, alone in her old age. And I knew, of course, that two women could not share a house, unless mother and daughter; our chief accountant had tried just that, with his mother and wife, and one went for the other with the kitchen knife.

The subsidiary company was by then doing quite well and the shareholders, requiring capital for major new plant investment at their main metallurgical works, decided to sell it. In fact, the company was purchased by an American group at five times the net asset value, paying the balance for the goodwill. Being sixty at the time, I was moved to a much quieter backroom job at the main head office, dealing with patents and market research, which suited me perfectly as a ten-year transition to retirement. Once again I could thank my good fortune for providing the right opportunity at the right time.

Mary ceased to be my secretary—in fact, I had no personal secretary in the new semi-retirement job—and for fourteen years we were on Christmas-card terms, while Marie Ivanovna, in her eighties, naturally required much attention. However, Mary's memory, far from fading, seemed to grow, and in 1983, having lost Marie Ivanovna two years earlier, I telephoned Mary (speaking from memory, impersonating a computer software salesman), and after that we met every few weekends, visiting museums and exhibitions or going to the opera or theatre. After some two years we felt it would be even more rewarding sharing all of our life and Mary retired from her office work and we were married in 1986, shortly before Lent, at the Catholic Church in Surrey (Mary was a Catholic by birth) to whose congregation Mary belonged. The wedding, attended by some hundred good friends, colleagues and neighbours, proved a memorable occasion, and the beginning of a new chapter in our lives. Some day—who can tell?—it might form the subject for a new book.

Select Bibliography

Edward Crankshaw, *The Shadow of the Winter Palace*, London, 1976, p.286.

Brian Crozier *et at.*, *This War Called Peace*, London, 1984.

K. Fitzlyon and T. Browning, *Before the Revolution*, London, 1977, p.53.

F. A. Hayek, *The Road to Serfdom*, London.

Fred Hoyle, *Energy or Extinction*, London 1977.

Maldwyn A. Jones, *Destination America*, London, 1976, p.17.

Thomas Keneally, *Schindler's Ark*, London, 1982.

Alexander Kérensky, *The Kérensky Memoirs*, London, 1966, pp.14, 85, 158–62, 308, 498.

Golda Meir, *My Life*, London, 1975, pp.5, 230.

A. Rybakov, *Heavy Sand*, London, 1970.

Leonard Schapiro, *1917—The Russian Revolutions* and *The Origins of Present-day Communism*, London, 1984.

G. Schoenberner, *The Yellow Star*, London 1969.

Nikolai Tolstoy, *Victims of Yalta*, London, 1979.

Bernard Wasserstein, *Britain and the Jews of Europe 1939–1945*.

K. W. Watkins, *The Paradise Builders* and *Political Strikes*, London, 1984.

Index

Abdullah of Jordan, King 227
Abramovicz, J. 37
Achilles 197
Admiralty in St Petersburg 51
Adrianople 22
Adriatic, the 22
Advent 59
'Aerial Trafalgar', the 189, 190
Aesop 86
Afghanistan 70, 74–5
Africa 20, 77
  Corps 205
  European settlement in 43
  German colonies in 150
Aggression pact, non- 183
Agricultural settlements 39
Ajax 197
Alaska 9
Albania 22, 80
Albert, Prince 84
Alechem, Sholem 37
Alexander I, Czar 8, 17
Alexander II, Czar 9–10, 16–19, 21–
  3, 74, 93, 98
Alexander III, 18–19, 22, 26–7, 36,
  50, 57–8, 89, 95, 100, 116
  the anti-Jewish policy of 24
Alexandra Feodorovna, Empress 88,
  90
Alexandra, Queen 116
Alexandria 4, 20

Alexei 31–2, 34–5, 133
Alice of Hesse, Princess 88
Aliens Act of 1905 38
Allenby, Field-Marshall E.H.N. 41,
  226
Allende 150
Allied Control Commission 151
  Forces in Crimea 124
  Tribunal 218
Alma, the 125
Alps 98
Alsace 28
  -Lorraine 78
Altmark 153
Amalfi 116
Amalia, Aunt 74, 86, 115, 117, 143
America 9, 52
  emigration to 43
  in the war 203
  North 59, 142
  Russian–Jewish groups in 136
  slavery in 17
American
  Civil War 17
  -Jewish relief agencies 179, 225
  Jewry 165
  Lend–Lease supplies 191
  Pacific Coast, the 9
  Pacific Fleet 202
America's restricted hotels 152
Ammonites 45

Amsterdam 66
Amu Darya 75
anarchists 45
Anatevka 38
ancestral landscape 13–26
Anglo-American Force 205
  -French military action 176
  -Jewry 44
Ankara 132
anti-Bolshevik 212
  -Bolshevik division 206
  -Hitler alliance 222
  -Jewish 152, 155
  -Jewish agitation 41
  -Jewish armouries 35
  -Jewish backlash 225
  -Jewish camarilla 52
  -Jewish campaign 161
  -Jewish legislation 163
  -Jewish measures 57
  -Jewish *pogróm* 133
  -Jewish policy 90
  -Jewish riots 26
  -Jewish stance 171
  -refugee 195
  -Russian ideology 200
  -semites 45
  -semitism 41, 153, 157, 166, 200,
    225
  -Slavonic ideology 200
  -war party 189
Antioch 20
Apfelbaum, Grigory 101
Arab conquest 39, 41
  Legion of Transjordan 227
  population 42
  rule 39
Arabic Jews 228
Arabs, standard of living of 42
Aral Sea 75
Arandora Star 193
Arras–St Quentin Line 106
Archangel 9, 34, 120
  arctic route to 81
Arcos 144
Ardentine Caves 112
  massacre in 217
Argentine 142
  colonies in 39
aristocracy 111

Ark Royal, HMS 203
Armenian Church 58
  Community 108
Armenians 6
  extermination of 217
  genocide of 157
  massacres of 42
Armistice 119, 188
Army Medical Corps 87
Arnold, Matthew 233
Aryans 162
Ash, Sholem 37
Asia 3–4, 9–10, 69, 142
  Central 69, 74, 119
  war in 216
assassinations 37
Association of Jewish ex-Servicemen
    162
Assumption 59
atheism, militant state 61
Atlantic, Battle of 197
atom bomb, first 244
atomic bomb exploded 246
  energy, peaceful use of 247
Attlee, Clement 221
Auerbach, Berthold 196
Aurora 103
Auschwitz 52, 207, 209, 211–12,
    214, 224
  deportations to 167
  freed 216
Australia 20
  chain gangs in 23
  transportation to 23
Austria 7–8, 21–2, 28, 32, 76, 78,
    80, 118, 172
  anti-Jewish movements in 19
  declaration of war 76
  -German position 81
  liberal press in 42
  serfdom in 16
Autonomism 44
Azerbaijan 106

Baal 72, 74
Babi Yar 208
Babylonia 72
Bad Homburg 63–4
  Ischl 41
    cure at 28

hotel at 32
Baden-Baden 63
Baikal 50
Bakhchisarai 4, 98
Baku 130, 146, 201
  oilfields 98, 106
Bakunin 45
Balaclava 125
Balfour Declaration 96, 165, 168,
  170
Balfour, Lord 168, 226
Balkans, the 22
  Christian people of the 20
  mountains, the 22
  position in the 80
ballistic missiles 215, 244
balloon barrages 184
Baltic, the 6, 8, 52, 100, 117
  Coast, the 9
  Fleet 51, 91, 101
  mini-states 118
  provinces 49, 120
  states 186
Bapaume 106
barin 48
Basel 41
Bastille 111
Batu 3
Batum 22, 106
Bechuanaland 167
Becquerel, A. H. 243
Begin, Menachem 40, 106
Behring, Emil Adolf von 84
Beilis, Mendel (Menachem) 46
'Beiunskys' 196
Bela Kun 122
Belgium, invasion of 78
  neutrality of 78
Belgrade attacked 76
Belsen 216
Beria, Lavrenti 245
Bering, Vitus 9
Berlin 22, 29, 52, 64, 66, 99, 107,
  146, 174
  Congress of 22, 26
  court case in 35
  humiliation of 23
  Jewish press in 42
  technical high school in 155
Bernstein, Eduard 102

Berufsumschichtung 163
Bessarabia 198
Bevin, Ernest 225–6
Beumelburg, Werner 151
Bismark, Otto, Prince von 22, 77,
  197–8, 203
Bizerta, French fleet at 124
Bizet 71
Black Death, the 4–6, 16, 47, 93,
  179, 207–9, 219, 224
  Hundreds 34, 91, 121, 133
  market 98, 192
  Sea, the 4, 6, 9, 13, 22, 122, 129,
  170
    Allied base on 16
    British in the 126
    Fleet 51–2, 54, 120, 124
Blanche 141
Blitzkrieg 187
Blue and White Flag 41
Boer War 52
Boeing Flying Fortresses 204
Boer War 52
Bohr, Niels 243–4
Bokhara 70
Bolshaya Alexéyevskaya 61
Bolshevik army, anti- 120
  bureaucracy 112
  coup 80, 104
  emigrés 71
  folklore 103
  government, Hungarian 122
  headquarters 103
  insurrection 116
  Party, Control Committee of 106
  propaganda 103, 107
  Revolution, the 23
  rule, under 107
  Socialists, non- 119
  take-over 104
  terror 135
  uprising 99
Bolsheviks, the 32, 92–102, 105–6,
  114, 119–20, 122–3, 126, 133,
  135, 143, 146, 173, 183
  anti- 121
  escape from 133
  fighting the 121
  flight from the 111–26
Bolshevism 150, 198

Bolshói socialist 100
  theatre 67, 71, 86
Borkum 152
Borysthenes of the Ancients 13
Bosnia 16, 22, 76
Bosphorus 80, 98, 129
bourgeois 111
bourgeoisie, liquidation of the 112
Brandenburg 7, 153
Brest-Litovsk 77, 93, 106–7, 111–12,
  124, 139, 154, 200
  Diktat, cancellation of 118
Brindisi 80, 123
Bristol 4
Britain 22, 46, 57, 77, 132
  at war 78
  Battle of 189
  civil defence in 190
  immigration to 38, 171
  Japanese alliance with 50
  post-war 221
  stands alone 188
British Admiralty, the 16, 129
  Army 106
  Colonial Office 168
  Commonwealth 222
  -controlled ports 51
  East Africa 8, 165
  Eighth Army 205
  Empire, slavery in 17
  Expeditionary Force (BEF) 187
  evacuation 126
  Government, the 23, 43, 99, 105
  Mandate 42
  marines 125
  Mediterranean Fleet, the 21, 80
  naval blockade 117, 183, 205
  naval supremacy 44
  pro-Turkish policy 20
  radar 189
  rearmament 176
  restaurants 192
  Ultimatum 78
Bronnen, Arnolt 151
Bronstein, Leo (*see* Trotsky)
Brooklyn Navy Yard 190
Bruning, Dr 160
bubonic plague, the 3–4
Buchanan, Sir George 92
Buchenwald 216

Bukhárin, Nicolai 105
Bukovina 186
Bulgaria 20, 22, 80–1, 169
Bulgarian attrocities, the 20, 42
  children, upbringing of 61
  Rushchuk 80
bureaucracy, high 111
Burnham, James 231
Burschenschaften 156
burzhúy 111–12
Butter Week 59
Büyükada 130
Byzantine dynasty 20
  Emperor, the 9
  Empire, fall of 9
Byzantium 13
Byelorussia 6–7, 11, 13, 44, 56, 106,
  108
  Voksál 64

Cadets, the 91, 99, 101, 105, 119
Caesar, Catholic 10
  Orthodox 10
California 9
Caprivi 77
Carlsbad 63
Caruso, Enrico 71, 76
Casement, Sir Roger 100
Casimir the Great, King 6
Caspian, the 3, 69, 74
  railway, trans- 75
Cathedral of the Assumption 36
Catherine the Great 4, 7, 9–10, 18–
  19, 23, 88
Catholic, becoming a 231
  Centre Party 153
  Church's Jewish roots 234
  Church, Universal 234
  priests, murder of 25
Catholics, Polish 10
Caucasus, the 22, 28, 69, 96, 98,
  106, 08, 200
Cayenne 23
censorship 17
Cesaréwitch Alexis 89
  Nicholas 18
Chaliapin 71, 86
Chamberlain, Neville 169, 176–77,
  182, 184
Charlotte, Princess 10

Charlottenburg 155
Chéka 108
  terror 136
Chekhov, Anton 32
Chekists 133
Chemistry, Candidate of 50
Cheminitz 146
Cherkassky Row 85
Chernigov 27, 134
Chernyakhovsk 78
Chicago 74
children, sacrifice of 45
China 3, 9, 74
Chiva 74
Chmielnicki 25, 88
Chovevé Zion 40
Christ 94–5
  -killers 34
Christian churches 58
  orthodox faith 58
Christians, early 45
Christianity 5, 9, 19, 58
Church and Nation, relationship of 58
Churchill, Winston 99–100, 120–21,
    168–9, 176, 188, 193, 198–99,
    202–3, 221
CID 174
Citizen's Committees 82
Civil Defence 190
  Service 142
civil liberties 45, 54
  rights 36
  war 119, 121, 135
class war 109
Clemenceau, Georges 118–20
Cohanim, the 5
Cohen, Hermann 232
collectivisation 199
Cologne 64
  the Jewish community in 5
Comintern 201
commerce, development in 56
Communism 151
  spread of 231
Communist Party 199
compensation payments 236
Compiègne, Forest of, 117, 188
concentration camps 23–4, 164–6,
    181, 224
Congress of Berlin 76

conscription, selective 10
  the twenty-five-year 10–11
  universal 10
Constantine, Caesar 19
  the Great 5, 16
Constantinople 10, 20–21, 23, 91,
    129–31, 134, 137, 142
  fall of 9
  refugees in 132
  Russian claim to 19
  Russian entry into 21
Constanza 169
Constituent Assembly 105, 119
constitution, suppression of the liberal
  19
Co-prosperity sphere 246
Corday, Charlotte 112
Cordoba 66
corpses, the catapulting of 4
Cossacks 36, 53
  guards 88
  rebellion 88
  revolt of the 25
Council of Nicaea 94
Cracow 6–7
Crimea, the 4, 16, 21, 28, 70, 92, 98,
    106, 112, 115–6, 118, 120, 125,
    130, 137
  Allied forces in 124
  dácha in 36
  entered by Bolsheviks 123
  Express 115
  fate of the 123
  Jewish settlement in 39
  life in the 122, 133
  white troops in 124
Crimea coast 96
  Horde, the 4
  War, the 16
Cripps, Sir Stafford 221
currency stabilisation 149
Curzon, Lord 120
Czar 20, 44, 51–2, 77, 83, 90, 92,
    104
  abdication of 54, 111
  accession of new 36
  anti-Jewish 58
  at Mogílev 88
  death of the 92
  duty to the 35

Czar (*cont.*)
  enemies of the 34
  -Liberator, the 10, 24
  petition to 53
Czargrad, exile in 129–38
Czarist loans 133
Czar's government 72, 91
  murder of 18
Czárskoye Seló 89, 92, 103
Czechoslovakia 172, 177
  rape of 182

Dachau 216
Daily Worker, the 189
Dairen 50
Daladier, Edouard 176
Danube, the 21, 80
Dardanelles 21, 125
Das Schwarze Korps 165
Davos 69
Dawes Plan 149
D-Day 215
death camp 209
Decembrists 53
  of 1825 45
de Gaulle, General Charles 119
Deir Yassin 227
Deníkin, General 119–22, 124,
  132–3
Denmark 125
deportations 23
  mass 186
Der Judenstaat 41
Deronda, Daniel 40
*Der Zukunftsweg einer deutschen
  Aussenpolitik* 200
destroyers, Japanese 50
destruction, orgy of 34
Deterding, Sir Henry 114
Dictatorship of the Proletariat 108
Dimitrov, Georgi 189
Dinter, Artur 151
diphtheria 84
Directorate 119
disarmament movement 176
  unilateral 49
displaced persons 8
dispossession, Socialist methods of 13
Disraeli, Benjamin 19–23, 51–2
Divine Revelation 72

Dizengoff Square 170
Dnieper 6, 13, 27, 56, 93
Dolchstross 165
Don Pacifico incident 94
doodlebugs 214
Dreyfus, Captain Alfred 41, 46
Dresden 66, 82
Dubnov, Professor 44
Dühring, Eugen 152
Duckwitz, Dr 210
Dúkhonin, General 104
Duma, the 24, 54, 90–1, 104
Dunhuang 42
Dusterberg 152
Dvina 56
Dvinsk 93, 118
Dzerzhínsky, Felix 108, 175

East Prussia 78
Easter *pogróm* 37, 94–5
  Rebellion 100
Eastern Front 201
Edict of Toleration of the Old
  Believers 54
education, spread of 57
Edward I 5
Edward VI 65
Edward VII 45
Egypt, British occupation of 20
Egypt's attack on Israel 32
Eichmann, Karl 52, 209–10, 212,
  214
Eight Stars flag 41
Einsatzgruppen 208
Einstein, Albert 243
Eisenhower, Dwight D. 205
Eisenstein, Sergei 183
Ekaterinburg 92
El Alamein 205
Elder dam 204
Eliot, George 40
emigration 38, 40, 58
Emir Abdullah 168
Enabling Act 160–61
'Engelsianism' 104
England 4–5, 27, 58–59, 66, 132
  abolition of serfdom in 16
  Jews expelled from 5
England's relations with Russia,
  Tudor 9

English legal system 223
Entente Cordiale 45
Epirus, Greek 80
Eshkol, Levi 40
Estonia 49, 51, 106, 118, 122
Eupatoria 97–8, 129
Europe 4–5, 40, 57
  British policy in 45
  Central and Western 3
  conquest of 177
  dechristianisation of 217, 233
  Eastern 6, 11, 13, 118, 200
  liberation of 215
  non-communist 222
  reconstruction of Western 235
  Western 59, 132, 142
European backlash 40
  Jews, East 6
  Jewry, destruction of 207, 217
  peninsular, the 3
  plain, North 64
  refugees 149
  war, east 78
evacuation 122
Evening Standard 192
Evian-les-Bains 169
Examination Board 49
execution, mass 208, 224
Exodus 95
explosives, high 53

factory workers' grievances 54
family business, liquidation of 28
  names, bearers of 5
  the saving of the 3
Far East 50–51, 69
  commanders in 53
  disasters in 45
  Russian fleet in 50
Fasanenstrasse, Synagogue in 166, 191
father 49–55
father and mother engaged 65
  married 66
father and mother's house 67
  and mother's honeymoon 66
  expelled 178
father's death 238–9
  export business 146, 148
  investments 149

  progress 54
  stolen property, restitution of 235
Father Gregory (*see* Raspútin)
February Revolution 25, 90–91, 93, 104
Ferdinand, Archduke Francis 76
Ferdinand of Coburg 81
Fermi, Enrico 244
Fiddler on the Roof 37–8
Fifth Column 188, 193
Fighter Command 189
Finland 100, 102, 106, 118
  Gulf of 56
Finlándski Voksál 103
Fioraventi 36
First Army 78
Fischer's 68
Fladers 103
Flex, Walter 151
flogging 24
flying bombs 214
Foch, Marshal Ferdinand 117, 188
food rationing 191
  shortage 98
forced labour camp 133
France 10, 21, 23, 28, 41, 46, 77, 86, 132
  anti-Jewish agitation in 41
  fall of 187
  Jews in 212
  relatives in 211
  travel to 29
Francis-Joseph, Emperor 28, 210
Franco, General Francisco 66, 211
Franco-German Frontier 187
  -Prussian War 28, 53
  -Soviet pact 176
Frankfurt Express 64
Frederick the Great 7
Frederick Willian III, King 10
freedom of speech 102
French fleet 124
  Huguenots 217
  Police 213
  Revolution 16, 18, 111
French, Sir John 83
Frick, Wilhelm 155, 162
Friedenau 149
Fritsche, Werner von 218
Fungus 61, 82, 143

Gaelic League 43
Galicia 7, 19
Gallieni 78
Gallipoli coast 21
Gapon, Father 53
Garibaldi, Giuseppe 119
gas chamber, mobile 32
    first use of 99
Gdansk (Danzig) 7
Genghis Khan 3
Genoa 3–4
genocide 42, 218
George V, King 92, 116
George, Stefan 151
General and the Greengrocer 93
    Election 103, 221
    Headquarters 104
Geneva 143
    Convention 206
Gentiles, Avenue of Righteous 219
German advance 93
    Army 3, 105, 117–18
    army of occupation 119
    attack 81
    defence against 45
    blockage 83
    capitulation 216
    declaration of war 77
    colonies, loss of 150
    freighters 51–2
    General Staff 77–8
    Government 147
    Hamburg America Line 51
    High Command 78–9, 99–100,
        103–4, 117, 147, 149, 165, 189
    invasion 47
    intervention 98
    –Jewish Claims Conference 235
    Jewry 152, 171
    Jews 153, 165, 211–12
    losses 189
    National Socialists 112, 121
    occupation 93
    occupation-line 114
    rearmament 175–6
    recovery 149
    refugees 195
    Reich 178
    Revolution 165
    Social Democrats 102

    –Soviet pact 183, 186
    State Prosecution Service, Federal
        218
    surrender 117
    unification 19
    war crimes 216, 218
    war industries 205
    War Ministry 166
    warships 98
Germans in Shanghai 206
Germany 4, 21, 28, 58, 63, 86
    at war 78
    capitulation of 244–5
    Easter *pogróms* in 94
    exile in defeated 146
    Jewish community of 5
    liberal press in 42
    naturalisation in 154
    Navy League 790
    Nazi 169
    peace treaties with 139
    post-war visit to 238
    propaganda from 192
    school fees in 148
    ultimatum to 78
    war declared on 10
    war-shattered 224
    war with 109
    Western 5
    worldwide blockade of 102
Germany's reconstruction 151
Gestapo 116, 160, 162–3, 179, 180,
        182–83, 212–13
    headquarters 32
ghetto uprising, Warsaw 211
ghettos 207
Gibraltar 20
Gide, Andrea 231
Ginzberg, A. 43
Gladstone, William Ewart 20
Glubb, General Sir John 227
Gobineau 37
Godunov, Boris 15
Goebbels, Dr Joseph 35, 158, 161,
        176, 218
Goering, Hermann 176, 218
Gorchákoff, Prince 22
Gordon, Lord 26
Gorky 69
Golda Meir 11

Golden Horde, the 3–4
  Horn 129
Gounod 71
government, constitutional 17,36
  demand for 45, 53
Government, Czarist 91
GPU 108
Grade, Lord 38
Graf Spee 197
Granada 66
Grandfather's marriage 27, 57
  death 60–2
  success 60
Grand Hotel 130
Grandmother's dowry 57
  Russian maid 64
  stroke
grandparents, the 27–48, 61
Grand Tour of Europe 66
graves, mass 208
Greece 22, 169
  neutral 80
  Easter *pogróm* in 95
Greek culture 49
  Hellenic Empire, the 4
Greens, the 121
Griebnitz Lake 153
Grimm, Hans 150
Grisha 133
Grodno 7, 93
Grozny 201
Guchkov 91, 101
Gulag labour camps, the 24
Günzburg, Baron Horace 43
Gurion, David Ben- 40

Haam, Achad 43
Hadrian 96
haemophilia 89
Haggadáh 95
Hagia Sophia 19
Halifax 102
Hamid, Abdul 42
handkerchiefs, allocation of 24
Hannukáh 87
Harbin 142
Harrow School 141
Hasid, Judah he 39
Haw-Haw, Lord 192
Hayek, F.A. 231

Hebrew 43, 49
Heine, Heinrich 94
heirless property 237
Helène, Aunt 115–16, 123, 130–31,
  133, 212–13
Hellenic Empire, the 5
Hercegovina 22
Herzl, Theodor 40–3, 157
Hess, Rudolph 218
Hesse 19
Heydrich, Reinhard 209
Himmler, Heinrich 169, 175, 199,
  209, 212, 218
Hindenburg, Paul von 53, 79, 160,
  162, 175
Hiroshima 202, 246
Hirsch, Baron von 39
Hitler, Adolf 6, 11, 23, 40, 66, 77,
  89, 105, 111, 121, 155, 160–63,
  165–7, 175–7, 182–3, 189, 193,
  199–200, 212, 218, 222
  literature, ant- 183
Hitler's legacy 224
  neo-Leninists 210
  Reichschancellor appointment 158
  rise 157
  suicide 216
Hoffman, Captain Max 53
Hoffman, General 79, 93–4
Hohenzollern 19, 163
  Oberrealschule 148
Holland 117
Holocaust 218
Holy Baikal, the 23
  Land, Jewish Colonies in 41
  of Holies 39
  Patriarch, the 21
Home Guards, the 188, 194
Homer 49
Hong Kong 203
Hood, HMS 198
Hoover, Herbert 136
Horel Eden 80
Horthy, Admiral 122, 211
Hosanna the Great 32
Hötzendorf, Marshal von 77
housing quota 110
  shortage 147
Hugenberg 160
Hungary 3, 122, 169

Hungary (*cont.*)
    deportations from 211
    serfdom in 16
hydrogen bomb 246–7
hydrophobia, symptoms of 29
hyperinflation 148, 150

ICA (*see* Jewish Colonisation Asso-
    ciation)
illiteracy, fight against 57
Ilyitch, Vladimir 100
immigration, anti- 38
    to Britain 38, 170–1
immigrants, illegal 225
Imperial Ballet 71
    Commission, the 27
    Crown 44
    Family 92
    Manifesto of 1861 17, 54
    residence 36
Independence, War of 41
India 20
    North-west
    Congress Party of 105
Indochina, French-controlled 51–2
Industrial Revolution 56
industry, development in 56
influenza 116
Inkerman Heights 125
inoródtsy 34
Insterburg castle 78
Ireland 58
    conquest of 9
Irkutsk 69
irrigation schemes 75
Isaac, Uncle 47–8, 50, 72–3, 81,
    132–3, 135
Island 20, 72
Israel 14, 57, 168, 171, 177
    attacked by Jordan 229
    evacuations in 72
    government, the 14
    Heroes Cemetry in 14
    Jewish resettlement of 40
    pioneers in 44
    President of 40
    repossession of 39
    return to 43
    State of 227
Italy 80, 132, 169

    victory in 205
Ivan III, Prince 20, 36
Ivan the Terrible 9, 100
Ivánovo Vosnesénsk 58, 69

Jacob, Uncle 212
Jacques, Uncle 74–5, 115, 123, 130
Jadwiga 6
Jaffa 39
Jagiello 6–7
James, cousin 144
Janiberg, Khan 4
Japan 52
    crisis with 203
    German spy in 210
    war against 245–6
Japanese Army 53
    attack 50–51
    Fleet 50, 52
    secret police 206
    war 53
Jerusalem 19–20
    destruction of 72, 96
    Grand Mufti of 170
    Jewish presence in 39
    next year in 39
    travel to 39
Jew-hater 37
Jewish Agency 170
    'Archbishop's palace' 94
    armouries, anti- 35
    business, boycott of 162
    Candidate 157
    cemetry 35
    colonies 41
    colonisation 42
    Colonization Association (ICA) 39
    conspiracy 52
    dietary laws 72
    emigration 38, 170
    families 36, 62, 95
    family names 6
    households in Russia 42
    immigrants, the 6, 170
    mass settlement 42–3, 57
    millionaires in Russia 42
    -owned assets 181
    philanthropists 44
    policy, anti- 22–3, 90
    population 19, 37, 40, 57, 88, 228

press 42
property 237
Quarter 39
refugee problem 170, 193, 204, 211
Refugees' Committee 175, 177
relief organisations 163
repatriation movement 40
resettlement 39–40
rural outlook 38
settlement in Palestine 43
travel-restricted 24
world conspiracy 23
world government 35
youth, idealism of 43
Jewry, American 165
  German 152
  Russian 45
Jews 60
  emancipation of 40
  exclusion of 24
  expelled 39, 96
  German 11
  in Poland 7–8, 10–11, 39, 224
  in Russia 43, 45, 207, 209
  killed 37
  Lithuanian 10–11
  misery of the 40
  murder of 5, 25, 121, 217
  of Hebrew stock 5
  of Israel 229
  of the Pale 42
  of Western Europe 42
  persecution of 66
  restriction on 17
  sephardi 211
  smuggled across Pyrenees 66
Johannesburg 74
Johnson–Lodge Act 154
Jordanian Arab Legion 229
Joseph II 16
Joyce, James 232
Judaism 4–5
Judennot, 40, 44
Jünger, Ernst 151
Junkers Bros 71, 176

Kagga (now Feodosia) 4
Kagen, Eliah 62–5
Kaiser 44, 77, 93

abdication of 117, 165
  threats of the 51
Kaiser's 'Contemptibles' 106
Kaltenbrunner 210
Kama 70
Kamenev 101
Kaplan, Fanny 111
Karakum desert 75
Katyn Forest 208
Kensington Gore 144
Kérensky, Alexander 46, 75, 89–105, 112, 118, 150
  currency 149
  Government 119
  money 130
Kereski, Herr 153
KGB 108
Khanates 74
Kharkov 47, 60, 114
Khiva 70
Khody'nka field 36
Khomeini period 5
Kiel, mutiny of sailors at 165
Kiev, 3, 9, 13, 56, 121, 133
Kishinev 37
  pogróm 43
Kislovdsk 98
Kitchener, Lord 81
Kizil Adalar 130
KKL Fund 41–2
Klaipeda 118
Kluck, von 79
Koestler, Arthur 231
Kokand 74
Kolchak, Admiral Aleksandr 120–2
Konigsberg 78
kosher dietary laws 74
  household 71
  intricacies of 73
  restriction 73
Korczak, Janusz 219
Korea, 50, 69, 52
Kornílov, Admiral 125
Kotel 39
Kommissariats 200–1
Kovno 7, 93, 118
Kremlin 107
Kristallnacht 166
Kronstadt 101
  Red Sailors of 107

Kropotkin, Prince 45
Krupp 156, 206
Krylóv 86, 111
Kunin family 57
Kurchatov 245
Kurfurstendamm 158
Kurpark 65
Kursk 114, 121
Kurski Voksál 113
Kastner, Erich 150

labour camps 59
Labour Party Conference 120
La Fontaine, Jean de 86
Lahmann, Dr 82
Lake Geneva 80
    Ilmen 8, 69
Lancaster bombers 204
Landsmannschaften 156
Lansbury, George 107
Latvia 51, 93, 106, 118
Lausanne 151
Laval, Pierre 213
Lazarus, Emma 154
League of Nations 149, 168
Le Havre 135
Lenin 23, 27, 60, 71–2, 92, 99–101,
    104–9, 111, 113, 118–19, 121,
    126, 133–4, 136, 160, 166, 178
    coup 103
    Hills 83
Lent 59
Lenten diet 59
Leo, Uncle 46–7, 133
Lermontov 98
Leshonó haboóh b'Jerusholáim
    39
Letts 109
Levites, the 5, 14
Libava 51
Lidice, destruction of 217
Liebava 93, 118
Liepritz Lake 153
Lilienblatt, Dr 172, 188, 194–5
Lithuania 6–7, 11, 13–14, 20, 44, 47,
    93, 106, 118
Lithuanian Jews, the 8
'Litvaks' 27
Litvinov 183
Livadia 36

living, standard of 57
Lloyd-George, David 120
London 4, 22, 141, 174
    Conference 149
    new attack on 214
Lodz 58, 93, 148
Lord's Judgement, Ten days of Awe
    of the 32
Lorraine 28
Los Angeles 74
Low Countries 193
Luba 133
Ludendorff, General Erich 79, 93,
    103, 105–6, 117–18, 146, 149,
    165, 182
    –Hitler coup 150
    –Lenin coup 103
Lueger, Karl 40
Luftwaffe 183, 215
Lu-shun, Chinese 50
Lustiger, Cardinal 224
Lvov, Prince 91, 95
Lycée Janson de Sailly 141–2

McAdam, John 15
Macedonia 21–2, 80
Machol, Kurt 167–8
MacMichael Sir Harold 170
Madagascar 51
Madrid 66
maecenas 71
Maginot Line 187
magnetic mine 198
Maimonides 30, 66
Makhno 121
Malaya 20
Malorussia 6–7, 11, 25, 47, 59, 106,
    112, 114, 121
Malta 21, 125
Maly theatre 67
Manchuria 50, 69, 81
Manchuria, disasters in 33, 76
    evacuation of southern 52
    Russian army in 50
Mandate 225–6
Mandatory Authority 170
Mann, Thomas 151
Mannerheim, Field Marshal Carl
    Gustaf 211
Marat, Jean Paul 112

Margraves 153
Marie Antoinette 88
Maria, Aunt 47
Marie Feodorovna, Dowager Empress 116, 123–5
Maria Ivanovna 86, 96, 98, 108, 113–16, 131–133, 140–41, 148, 154, 167, 173, 175, 182, 192, 194, 221, 248
Mark Brandenburg 154
mark, value of 147
Marmara, Sea of 21, 130–31
Maronite Christians 217
  Church 58
marriage contract 65
Marseilles 135, 137, 139
marshes, draining of 40
Martel, Charles 20
Martindale, Father 233
Marx, Karl 23, 104
Marxist doctrine 101
Marzabotto 217
  folklore 54
Masé, Dr 45, 74
Mass, sacrament of 23–4
massacres of civilians 136
Materialkrieg 117
Matthew, Uncle 61–2, 68, 70–71, 82–3, 117, 133, 140–42, 144, 175, 212–13, 239–40
Masurian Lakes 53, 79
Mediterranean, the 4, 20
  the Easter 22
  Fleet 94, 130
Meir, Golda 228
Melbourne 74
memorial monuments 218–19
meningitis 144
Mensheviks 100–1, 105, 111, 119, 160
Ménshiy 100
  socialists 100
Merv, Russian troops at 75
Mervousness 75
Mesoptamia 135
Messiahs, false 39
mesusahs 64
Michael, Grand Duke 90–91, 93
Middle East, the 4, 77, 106
  British policy in 226

milch-cow, purchase of 3
military coup 101
Military Revolutionary Committee 101
militia, armed 101
Milyukóv, Professor 91, 101
Minin, monument to 82
Ministry of Supply 194–5
Minsk 7–8, 38, 63, 82
  train to 29
Mirbach, Wilhelm von 111
Misráim 96
Mitsubishi aircraft 203
mixed marriages
Mogilév 7, 13–15, 22, 28–9, 35, 40, 46–7, 56, 63, 65, 90–91, 104, 112, 116, 133–4
  daily life at 30
  law and order in 34
Mohammed 72
Mohne dam 204
Moiseiwitsch 38
Moloch cult 45
Molotov 101, 183
Monaco 213
monarchy, absolute 18
  overthrow of 45
Mongol invasion 6
  rule 6
Mongolia 3
Mongols, the 9
Monte Cassino 205
Montefiore, Sir Moses 14–15, 39, 43
  journeys to Russia 14
Montenegro, independence of 21
Montgomery, General Bernard 205
Montparnasse Cemetery 140
Montreaux, hotel share in 132
  move to 80
Montrose, HMS 123–4
Morósov 61
Morósovs 71
Mosaic Law 232
  prohibitions 72
Moscow 3–5, 9–10, 13, 24, 27, 36, 53, 57, 59–60, 62, 65, 67, 70, 74, 76, 98, 108–17, 116, 119, 137, 143
  childhood in 67–75
  Committee 82

Moscow (*cont.*)
  dressmakers 68
  Imperial Acadamy of Commercial
    Sciences 96
  Jewish families of 95
  life in 58, 104
  merchants 71
  opera in 71
  Rabbi of 45
  Synagogue 61–3, 65
  wartime 81, 84
  winter in 85, 136
Mosley, Sir Oswald 189
mother 63–5
  death of 139–40
mother's medical treatment 132
  marriage contract 65, 71
  people 56–66
  private philanthropy 71
  wardrobe 68
Movement of Return 40
Moyne, Lord 170
Mozart, Wolfgang Amadeus 71
Mukden 50
Mulberry Harbour 215
Mulhous 64–5
  diploma 55
Müller, *Geheimrat* 163
Munich 176–7, 189
  Agreement 176
murders, ritual 45–6
  mass 23, 146, 209, 216–7
Murmansk 105, 120
Muscovy 11, 57, 200
  Company, the 9
  Princess of 10
Muslim Legion 170
Mussolini, Benito 176, 187–8, 205
muzhik 63

Nachímov, Admiral 125
Nagasaki 246
Nansen, Fridtjof 143
  Passport 143, 173, 179, 231
Napoloeon 15, 104
Napoleonic invasion 15
Nasser, Gamel Abdel 229
National Labour Corps 176
  Home 165
  Party 152

Socialism 160, 215
Socialist 135, 163–4, 177, 180–81,
  193, 197, 199, 207–8, 236
Socialist activities, anti- 163
Socialis crimes 218
Socialist extermination programme
  169, 217–18, 224
Socialist German Workers' Party
  160
Socialist Germany 106
Socialist leaders 175, 218
Socialist mass murder 216
Socialist, rise of 157
Socialist rule 166
Socialist rulers 201
naturalisation 222
Negrosco 135
Nemirovich-Danchenko 134
Neue Freie Presse 41
Neumark 154
New York 38, 46, 74, 102
New York's East side 37
  sweatshops 38
Neuwied 103
Neva 103
Nicaea 19
Nice 135
Nicene Creed 19
Nicholas I 10–11, 14, 16–17, 19, 27
Nicholas II 36, 46, 51, 54, 57, 95
  abdication of 91
Nicholas and Alexandra, marriage of
  89
Nicolaewitch, Grand Duke Nicolai
  81, 125
Nicopol, the Battle of 20
Night of the Broken Glass 166
nihilists 45
Nizhni Novgorod Fair 69–70
NKVD 109
Nord Express 64
Norderney 152
Normandy 9
  Allied landing in 214
Norsk Hydro 244
North Sea, the 8
Northern Command Headquarters 91,
  103
Notre Dame Cathedral 219
Nóvaya Basmánnaya 67

November attack 165
Novgorod 8, 56–7
  the Great 69
Novorossísk 124, 130, 132
  tragedy at 126
Nuremburg 218
Nurnberg, Jewish community of 5
  Laws 163, 165

Observer corps 188
Ocamo, SS 125–6, 129–30
Octobrists 91, 101, 105
Odessa 11, 80, 98, 102, 120, 130,
    182
  forces at 124
  tragedies at 126
Odra (Oder), the 6
Ogadai, death of 3
Oka 69–70
Old City, Jews excluded from 39
Oleg (Helgi) 9
Olga, Aunt 134, 213
Omsk 119
opera in Moscow 71
Operation Sealion 189
Oppenheimer, Robert 244
Oradour 217
Oranienburg 213
Orékhovo Zúyevo 97
Orel 121
Orenburg 75
Orient Express 143
origins, family 1–12
Orsha junction 63
  journey to 29
ORT 44, 61–2, 71, 87
orthodox Christians, non- 60
  Church 10, 17
  Church, conversation to 37
  Empire 11
  faith, the 20
  Jews 39
  midnight Mass 60
  patriarchs, the four 20
  Russian policy 20
Ostland 200
Ostmarkenverein 19
Oxford Union 176

Pacific, the 9

loss of colonies in 150
new naval power in 52
Pahlen Commission, the 25
Pahlen, Count 24
Pale of Settlement, the 10, 24, 38,
    46, 56–7, 61, 93, 108, 192, 207
Pale divided from Moscow 82
  Jewish misery in the 44
  Jewish population of 37–8, 43
  life in the 37
  poor Jews of the 42
  residence outside the 38
Paleologus, Constantine 20
Palm Branch Procession, the 32–3
Palmerston, Lord 94
Palestine, Arab immigration into 42
  Arab population in 42
  Arabs 228
  British administration of 225
  British forces in 52
  illegal immigrants into 169
  Jewish emigration to 170
  Jewish settlement in 43, 224
  Mandate for 168
  Second Partition of 169
  transjordanian 42
  waste-land in 41
Pamirs 74–5
Panzers 176, 186
Papen, Franz von 160, 182, 218
parliamentary system, English 68
  two-party systems 36
Partition, the First 10–11, 13, 56
  the Third 11
Paris 29, 64, 66, 79, 135
  capture of 77
  Commune 54
Paschal Meal 39
Páshkovo 31
Passover 45
  celebrations 95
  in Moscow 94
Pasteur, Dr Louis 29, 84
Paul I 18–19, 90
Paulus, von 202
peasants, emancipation of 56
  liberation of 16
Peace Pledge Union 176
peace revolt 190
Pearl Harbor 50, 202, 206

Peel Commission 169
Peenemunde 214
  destruction of 204
Pellepoix 213
Pentateuch 72
Perekóp 122–3
Perelman, Elieser 43
Perkins 70
Pérovskaya, Sophie 18
persecution, political 38
Persia 70, 74, 98
Persian Gulf 81
Peshkov Maxim 69
Pétain, Marshal Philippe 119, 188,
  213
Peter the Great 9–10, 45, 49, 106,
  108
Peter III 18
Peter and Paul Fortress 111
Petersburg 23–5, 28, 33–5, 43–5, 52–
  3, 57, 59–61, 83–4, 93, 100,
  103, 105, 108. 119
  Admiralty in 51
  Bolshevik rising in 99
  corrupt government in 72
  Czar's return to 91
  government 53
  Jewish community in 90
  report to 35
  Soviet 101
Petition of Rights 54
Petlýura 133
  pogróm 121
Petróvka 67
Philistines 39
Phoenicians 45
phoney war 187
Piast, anciant dynasty of the 6
Piccadiliy Hotel 144
Pikes 61
Pinsk 7
Pioneer Corps 192
Piraeus 80, 94, 123
Pittsburgh 117
plague, spread of 4
Pland 186
Plehvé 37, 43, 57, 109
  reign of 66
Plekhanov Georgii 45
Plevna 20

PLO (Palestine Liberation Organisa-
  tion) 228
Pobedonóstsev 18–19, 22, 25–6,
  36–7, 50–51, 57
pogróms, the 25–6, 33–5, 37, 44,
  46–7, 64, 81, 94–5, 121, 133,
  136, 166
  badge of the 45
  Easter 37
poison gas 202
Poitiers 20
Pojársky, monument to 82
Pokrovskaya Manufactura 70
Poland 3, 6–8, 11, 40, 58, 93, 106
  Catholicism in 8
  Jewish population of 40
  Jewish youth of 40
  partition of 106, 183, 186
  Soviet-occupied 186
Poles, Catholic 32
  loss of indendence of the 11
  murder of 25
Poliakoff 45
Polish cavalry destroyed 186
  Crown, the 11, 25
  estate owners 46
  extermination camps 209
  fighter pilots 189
  Government
  invasion 82
  Realm, the 13, 56
  Realm, destruction of 40
  resistance broken 186
  Underground 213
political assassinations 45
  freedom 54
  hostility 39
  oppression 57
  persecution 38
  ruling class 111
'Pollaks' 27
Pomerania, serfdom in 16
Pomorze 6–7
Port Arthur 50, 52–3, 202
Potémkin 54, 124
Potsdam 153
Poverkhovsky 60–62, 67, 70, 80, 82,
  109, 141, 144, 213
  family 63
  Grandfather 67

Grigory 57
  office 85
  shares 71
Poverkhovsky's cook 74
Poznan (Posen) 7
Prague, Jewish cemetery in 35
Prelestnaya 9
Preuss, Dr 172
Prince of Wales, HMS 203
Princes Islands, the 21, 130
Prinkipo 130–2, 137–8
  life on 133
prisons 59
prisoners-of-war 193
prohibition 23
prohibitions, Mosaic 72
'Project Manhattan' 244
proletariat, dictatorship of the 120
Promised Land, Jewish resettlement
  in 39
propaganda 35
property, confiscation of 23
Protocols of the Elders of Zion 35
Prussia 7–8, 28
  anti-Jewish movements in 19
Prussian militarism 149
  military traditions 78
Pskov 57–8, 103
Pumbedita 72
punishment, corporal 24
Purim 87
Pushkin, Alexander 108
Putilov munitions factory 53
Pyrenees 98

Queen Elizabeth 204
Queen Mary 204
Queen Victoria 45

Rabbi of Bacharach, The 94
Rabbi of Rome, Chief 213
  of Moscow 74
Rabbi, the Fiscal 33
Rabbinowicz, S. 37
rabid dog incident 29
rabies, cure from 29
Rachel's Tomb 14
Rachmaninov, Sergei 71
racialism 151
Railway Age, the 27

railways, system of strategic 28
Ramsgate 14
Rapaport, Nathan 229
Rashi 30
Rashid Ali rebellion 170
Rasp\u00fatin, Gregory 89–90, 104, 116
rationing 134, 221
Reamur scale 85
rebbe 38
Red Army 108, 120, 175, 183, 199
  Cross, International 206
  Cross, Russian 86
  Gate 67
  Guard 101–3, 105, 109, 125, 136
  Sailors of Kronstadt 107
  Terror 112
Reds 124
refugee-help organisations 129
  industries 171–2
rehabilitation at home 46
Reich, Third 146
Reichsbank 164, 171, 235
Reichschancellor 158, 160, 175
Reichsführer 175
Reichskommissariat 200
Reichsrat 154–5
Reichstag 153, 160–61, 164
Reims, capitulation at 216
religions, suppression of non-conform-
  ing 10
Rennenkamp 79
repression, political 37
Repulse, HMS 203
resistance 213
Return to Israel 43
Revel 45–6, 51, 118
Revolution, 1905 54
revolutionaries, professional 54
'revolutionary attitude' 45
  terrorism 37
Rhine 5
Rhineland, demilitarisation of 151,
  176
Ribbentrop, Joachim von 183, 198
Riga 56
  murder of Jewish population 44
Right-wing party 119
Rilke, Rainer Maria 151
Rindfleisch pogróm 5
rioting and looting 34

Ritters Park Hotel 65
  Marne 79
road-building business, the 27
roads, the surfacing of 15
Robespierre, Maximilien 28
rocket, V2 215
Róhm, Ernst 161, 175
Rollo 8
Roman conquest, the 4, 39
  culture 49
  Empire, the 5, 16, 19
  Empire, Eastern and Western 10
Romania 40, 80, 169
  German-occupied 169
  independence of 21
  oppressed Jews of 43
Románov dynasty, end of 92
  Michael 93
Rome 66
  liberation of 215
  Third 10
Rommel, Erwin 205
Roosevelt, President Theodore 52,
    160, 188, 190, 203
  letter to 243
  residence of 36
Rose 61
Rosenberg, Alfred 79, 82, 200–1
Rosenfeld, Leo 101
Rothschild, Baron Edmond de 40, 45
Rothschilds 162
Royal Air Force, the 3
  Navy, the 3, 102
Royal Oak, HMS 189
royalty, intermarrying of 19
Rozhdestvensky, Admiral 51–2
Rumelia, Eastern 22
Runstedt, Karl von 78
Rurik 8–9
  dynasty, the 9
Rurik's Russian Empire 13
Rus 9
Russia 7, 10, 15, 23, 29, 46, 50
  advance of 74
  army of occupation in 119
  Black Death in 208
  Bolshevik take-over in 104
  Central and Eastern 10
  colonies in 39
  Czarist 13

deaths in 136
declaration of war on 77
Eastern 69
European 201
German attack on 81
history of 54, 56
home-grown cotton in 75
Jews in 25
Left-wing socialists in 160
persecution of Jews in 45
pre-partition 10
public opinion in 46
second Front in 120
serfdom in 17
slavery in 17
suffering in 121, 135
tragic fate of 122
war declared on 78
Russian Armies, annihilation of 53
  Army 28, 79, 81, 117, 132
  methods 53
  mobilisation of 77
  battleships 50
  Czar, the orthodox 10
  disasters, early 79
  Dissenters 54
  emigrés 99
  Empire, the 7
  farmer class 46
  Federation 118
  fleet annihilated 52
  Foreign Ministry 102
  Front 105
  government, the 13
  immigrants, life of 37
  industry 57
  –Jewish community 38
    Groups 136
  Jewry 45
  Jews 207–8, 224
  movement, anti- 93
  Orthodox church 46, 58
  People, Union of the 34–5, 45
  prison camps 106
  prisoners of war 20
  Red Cross 86–7
  refugees 132, 142, 147, 149, 154,
    211
  Revolution 102
  ruling class 45

Siberian Bank 71
state, foundation of the 9
supremacy 34
suzerainty 118
war losses 51
warships 51
Russia's borders 118
mobilisation 78
'Russification', policy of 19, 50
Russo-Japanese War 53
–Turkish War, Tenth 20
Rutherford, Lord 243
Ryan, Miss 96
Ryo-Jun, Japanese 50

Sacher, Hotel 76
Saint Alexander Nevski 59
Andrew's Cross 124
Bartholomew Massacre 217
George 124–5
Louis 168
Olga 59
Paul 59
Peter 59
Petersburg 10, 16, 21, 27
Sergius 59
Vladimir 9, 59
Sakhalin 23
Solomon, Ernst von 151
Salonika 22, 80
Samarkand 70, 74–5
Samsonov, General 78–9
Sandomír 27
Sandomírskys, the 27
San Francisco 9
San Stefano 131
Treaty, the 21–2
Sarajevo 76
Saratov 48, 133, 135
Sassnitz 100
Scandinavia 13
Scapa Flow 189
Schacht 218
Schieber 147
Schiller, Friedrich von 159
Schleicher, General von 160, 175
Schlieffen, Count Alfred von 77
legacy 187
Plan 77–9, 198, 203
Schlippe, von 181

Schmerling 14–15, 29, 134
bank, run on 47
Boris 22, 63–4
boys, the 46
family home, the 15
family's daily life 30
family's Sabbath 31
family's summer 32
house, 34–5, 63, 134
Moses 27
Solomon 14–16, 22, 25, 27, 32,
38, 63
Schmerlings, death of 238
pre-partition 14
Schoneberg 148
Schwenden 164–5, 171, 173–5, 183–
4, 188
brothers 193
company, work with 237
enterprise 182, 221
factories returned 236
Laboratory 194
Scriabin, Vyacheslav 101
Sebastopol 98, 115, 124–5, 130
Second Pacific Squadron 51
Partition 118
Russian Army 78–9
secret societies 45
Sedan, the debacle of 28
Seder 96
sephardi 228
sephardim 138
Sephorim, Mendele Mocher 37
Serbia 22, 80
independence of 21
war on 76
Serbian secret society 76
serfdom, Imperial Committee on 17
serfs, emancipated 18
Sergei, Grand Duke 95, 109
Seville 66
Shaftesbury, Earl of 41
Shakespeare, William 56
Shamil 98
Shanghai 180–1
sister in 205
Shapiro, Leonard 186
Shinwells, the 38
Siberia 23, 69, 119–122, 137
the exiles in 23

Siberia (*cont.*)
    transportation to 23
    western 9
Siberian furs 113, 132
Sieffs, the 38
Silesia 6
Simferopol 115
Simon, cousin 134, 213–14
Simon, Fr Ralph 233
Simbirsk 100
Simeiz 123
    villa at 115–16
Sinclair, Upton 69
Singapore 120
    capture of 50
    fall of 202, 206
    slaughter, mass 53
    ritual 72
slave-labour camps 214
slavery 17
Smirnov brothers 69
Smolénsk 13, 15, 29, 56, 62
    First Merchant Guild of 16, 25, 47
        63
Smolny Institute 103
Sobinov 71
Socialist ideology 54
Socialists 45
Society of Manual Trade 44
Sokólniki 84–5, 98
Solzhenitsyn, Aleksandr 245
Somme, River 99
Sophie 20, 47, 208
Sophie, Empress 36
Sorge 201
Soskices, the 38
South America, anti-Jewish armouries
        in 35
Southey, Robert 86
Soviet-occupied Poland 186
    repatriation crime 230
    socialism 120, 198–9, 201
    Socialist Government 120
    tyranny 101
    Union 186
Soviets 101
Spain 9–10, 58, 66, 116
    victory in 142
Sparrow Hills 83
Spartakist rebellion 102

Special Operations 192
Spender, Stephen 231
Spitfires 189
Spreewald 154
SR (Peasants Party) 105, 119
Stalin, Josef 183, 198, 202
Stahlhelm 160
    Ex-Serviceman's Organisation 152
starvation 134
State of the Jews, the 41
Statue of Limitations 218
Stauffenberg, Klaus Schenk von 214
Stinnes 156
Stock Exchange collapse 159
Stocker, Adolf 41, 152
Stoessel, General 51
Stolypin 46
Straits, the 20, 51–2
Streicher, Julins 218
Stresemann, Gustav 149
strikes, student 50
    university 54
Stroganoff, merchant adventurer 9
Struma 169–70
Sudanese Mahdi 98
Suez Canal, the 20, 22, 43, 170
suffrage, universal 44
Sultan, the 22
    Janissaries of the 10
Summit of the Three Noes 229
Supplication, Services of 32
supply services, corruption in 53
Supreme Headquarters 103
Sura 72
Susanin, Ivan 134
Suvorov, HIMS 51
Sverdlov, Yakov 92, 101
Sverdlovsk 92
swamps, malaria-infested 40
sweatshops 38
Sweden 9, 100, 103, 117, 210
Switzerland 70, 76, 82, 132
    Russian emigrés in 99
    trapped in 79
Sword of Damocles 39
Syr Darya 75
Syria, excavations in 72

Tableau d'Honneur 142
Taganka 60–1, 63, 66

household 62
Taganrog, synagogue at 17
Tallinn (*see* Revel)
Talmud, the 72
Tammann, Professor 50
Tannenberg 53, 79, 175
Tartar *Lebensraum* 3
Tartars, the 3, 9, 21, 59–60
Tartu 50
Tashkent 74–5
Tasmania, chain gangs in 23
    transportation to 23
Tawje the Milkman, 37
Technical Institute of Mulhouse 55
Technion in Haifa 43
Technische Hochschule 174, 240
Tel Aviv 40, 170
Tel Hai, Jewish settlement of 53
Temple Mount 39
Temporary Regulations of 1882 24,
        37, 40, 46–7, 52, 57, 75, 81–2,
        91, 95–6, 108, 134
    abolition of 36, 90
Ten Commandments 64
Ten Days of Awe 32
Ten-hour Bill 41
Terezin 207
terrorism, revolutionary 37
Teuton 59
Teutonic Knights 49
    Orders, the 9
Third Partition 118
Thrace 22
Thuringia 155
Thyssen, August 162
Tiflis 98
Tirpitz, Admiral 44
Tobolsk 92
Togo, Admiral 52
Torgau 216
Toronto 74
torture 23
Toulon 16
Tours 20
Transjordan 168
Trans-Siberian Railway 50, 57
Travers, P.L. 86
Treaty of Brest-Litovsk 106–7
    of London 78
    of Ninfeo, the 4

terms of 52
    of Versailles 107, 151
trial by judge and jury 17
Triumph, HMS 225
Trocadera 142
Trotsky 102–3, 107, 138, 187
Trotskyites 99
Trudovik 91, 105
Trumpeldor, Joseph 52–3
Tsaritsyn 201–2
Tsushima 52, 103
Tucholsky, Kurt 151
Tukhachevsky, Marshal Mikhail 183,
    199
Tunis 124
Turgénev, Ivan 23
Turkey 22, 28, 80, 98, 106, 169
    Jewish settlement in 39
Turkish conquest 39
    infidels 19
    massacres 61
    prisoners 61
    rule 41
    suzerainty 4
Turks, the 9
typhus 117, 135–6

U-boats 197, 199
    warfare 99, 190–1
Ufa 119
Uganda option 43
Ukraine 146, 200
Ulyanov, V. (*see* Lenin)
Uncles, the 46
unilateral disarmament 49
United Nations 226
United States of America 46, 100
    Air Force 204
    entry into the war 99
    Government 179
    immigrants into 154
    Navy 190
University of Dorpat 49
Urals, the 3, 69, 119, 121
'Uranian Commission' 245

Valdai Hills, the 13, 56
Varna 16, 129
Vatican 46, 213
    temporal policies 234

Velodrome d'Hiver 212
Venice 66
Venezuela 126
Verdi, Giuseppe 71
Verdun 99
Versailles 40, 106, 118, 159, 176
　Palace of 139
Vichy France 169
Victoria, Queen 22, 88
Victorious, HMS 203
Vienna 22, 28, 76
　the Congress of 7–8, 10
　'Jewish' press in 42
Vietnam, Soviet-controlled 51
Vikings, the 8
Vilna 8, 32, 93, 118
　transfer of 11
Vinogradskaya 53, 96
　Anna 61
　Gymnasium 61
visas 132, 137, 154, 165, 168, 173,
　178–9
Vistula 27
Vítebsk, city of 7, 29, 56–8, 61, 63
Vladikavkás 98
Vladimir 23, 93, 97
Vladimirka, chain gangs on the 23
Vladivostok 50–52, 81, 113, 120
Vlasov, General 206
Volga, the 3, 56, 69–70, 119, 202
　region 136
Volóvnik, Uncle 121
Volunteer Armies 120
Voznesensk, Ivanovo 70

Waffen SS 211, 217
Wall Street crash 159
Wannsee Conference 209
war 76–87
　civil 137
　crimes 217
　Loan 82
　of Independence 41, 226
　outbreak of 194
　Six-Day 227, 229
warfare, bacteriological 4, 99
　chemical 99
　chemical and germ 245
　deterrent, chemical 202
Warsaw 29, 57, 60, 64, 82, 93, 106, 144

Duchy of 7
Express 62
ghetto uprising 211
victory parade in 186
wartime in England 186–220
Washington 120
Waterway, Great 56
weapons, V1 and V2 204
Wehrmacht 217
Weimar 149
　Constitution 160
　Republic 157
Weinstocks, the 38
Weisser Hirsch 82
Weizmann, Professor 40, 226
Werfel, Franz 151
West Bank territories 42
West, Rebecca 192
Western Front 99, 105
　Powers 132
White Armies 121, 133
　Guards 120, 125
　Paper 169, 226
　Sea coast, the 9
　troops 124
　Volunteer army 212
Whites, defeat of the 122–3
Wiesenthal, Simon 218
Wilenkin, Alexander 105
　Grigory 52, 57
Wilhelmstrasse 180
Wilmersdorf 148
Wilna 7
Windsor Castle 84
Winter Palace, audience at 45
　storming of the 103
Wissotzky, Basil 43, 45, 74
Witté 52, 57
Wohlfahrtsamt 160
Wolfsons, the 38
Woolton, Lord 191
Worker's and Soldier's delegates 101
World War I 25, 40, 52, 54, 66, 100,
　102, 114, 175, 182, 187, 190,
　199, 200
World War II 66, 98, 150, 153, 160,
　222, 229
Wrángel, General Carl Gustaf 120,
　124
Württemberg 19

Yad Vashem 218
Yalta 98, 115, 123
  Conference 36, 231
Yalu river 50
Yar restaurant 83
Yehuda, Ben 43
Yellow Sea 50
  Star 167
Yevtushénko, Evgeniy 208
Yiddish 41
Yiddish–German 49
Yokohama 113
Yom Kippur 32
York 4
Young Plan 151
Ypres 99
Yudénich, General 120–22

Yugoslavia 76, 132, 169
Yuriev 50
Yusupov, Prince 90

Zagorsk 97
Zangwill, Israel 43
Zinoviev 101
Zion, Friends of 40
Zionism 39
Zionist Congression 41, 43
  movement 43
Zionists 42
Zméevka, Battle of 121
Zolli 213
Zweig, Stefan 151
Zwi, Sabbatai 39
Zyklon B gas 207

Mme Eugénie Lang
    one of the unsung heroines
of occupied France
                    GS

Certainly never was! –
From her to the Nortons, with love,
and the hope that this book
will answer all David's questions.
                        T.L.
1988